From Music to Sound

From Music to Sound is an examination of the six musical histories whose convergence produces the emergence of sound, offering a plural, original history of new music and showing how music had begun a change of paradigm, moving from a culture centred on the note to a culture of sound. Each chapter follows a chronological progression and is illustrated with numerous musical examples. The chapters are composed of six parallel histories: *timbre*, which became a central category for musical composition; *noise* and the exploration of its musical potential; *listening*, the awareness of which opens to the generality of sound; deeper and deeper *immersion* in sound; the substitution of composing *the* sound for composing *with* sounds; and *space*, which is progressively viewed as composable.

The book proposes a global overview, one of the first of its kind, since its ambition is to systematically delimit the emergence of sound. Both well-known and lesser-known works and composers are analysed in detail: from Debussy to contemporary music in the early 21st century; from rock to electronica; from the sound objects of the earliest *musique concrète* to current electroacoustic music; from the *Poème électronique* of Le Corbusier-Varèse-Xenakis to the most recent inter-arts attempts.

Covering theory, analysis and aesthetics, *From Music to Sound* will be of great interest to scholars, professionals and students of Music, Musicology, Sound Studies and Sonic Arts.

Supporting musical examples can be accessed via the online Routledge Music Research Portal.

Makis Solomos was born in Greece and now lives in France, working as Professor of Musicology at the Université Paris 8 and as director of the research team MUSIDANSE. He has published many books and articles about new music, and he is one of the main international specialists of Xenakis' music. Extending this book, he is now developing the frameworks for an ecology of sound and music.

Routledge Research in Music Series

Music Video After MTV
Audiovisual Studies, New Media, and Popular Music
Mathias Bonde Korsgaard

Masculinity in Opera
Edited by Philip Purvis

Music, Performance, and the Realities of Film
Shared Concert Experiences in Screen Fiction
Ben Winters

Burma, Kipling and Western Music
The Riff from Mandalay
Andrew Selth

Global Percussion Innovations
The Australian Perspective
Louise Devenish

Double Lives
Film Composers in the Concert Hall
James Wierzbicki

John Williams
Changing the Culture of the Classical Guitar
Michael O'Toole

Paul Dukas
Legacies of a French Musician
Edited by Helen Julia Minors and Laura Watson

The Consolations of History in Richard Wagner's Götterdämmerung
Alexander Shapiro

From Music to Sound
The Emergence of Sound in 20th- and 21st-Century Music
Makis Solomos

For more information about this series, please visit: https://www.routledge.com/Routledge-Research-in-Music/book-series/RRM

From Music to Sound
The Emergence of Sound in 20th- and 21st-Century Music

Makis Solomos

LONDON AND NEW YORK

First published in English 2020
by Routledge
2 Park Square, Milton Park, Abingdon, Oxon OX14 4RN

and by Routledge
52 Vanderbilt Avenue, New York, NY 10017

Routledge is an imprint of the Taylor & Francis Group, an informa business

© 2020 Makis Solomos

The right of Makis Solomos to be identified as author of this work has been asserted by him in accordance with sections 77 and 78 of the Copyright, Designs and Patents Act 1988.

All rights reserved. No part of this book may be reprinted or reproduced or utilised in any form or by any electronic, mechanical, or other means, now known or hereafter invented, including photocopying and recording, or in any information storage or retrieval system, without permission in writing from the publishers.

Trademark notice: Product or corporate names may be trademarks or registered trademarks, and are used only for identification and explanation without intent to infringe.

Based on the French edition published by Presses Universitaires de Rennes, 2013
De la musique au son. L'émergence du son dans les musiques des XXe-XXIe siècles
Translation from French by John Tyler Tuttle

British Library Cataloguing-in-Publication Data
A catalogue record for this book is available from the British Library

Library of Congress Cataloging-in-Publication Data
Names: Solomos, Makis, author.
Title: From music to sound: the emergence of sound in 20th- and 21st-century music / Makis Solomos.
Description: New York: Routledge, 2019. |
Series: Routledge research in music | Includes bibliographical references and index.
Identifiers: LCCN 2019029795 (print) | LCCN 2019029796 (ebook) |
ISBN 9780367192136 (hardback) | ISBN 9780429201110 (ebook) |
ISBN 9780429577123 (adobe pdf) | ISBN 9780429572906 (mobi) |
ISBN 9780429575013 (epub)
Subjects: LCSH: Music–20th century–Philosophy and aesthetics. |
Music–21st century–Philosophy and aesthetics. | Sound (Philosophy) |
Noise (Philosophy) | Listening (Philosophy) | Tone color (Music)
Classification: LCC ML3877.S6 2019 (print) | LCC ML3877 (ebook) |
DDC 781.2/3–dc23
LC record available at https://lccn.loc.gov/2019029795
LC ebook record available at https://lccn.loc.gov/2019029796

ISBN: 978-0-367-19213-6 (hbk)
ISBN: 978-0-429-20111-0 (ebk)

Typeset in Times New Roman
by Deanta Global Publishing Services, Chennai, India

Supporting musical examples can be accessed via the online Routledge Music Research Portal:
www.routledgemusicresearch.co.uk
Please enter the activation word RRMusic and your email address when prompted. You will immediately be sent an automated email containing an access token and instructions, which will allow you to log in to the site.

With the support of MUSIDANSE (Université Paris 8)

Contents

Foreword ix

Introduction 1
Sound, the audio culture and artistic practices focussing on sound 1
The emergence of sound in music 3
A plural history: from timbre to sound–space 6
Points 10
Acknowledgements 12
Notes 13

1 On timbre 14
'Timbre' 14
    Defining timbre 14
    From the origins of the word to Rousseau 14
    Romantic musicians, orchestration treatises and positivists 16
    Timbre as phenomenon of perception: a 'map of timbres' 18
    Towards the dissolution of the concept of timbre 20
Substituting timbre for pitch 21
    Towards the emancipation of timbre 21
    Klangfarbenmelodien 24
    Timbre as central category 28
    The utopia of a language of timbres 30
Extending harmony in timbre 32
    Harmony and timbre 32
    Chord-timbres 33
    Composing timbre 35
    Thresholds of perception 37
Timbre and sound 40
Chapter 1 online examples 43
Notes 44

2 On noise — 46

On noise 46
   Noise as nuisance 46
   Musical noises 47
Two histories of music 48
Dissonance 53
Bruitisms 55
   The bruitist dilemma 55
   'Organised sound' 57
Musiques concrètes 60
   Making noise musical 60
   The musical potential of noise 64
Revolt, protest and social criticism 65
   Free jazz 66
   Rock 67
   'Touching a sound' 69
Noise and sound 72
   Industrial music, metal, rap, New York Noise, radical improvisation... 72
   Noise and construction 74
   Electronic noises and Noise 77
   Noise and sound 80
Chapter 2 online examples 81
Notes 82

3 Listening (sounds) — 83

Liberating listening 83
   Happy new ears 83
   Refocussing on listening 84
   Free listening 87
Phenomenology of listening 89
   A treatise of listening 89
   For a phenomenology of listening 90
   The four ways of listening 91
   Reduced listening and the sound object 92
A multiplicity of ways to listen 93
   Acousmatic 93
   Composing from what one perceives 96
   Listening and time 101
   Authentic listening 103

   Amplified listening 107
   Equipped listening 110
  Chapter 3 online examples 112
  Notes 113

4 Immersion in sound   114
  The 'inner' life of sound 114
  About 'immersion' 120
   Immersive sound–space 120
   Immersion and 'oceanic feeling' 122
   Dionysian immersion 124
  The 'depth' of sound 126
  The 'abyss' of sound 129
  Chapter 4 online examples 134
  Notes 135

5 Composing sound   136
  The question of material 136
   *The historicity of material and the notion
    of material 136*
   Refocussing on material 137
   Composing the material 138
  Composed resonances 139
   Change in listening 139
   Éclats 148
   Electroacoustic resonances 154
   *From rock to disco: the studio as site for the
    composition of sound 156*
   Electronic auras 160
  Composed sonorities 163
   'Sonority' 163
   Organised sound (2) 163
   Continua 170
   Textures, surfaces, masses 172
   Process 176
  Micro-composition 181
   Sound syntheses 181
   The granular paradigm 190
  Chapter 5 online examples 197
  Notes 199

6 Sound–space 201

Representational space as operatory category 201
Composing the physical space 203
    Towards the composability of space 203
    Varèse and the pioneers of the 1950s and 1960s 204
    The 1970s and 1980s 209
    The 1990s–2000s 212
    The composed sound–space: a typology test 217
Music, sound, place 219
    Music and architecture 219
    Sound installations and 'audible ecosystems' 224
    Towards the ecology of sound 230
Chapter 6 online examples 235
Notes 236

Conclusion 237

References 243
Index 270

Foreword

Makis Solomos is a Greek and French musicologist, well-known as a Xenakis scholar and also for his contribution to the study of several aspects of new music's theories and practices. *From Music to Sound* was first published in French and offers one of the very first syntheses on a topical subject: the emergence of sound with the importance that it has today. While the topic of this book is 'sound' it should be distinguished from a burgeoning literature on 'sound studies' by its focus on music as traditionally defined. Overall Makis Solomos focusses on innovative (even 'experimental') music practices, not only those of 'classical art music' but relating also to a wider range of music genres and their interactions.

Solomos has identified a central characteristic of the development of western music as one of a steady 'turn' towards sound quality itself as a key carrier of musical meaning. He grounds his presentation on historical developments in the interaction of musical materials, instrumentation and the space (including architectural) dimensions of musical life. But in the 20th century he argues for a much greater and deeper engagement with sound itself (its plastic and aesthetic nature in many forms) as the primary articulator of the musical 'argument'. Emerging clearly in the first half of the century this becomes intensified and explicit in the second half and through till today.

The foundation and development of electronic music practices plays a major role – for the first time the composition *of* timbre seemed within sight. For a while in the 1960s and 1970s it looked as if there were an explicit interaction of the new studio practices with techniques across the board – the sonic innovations of Xenakis, Ligeti, Stockhausen, Cage, Reich and Oliveros (and many others) were not confined to their electroacoustic output. Their writing for instrumental ensembles often bore close resemblance to the behaviour of oscillators, impulse and noise generators, filters, tape echo and the like. Even more so, the later spectralist composers utilized sound analysis as the basis for compositional models.

While the early literature showed an openness to cross all these boundaries, there developed a divide between discussion of sound in instrumental composition on the one hand and electroacoustic practices on the other. To reinforce this, in discussing the notion of *timbre*, classic psychoacoustic research (from the first generation of computer-enabled synthesis) focussed on sustained instrumental sound, while the post-Schaefferian project, that included *ab initio* a greater attention to noise and time-domain aspects of sound, intensified its strong relationship to the electroacoustic studio. Thus detailed consideration of timbre, harmony, noise and sound, space and immersion in a single volume is long overdue. This book brings together many strands of thought that have developed concurrently – Solomos has created an innovative synthesis in which the whole compound is much greater than the sum of its elements.

Makis Solomos elaborates his core argument through what he calls six 'histories': which of course overlap and interact. The first two chapters look at developing approaches to *sound quality*. Firstly *timbre* (Chapter 1), which has progressively become a central focus of western music composition: Solomos looks at the various shades of meaning (the English and French usages are by no means synonymous while the German *Klangfarbe* has its own history) – although the core direction of travel seems almost universal. Related to this development is a parallel and increasing engagement with *noise* (Chapter 2) and the exploration of its musical potential; here, definitions range from the acoustic to the social and psychological – and the discussion shows how all have contributed to the new materials of music.

The third Chapter (*listening*), is rightly placed at the centre of the book. In many ways other chapters may be seen as part of a constellation around this core – the author himself describes the chapter sequence as 'forming part of a spiral of ideas mutually reinforcing'. The different modes of listening are products both of evolution and of cultural history – *what do we listen out for and how?*

But there are paradoxes, too: the opening up of awareness to sound in itself is in many ways in conflict with our increasingly noisy environment (as Murray Schafer argued); this relates to the next topic (Chapter 4): the increasingly intensive *immersion in sound*. Solomos develops a psycho-sensual approach – he talks of seeking out the sound's inner life, its heart, through immersion and envelopment, 'sinking into the abyss' of sound through amplification and the microphone as microscope, spherical auditoria and surround-sound systems in composition and performance. A desire for the comfort of our amniotic state seems never far away. Solomos also brings together psychological, social, organic and inorganic metaphors for this increasingly 'deep' engagement with the material.

In Chapter 5 (*composing sound*) – he examines the evolution of the composition *of* sounds to replace composition *with* sounds. Yet he goes well beyond our traditional interpretation of this phrase as 'composing sounds = sound synthesis'. His view is much more holistic – the 'sound' of Webern and Varèse, for example, is built from specific techniques of developing musical material, instrumentation and performance practice. Electronic resources are included, of course, from all the many traditions of electroacoustic music but his approach reunites the fragmentation of earlier discussions and publications.

Finally, in Chapter 6, Solomos presents an examination of *sound–space*, which goes into much detail beyond issues of immersion dealt with in Chapter 4. He balances deftly in moving between the more abstract (Newtonian) space of some compositional approaches and the socially situated space of the 'place and site sensitive' work traditions. Once again he undermines any simplified divisions and shows us the underlying mechanisms that follow from elements of all previous chapter topics.

It is in crossing, combining and converging that these histories have ended up provoking the change of paradigm that we have steadily witnessed, as we go from a musical culture centred on *notes* to a culture of *sound*. A great strength in this approach is to paint a much 'bigger picture' of the sonic relationships of electroacoustic and classical instrumental music on the one hand, and more popular practices on the other. While Makis Solomos understandably says he approaches his theme not as historian but as a musicologist there is a great sense that we have, as a result of this book, a much better grasp of some of the 'big ideas' of the music of this era. We will eventually join this up with developments in the other arts, sciences and technology to understand our culture better.

Simon Emmerson

Introduction

Sound, the audio culture and artistic practices focussing on sound

Today, sound accompanies the life of human beings as never before: everything happens as if the spaces in which we live have been fitted out with a permanent sound system, causing a hypertrophy of our sound environment. From sound pollution suffered to music carefully chosen for listening with headphones, from supermarket music to the most beautiful moments of a concert, from the untimely ringing of a cell phone to planning a moment of silence from time to time as one sound possibility amongst others... sounds continuously pour out, mixing with one another, provoking mask effects or increasing ten-fold, becoming deafening or, on the contrary, pleasantly mysterious, weaving a sprawling polyphony that no composer would have dared plan. Music, in particular, has turned into an immense flow of sound, a planetary tsunami that is devastating for some, or a nurturing, universal amniotic fluid for others. Thanks to recording and technological progress, it has become possible and unavoidable to listen to it wherever one is, constantly. And thanks to globalisation, one can theoretically listen to whatever one wishes – or does not wish. Thus, we live in a ubiquity of music and sound that solicits continuous listening (see C. Pardo Salgado, 2011; A. Kassabian, 2013).

Whether it is a question of music or surrounding noises, one of the reasons leading to speaking about *sound* is that this auditory phenomenon, whose omnipresence we have just stressed, enjoys a certain *autonomy*. Thus, in the multimedia industry, sound design attaches sounds to electronic apparatuses which, otherwise, would produce no or very little sound: if the user ends up associating them with the object or action, he could also hear them for themselves. As for music, in the previous examples, it becomes a *sound* flow because it seems to be only the consequence of no event, other than pushing a *play* button: everything happens as if no one was playing and that it should be interrupted just as abruptly. For, indeed, recording, substituting for memory, has made possible something that was not imaginable in the past: capturing a sound, freezing it, reproducing it and repeating it. Pierre Schaeffer, the inventor of *musique concrète* – one of the first musical trends resolutely focussed on sound – liked to say that it became possible thanks to the accident of the 'closed groove' (P. Schaeffer, 2012: 39):

repeated, a noise ceases to be heard as the 'sound-of' (reference to its cause) to be sounded in itself and appreciated as such, owing to its intrinsic morphology. In a text written in 1946, before the birth of *musique concrète*, the same Schaeffer (2002: 82–84; our translation) underscores the 'microphone effect':

> The microphone gives events [...] a *purely sound* version. Without transforming sound, it transforms listening. [...] The microphone can confer the same importance then, if it pushes the magnification further, the same dimension of strangeness to a whisper, a heartbeat, the ticking of a watch.

Thus, with the technologies of sound reproduction, a new culture was born, which can be described as 'audio' – 'a culture of musicians, composers, sound artists, scholars, and listeners attentive to sonic substance, the act of listening, and the creative possibilities of sound recording playback and transmission' (C. Cox and D. Warne, 2004: XIII). In traditional culture, sound is only a *result*, sometimes less important than the music itself. Musicians must always adapt to acoustic conditions that can only be imperfect and are sometimes obliged to put up with surrounding noises. They can produce the most beautiful music with the ugliest sound, be it due to the quality of the instruments or the space with which they are playing, or else the quality of the recording or of the reproduction diffusing them. It is said that music does not reside in sound, that it is found in the musicians' gesture and in its internal structures, or even in the pure musical intention. Thanks to the score, classical musicians have developed 'inner hearing', by which they can hear music without any sound being produced. As concerns the listener, the 'structural listening' theorised by Theodor W. Adorno (1976: 1–20) – listening that aims to define the internal organisation of the work, of which the characteristics are sometimes not present as sound events – represents, in a sense, the ideal of this culture. The new audio culture overturns the perspective. Focussed on sound – or, more precisely, on 'fixed' sounds, to borrow the terminology of Michel Chion (2016: 136) – and listening, it develops gestures, structures, intentions, meanings or emotions directly in what was previously considered only an epiphenomenon. This does not, of course, mean that there is nothing 'beyond' sound or that sound has become an end to itself for, as the feminist electronic musician Tara Rodgers (2010: 5) wrote, 'sounds are points of departure to realms of personal history, cultural memory, and political struggle'.

The importance of the audio culture is well established. It is at the heart of this new discipline – or, rather, interdiscipline – that sound studies have developed. An increasingly large amount of work is questioning sound and its place in culture according to extremely varied directions. Some studies are concerned with the emergence of audio culture and its inextricable relation with technologies of sound reproduction (see J. Sterne, 2003). Others are developing the concepts of sound 'ambiance' (see J.P. Thibaud, 2016; C. Guillebaud, ed., 2017) and sound 'atmosphere' (see G. Böhme, 2017) or even link sound studies with affect studies (see M. Thompson, I. Biddle, eds., 2013). The pioneering essay by the Grenoble natives Jean-François Augoyard and Henri Torgue (eds., 2005) proposes a general morphological analysis of the world of sounds, whereas the artist and theorist Brandon LaBelle studies how sound constitutes territories (B. LaBelle, 2010) or composes forms of resistance (B. LaBelle, 2018). Other studies deal with soundscapes of powerful historical moments (see C. Birdsall, 2012), envisage an interdisciplinary history of the notion of vibration (see S. Trower, 2010) or a history of music as provoking illnesses (see J. Kennaway, 2012), question the presence of sound in places such as hospitals (see T. Rice, 2013), propose exhaustive studies of listening to music in the car (see K. Bijsterveld et al., 2014)... The avenues are infinite.[1]

The importance of audio culture can also be measured in the abundant development of a group of practices focussed on sound, ranging from the functional to the artistic. In the purely functional, we will mention background music, advertising music, sound logos, sound design – 'Muzak', of which the name of the homonymous American firm, founded in 1922, remains emblematic. If Muzak – of which Érik Satie had predicted the use of sound with his famous '*musiques d'ameublement*' or 'furniture music'[2] – remains, quite felicitously, a foil for a number of people today, other functional practices of sound tend to develop, their natural limit being the fact that sound is more present, and thus more cumbersome, than the image.

As for artistic practices centred on sound, they are manifold, heterogeneous and varied, evolving at high speed. Evolving just as rapidly is their categorisation. We could evoke the relatively recent art of sound installations and sound sculptures, the realisations stemming from field recordings that display an artistic will, soundwalks, artistic works in relation to acoustic ecology or various types of sound performances. We could also mention sound practices that are developing within other arts, in particular visual arts, cinema, dance, theatre, poetry and literature, performance... not to overlook digital and multimedia arts. Finally, there exists a new art centred entirely on sound: sound art. This recent generic expression – sometimes we still hear talk of 'audio art', 'sonic art', etc. – is increasingly theorised.[3] It designates a set of heterogeneous practices on the level of artists of today who claim to represent it as much as those of the past, whom theorists consider the ancestors of the genre. Some of the artists who embody it come from the visual sphere and produce sound works often in relation with images, visual objects or spaces. Another part is of acousmatic – purely auditory – allegiance and sometimes comes from the art of recording, evoking in a sense what, in the 1960s, François-Bernard Mâche (1998: 79) called '*phonographies*'. But others categorised as 'sound artists' could perhaps be apprehended as belonging to what continues to bear the name *music*.

The emergence of sound in music

What about music, which is the object of this book? Might it have remained outside this vast movement refocussing on sound? Might it have taken refuge in what would be specifically musical, which would distinguish it from 'simple' sound? This is certainly the case with some of today's musical trends, in which sound remains an inert matter, animated by traditional notions of melody, harmony, rhythm or instrumentation. But, in a number of other cases – which go beyond the divisions between musical genres – it is, quite to the contrary, *music itself that has profoundly contributed to this refocussing on sound*.

In contemporary music, whether instrumental or mixed with electronics, this decisive transformation is expressed by, amongst others, the very extensive work on timbre, and the extraordinary innovations, as regards extended techniques and orchestration. A composer such as Giacinto Scelsi went so far as hypostatising sound:

> You have no idea of what there is in a single sound! There are even counterpoints if you will, gaps of different timbres. There are even harmonics that give totally different effects, which not only come out of sound but enter the centre of sound. There are concentric and divergent movements in a single sound. That sound becomes very large. It becomes a part of the cosmos, however minimal. There is everything inside.
>
> (2006: 75; our translation)

In electroacoustic music – from the earliest *musique concrète* or electronic music to current space–sound research, by way of the notion of 'sonic art' defended by Trevor Wishart (1985) – sound is both material and form, formal and narrative model, insignificant matter and mysterious sound body with multiple connotations… Whether working on treatments or synthesis, sound determines it through and through, the fundamental questions become: What is a sound? Where does it begin? Where does it end? (see R. Meric, 2012.) In various types of 'experimental' music of yesterday or today – the sense of the expression 'experimental music(s)' is constantly evolving: compare, for example, Pierre Schaeffer (ed., 1957), Michael Nyman (1974) and Jennie Gottschalk (2016) – the turning point towards sound gives rise to what could be called, generically speaking, a 'sound-based music' (see L. Landy, 2007a). As for the diverse current types of electronic music, popular or experimental, it is obvious that sound constitutes their very substance. But sound has become fundamental in numerous other musical genres. In forms of popular music such as rock, disco, funk, rap, pop, world music… studio work has led to bringing out the role of the engineer and producer, who create sound treatments and arrangements constituting much more than window-dressing and resulting in albums whose interest is 'no longer just about the songs any more, but about the sound' (D. Levitin, 2007: 2). Baroque purists have also developed the idea of sound as an additional element to an extreme. In their realisations, sound effects add spice to scores heretofore imagined in a somewhat disembodied way: what is there in common between *The Four Seasons* played by an orchestra – even the best – of the 1950s to 1960s and the same *Four Seasons* reinvented by Il Giardino Armonico? In jazz, 'when we use [the word "sound", it] is much broader than "sonority"; it is basically like personality; it is a whole; it is practically the style' (P. Carles, 2001: 67). We find the same use in flamenco – 'You should understand this: each song or each style of flamenco has a different sound, and what you must do, what you normally do, is to get involved into that sound' writes Paco Peña (in D. Bailey, 1992: 15).

Such is the subject of this book: showing that sound has worked its way into being a central issue of music. From Debussy to contemporary music in this early 21st century, from rock to *electronica*, from the sound objects of the earliest *musique concrète* to current electroacoustic music, from the *Poème électronique* of Le Corbusier-Varèse-Xenakis to the most recent inter-arts attempts, sound has become one of the major wagers – if not *the* major wager – of music. Everything has happened as if music had begun a change of paradigm: we are going from a musical culture centred on the note to a culture of sound. And it could be wagered that this radical change is at least as founding as the revolution that, at the beginning of the 17th century, gave birth to tonality: as regards the most advanced music of the 20th century, we notice with distance that the adjective 'atonal' corresponded only to its potential for destruction of the past, with the refocussing on sound constituting the constructive side.

The hypothesis that will be defended is that this change of paradigm came about within music itself, i.e., according to an evolution unique to it, in its technical stakes, aesthetic content and reception. Certainly, outside factors intervened. That is particularly the case with technology, which, as has been seen with recording, is central to audio culture. However, if we exclude cinema, the birth of which is linked to technology, music is the first art to have appropriated technology, this becoming a natural extension of musical technique. In numerous types of music today, it is impossible to make the distinction between 'technique' and 'technology'. Modern musical culture and audio culture, both centred on sound, have developed at the same pace and converged progressively. Far from disappearing in favour of a triumphant audio culture, musical culture, which had reached its apogee with Romanticism, has precisely been revitalised thanks to a refocussing on sound by, of course, transforming itself radically.

This change of paradigm might be thought of as the equivalent of a phenomenological reduction. This explanation has often been favoured by the few musicologists or philosophers of music who, in the past, took note of this refocussing. As Daniel Charles, specialist on John Cage, wrote: 'Everything happens as if, nowadays, music were discovering this matter never yet isolated for itself, and which, however, seems to constitute the very condition of its edification: that of the appearance of sounds' (D. Charles, 1978: 27; our translation). Indeed, with several musicians, the attraction of what is purely sound looks like a return to the sources: 'There is, with Webern, like a metaphysical need to put aside all artifice to achieve the primordial and fundamental, to surprise musical thinking at its very birth' wrote Gisèle Brelet (1968: 256; our translation).

The phenomenological explanation remains valid for numerous types of music. But the refocussing on sound cannot always be thought of as 'reduction'. More generally, it could be described as 'emergence'. In its fullest sense, as developed in certain trends of the cognitive sciences, physics, biology, etc., this word designates an evolution, which, starting from a critical threshold of complexity, generates new properties. For example, going from music centred on tonality to a music of sound does not necessarily mean that the latter simply substitutes for the former. That can also occur when – as with spectral music – the work on pitches, by its increasing complexity, produces objects that end up no longer perceived as chords but as composed sounds. In this book, the word 'emergence' will most often be taken in the weaker sense, designating, on the one hand, the fact that refocussing on sound happens through a progressive and inner evolution to music, and that, on the other, this evolution proceeds by way of increasing complexity.

A plural history: from timbre to sound–space

This book proposes tracing the history of the emergence of sound in music itself. It will go back to the beginning of the 20th century – with a few incursions into earlier periods – and arrive at this early 21st century, the transformation not yet being finished. The milestones marking this history are quite numerous. For the pre-1945 period, we can mention the colourist approach to harmony of musical Impressionism, the concept of melody of timbres put forward by the Second Vienna School, Italian bruitism, Édgar Varèse and his famous definition of music as 'organised sound'… In the post-1945 period, we can turn our attention to the aforementioned *musique concrète*, to the beginnings of electronic music, to serialism and the composed sonorities of Iannis Xenakis, to the refocussing on listening carried out by John Cage. In the 1960s and 1970s, digital sound synthesis opened new paths, at the same time, free jazz and rock were also emancipating sound, in the same way as minimalism or the pioneers of live electronics. The development of extended playing techniques of avant-garde instrumental and vocal music continued the expansion of sound in the 1970s and 1980s. Then came the threshold explored by spectral music, the sound parasitosis of 'industrial music', the exploration of space, the rediscovery of consonance by post-modernity, which does not re-establish the functionality of tonal music but plunges the listener into the meditative sensuality of sound, ambient music, the development of real-time electronics and mixed music, the birth of different types of (popular) electronic music.

How does one narrate the history of this emergence? Is it possible to establish a linear chronology of it, as has just been done, and as histories of music do in general? The complexity of the notion of sound imposes another strategy. In fact, throughout this book, the reader will be able to ask him- or herself: What is sound for music? Might it be 'timbre'? Can it be reduced to the idea of 'colour'? Could it be assimilated to its physical description? Moreover, is it possible to treat it without speaking about space? Another question, to which theorists responded positively for centuries: Must we limit sounds to those called 'musical', eliminating noises? On a different note: Can we envisage sound as object, i.e., as an entity external to our perception? Constituting a complex notion, sound combines several aspects, encompassing the notions of timbre, colour, noise and space… Its development in music goes via several paths, and it is therefore impossible to establish one single line. That is why this book is made up of *several* histories, six in all, each representing the subject of a different chapter. 'Sound' is not the prerogative of just one of these histories; it results precisely from their combination. Their interaction produces the singular history of the emergence of sound.

The opening chapter deals with the notion of *timbre*. First of all, the fascinating history of this notion will be analysed. From Jean-Jacques Rousseau's (1995) *Dictionnaire de musique* (1767) up to current research on visual mappings for acoustic timbre features (see S. Soraghan et al., 2016) or the use of audio descriptors (see K. Siedenburg et al., 2016) by way of Hermann von Helmholtz's (1895) *Die Lehre von den Tonempfindungen* (1862) or work on the 'map of timbres' concept (J. Grey, 1975), this notion has ended up by designating a *phenomenon of perception*. Then, it will be shown how, in the history of music, timbre becomes increasingly important, thanks to the simultaneous development of two complementary paradigms. The first tends to *substitute timbre for pitch*; arriving at the utopia of a language of timbres, it comprises several decisive stages, such as the birth of orchestration, the development of orchestration in the 19th century, the concept of *Klangfarbenmelodie* or the frenzied multiplication of new playing methods in post-war instrumental music. The other major paradigm is presented as a *prolongation of harmony in timbre* and is displayed in the colourist harmony of Richard Wagner, or the timbre-chords of Claude Debussy or Olivier Messiaen, the attempt at composing timbre in Karlheinz Stockhausen's earliest electronic music, the timbre-harmony fusion of spectral music or the orchestration assistance software developed at Paris's Institut de Recherche et Coordination Acoustique/Musique (IRCAM). This great adventure of timbre, sometimes considered 'French' – even though Claudio Monteverdi constitutes one of its origins, Wagner is a missing link, and Jonathan Harvey contributed to it… – is perhaps that of the six histories which can henceforth be considered achieved, an affirmation that, of course, does not invalidate ongoing research on the concept of timbre or today's music of timbre.

Second history: music's progressive acceptance of *noise*. Over the past few years, noise is at the centre of numerous interests in media sciences or human sciences (see M. Thompson; 2017; G. Hainge, 2013; H. Schwartz, 2011; M. Goddard, B. Halligan, P. Hegarty, eds., 2012). A *noise* trend also runs through a broad spectrum of today's music. But noise is not a discovery of today's music: as this chapter shows, we can trace a history of music tending towards its integration. Although it is true that, for a long time, theorists considered it the opposite of so-called 'musical' sounds, it innervated music unofficially, either through the needs of imitative music (thus, Jean-Philippe Rameau composed a 'noise of sea and winds' in *Hippolyte et Aricie*), or through dissonance that developed up to the 'cacophonies' of the polytonalities of Igor Stravinsky and Charles Ives or Arnold Schoenberg's free atonality. With the bruitism of a Luigi Russolo, the sound research of Varèse, then with *musique concrète*, it made a grand entrance in music. It then developed in avant-garde music and tended to present itself – in free jazz, historic rock or with a Lachenmann – as social criticism. And it is henceforth spreading in industrial music, metal, rap, 'New York Noise', radical improvisation, the new Russian constructivism, 'Japanoise' and simply 'Noise'. We can say, at the conclusion of this history – which is not yet finished – that the exploration of sounds of indeterminate pitch not only enriches the musical material but, in addition, changes our very conception of music. As regards the intention of this book, the increasingly intensive lack of differentiation between the so-called 'musical' sound and noise opens wide the door of sound apprehended in its full generality.

The opening up to sound in its generality is synonymous with a new way of apprehending music, i.e., *listening*. That is why the third chapter draws a history of musical listening. Some continue to assert that advanced music of the 20th century is 'difficult' (for the public) but, in truth, that is valid only if the listener hopes to again find in it what characterises music of the past or types of music described as 'easier': melody, harmony, standard forms, etc. The refocussing on sound went hand in hand with a profound change in listening, which, precisely, allows for appreciating the morphological sound inventiveness of music that is sometimes complex in its elaboration but can be easy and pleasant to listen to if we hone our ear to appreciate these morphologies. This chapter first proposes a particular development on two contemporary figures who, without being the sole pioneers to have broached the question of listening in modern music, offer the advantage of posing, by their complementarity, fundamental questions. First of all, there is John Cage, whose amusing witticism 'happy new ears' opened the path of free listening; then Pierre Schaeffer who, by his phenomenological approach, aimed at reinventing what civilisation had buried. The chapter goes on to examine several strategies towards developing listening in recent forms of music: acousmatic, composition starting from what is perceived, minimalism, 'authentic' listening, amplified listening or equipped listening.

The fourth history is devoted to one of the most frequent entries in sound: sound *immersion*. Today, the word 'immersion' tends to designate virtual reality and serves as publicity for speaker systems, which, by their quality, highlights the literally sonic aspects of the types of music they reproduce – deep basses, spatialisation effects, etc. But its meaning can be expanded to include thoughts and discourses that sometimes accompany the refocussing on sound. Following Edgar Varèse (1983: 184), numerous composers of instrumental music and, even more, of electroacoustic music, evoke the existence of an *inner life* of sound. They thereby emphasise the fact that, unlike the music theory notion of note, reducible to a point, a sound is endowed with a 'thickness', which can be 'listened to' by 'diving' into it. Next, several types of sound immersion are analysed: 'sound–spaces' – of which this first mention prepares the book's final chapter – in the literal sense (musical-architectural projects such as the auditorium of the German pavilion at the Osaka World's Fair in 1970 used by Stockhausen) or the figurative (static music of the 1960s and 1970s: Ligeti, minimalism, psychedelic rock...); immersion generating a sort of oceanic, intensely close feeling, which characterises, for example, ambient music; the Dionysian type of immersion that a Xenakis convokes in the *Diatopes*. The chapter continues with the analysis of the project of one of the purest musicians of sound, Scelsi, who has already been mentioned above, a project that evokes the idea of a sphericity of sound; this idea opens wide the door to a *spiritualistic approach*, one that is sometimes associated with the becoming-sound of music. Then a few famous 'mystical' trends are examined with sound musicians: Alexander Scriabin, La Monte Young, John Coltrane, Gérard Grisey, Jonathan Harvey and Glenn Branca...

In a way, the fifth chapter, owing to its scope, constitutes a book in itself. It narrates the very dense history of what could be described as musical constructivism – substituting for or prolonging the organicist paradigm that dominated Romantic music – where, to borrow Risset's famous phrase, *the composition of sound* replaces composition *with* sounds.[4] If we sometimes continue to assert that music cannot be 'limited' to sound, it is because the latter is apprehended as inert matter, devoid of all subjectivity, like a simple vibration that has no need of humans to exist. Yet, precisely, one of the royal roads leading to refocussing music on sound consists of thinking of it as susceptible to being constructed, as a composable entity. The chapter first focusses on the question of the *progress of material* that has run through the 20th century, from dodecaphony up to the most advanced research on sound synthesis, a question that has played a decisive role in the theoretical debates accompanying the history of the emergence of sound – one will think in particular of the Adorno school. It goes on to develop the idea of *composed resonances* to study well-known pieces of music, which are still not commonly broached from the angle of sound. Thus, dealing with dodecaphonic and serial music, it defends the hypothesis that, in certain works, the compositional hypercomplexification of classic 'parameters' (pitches, rhythms...) constitutes a sort of 'infrastructure': this work is worthless in itself but serves for composing sonorities – Anton Webern's *Symphony Op. 21* and Pierre Boulez's *Le Marteau sans maître* are analysed in this sense. The idea of composed resonance is also applied to the analysis of a few historic pieces of electroacoustic music, as well as to the role played by the studio in pop music spanning rock of the 1960s and 1970s up to disco, along with certain mixed instrumental-electronic music productions in which electronics appear as a sort of 'aura' of the instrumental parts. Next, we develop the idea of *composed sonorities* to analyse instrumental musical works appearing openly as composition-of-sound. A first model is provided by Varèse's *Ionisation*, pure music of sound textures, even though it is possible to continue to envisage a thematic reading of it. Other types of music, from Ivan Wyschnegradsky to composers of today, are apprehended from the same viewpoint, through the question of the continuum that has developed throughout this history of the emergence of sound. Then comes the notions of texture, mass and surface, explored with the work of Xenakis. The idea of process closes this part and allows for broaching two musical trends that have strongly developed sound-based music: minimalism and spectral music. The last part of the chapter apprehends the *micro-composition* of sound, i.e., sound syntheses. First offering an historical panorama of the development of the latter, then focussing on a particular method, the synthesis or granular 'sensibility',[5] it supports the hypothesis that sound synthesis embodies the possibility of generalising the *praxis* of composition by thinking the entire work as composed sound and subsequently tending towards the unification of diverse timescales, from the material to the overall form.

The six histories presented in this book are interwoven in a spiral. The first, dealing with timbre, is already accomplished whereas the last is, at present, fast developing: it is the history in which music and sound extend in *space*. Although, in recent years, the expression 'sound space' has found a terrain for interdisciplinary development, going from sound studies to studies of environmental ecology, by way of the theatre and other performing arts, geography, urbanism and architecture, design, ethnology and sociology... (see, amongst others C. Guiu et al., ed., 2014; G. Born, ed., 2013), it was in music that it first materialised, thanks to a long history making its way towards the *composability* of the sound space. To tell the truth, space has always been a part of music, if we think about traditional forms of music; however, the generalisation of the Italian-style stage, which went hand in hand with the birth of tonal music, has neutralised it. That is why the modern history of this composed space began with orchestral writing of the 19th century (Berlioz or Wagner), continuing in crescendo with Ives, Varèse, Stockhausen, Xenakis, Emmanuel Nunes, the set-ups of electroacoustic music, ambisonics, wavefield synthesis and, at the present time, giving rise to a very high number of realisations whether technological or artistic. But there is also, alongside this history, a history of space as a tool of *representation*, with which the chapter opens: in this sense, space constitutes a new operating category, allowing for thinking, composing and listening to music. These two complementary histories allow for developing the *sound–space* hypothesis: the emergence of sound is also emergence of space; the types of today's music are not only sound-based but are also sound–space-based. Had this book been written 30 years ago, it would have stopped here. But the latest musical evolutions in the emergence of sound certainly justify that the history of sound–space be pursued in order to include here discussions about relations between music and architecture, about realisations in terms of sound installations and 'audible ecosystems', about music of soundscape-based composition stemming from acoustic ecology, field recording or soundwalks.

Points

Even though narrating a history, this book was not written by a historian. It will not deal much with the context that accompanies the emergence of sound in music. A history of this emergence told by a historian would grant a large place to audio culture in all its manifestations: radio practice, discophilia, peer-to-peer downloads... It would deal at length with the history of sound technologies: recording, digital audio techniques... It would insist on the history of musical institutions favouring the emergence of sound: research centres for 'art' music, recording studios for popular forms of music... Rather, this book is written by a musicologist whose object of study is music itself – and, through it, the multiple experiences to which it invites, heightening our senses, our sensibility and intellectual faculties, developing our memory and forecasting capacities, and increasing our imagination by enabling us to tame our emotions to go in search of the unknown. For a number of types of music broached, the musical *work* – in the sense of process or project – constitutes the special place where the experience of music occurs: this history of the emergence of sound will be, in large part, a history of musical works.

Of course, we shall also take into account musical techniques and technologies, musical theories as well as other specifically musical manifestations.

There are very many writings on the subject of the emergence of sound in music, dealing with one of its aspects (timbre, noise, space…), particular composers or specific works. They will be mentioned in due course and grouped in the bibliographic section. The present book proposes a synthesis, one of the first of its kind, since its ambition is to delimit the emergence of sound systematically and globally. Moreover, the principal musical genres studied here are in relation with the types of music in which the author specialises, the so-called 'art' or 'highbrow' music – 'contemporary', 'avant-garde', 'experimental' kinds of music… But it is important to specify, as has already been done, that the refocussing on sound goes beyond the division between musical genres – hence the incursion into a few other fields. It should be pointed out that, sometimes going into detail of the musical works, this book could be inspired by analytical methods developed in the framework of electroacoustic music[6] – which remains to the present day the most developed sound-based music (and even sound–space-based music).

The synthesis that this book attempts has necessitated several years of research. Prior to the actual writing, specialised work that I carried out nourished the thinking, making it evolve and leading to the necessary distance. During the writing, I undertook further research to try to provide as broad a view as possible, with hopes of not skipping over too many things. At times, this quest looked like a bottomless pit: each time that I advanced in one area, another, unknown, appeared. Although it is customary to warn the reader that no synthesis can be exhaustive, here it will not be a simple oratorical precaution. Despite the large number of musical trends and musicians mentioned, several others, equally pertinent, are absent. But this confirms the scope of the subject: the change of paradigm under discussion concerns practically all music going back at least a century! Besides, this book sometimes refers to little-known or unknown musical works next to others more frequently mentioned by musicologists and music lovers. It also seeks a balance between sections comprising analytical developments and others of a more synthetic nature – it hopes to address the general public and specialists alike.

The English version of the book, which the reader has in hand, is quite different from the original French version. On the one hand, this is an abridged version: for the needs of the English edition, a good number of analyses, developments and musical examples had to be deleted or reduced. On the other hand, I have sought a new balance of musical references by eliminating some and introducing others which will be more familiar in the English-speaking world. Above all, I sought to introduce several references that were forgotten in the French version. That version having come out in 2013, I have had the time to receive several reactions. The most frequent comment – after the customary praise – consisted of pointing out to me musicians whom the book did not mention or not sufficiently. What I initially took as criticism is, in the final analysis, praise: it would seem that this book succeeds in whetting the musical appetite, stimulating a desire to hear different types of music developing in several directions and sometimes ill known – so it is to help me go in that sense that my readers were giving me new trails! Of course, it still remains just as incomplete. Final point: in the English version, certain examples are given in e-resource.

Acknowledgements

The gestation, writing and completion of the French version of this book spanned several years. Without the encouragement and support of friends, colleagues and students, I would never have put the final full stop. Indeed, I interrupted it on several occasions, discouraged by the scope that the research was taking and by the domains that I was obliged to broach, without always being a specialist in them. So as not to give up on it, I subconsciously deployed a childish strategy but one that eventually paid off: I spoke about it with friends, colleagues and my students as a book I was on the verge of finishing, so it was indeed necessary to keep my promise and finish it!

Amongst the friends and colleagues who helped me keep this promise, I would first like to mention those who were willing to read me with a critical eye. Roberto Barbanti, Agostino Di Scipio, Carmen Pardo Salgado, Jean-Claude Risset and Horacio Vaggione reread important passages on the level of ideas. My other readers were called upon for their competence in particular fields: Ramón González-Arroyo, Olivier Baudouin, François Bayle, Marie-Hélène Bernard, Kevin Dahan, Didier Guigue, Roseline Kassap, Elisavet Kiourtsoglou, Guillaume Loizillon, Mario Lorenzo, Frédéric Maintenant, Frédéric Saffar and Benoît Tarjabayle. May these friends and colleagues be reassured: if there remain any ideas that are still blurred or data that are erroneous, I alone am responsible!

I would next like to name my Xenakian connections, especially Rudolf Frisius, Benoît Gibson, Peter Hoffmann, James Harley, Antonios Antonopoulos, Anne-Sylvie Barthel-Calvet, Elisavet Kiourtsoglou, Anastasia Georgaki, Kostas Paparrigopoulos, Curtis Roads, Stéphan Schaub, Dimitris Exarchos, Reinhold Friedl and Charles Turner, with whom discussions often deal with themes that this book crosses – moreover, it is in my doctoral thesis, dedicated to Xenakis, that the issue of refocussing on sound appeared. Another network that played an important role consists of my colleagues and co-founders of the review *Filigrane. Musique, esthétique, sciences, société*, Joëlle Caullier, Jean-Marc Chouvel and Jean-Paul Olive, for this periodical was born practically at the same time I was beginning this book. Thanks, too, to the colleagues who wrote reviews of the French edition or participated in debates when the book was published: Jacques Amblard, Claude Chastagnier, Élie During, Christine Guillebaud, Christophe Franco-Rogelio, Mihu Iliescu, Martin Laliberté, Philippe Lalitte, Tom Mays et al. Other friends and colleagues have more or less followed this project, supplying me with ideas and discoveries or, quite simply, encouraging me: it would be impossible to mention them all here without risking overlooking some.

Finally, my students at the Université Paul Valéry, then the Université Paris 8, played a fundamental role. Many of the ideas in this book were tested on them and benefited from their remarks and their own experiences. Some of the oldest are now friends or colleagues. I would like to name, in particular, a few PhD students, present or past: Renaud Meric, Frédérick Duhautpas, Sara Bourgenot, Guilhem Rosa, Jose-Luis Besada, Alejandro Reyna, Louisa Martin Chevalier, João Fernandez, Stephen No, Ariadna Alsina, Alejandro Gómez Villagómez, Kumiko Iseki, Namur Matos Rocha, Dimitra Papachristou, Riccardo Wanke, Daniel Mancero, Federico Rodriguez, Anastasia Chernigina and Antoine Freychet.

For the English version of the book, my warm thanks to John Tyler Tuttle, who had the patience to translate it and to do so in several stages. Many thanks also to Heidi Bishop and Laura Sandford of Routledge, who have accompanied its realisation. And I would especially like to thank Simon Emmerson who agreed to write the foreword, thereby offering an introduction to English readers.

The French edition was dedicated to my daughter, Ειρήνη, who 'will always have the age of this book', as it was written. The present edition owes much to Isabelle, were it only because she encouraged me to take the plunge.

Notes

1 Numerous collective publications explore several directions simultaneously: see T. Pinch et al., ed., 2012; J. Sterne, ed., 2012; C. Guiu et al., ed., 2014; M. Bull et al., ed., 2016; M. Bull, ed., 2018.
2 'We wish to establish a form of music designed to satisfy "utility" requirements. Art does not come into these requirements. "Furniture Music" creates vibration; it has no other purpose; it fills the same role as light, warmth, and comfort in all its forms' (E. Satie, 1997: 200).
3 To mention only a few works: see H. de la Motte, ed. 1999; A. Weiss, 2000; A. Licht, 2007; S. Kim-Cohen, 2009; F. Dyson, 2009; S. Voegelin, 2010; C. Kelly, ed., 2011; P. Price, 2011; P.Y. Macé, 2012; A. Carlyle et al., eds., 2013; B. LaBelle, 2015; T. Gardner et al., eds., 2016; A. Castant, 2017; M. Cobussen et al., eds., 2017.
4 'One of my early desires as a musician was to sculpt and organize directly the sound material – to compose the sound itself, instead of merely composing with sounds' (J.C. Risset, 1992: 591).
5 The expression 'granular sensibility' is used by Horacio Vaggione (2005: 348).
6 See, amongst others: D. Smalley, 1986; S. Emmerson, ed., 1986; T. Licata, ed., 2002; S. Roy, 2003; M. Simoni, ed., 2006; S. Emmerson, L. Landy, eds., 2016; C. Roads, 2015; A. Bonardi et al., eds., 2017.

1 On timbre

'Timbre'

Defining timbre

The history of the notion of 'timbre' gave rise to an extraordinary adventure: although it appeared progressively, it ended up becoming a central category in music in the latter half of the 20th century. But it is a difficult notion to define. By timbre, does one mean the 'colour' of a sound ('a shimmering timbre') or else its cause ('the timbre of a violin *pizzicato*')? Can it be measured? Even today, it is often given a negative definition: in sound, timbre is something that is not pitch, duration, intensity or spatial position.

A definition that henceforth seems to have emerged introduces an important idea: timbre is 'that *attribute of auditory sensation* in terms of which a listener can judge that two sounds similarly presented and having the same loudness and pitch are dissimilar' (American Standards Association, quoted in A. Bregman, 1990: 92; our italics). Here let us sketch the history of the concept of timbre to understand why this definition has imposed itself and to ask the question of whether this concept still constitutes a useful notion.

From the origins of the word to Rousseau

The French language is the first to have used the specific word *timbre*. Certain languages would subsequently use the same word (*timbro* in Italian, *timbre* in Spanish and English, *tembr'* in Russian), whereas others would make use of the composite expression 'colour of sound' (*Klangfarbe* in German, *tone* or *sound colour* in English – words used in parallel with 'timbre' – ηχόχρωμα in modern Greek, *yinse* in Chinese...).

The French word has a long, abundant history. In the Middle Ages, it had several meanings, some of which were already musical: 'Timbre 1: a sort of tambourine / sort of bell / head / coat of arms. Timbre 2: trough, fountain / vase, jug. Timbre 3: furrier's term, marten or ermine skin, etc. *Timbrer*: to make resonate (a *timbre*) / call someone with the sound of a drum / play the *timbre* / resonate' (F. Godefroy, 1994; our translation). As for its musical sense, it would seem that the word ended up designating a bell: 'A sort of round bell which has no clapper inside and is struck on the outside with a hammer. The *timbre* of a clock. *Timbre* of an alarm clock. The timbre of this clock is quite good', one can read in the first edition of the *Dictionnaire de l'Académie française* (1694; our translation).

The modern musical sense does not appear until the fifth edition of that dictionary (1798), which, after the repeat of the previous definition, adds: 'It is sometimes said for the sound made by the *timbre*. This *timbre* is too brilliant' (our translation). However, this modern notion seems to have already been present, even without the usage of the word, as attests Marin Mersenne's famous *Harmonie universelle* (1636–1637). It is possible to advance the hypothesis that the meaning of the modern sense was initially limited to the voice (see H. Xanthoudakis, 1992: 24–25). We would therefore have the following evolution outline: bell > sound quality of the bell > sound quality of the voice > sound quality in general. Regardless, let us observe that the word will always maintain the idea of a *cause*, i.e., the origin of a sound (a bell, a voice and, by extension, a musical instrument) – an important observation for henceforth underscoring its limits.

Jean-Jacques Rousseau seems to be the first to have officialised the usage of the word in its modern sense, integrating it in his *Dictionnaire de musique* (1767), which assembles what he had written for Diderot and d'Alembert's *Encyclopédie*. The word ('tymbre') is encountered several times. In the entry devoted to it, its definition proposes a first typology: 'One thus calls, by metaphor, this quality of the sound by which it is shrill or soft, dull or bright, dry or mellow' (J.-J. Rousseau, 1995: 1135; our translation).

In the definition given for 'sound', it is placed as the third 'object', the third 'part' to consider, alongside 'tone' (or 'elevation') and 'force' (Ibid: 1047), and one discovers one of the definitions still used to the present day:

> As for the difference found […] between sounds by the quality of the timbre, it is obvious that it is due neither to the degree of elevation nor even to that of force. No matter how much an oboe puts itself in unison with a flute, it will have to sweeten its sound to the same degree; the sound of the flute will still have that *je ne sais quoi* of mellowness and sweetness; that of the oboe, a *je ne sais quoi* of roughness and harshness, which will prevent the ear from confusing them; not to mention the diversity of the timbre of voices.
>
> (Ibid: 1053; our translation)

To which Rousseau adds:

> However, no one, so far as I know, has examined sound in this part; which, as well as the others, will perhaps find itself having difficulties: for the quality of the timbre can depend neither on the number of vibrations, which makes the degree from low to high, nor the size or force of these same vibrations, which makes the degree from strong to weak. So it will be necessary to find in the sound body a third cause, different from these two, to explain this third quality of sound and its differences; which, perhaps, is not too easy.
>
> (Ibid: 1053; our translation)

16 On timbre

Rousseau relates what, in current terms, we would call a *sensation*, with *physical* causes. The (sensation of) pitch ('tone' or 'elevation' in his language) stems from the number of vibrations, the (sensation of) intensity of their 'force'; hence his hypothesis: timbre must have a cause, which is to be sought in the sound body. This hypothesis will be taken seriously by the positivists of the 19th century.

Romantic musicians, orchestration treatises and positivists

In the 19th century, the word entered the French language but was still little used – it was above all in relation to the voice. Italians still preferred to speak of *colore de' suoni* (see P. Lichtenthal, 1826). In German, *Klangfarbe*, and sometimes *Tonfarbe*, gradually established themselves: Gustav Schilling (1838) noted for *Tonfarbe*: 'more commonly *Klangfarbe*', whereas *Klangfarbe*, as we shall see, became a keyword in Helmholtz's famous treatise *Die Lehre von den Tonempfindungen*. As for English, a plurilingual musical dictionary of 1871 notes that 'timbre' is a French word signifying 'the quality of tone' (J. Hiles, 1871).

In their writings, the Romantic musicians integrated the word only gradually. One would expect it in Schumann's exceptional 1835 analysis of Berlioz's *Symphonie fantastique*, but it never occurs, whereas we have many other rich expressions such as in these sentences: 'Admittedly, Berlioz blanches at nothing that makes *a tone, a sound, a noise or a clang*. He uses muted trombones, and horns, and harps and English horns and even bells' (R. Schumann, 1965: 84; our italics).[1] Some 20 years later, Liszt used the concept and term more commonly – the French term, for most of his articles were originally in French – but he continues to utilise general expressions such as 'sonority', 'sound', 'colour' or 'shade' (see F. Liszt, 1995). During the same period, in *Oper und Drama* (1852), Wagner used the word *Klangfarbe* fairly frequently. In Berlioz's memoirs, we find the French word some twenty times in reference to the voice or instruments – for example, when explaining that he attended performances at the Opera armed with scores: 'In this way I began to see how to write for the orchestra and to understand something of the accents and timbres, as well as the ranges and mechanisms of most of the instruments' (H. Berlioz, 1969: 98; our translation).

The slow introduction of the word 'timbre' during the 19th century is also attested to by orchestration treatises. It is not to be found in Louis-Joseph Francœur's *Diapason général de tous les instruments à vent* (1772), the first book that, according to James E. Perone (1996), can be described as an orchestration treatise. This is also the case with its extensive revision by Alexandre Choron (L.-J. Francœur et al., 1813). The treatise by Georges Kastner integrates, albeit timidly, the word: once for voices and, more often, for string effects; for example, one reads: 'The *mute* [...] gives the violin a veiled, mysterious, plaintive timbre [...]'. But Kastner can also use periphrases: '*sul ponticello*: it is a kind of sound [...]' (G. Kastner, 1835: 6; our translation). Berlioz's extraordinary treatise (1843; 1993) does not use it a single time, preferring the words 'instrument' and 'sound'.

At the end of the century, orchestration reaches its apogee. Rimsky-Korsakov's treatise envisages complex operations such as 'the amplification and elimination of tone qualities': amplification is 'the operation which consists of contrasting the resonance of two different groups (or the different timbres of one and the same group), either in sustained notes or chords, [... to transform] a simple into a complex timbre, suddenly or by degrees' (N. Rimsky-Korsakov, 1964: 109). Staggeringly modern, in the 'artificial effects' paragraph, it prefigures the 'auditory illusions' that will be explored much later with electronic music, in particular by Jean-Claude Risset. Herein, Rimsky-Korsakov mentions 'orchestral operations which are based on certain defects of hearing and faculty of perception' and gives as an example glissandos in scales or in arpeggios played in a particular way (Ibid: 116).

Orchestration treatises of the 20th century will further refine the art of orchestration and systematise the use of the word 'timbre'. Let us mention the treatise of Charles Koechlin who, in his overabundance of adjectives and pieces of information, brings to mind the attempts of the acousmatic school of the 1970s to 1980s to define timbre with the help of language; dealing with the timbre of the flute, he writes:

> We would be unable to define it in a single word. If it is only a matter of sonority, you know that it is particularly *transparent;* crystalline and translucent (especially in the first notes of the *upper register* [...]) or as *immaterial* in the *medium*, in light staccato.
>
> (1944: 12–13; our translation)

Staying in the 19th century, the concept of timbre was analysed by musicologists and scientists alike, like Ernst Chladni or François-Joseph Fétis. Amongst the scientific works, it is Helmholtz's that stands out, in particular his *On the Sensations of Tone as a Physiological Basis for the Theory of Music*, first published in 1862 and still read today. Helmholtz innovates by proposing to substitute a 'physiological' acoustics for a 'physical' acoustics: a new acoustics, 'the aim of which is to investigate the processes that take place within the ear itself' (H. Helmholtz, 1895: 4). He would thus also study timbre in keeping with hypotheses about the hearing apparatus and the description of the ear. However, his definition is physicalist: 'We have seen that force depended on amplitude, and pitch on rapidity of vibration: nothing else was left to distinguish quality of sound[2] but vibrational form (H. Helmholtz, 1895: 65), he writes, localising timbre in the physical phenomenon itself and not in perception. Moreover, with him, the analysis of the sound wave occurs uniquely in keeping with the spectrum, and, above all, limited to the supposedly stable part of the spectrum. Admittedly, he does envisage studying the attack and extinction transients (the way sounds 'begin and end': Ibid: 66), but he describes them as 'peculiarities of musical tones' (Ibid: 66), before concluding: 'When we speak in what follows of musical quality of tone, we shall disregard these peculiarities of beginning and ending, and confine our attention to the peculiarities of the musical tone which continues uniformly (Ibid: 67). By 'simplifying' timbre in this way, Helmholtz pursues the trail already blazed by Joseph Fourier, a path that will seem the best until the first works on the synthesis

18   *On timbre*

of sound which will show its aporia. Eliminating any trace of noise (the transients) from timbres and therefore from sound indeed constitutes a Helmholtzian project, which also explains his conservative positions on dissonance.

Timbre as phenomenon of perception: a 'map of timbres'

Research on timbre, which continued throughout the 20th century, became aware of the fact that Rousseau's premonition – 'which, perhaps, is not too easy' – concerning the search for a *physical* cause for the sensation of timbre was indeed founded. This is why a new line of research is taken with the birth of psychoacoustics, particularly in the latter half of the century. With it, timbre becomes a phenomenon of *perception*. So, it is no longer a matter of localising it in sound itself but in the way in which the listener apprehends the sound. Thus – to mention a distinction that Pierre Schaeffer (2017: chapter 10) was one of the first to develop – we must differentiate between frequency and pitch: the former concerns acoustics, the latter psychoacoustics; frequency is linked to the object that the sound constitutes, whereas pitch stems from listening. As concerns timbre, from the acoustics side, we will limit ourselves to the form of the sound wave. On the other hand, research on perception will be developed, the word 'timbre' itself henceforth designating more its perception than its physical reality – the notion of 'quality of sound' taking on its full importance.

Another adventure also leads to the perceptive definition of timbre: the synthesis of sound based on the analysis of real sounds. Here, special mention must be made of the work of Jean-Claude Risset. In the mid-1960s, thanks to the computer, Risset analysed trumpet sounds in a detailed manner. Then, by their (re) synthesis, he showed that the data of the analysis of a real trumpet sound has no equal value for perception, i.e., so that the listener recognises the perceptive entity he calls trumpet timbre. In particular, he observes that, for the ear, the most pertinent feature is the fact that 'the proportion of high harmonics of the spectrum is enriched thanks to intensity' (J.C. Risset, 1991: 243). Which led him to the following conclusion:

> Auditory perception is highly specific: ignoring certain physical aspects almost completely, it is extremely sensitive to others. The 'psychoacoustic' relation between the physical structure of the sounds – which can be specified on the computer – and the structure perceived –, the one that matters for the listener, is much more complex than is generally thought, as shown by the specificities of musical practices [...] or auditory illusions and paradoxes.
> (Ibid: 244; our translation)

Research founding a psychoacoustics of timbre developed in the 1960s (for a synthesis of these works, see J. Hadja et al., 1997). The earliest works take up Rousseau's idea: categorising timbres according to more or less well-defined axes, corresponding to (qualitative) aspects of timbre determined by verbal metaphors (see T. Rossing, 1990: 126). For quite some time, Fritz Winckel's book published in 1960 would remain a pioneering work. Whilst continuing to lie within the side of a physics of timbre – in addition, limited, as with Helmholtz, to the stable part of the spectrum – Winckel developed hypotheses leading him to the idea of timbre as a perceptual phenomenon. Starting from the analysis of vocal sounds, he developed a formantic theory of timbre and, postulating that every sound, whether vocal or instrumental, can be described by formantic peaks, he constructed 'formantic diagrams' on two axes (one for each peak) in which a given point corresponds to a precise timbre, an idea that led him to the notion of '*metric of timbres*' (1967: 15). 'Metric of timbres': the ambition is clearly displayed; it is a matter of elaborating what will subsequently be called a '*map of timbres*'.

The idea of a 'map of timbres' – or a 'space of timbres' – developed towards the end of the 1970s. Indissociable from the compositional project that seeks to construct a continuum of timbres, it aims to arrive at a general topology of timbre: with this idea, 'one can [...] propose geometric models of subjective timbre space representing individual sounds like points in space: sounds deemed very dissimilar are far away one from another, and sounds deemed similar, close' (J.-C. Risset, D. Wessel, 1991: 123; our translation). The method for giving concrete expression to this ambition was the multidimensional scaling, a method that had already been applied in other disciplines. In this domain, the pioneering works of Reiner Plomp, John Grey and David Wessel remain references. Let us briefly comment on John Grey's studies (1975, 1977, 1978).

Grey based his experiments on listening to instrumental sounds, which, after computer analysis, were re-synthesised and equalised – same pitch, loudness (i.e. subjective intensity)[3] and subjective duration – in order that they might be compared in terms of timbre. Listeners (experienced musicians) evaluated the degree of similarity of these timbres in comparing them by pairs. For the multidimensional computer analysis of data provided by these listeners, Grey chose to limit himself to three dimensions. One thus obtains a graph of three axes in which each timbre has a precise position and where variations of distance indicate the degree of similarity or dissimilarity (see **Example 1.1**).

In Grey's experiments, unlike tests based on axes defined beforehand thanks to verbal expressions, the listeners judged only the degree of similarity of timbres on an abstract scale: the axes thus constitute abstract dimensions. This is why they must be *interpreted*. Grey chose to try to relate them to physical properties of the timbres. With the help of spectral analyses as well as new experiments wherein the re-synthesised timbres were modified in order to confirm the interpretation, he proposed putting the vertical axis in relation to the distribution of spectral energy (the 'brilliance'). Thus, the timbres at the top of the graph seem to be those whose spectrum is narrow and possesses a maximum of energy at a relatively low frequency (cases of the horn or cello playing *sul tasto*); inversely, the muted trombone and oboes are localised at the bottom. The horizontal axis is indexed to the degree of variation of the spectral envelope and to the degree of synchronicity of the attack of the partials, which explains why the saxophones, English horn and clarinets are on the left and the flute and cellos on the right: for the former, the partials are relatively synchronised, and the envelope varies little; the opposite for

On timbre

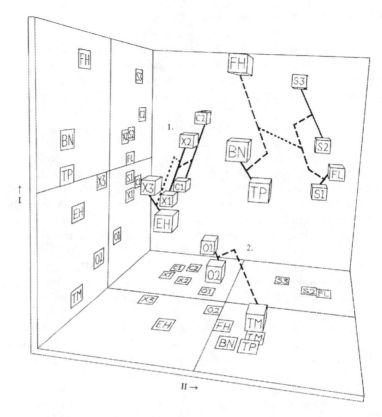

Example 1.1 Tridimensional representation of 16 instrumental timbres according to Grey's experiments evaluating their degree of similarity (after J. Grey, 1975: 62). © By kind permission of John Grey. Caption: bassoon (BN), E flat clarinet (C1), bass clarinet (C2), English horn (EH), flute (FL), French horn (FH), two different oboes (O1, O2), cello *sul ponticello* (S1), normal cello (S2), cello *sul tasto* (S3), trombone with mute (TM), trumpet (TP), soprano saxophone playing *mf* (X1), soprano saxophone playing *p* (X2), soprano saxophone playing *f* (X3).

the latter. Finally, the axis in depth is interpreted as a trait relative to the attack transient: instruments such as clarinets, saxophones, cellos and flute are towards the rear, as their attack is noisier.

Towards the dissolution of the concept of timbre

One of the questions raised by these works concerns the interpretation of the axes. Thus, Grey's vertical axis – which, however, is already found with Rousseau: it concerns the timbres judged according to whether they are 'dull' or 'bright' – did not satisfy John Pierce, who wrote: 'It is not just entirely clear what is represented by the up-and-down spectral energy dimension. Perhaps this is a sort of average of the frequencies of the partials, weighted by their computed loudness' (J. Pierce, 1992: 199). But it is the interpretation of the third axis (depth of the graph) that was most contested for it 'has not yet been explained very well' (C. Hourdin et al., 1997: 52). This is doubtless why the idea of a map of timbres, as appealing as it may be, has gradually been abandoned.

The failure of this utopia – a general topography of timbres – is not insignificant. Today it is the very notion of timbre that seems to have become questionable, and we are moving towards the dissolution of the concept. Indeed, timbre turns out to be elusive as much on the physical as on the perceptual levels. To tell the truth, if it designates the *quality* of the sound, we may wonder whether it is necessary to have a specific word and whether it would not be preferable to speak quite simply of 'sound'. In current language, do we not speak of the 'sound' of Xenakis, Miles Davis or Harnoncourt to designate this famous sound quality?

Upon closer examination, the notion of timbre is useful only as regards the *cause* of the sound: for example, when one speaks of the timbre of a violin's *pizzicato* or the timbre of the clarinet's 'pipe' register (low register). As Michel Chion (2016: 174) wrote, 'this empirical notion that is timbre proves to designate nothing other than that which makes us identify such and such source type rather than another. It is thus a fundamentally causalist notion'.

Finally, to get back to the classic definition, the notion assumes that one can isolate aspects of sound such as pitch, intensity, duration or spatial position (quantifiable aspects) from timbre (quality), since the latter is supposed to mark what differentiates two sounds having the same pitch, intensity, duration, etc., but played by different instruments. That assumes that the notion can apply only to sounds in which pitch constitutes an important element, consequently fixed-pitch sounds. Similarly, it can only be pertinent in relation to sounds evolving little in time. Finally, it requires that the sounds be known in advance. But music works increasingly with sounds that do not meet any of these three criteria: the new sounds can be *bruiteux* (without fixed pitch); they can evolve considerably over time; and, above all, they are not predetermined. In electronic music, a large share of the sounds is to be discovered by the listener; we are no longer dealing with circumscribed objects, whose causality is clear – 'timbres' – but with this dynamic process that is sound in general, a process that is not only complex, but also heterogeneous. In the final analysis, the word 'timbre' turns out to be less pertinent than the more general term of 'sound'.[4]

Substituting timbre for pitch

Towards the emancipation of timbre

After having sketched the evolution of the concept of timbre, let us broach its musical history, a very dense history in which this notion would, in the latter half of the 20th century, end up becoming a central category of music before

22   On timbre

beginning to wane. This history is, in fact, two-fold for one can distinguish two paradigms – between which numerous bridges exist: the first will be called *timbre-object*; the second could be compared to the notion of 'sound colour' and the history of its emergence is presented as an *extension of harmony in timbre*.

The history of the first large paradigm is linked to the history of orchestration which, itself, emerged progressively through the extraordinary 'progress' – the word appears in Berlioz's *Treatise on Instrumentation* – that European instrumental music experienced starting with the beginnings of Baroque. Monteverdi's *L'Orfeo* (1607) is doubtless the first work to indicate its instrumentarium at the beginning of the score (see **Example 1.2 online**). In Baroque music, orchestration witnessed advances, for example, with Bach's *Brandenburg Concertos*. The beginnings of the Classical era saw the birth of the modern orchestra with the Mannheim School, formed in 1750 by Johann Stamitz.

In Romantic music, two conditions allowed for the blossoming of the art of orchestration: homogenisation of instruments and erosion of the specific functions reserved for precise categories of instruments. Thus, combinations of instruments were henceforth possible aiming at producing new, literally unheard-of, overall sounds. By putting the accent on orchestration, Berlioz was one of the first composers to move towards the *emancipation* of timbre (see J.-P. Bartoli, 1986). Let us mention here the famous passage in the 'Dream of a Witches' Sabbath' from the *Symphonie fantastique* (1830) (see **Example 1.3**), where bassoons, clarinet, flute and piccolo are juxtaposed by overlapping – in addition, in keeping with the spiral rise and doublings of the strings, which muddles analytical perception. Not only is the sound object resulting from fusion new; furthermore, the continuity is almost total: one can practically speak of melody of timbres before the term was coined.

With the Romantic composers, the search for dramatic expression gave rise to an 'energy' type of relation – in the sense of Hanslick's famous book *On the Beautiful in Music* (1854). This is why musicians resort not only to original instrumental combinations but also to veritable orchestral writing, so that the orchestra becomes significant at every moment and not only occasionally as with the 'word painting' of Baroque aesthetics. Here, the notion of timbre turns an additional corner: it henceforth participates in the 'music' itself, the musical writing rising to the status of compositional category.

This would be the case with Wagner. As Adorno wrote (2009: 60), 'if Wagner learns about the emancipation of colour from line from Berlioz, his own achievement is to win back liberated colour for line and to abolish the old distinction between them'. Yet, Adorno adds: 'the colouristic sensibility of Wagner the orchestrator is the complement to the sensual susceptibility of the man who wrote the letters to the milliner' (Ibid: 61). Amongst the German musician's innumerable strokes of inspiration, let us mention, with Ligeti, the 'rustling' of his orchestra:

> There was already a blurring and art of movement [*Verwischung und Bewegungsfarbe*] in certain rustling' [*rauschenden*] pieces for orchestra from the apogee of Romanticism, in the 19th century, without anyone being aware

Example 1.3 Hector Berlioz, *Symphonie fantastique,* 'Dream of a Witches' Sabbath': measures 9–12.

of this phenomenon at the time. We find, for example, in the 'Feuerzauber' [Magic Fire Spell] at the end of Wagner's *Walkyrie* the following flickering effect [*Flimmereffekt*]: the individual figures in the violin parts are so difficult to play at the indicated speed that each violinist inevitably makes negligible rhythmic errors. That produces minuscule temporal fluctuations between the figures of the different violins, for the errors are not synchronous [...] This particular orchestral brilliant [*Orchesterglanz*], which is not the sum of the individual instrumental colours but a new quality, relies on the fusion of successivity [*Sukzessionsverwischung*]. I did not understand how this particular quality of timbre was produced until after having experienced Koenig's sequences of sounds in the electronic music studio.

(G. Ligeti, 2007, I: 253–256; our translation)

The 20th century would considerably develop the idea of an emancipation of timbre. Not only would the latter henceforth constitute a compositional category; in addition, it would tend to become a central category. Thus, the ambitious project developed where there is a question of *substituting timbre-(object) for pitch*, the latter having been the central category in the past. It is this extraordinary project that governs the elaboration of the famous concept of 'melody of timbres'.

Klangfarbenmelodien

The expression 'melodies of timbres' (*Klangfarbenmelodien*) was coined by Schoenberg at the end of his *Theory of Harmony* (1922), written in 1911 and revised in 1921. Therein, Schoenberg puts forward the hypothesis – pure *Zukunftphantasie* (Futurist fantasy), to use his own term – that although *melodies of pitches* (what are simply called 'melodies') existed in the past, henceforth, nothing prevents envisaging melodies *of timbres*. Let us listen to him in conclusion of the very chapter, entitled 'Aesthetic Evaluation of Chords with Six or More Tones':

In a musical sound (*Klang*) three characteristics are recognized: its pitch, color [timbre], and volume. Up to now it has been measured in only one of the three dimensions in which it operates, in the one we call 'pitch'.... The evaluation of tone color (*Klangfarbe*), the second dimension of tone [*Ton*], is thus in a still much less cultivated, much less organized state than is the aesthetic evaluation of these last-named harmonies.... Anyway, our attention to tone colors is becoming more and more active, is moving closer and closer to the possibility of describing and organizing them. At the same time, probably, to restrictive theories, as well....

The distinction between tone color and pitch, as it is usually expressed, I cannot accept without reservations. I think the tone [*Ton*] becomes perceptible by virtue of tone color, of which one dimension is pitch. Tone color is thus the main topic, pitch a subdivision. Pitch is nothing other than tone color measured in one direction. Now, if it is possible to create patterns out of tone colors that are differentiated according to pitch, patterns we call 'melodies', progressions, whose coherence (*Zusammenhang*) evokes an effect analogous to thought processes, then it must also be possible to make such progressions out of the tone colors of the other dimension, out of that which we call simply 'tone color', progressions whose relations with one another work with a kind of logic entirely equivalent to that logic which satisfies us in the melody of pitches....

'Tone-color melodies! How acute the senses that would be able to perceive them! How high the development of spirit that could find pleasure in such subtle things! (A. Schoenberg, 1978: 421–422).

This passage provoked a great deal of debate, for certain formulations in it are ambiguous. The ambiguity lies in the double definition that Schoenberg gives the word 'timbre' (*Klangfarbe*, translated in the quoted American edition by 'tone color'), as the following phrase implies: 'tone colors of the other dimension, out of that which we call simply 'tone color'. Thereby, this passage offers two very different interpretations: one will be developed in the lines below; the other will fall within the second paradigm, which will be broached later on. For the time being, let us limit ourselves to the definition of timbre for which Schoenberg wrote: 'that which we call simply "tone color"', i.e., the timbre-object we are speaking of here. It is in interpreting the word 'timbre' thus that these lines from *Theory of Harmony* can be considered founding in the ambition of substituting timbre for pitch.

According to this interpretation, melody of timbres would consist of producing a succession of new types of objects (the timbres), which could create a new organicity (a 'melody') just as functional ('coherence') as a succession of pitches in a melody (in the traditional sense of the term) – and the stakes could doubtless be extended by speaking of 'chords' of timbres, 'counterpoints' of timbres and so on. Again, according to this interpretation, the delicate assertion that 'tone color is thus the main topic, pitch a subdivision' would refer not to an acoustical definition but to an overturning of *musical priorities*: musically speaking, in the past, timbre was subject to pitch (this having constituted the 'main topic'); it would henceforth then be a matter of inverting this order of submission, adjusting pitch to timbre, first thinking timbre and subordinating pitch to it.

Commentators who subscribe to the interpretation that has just been given of the 'melody of timbres' concept agree in viewing the third of the *Five Pieces for Orchestra, Op. 16* as an illustration of this concept. The set of pieces was composed in 1909, 2 years before the completion of *Theory of Harmony*, and published in 1912. The 1922 revision adds titles for the pieces, which can back up the present interpretation, the subtitle of the third being '*Farben*' (Colours).[5] In a traditional melody, timbre remains constant or changes very little: to associate pitches, in principle discontinuous, the ear needs a continuity, that of the 'support' of these notes, i.e., the instrument, the timbre-object. In the opposite situation, where timbres change constantly, the continuous support would be pitch. Transforming pitch into a region of timbre, subordinating the former to the latter, would then signify: running through the timbres whilst remaining tied to the same pitch or to a few pitches. That is what happens in 'Farben', where the pitches change little while the orchestration explores all its possibilities.

The entire piece can be analysed as a slow flux based on a five-part canon sometimes punctuated by very brief motifs. The canon itself is made up of very slow conjunct melodic movements, which transform a single chord by progressively leading it to its transpositions: 'Thus the piece does turn out to be, in a sense, one "changing chord" – one great five-strand organism that ever so slightly crawls, snake-like, through all 44 measures', writes Charles Burkhart (1973–1974: 147) in his highly detailed analysis of the piece. On the other hand, the instruments change constantly with overlapping, colouring this changing chord differently. One can count fifteen colours (timbres) corresponding to the instruments present. One should also take into account the 'sub-colours', i.e., different registers for the same instrument, the use (or not) of mutes for the brass and strings, playing methods of the latter (*arco, pizz.* or *harm.*) and the fact that they can play in solo, *divisi* or in *tutti*. In the first twelve measures, the colours of the four upper voices of the canon change every minim, making the two fixed quartets alternate (the bass exchanges two same instruments every crotchet). Measures 13–25: the colours of the four upper voices change with every minim, this time without the quartets repeating themselves (for the bass, the changes take place every crotchet with few repetitions). **Example 1.4 (online)** gives a reduction of this passage. Measures 32–44, which end the piece, bring changes of colour for all the voices at the minim, without repetitions.

As regards what has just been said, it is still possible to miss out on the notion of melody of timbres and apprehend 'Farben' as 'an Impressionistic mood piece – Schoenberg's last – of extreme sensitivity', as Adorno wrote (1927: 338) in one of the very first analyses of *Opus 16*, or else, to see the simple influence of painting therein (E. Doflein, 1969: 203). But the same does not apply to the piece's central passage: measures 25–29. In fact, a *series* of timbres has been detected in it – at a time when Shoenberg had not yet applied the series concept to pitches! **Example 1.5** provides the reduction. In this passage, the instrumental changes speed up. The five voices, from the second part of measure 25 up to the beginning of measure 27 are followed by eleven different timbres, with a few exceptions. Let us call the succession of eleven combinations of timbre thereby produced the 'original series'. If we henceforth forget the lower voice and keep only the quartet formed by the four upper voices, what follows constitutes the retrograde of this series, with a brief inversion in the middle, the omission of the sixth element of the series and a few differences. Then, in measure 29, the original series is repeated in an order that is perfect this time (albeit always with a few differences). Finally, the very end takes up the first three elements of the original series. In addition, by taking into account the first minim of measure 25 and the last semiquaver of measure 28 (strings primarily in harmonics), we even obtain a series of twelve combinations of timbres…

Although, despite certain commentaries, the famous B of Act III, sc. 2 in Berg's *Wozzeck* (1917–1921) – a note that goes from one instrument to another throughout the whole scene ending up with a general B in the orchestra – constitutes more of an unusual expressive means, to the extent of the drama that unfolds, than a melody of timbres, the other student of Schoenberg, Webern, would radicalise the experiments as regards the melody of timbres, whereas Schoenberg seems to have abandoned them after *Theory of Harmony*. With Webern, timbre

On timbre 27

Example 1.5 Arnold Schoenberg, *Five Pieces for Orchestra*, 'Farben': measures 25–29: reduction. For the various conventions, see example 1.4. Not indicated are the instruments not participating in the canon. The numbers indicated between the measure numbers and the instrumental combinations (numbers at the top) correspond to the elements of the series of timbres. The differences (instruments) are in bold.

and its structuring are outstandingly limpid, thanks to pointillist, silent writing, poles apart from Wagner's orchestral fusions. He did not realise the simple version of the melody of timbres either, which presupposes a neutralisation of pitch, except in a few passages of his works, some of which are contemporary with Schoenberg's Opus 16 – in this regard, the *Six Pieces for Orchestra, Op. 6* (1910) and *Five Pieces for Orchestra, Op. 10* (1911–1913) are often mentioned. But he pursued the quest of an emancipation of timbre and an empowerment of its structuring. For example, his later pieces for orchestra, in particular the first movement of the *Symphony, Op. 21* (1928), may be played in a reduction where the instruments would still produce unisons: the result would admittedly be poor but doubtless less so than a piano transcription! Moreover, when speaking about timbre, it is always necessary to evoke the little marvel that is Webern's orchestration of the Fuga (Ricercar a 6) from Bach's *Musical Offering* (1935). In **Example 1.6 (online)**, we find an excerpt from the original (Bach), corresponding to the third entrance of the subject in the exposition; **Example 1.7 (online)** shows Webern's arrangement of this passage.

Timbre as central category

In the post-war period, compositional research on timbre went through an extraordinary acceleration. Numerous pieces of instrumental music, either in a few passages or in their entirety, took up the idea of melody of timbres in its simple version, i.e., with neutralised pitches, and refining it. Thus, the *Four Pieces for Orchestra* (1959) by Giacinto Scelsi, subtitled '*su una nota sola*', takes this concept literally: each piece works on only one note: F, B, A flat, A natural, respectively; here, pitch becomes the 'support' of timbre (see G. Castagnoli, 1992). We might also mention the seventh etude from Elliott Carter's *Eight Etudes and a Fantasy* (1950) as well as works by less well-known composers such as Zoltán Jeney, Björn Wilho Hallberg, Sune Smedeby and many others.

If one is interested in research that does not necessarily go via the neutralisation of pitch, there is quite a vast body of instrumental works in which timbre tends to emancipate itself and give rise to a structuring whose relevance in the musical hierarchy is stronger (in listening or in the very writing) than that of the organisation of pitches. Thus, integral serialism, in its pointillist phase, prolonged Webern's research, producing works of a constantly varying timbral glittering. Moreover, composers, serial and non-serial alike – Berio, Nono, Maderna, Messiaen, Ohana, Donatoni, Carter, Ligeti, Xenakis, Takemitsu, Penderecki, Crumb, Nguyen-Thien Dao, Mâche, Ferneyhough, Sciarrino, Taira, Kurtág, et al. – realised unprecedented structurings of timbres that also go in the direction of an autonomous, thought-out organisation of timbre. In addition, the 'open' works as well as the musical theatre works of a Kagel or a Globokar lead to timbral combinations that place timbre at the centre of the musical fabric. Finally, the arrival or generalisation of new musical means contributed to placing the timbre-object at the centre of writing preoccupations: percussion, new playing methods and, of course, electroacoustic music; with the latter, however, the notion of timbre tends to dissolve into the more general notions of noise or sound. To back up what has just been said, here are three examples, almost chosen at random and belonging to three different eras.

The first (see **Example 1.8 online**) is an excerpt from *Nones* (1954, for orchestra) by Berio, dating from the period of serial pointillism. From the writing standpoint, timbre is not autonomous here; it is even subject to pitches. In fact, the solo violin plays in retrogrades of the original series of pitches, the other instruments accompanying it with a rather complex serial variation of it (see D. Osmond-Smith, 1991: 16–18). However, the listener, hardly able to consciously follow the pitch relations, will more probably follow the sparkling sound of the extremely delicate timbral fabric, in the subtle blend of sound points as much as in their individual elaboration (*suono d'eco* – 'sound of echo' – for the clarinets, variations of playing methods and divisions for the strings).

Brian Ferneyhough's *Unity Capsule* (1975–1976, for solo flute, first performed by Pierre-Yves Artaud), illustrates the musical integration of a plethora of 'new' playing methods for wind instruments, which were introduced, starting in the late 1960s, thanks to the work of young instrumentalists and their collaboration with composers. It would take several pages to explain all the signs of the score symbolising these new timbres (see **Example 1.9**). One of the reasons for the success of this piece lies in the fact that it does not settle for a linear 'catalogue' of playing methods: 'In the further course of the composition the permutation and recombination of these, and many other levels of articulation, produces a truly polyphonic tangle which performers must unravel according to their own proper habits, abilities and inclinations', notes Ferneyhough (1980: 106).

At the beginning of the first movement of François-Bernard Mâche's *L'estuaire du temps* (1993, for solo sampler and large orchestra), the sampler emits recordings of sounds stemming primarily from Nature; the score indicates 'undertow', 'shingles', 'rain stick', 'black grouse decoy', 'barn-owl, 'stereo wind' and 'Arctic wind'. We first hear the sampler in solo, then the orchestra enters with, in the successive episodes, the different components imitating the sampler. In **Example 1.10**, four muted horns, a semitone apart, provoke very gentle vibrations, joined by the flutes and trombones, whilst we hear the wind in the sampler: a near-perfect timbral fusion is thus obtained between orchestral and natural timbres.

The emergence of timbre as a central category also occurred in all these musical attempts seeking more than the neutralisation of pitch: its destruction. From this come new 'objects' aimed at substituting for pitch, result, which we can, therefore, relate to timbre-objects. The excerpt from Penderecki's *De natura sonoris No.2* (1971, for orchestra), given in **Example 1.11 (online)**, strongly but not totally limits the universe of fixed pitches: the strings play *glissandi* or in clusters, the flexatone slides constantly, the bells and piano play the highest note possible, the other instruments do not play fixed pitches. Above all, it consists of

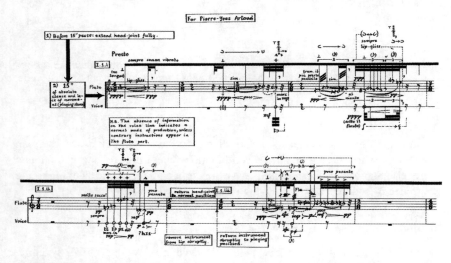

Example 1.9 Brian Ferneyhough, *Unity Capsule*: beginning (B. Ferneyhough, 1975).
© By kind permission of Peters Editions.

30 *On timbre*

Example 1.10 François-Bernard Mâche, *L'estuaire du temps*, 1st movement: measures 35–36. © By kind permission of Editions Durand. Instruments: flutes, horns, trombones, sampler (programme I: the notes indicated do not correspond to fixed pitches but to different sounds and their transposition).

a combination of objects clearly differentiated by their sound qualities, the plan of the entire work relying on such a combination. These new objects can receive the generic name 'noise', and that is why they join another history leading to the emergence of sound, a history to which Chapter 2 is devoted.

The utopia of a language of timbres

The fact that the timbre-object became a dimension of writing and/or listening entailed three consequences, to wit: first of all, its history reached an outcome: the instruments, their particular playing methods, combinations, superimpositions or fusions, i.e., everything that could be included in the 'timbre' category was emancipated. The same is true of the new objects (clusters, noises, etc.), which can be related to the timbre-object. In that way, timbre is no longer a support – the support for emitting notes and rhythms – tending to constitute an end in itself. Secondly, a logical consequence of this emancipation, timbre tended to become a central category, if not *the* central category. Although one could already find beautiful the Schoenbergian or Webernian *Klangfarbenmelodien* due to the simple succession of timbres, timbre comes off as a federating, or even unique, element of the musical discourse in innumerable post-war works. Thirdly, that timbre became a parameter of writing also signifies that, generally speaking, one would try – if we except the positions of a Cage who refused any idea of relation – to structure it.

It is on this last point that the timbre-object turns out to be a fragile category. Emancipating it and putting it at the centre of imperatives was a relatively simple story, which, to simplify, leads from the earliest Romantic orchestrations to the 1970s. On the other hand, the idea of *structuring* it proved to be more delicate. With this idea, the ambition is to assign to it the role played in the past by pitch; in other words, trying to found a *language of timbres*. Yet, in music, the notion of 'language' is closely linked to pitch and tonality. The latter stems precisely from integrating and assimilating the structure of the (spoken) language. Numerous elements of tonality constitute a copy of linguistic structures: minimal element (note), phrases, etc. The tonal system has extraordinary functionality and cohesion, having assimilated the logic of language. Yet, that was possible since its minimal element, pitch, lent itself to it. As for the timbre-object, it can hardly found a language: unlike pitch, it cannot pass for a minimal element, being too complex. By definition, it constitutes the element that characterises a sound qualitatively; it is in no way neutral, and the association of timbres stems from a highly evolved art: orchestraton. Where, with pitches, one barely begins to make music when a few notes have been assembled (melodic phrase), with timbre, we are already dealing with great refinements if we succeed in realising a brief melody of timbres. Generally speaking, pitch can establish a *play of differences* – which constitutes the definition of the notion of language – whereas each timbre-object constitutes a world in itself.

Another important moment in research on timbre also illustrates the difficulty of structuring it: the quest for a *continuum* of timbres, which was frequently encountered after the war. The electroacoustic medium was able to favour this research since sounds are better controlled in it, either by creating or by transforming them. Thus, Stockhausen's first electroacoustic masterpiece, *Gesang der Jünglinge* (1955–1956), works on the continuity of electronic sounds, that of vocal sounds, and, finally, the continuity of all; or else, *Diamorphoses* (1957) by Xenakis elaborates subtle transformations of white noise thanks to, amongst others, variations of density (see Chapter 2). Another example, from the repertoire of the 1970s: the piece entitled 'Géologie sonore' from Parmegiani's *De natura sonorum* (1974–1975) (see **Example 1.12 online**).

This research – and much other – prefigured the idea of the map of timbres, an appealing idea but which, as has been said, turned out to be problematical.

32 On timbre

More generally, the effort to establish a classification of timbres according to a continuum runs up against the following difficulty:

> [...] When one wants to organise colours or timbres [...], one can classify them from the point of view of certain criteria. What one cannot do is have a single classification, as with pitches: when one goes from a low pitch to a high pitch [...], one always crosses the same pitches in the same order [...] Whereas if one wants to go, for example, from a clarinet timbre to a 'ssss' timbre [...], there are several possible ways; for example, from the clarinet one can go to the violin, and then, in a continuous manner, from the violin to the 'ssss' timbre [...] But one can take another path: starting from the clarinet, going through a noise of Niagara, then to a trumpet, and finally ending up again at 'ssss' [...]
>
> (I. Xenakis, in F. Delalande, 1997: 46–47; our translation)

The fact that, on the musical as much as on the scientific levels, one can hardly order timbres in a univocal way, in the manner of a continuum of pitches (or of rhythms), signifies that it is hardly possible to found a play of timbral *differences* as could be done with pitches, i.e., a language.

Extending harmony in timbre

Harmony and timbre

The second paradigm associates 'timbre' with *harmony*. The history of this association is old and goes by way of a mediation of the notion of 'colour'. Indeed, before being linked to timbre (*Klangfarbe*, *tone* or *sound colour*), colour was linked to harmony – and this is sometimes still the case today. This applies to Rousseau in his argument with Rameau, who wished to base music on harmony, whereas Rousseau defended melody. To give weight to his argument, he established a parallel with painting, in which there existed a consensus in his era, stating that draughtsmanship was more important than colour. Comparing melody to draughtsmanship and harmony to colour, he thereby succeeded in convincing (see Rousseau, 1995: 413–414). This association is doubtless even older: it will be necessary to wait for the definitive consolidation of tonality – i.e., *functional* chord progressions – for musicians to stop assimilating harmony with colour and make timbre correspond to the latter. Thus, the madrigals of a Gesualdo implement, in relation to the theory of affects, a colourist conception of harmony.

The dissolution of tonality will again allow chords to free themselves from their functionality and become, in a way, pure 'spots' of colour: *chord-timbres*. Also, as of the late 19th century, this second paradigm of timbre appeared, undergoing an extraordinary development during the 20th century, competing with the paradigm embodied by timbre-object. Whereas the latter aims at substituting timbre for pitch, timbre-harmony – which could also be called *spectrum-timbre* – develops the project consisting of *extending harmony in timbre*.

Chord-timbres

The colourist use of harmony even subsists in the frameworks of the functional harmony of Classicism, but it is Romanticism which again gave it a place of honour. With Wagner, it became an intrinsic given of the musical discourse. One of the first Wagnerian musicologists, Ernst Kurth (1923), analysed this phenomenon with precision, showing how dissonances constitute a 'sound effect' with the German musician, at the same time that harmony can play an 'energetic and no longer 'functional' role. This can be illustrated by the opening measures of the Prelude to *Tristan* (see **Example 1.13 online**): the famous 'Tristan chord', purely afunctional in the harmonic sense, as has often been said, arises like a *spot of paint*, moving in space and not in time (successive transpositions); the orchestration (timbre-object), it, too, reiterated with a few microvariations, reinforces this effect (see **Example 1.14 online**).

If we had to mark the most important milestones in a history of 20th-century music extending harmony in timbre, Debussy would certainly be considered the first: his music accentuates the timbre-harmony fusion by pushing the former even further towards the latter. With him, the most complex aggregates often sound like colours, timbre-harmonies. The phenomenon had already been observed in his lifetime: a well-informed critic, Edward Dent, referring to Debussy (as well as to Satie and Ravel), wrote in 1916:

> Dissonances of modern harmony stem [...] from the fact that we accept dissonant, as well as consonant chords, like effects of timbre [...]. We know that every particular note can be fragmented into these harmonic components and that timbre depends on their relative intensity; in this case, why would we not create new timbres synthetically, making several notes resonate together?
> (E. Dent quoted in E. Lockspeiser, 1980: 311–312; our translation)

In fact, certain Debussyst aggregates do not sound like chords, i.e., superimpositions of pitches, but like timbres created artificially. Their degree of dissonance – they are not necessarily classifiable chords 'spiced up' with dissonances, even though they can be analysed in that way – along with their disposition in the register and their afunctional progressions suggest taking them as objects in themselves, overall sounds, pure colours, timbres. In other words, with Debussy, the note, which is habitually apprehended on the side of *pitch*, can play the role of *frequency*: rather than existing to base a melodic or harmonic play, it is presented as the spectral component of a timbre. Such a 'timbre' – the inverted commas are necessary, for we are dealing with metaphor – which would be synthesised by the orchestra, is audible in the opening measures of *Jeux* (1913) (see **Example 1.15 online**). The reduction shown in **Example 1.16** brings out the harmony: the chords are derived from a whole-tone scale. But can we really speak of chords? The term *spectrum* would doubtless be more appropriate – 'It is in skilfully using the whole-tone scale that Debussy succeeded in realising this

34   On timbre

Example 1.16 Claude Debussy, *Jeux*, measure 5–6: reduction. Instruments: woodwinds (piccolo, two flutes, oboe, three clarinets and bass clarinet) on the two upper staves and strings on the lower stave.

spectral analysis of sound, which is almost a laboratory experiment', wrote Émile Vuillermoz (quoted by S. Jarocinski, 1970: 36), comparing this 'experiment' to Monet's with colour. The whole-tone scale in itself does not renew harmony; it only acts as a colour effect. In addition, in the very slow, static passage in question, we simply have a translation: the last two chords come from the sliding of a major third of the first. Here, Debussy appears like the direct ancestor of the electronic synthesis of sound and even of spectral music, which would transpose the results of the latter to instrumental writing.

Following on from Debussy, numerous 20th-century composers prolonged the slide of harmony towards timbre. The case of Messiaen is exemplary: in the footsteps of Scriabin but taking inspiration from synaesthesia, he theorised a parallel between colour and harmony precisely because his chords go in the direction of timbre. In the seventh movement of the *Quartet for the End of Time* (see **Example 1.17 online**), chords that can be classified follow one another in a totally afunctional way: they constitute pure colours. This phenomenon is reinforced by the fact that this succession is played three times, in transposition by a minor third (measures 1–3, 4–6 and 7–9). The composer's note is eloquent:

> As music uses thousands, millions of sound complexes, as these complexes of sounds are always in motion, constantly being done and undone, thus the corresponding colours give intermingled rainbows, blue, red, violet, orange, green spirals, which move and turn with the sounds, at the same speed as the sounds, with the same oppositions of intensities, the same conflicts of duration, the same contrapuntal whorls as the sounds.
> (O. Messiaen in H. Halbreich, 1980: 138; our translation)

The posthumous publication of his *Treatise on Rhythm, Colour and Ornithology* (O. Messiaen, 2002: chapter 3) will provide the correspondences he envisaged between modes with limited transpositions and colours on the one hand, and between chords and colours on the other. We might also mention numerous other composers such as Varèse, Ohana, Dutilleux, spectral composers; or Mauricio Kagel in his *Opus 1.991* (1991), in which

> chains of chords for families of homogeneous instruments (for example, piccolo, flute, alto flute) are derived from their characteristic spectrum. An accentuation of sound particularities occurs: the composition of chords highlights precisely the constituents shown by spectral analysis. A homophonic treatment accentuates the timbre concerned, precisely so as to bring out the singular duplications; harmony and timbre are elements impossible to distinguish, but in a state of reciprocal dependence. This technique offers multiple combinations and labyrinthine variants.
>
> (1993: 174; our translation)

In this history of timbre conceived as an extension of harmony, Schoenbergian *Klangfarbenmelodie* could also take its place. Indeed, it has been said that *Theory of Harmony* uses the word *Klangfarbe* in a double sense. We have treated the first, timbre-object, at length. The second is given in the previously quoted phrase:

> The distinction between tone color and pitch, as it is usually expressed, I cannot accept without reservations. I think the tone becomes perceptible by virtue of tone color, of which one dimension is pitch. Tone color is thus the main topic, pitch a subdivision. Pitch is nothing other than tone color measured in one direction.

Here, timbre would be taken in the sense of *spectral substratum* of sound. According to this interpretation, as writes Horacio Vaggione (2003a: 165; our translation),

> Schoenberg's questioning as to the structural aspects of sound (*Klangfarbe*) is mentioned in particular at the end of his *Theory of Harmony* [...] Having set out – perhaps under Helmholtz's influence, as Dahlhaus suggests – the principle of emancipation of dissonances and the non-subservience of dissonances ('distant' harmonics) to consonances ('close' harmonics) [...], he perceived in the idea of *Klangfarbe* – of spectral structure – a theoretical basis for justifying and, above all, developing this really new conception of the role of dissonances.

Composing timbre

At the very beginning of the 1950s, with the earliest electronic music, the spectrum-timbre hypothesis took shape. Indeed, the type of synthesis of sound with which one was working at the time is the additive synthesis, which is based on the postulate that timbre consists of a superimposition of sinusoidal waves. Nothing prevents

36   On timbre

comparing these 'pure' frequencies to pitches. Stockhausen was doubtless the first composer to theorise about the idea that one could henceforth *compose timbres as one composed chords in the past*. In his first electronic piece, *Studie I* (1953) (see **Example 1.18**), he tried to create complex sounds by superimposing up to six sines, which represented a 'tremendous job, given the rudimentary nature of the sounds used [the sines] and interminable manipulations necessary for transforming them' (M. Rigoni, 1998: 41; our translation). The sound result is rather weak – it could be compared to the sanitised reconstruction of post-war Germany – even though Stockhausen's positivism is accompanied by mysticism thanks to which he interpreted the poorness of the sounds obtained as 'purity' – 'This music sounds indescribably pure and beautiful!', he wrote at the time (K. Stockhausen, quoted by R. Maconie, 1990: 51). But it is the theoretical conclusions that are important here: with this piece, Stockhausen noted (1963: 42; our translation),

> I was returning to *the element* that constitutes the basis of all sound multiplicity: to the pure vibration that can be produced electronically and which is called a *sinusoidal wave*. [...] For the first time, it was possible in music to *compose*, in the true sense of this word, *timbres*, i.e., synthesise them from elements and, in so doing, let the structural principle of a music also act in the sound proportions.

The first digital syntheses of sound realised by Jean-Claude Risset at the end of the 1960s take up the idea of a composition of timbre similar to the composition of a chord. The beginning of *Mutations* (1969) (see **Example 1.19**) drops notes one by one, they then forming a *tenuto* chord. Next, we hear a synthesised sound that resembles a bell (or a gong). The ear does not immediately make the connection between the two events, first perceiving a chord (arpeggiated then *tenuto*), then

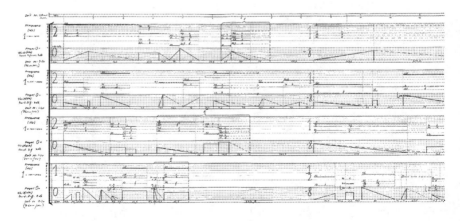

Example 1.18 Karlheinz Stockhausen, *Studie I:* 'score': page 1. © By kind permission of Stockhausen Foundation for Music, Kürten, Germany, www.stockhausen.org.

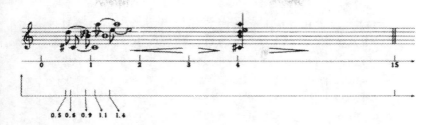

Example 1.19 Jean-Claude Risset: bell (or gong) sound 'composed like a chord' (*Mutations*) (J-C.Risset, 1991: 247). © By kind permission of Tanguy Risset.

a timbre. Yet, to obtain the notes of the chord, Risset used the frequencies of the bell's spectrum, thereby demonstrating the power of additive synthesis. Risset would write: 'the methods of additive synthesis allow for composing sounds like chords' (1998: 160; our translation).

The novelty of Risset's work, made possible by the most refined mastery allowed by the computer, lies in the idea of an *ambiguity*: one can go from harmony to timbre, or inversely, by an unbroken sliding as for the writing. The break is situated *from the point of view of perception*. Two different categories for perception – harmony and timbre – are no longer needed for writing. Too, the latter can play with the former: it can deceive the ear, come to terms with its defects and explore the thresholds of perception (see Chapter 3).

Thresholds of perception

Spectral music, initiated around the mid-1970s, invented this new type of harmonic-timbral writing, playing with and thwarting perception. It again rooted it – and this is significant – in instrumental music, whereas Stockhausen and Risset deduced it from the synthesis of sound: 'timbre', of which this is about, is again partly metaphorical. To understand the ambitions of this music, let us listen to Hugues Dufourt (1998: 182; our translation), the theorist of its beginnings: in spectral music,

> harmony turns into timbre. […] The interest of such a prospect obviously does not lie in a crystalline or set definition of the sound object but in the exploration of adjoining categories, hybrid objects, thresholds, illusions or continuous transformations.

The beginning of Gérard Grisey's *Partiels* (1975) – a work that, in a way, constitutes the musical manifesto of early Spectralism – illustrates this type of writing as concerns the timbre-harmony ambiguity. Attacks on a low E of the trombone and double bass (**Example 1.20 (online)** gives the second attack) alternate with chords in the instrumental ensemble. These spread out in time, and the entrances

2	1.0	12.	0,7026	22.	0,1876	32.	0,007	42.	0,1195
3.	0,2632	13.	0,7035	23.	0,3141	33.	0,0562	43.	0,1208
4.	0,5014	14.	0,0308	24.	0,0164	34.	0,0819	44.	0,0266
5.	0,5449	15.	0,2754	25.	0,0484	35.	0,168	45.	0,0502
6.	0,5437	16.	0,0095	26.	0,0538	36.	0,1121	46.	0,0198
7.	0,9649	17.	0,2392	27.	0,3454	37.	0,1963	47.	0,0298
8.	0,0044	18.	0,1949	28.	0,34	38.	0,1002	48.	0,0066
9.	0,2341	19.	0,3947	29.	0,4836	39.	0,0435	49.	0,0108
10.	0,4108	20.	0,2605	30.	0,2855	40.	0,0132	50.	0,0245
11.	0,8698	21.	0,6908	31.	0,0524	41.	0,0319		

Example 1.21 Tristan Murail, *Désintégrations*: formants of the piano's C_0 (first 50 harmonics) (T. Murail, 2004: 128). The numbers on the left indicate the rank of the harmonic, and those on the right its relative intensity (the most intense harmonic was arbitrarily given the value 1). The groups of partials constituting formants (zones of stronger resonance) are in bold. © By kind permission of Tristan Murail.

of the instruments are not simultaneous. In addition, they are close in their constitution: the ear – even an untrained ear – perceives them as a variation, an enrichment, a soiling of an E major chord. In fact, it is work on the harmonics of E. In other words, these chords can also be perceived as *spectra*: to borrow Gérard Grisey's terms (2008: 50–51; our translation), it is a 'hybrid being for our perception, a sound that, without yet being a timbre, is not fully a chord, a sort of mutant of today's music, stemming from the crossings carried out between new instrumental techniques and the additive syntheses created by computer'.[6]

In another classic of early spectral music, *Désintégrations* (1982–1983, for instrumental ensemble and tape), Tristan Murail uses spectral technique to merge orchestral sounds and electronics. Thus, the first section of the piece exploits a piano's C_0, of which **Example 1.21** gives the spectral composition (rank and relative intensity of the first 50 harmonics). After having selected the groups of partials constituting formants (zones of stronger resonance, framed in the example) and after having approximated them to the closest quartertone and transpose the whole on an A sharp (see **Example 1.22 online**), Murail uses it as a reservoir of absolute pitches to create aggregates. In his analysis of this passage, he notes:

> The resulting aggregate will sound not like a chord but like a unique object, a *timbre*. On the other hand, the instrumental orchestration of this object will create rather a 'harmony'-type sonority due to the individual richness of each instrument used (presence of harmonics in the instrumental sound, envelope of sound, vibrato, etc.). The overall result will nevertheless be somewhat

ambiguous since electronic sounds and instrumental harmonies will be heard simultaneously. Again, one can thus speak of 'timbre-harmony'.

(Murail, 2004: 130; our translation)

Spectral music did not limit itself to exploring the boundaries of harmony and timbre: it exploited all sorts of thresholds of perception. At its beginnings, it was accused of selling off 'writing', i.e., detailed work with the score, which had become – owing to long centuries of its evolution – autonomous and not necessarily aiming for an adequacy with perceived reality. The historic debate of the mid-1970s was played with waning serialism, presented at the time as the guarantor of writing. Opposing spectral music to serialism, Dufourt, in the first theoretical manifesto ('Musique spectrale', 1979), defined it as 'an aesthetic of transparency' (H. Dufourt, 1991: 294). We will add that the second spectral project consists precisely of achieving transparency from which perception begins working, this becoming, in a way, a parameter of writing. This is why Grisey preferred the term 'liminal' to the adjective 'spectral'. Regarding his cycle *Espaces acoustiques* (1974–1985) – including *Partiels* – he noted:

> The music of *Espaces acoustiques* can appear to be the negation of melody, polyphony, timbre and rhythm as exclusive categories of sound, in favour of ambiguity and fusion. Here, the parameters are only a frame of reference, and musical reality lies beyond, in the thresholds where an attempt at fusion occurs. *Liminal* is the adjective I would readily give to this type of writing: more readily, in any case, than that of *spectral*, often heard today and which seems too restrictive to me.
>
> (G. Grisey, 2008: 114; our translation)

To come back to the timbre-harmony ambiguity, it has been noted that the first spectral music again took it into the domain of instrumental music. More generally, one could say that this music was born from a transfer of studio techniques to the latter. Certainly, Grisey and Murail wrote a few mixed electronic-instrumental pieces, just like composers of the second spectral generation as well as other musicians who can be linked to it, such as Philippe Hurel, Kaija Saariaho, Pascale Criton, Jean-Luc Hervé, Marc-André Dalbavie, François Paris, Joshua Fineberg, Georg Friedrich Haas, et al. However, it turned out that one of the interests of Spectralism was the renewal of the art of orchestration: spectral technique constitutes a wonderful tool for mastering timbre-object – in a way, with this evolution of spectral music, the histories of the first paradigms of timbre tend to converge. Moreover, this return to instrumental music led, as has been said, to the inversion of the historical evolution leading from harmony to timbre: another interest of Spectralism was its renewal of the universe of pitches, especially through the integration of micro-intervals initially conceived as approximations of higher harmonics. One may wonder about the 'why' of these returns, which allow for establishing a relative parallel between the historic roles of spectral music and minimalism. The response is perhaps to be found in the context that, in the 1980–1990s, stimulated many 'returns to'.

But we should also question the *acoustic premises* of Spectralism. Indeed, the spectral view of timbre is essentially Helmholtzian: although the superimposition of primary elements (sinusoidal waves) for the synthesis of sound is presented as a superimposition of notes forming chords, it is because one is limited to the *stable* part of the spectrum. Timbre is essentially conceived as a *static* phenomenon: a timeless, periodic phenomenon. Certainly, Hugues Dufourt has always evoked the new acoustics, which is interested in transients and noises (see H. Dufourt, 1991: 289–290), but, in that he is perhaps more Varésian than spectral. Certainly, too, Grisey has sometimes 'transcribed' for orchestra sonagrams (dynamic representations of the spectrum, i.e., of its evolution in time); but those are very rare occurrences in his work.[7] The heart of the initial spectral project is marked by a static vision of sound: one might even go so far as to say that this project constitutes only a variant of the 'sound body' theory developed by Rameau, who deduced harmony from resonance, an operation made possible by a vision of sound outside of time.

Timbre and sound

At the beginning of the 21st century, musical explorations of timbre achieved extreme refinement. In the sphere of instrumental music, as well as in mixed electronic-instrumental music, orchestration, whilst preserving its purely empirical nature, made considerable 'progress', to take up the word used by Berlioz. As we have just seen, the advance in the sphere of orchestration techniques (in relation to the notion of spectrum-timbre) constitutes one of the major contributions of spectral music, explored not only by the second generation of spectral musicians, but also by a number of composers who cannot henceforth be described as spectral but were inspired by it. Generally speaking, it is difficult today to find a composer who would not pay attention to timbre, whose orchestrations would not sound 'right'. One example amongst many: **Example 1.23 (online)** provides an excerpt from *Le parfum de la lune* (2003, for solo violin and instrumental ensemble) by José Manuel López-López, a Spanish composer who can be placed in an impressionistic and spectral filiation, and who, in quest of sound poetry, works at going deeply into the sound matter thanks to highly refined writing of timbre. Henceforth, Chinese composers are also contributing to this history, which was occidental for a long time – Chen Qigang, Ge Ganru, Tan Dun, Xu Shuya, Xu Yi – and, more generally, Far Eastern, for, as writes Chen Yi (in M.H. Bernard, 2011: 287):

> in the traditional music of China, Korea and Japan, the isolated note is perceived as a sustained and flexible continuum. The isolated note is 'brought to life' by altering its loudness, timbre, even pitch, and by adding ornamental 'accretions' that nonetheless form part of its substance. [...] The commanding role of the isolated note not only implies a different relation to musical time, it also entails the predominance of timbre over pitch.

Finally, it is interesting to note that this work on timbre constitutes the 'modern' aspect developed by composers who are customarily classified as 'neo-classic', 'post-modern' or even 'neo-tonal' or who, having left the avant-garde, have progressively 'settled down' or become more subdued. This is especially the case with the orchestral repertoire, which tends to favour this type of writing. Let us mention composers as varied as John Adams, Thomas Adès, Pascal Dusapin, Oliver Knussen, Magnus Lindberg, Arvo Pärt and Wolfgang Rihm.

A certain number of composers have made the work on timbre the very substance of musical composition. Their work also goes via the integration of noise, and that is why they could also be mentioned in Chapter 2 of this book – such is especially the case with Lachenmann. Sciarrino's music (see **Example 1.24** for an excerpt from *Infinito nero* [1988] for mezzo-soprano, flute, oboe, clarinet, piano, percussion, violin, viola and cello) could constitute a perfect illustration of this type of research: 'Take existing instruments such as they are, but reviving them and, consequently inventing new sounds and techniques that established tradition prevented from choosing', writes the Italian composer (Sciarrino in G. Vinay, 2005: 155; our translation). By developing this approach, he hopes to deploy an 'ecological listening' that allows for better reproducing reality: 'By listening to reality with an insect's ear and a giant's ear, I try to reproduce it in a music of wind and stone. Those are listening experiments, which, more than any others, could be defined as ecological' (Sciarrino in G. Vinay, 2005).

Example 1.24 Salvatore Sciarrino, *Infinito nero:* measure 96–97 (S. Sciarrino, 1988).
© By kind permission of Editions Ricordi.

Example 1.26 Kenji Sakai, *Astral/Chromoprojection:* letter W. © By kind permission of the composer.

With other composers, the influence of electroacoustic music is important, as was already the case with spectral music. Thus, to a certain extent, in *Stress Tensor* (2009–2011, for flute/piccolo, clarinet/bass clarinet, piano, violin, viola, cello: see **Example 1.25 online**), Hèctor Parra took inspiration from the categories drawn up by Denis Smalley (1986) for analysing the latter, in order to create highly varied sound figures.

Since the beginning of the millennium, this work on timbre and orchestration has given rise to research in music informatics. In fact, certain realisations have been sufficiently formalised as to result in computing implementations that can assist the composer. Let us mention the Orchidée software, developed at IRCAM by researchers Grégoire Carpentier and Damien Tardieu (2011), under the supervision of composer Yan Maresz. The user introduces a sound sample into the programme, which analyses its characteristics then, after having specified the instrumentation at his disposition, proposes an orchestration able to simulate the sound sample. Jonathan Harvey used this program in *Speakings* (2008, for large orchestra and electronics). The second part of *Astral/Chromoprojection* (2008–2009, for percussion, ensemble and electronics: see **Example 1.26**) by composer Kenji Sakai carries out an instrumental transcription of electronic transformations heard in the first part.

However, like the utopia of founding a musical language on timbre-object, the very advanced explorations of spectrum-timbre have not led to a new universe but ended up taking the form of a renewal – admittedly, quite substantial – of orchestration. In the final analysis, it is a matter of increasingly advanced musical exploration of timbre – of its two paradigms – as it was a matter of the scientific attempt to define it: this category is linked to the universe of instrumental music. Timbre has meaning only for sounds whose pitch remains an important characteristic and which evolve little in terms of their sound quality (of their timbre). The types of music that extend beyond this framework – for example, by resorting to sounds where pitch disappears or else to an electronic set-up that produces sounds in constant variation (where, therefore, it is not possible to isolate recognisable entities that we shall call 'timbre') – necessitating other categories to be broached: we will speak of noise, or of 'sound' in general.

Chapter 1 online examples

Example 1.2 Claudio Monteverdi, *L'Orfeo:* list of characters and instruments.

Example 1.4 Arnold Schoenberg, *Five Pieces for Orchestra*, 'Farben': measure 12–16; reduction. The instruments: bcl, bass clarinet; bn, bassoon; cbn, contrabassoon; cl, clarinet; db, double bass; eh, English horn; fl, flute; hn, horn; ob, oboe; tba, tuba; tbn, trombone; tp, trumpet; va, viola; vn, violin; vc, cello. Playing methods: h, harmonic; m, mute; p, pizzicato. The numbers above the upper stave indicate the instrumental combinations in reference to the four upper voices. Areas of instrumental overlapping are not indicated (only noted are the instruments that attack the notes). Below the last line, the symbol 'C', followed by a number, indicates the transposition of the chord.

44 On timbre

Example 1.6 Johann Sebastian Bach, *The Musical Offering*, 'Ricercar a 6': third entrance of the subject.

Example 1.7 Anton Webern, orchestration of *The Musical Offering*: 'Ricercar a 6': measure 17–25.

Example 1.8 Luciano Berio, *Nones:* measure 40–46 (L. Berio, 1955). © By kind permission of Suivini Zerboni Editions. Instruments, from top to bottom: clarinets, timpani, bass drum, suspended cymbals, military drum, tam-tams, vibraphone, electric guitar, violin (solo), violas, cellos, double basses.

Example 1.11 Krzysztof Penderecki, *De natura sonoris No.2*: numbers 13 (end)-18 (beginning) (K. Penderecki, 1971). © By kind permission of SCHOTT MUSIC, Mainz. Instruments: metal block (mtbl), flexatone (flex), crotales (crot), cymbals (cyms), tam-tams (tam-t), bells (bell), piano (pf), violins (vn), cellos (vc), double basses (db).

Example 1.12 Bernard Parmegiani, *De natura sonorum*, 'Géologie sonore': first page of the 'score'. © By kind permission of INA/GRM.

Example 1.13 The Tristan chord.

Example 1.14 Richard Wagner, *Tristan und Isolde*, Prelude to Act I: measures 1–12.

Example 1.15 Claude Debussy, *Jeux:* measure 5–6.

Example 1.17 Olivier Messiaen, *Quartet for the End of Time*, 'Fouillis d'arcs-en-ciel, pour l'Ange qui annonce la fin du Temps': measures 1–12 (O. Messiaen, undated). © By kind permission of Editions Durand.

Example 1.20 Gérard Grisey, *Partiels:* 2 (G. Grisey, 1975). © By kind permission of Editions Ricordi.

Example 1.22 Tristan Murail, *Désintégrations:* spectrum transposed on A sharp (T. Murail, 2004: 129). © By kind permission of Tristan Murail.

Example 1.23 José Manuel López-López, *Le parfum de la lune:* measures 4–6 (J.M. López-López, 2003). © By kind permission of Editions Salabert.

Example 1.25 Hèctor Parra, *Stress Tensor*: measures 40–42 (H. Parra, 2011). © By kind permission of Tritó Edicions.

Notes

1 The German original, 'Ton, Klang, Laut und Schall' (R. Schumann, 1891, vol. I: 145), is translated as 'tone, sound or note, noise and sound'. The French translation, dating from the end of the 19th century, uses the word 'timbre': 'son, résonance, bruit et timbre' (R. Schumann, 1979: 146).

2 'Quality' and, further on, 'quality of tone' render, in this old English translation, *Klangfarbe*.

3 When loudness is not identical (cases of S1, S2 and S3 in **Example 1.1**), we consider it a matter of different timbres.

4 The critical position defended here does not, of course, invalidate the pertinence of work that continues to be carried out on the notion of timbre. This work goes in several directions: development of visual mappings for acoustic timbre features (see S. Soraghan et al., 2016), use of audio descriptors (see K. Siedenburg et al., 2016), research on orchestration (see A. Antoine, E. Miranda, 2017), adaptation of convolutional neural networks towards learning timbre representations (see J. Pons et al., 2017) and examination of

the neural underpinnings of musical timbre (see K. Patil et al., 2012). For a synthesis, see S. McAdams, Goodchild M. (2017).
5 The definitive revision of 1949 (published in 1952) bears the title 'Sommermorgen am See (Farben)' ('Summer Morning on a Lake [Colours]'). It would seem that the piece also received other titles: '*Akkordfärbungen*' ('Chord Colorations'), '*Der Traunsee am Morgen*' ('The Traunsee in the Morning') and '*Der wechselnde Akkord*' (The Changing Chord') (see B. Charles , 1973–1974: 141–142).
6 For a genetic analysis of *Partiels*, see F-.X. Féron (2010).
7 Jérôme Baillet (2000: 79) notes that only three passages in all of Grisey's work call for this kind of transcription.

2 On noise

On noise

Noise as nuisance

Noise has, incontestably, always constituted a nuisance. However, the first measurements of noises began to appear only some 40 years ago, i.e., at the time when urbanisation was peaking in rich countries. In *The Tuning of the World*, R. Murray Schafer (1977, chapter 13) compares studies carried out in more than two hundred cities in the 1960s and 1970s, studies that provide the number of complaints lodged according to the type of noise. In London (1969), in decreasing order the complaints were about traffic, construction building sites, telephones, office machinery, refuse vans, street repairs, trucks (lorries), sirens, ventilation machinery, voices, motorcycles, aircraft, doors, radios, railways and factory machines; but in Johannesburg (1972), complaints about animals and birds were ten times more numerous than those about any other source of noise. Specialised studies have come to light more recently. Thus, a report from the French Ministry of Justice (M. Cipriano-Crause et al., 1984: 32) noted that, at Fresnes prison, one of the largest in France, in an average day, 1,000 – highly noisy – door openings take place for exercise and 8,500 for distributions (meals, post, etc.). One wonders if the penal colony was not preferable, at least in terms of noises and whisperings in Genet's *The Thief's Journal* as imagined by John Zorn in *Elegy* (1992)...

It is certain that noise (in the sense of nuisance) has increased exponentially with industrial society. Benevolent Nature as imagined by Virgil in *The Georgics* is perturbed only by the noises of war. In the 18th century, the bell of Notre-Dame de Paris – which, it is true, weighed twelve tonnes – could be heard for several kilometres around (see D. Fortier, 1992: 18). It was during the same century that machines producing invasive noises made their appearance: sewing machine (1711), cast-iron tramway rail (1738), air cylinders with piston activated by a hydraulic wheel tripling the output of blast furnaces (1761), propeller (1785), gas engine (1791), etc. But the nuisance is not due solely to new sound sources:

> The industrial society, taken as a whole, is [...] noisier than old societies but, above all, it has modified the nature of noise. It has given birth to the acoustic

straight line, to the continuity of mechanical noises. [... In addition,] first the phonograph then other recording techniques freed sounds from their point of origin in time.

(L. Méric, 1994: 45; our translation)

This last remark is important because if post-industrial society is in the process of reducing the intensity of noises, it is, however, going even further in the sense of their delocalisation, which brings about considerable upheavals regarding our way of listening.

From the preceding paragraph, it will be understood that the harmful character of a noise does not necessarily lie in its nature but in its raised level of intensity: even a Brahms *intermezzo* becomes noise when played at maximum volume on a stereo system. In debates on noise pollution, the measurement of noise focusses on the reading of its intensity and not on its nature, even though the two are sometimes indissociable. This reading is not always easy to carry out. Moreover, the exact level of the pain threshold also varies according to the study. However, there is no doubt as to the physiological effects of over-exposure to intense sounds, which can range from auditory fatigue to deafness and also affect other parts of the brain such as the endocrine system or the immune system, more generally, the psyche (see A. Muzet, 1999: 35). Hence the increasingly frequent use of the harmful character of noise – of sounds in general – as a weapon. We shall mention only the breaking of the sound barrier at low altitude by Israeli fighter jets on several occasions in September 2005:

> Thousands of windows shattered, and cracks appeared in some walls. Palestinians 'compared the sound to an earthquake or a huge bomb'. They said that it gave the effect of being struck by a wall of air, that it was painful for the ears, that it could cause nosebleeds and 'leave you trembling'.
>
> (J. Volcler, 2011: 61, our translation; see also S. Goodman, 2010)

Musical noises

But what happens when noises do not have a high intensity? For example, when a pneumatic drill, muffled by a double-glazed window plays *pianissimo* and starts to resemble the beginning of the electroacoustic piece *Schall* (1994) by Horacio Vaggione? Or when, in the dark of night, the sounds of a gentle rain barely emerge distinctly? Literature abounds in descriptions of such non-harmful noises. Proust, 'who listened attentively to nocturnal sounds' (M. Chion, 2016: 10), includes a large quantity of them, which can be classified in three categories: for example, the violently opened window and aeroplane constitute a 'harbinger' of Albertine's flight; then there are 'completely dissonant noises as revelation of art'; finally come the 'auditory illusions' (see H. Masuo, 1994). Another literary study, entitled *Le bruit du roman* (M.T. Jacquet, 1995), compares noises

48   On noise

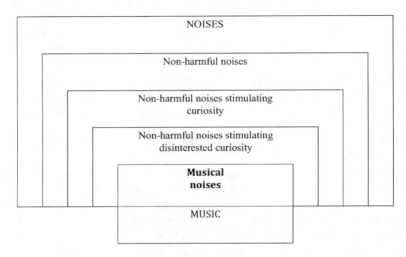

Example 2.1 Delimitation of musical noises.

described in *Le Père Goriot*, *Madame Bovary* and *Germinal* to draw conclusions as to the aesthetics of their respective authors.

In truth, few noises are harmful, yet, in the subset of non-harmful noises, some bring pleasure for they awaken our *curiosity*: they can be interpreted as signs or clues, as is the case with the noises about which we have just spoken. Within this new subset, we can define non-harmful noises stimulating a *disinterested* curiosity. With them, if we follow the Kantian definition of art, we enter the sphere of aesthetics. Finally, if we continue through on our delimitation of subsets, as proposed by **Example 2.1**, we end up at the final subset of noises, which constitutes the exclusive property of music and which is going to, henceforth, concern us.

Two histories of music

It is often said that 20th-century music was the first to welcome the universe of noises into it. Although it is true that recent music has fitted out an increasingly sizeable space for it, it would be erroneous, however, to assert that music of the past does not contain noises. To tell the truth, all music is brimful with noises, but only today's music proclaims them as such: in the past, theorists sought to exclude them from the musical field. So there are two histories of music: one, which is that of musical practice, contains – naturally, we might say – noises; the other, supported by theorists, long endeavoured to contrast them with the so-called 'musical' sounds.

The foundation of that opposition relies on an acoustical basis, due to the difference between periodic sounds, apprehended as 'musical', and non-periodic sounds, considered 'noises'. It is also musical, stemming from the listener's ability, cultivated by numerous musical traditions, to recognise, in periodic sounds – despite the portion of non-periodicity they contain – a complex element: a *pitch* of sound, i.e., what can be called a 'note'. For a long time, anything that could be sung, carrying one's voice to a fixed tone, was apprehended as a musical sound; as for the rest, it was thought of as *bruiteux* (where the acoustic nature is made up of noise), even though it was not necessarily *bruyant* (noisy); it is more a question of intensity, the latter's being high, which is not necessarily the case with the former.

This 'metaphysics' of sound – extracting from the vast universe of sound possibility a small set of fixed-tone sounds that will be thought of as the foundation of music – was built, like metaphysics itself, with the Greeks. Primitive peoples, such as numerous musical cultures surviving in Africa or the Aborigines of Australia, do not contrast musical sound and noise as violently, for they are less focussed on the notion of pitch. The concern of the ancient Greeks was to rationalise the supernatural and impose human order on it. Yet, bringing reason, *logos*, into music meant, precisely, delimiting a quantifiable, measurable aspect in the sounds – pitch – thanks to which we can compare sounds and put them in relation with each other. Music theorists would thus construct an edifice called Harmony, which does not enter here, having been sent back to Chaos. Pythagoras and his disciples would base an important part of their teaching on calculations of pitch and on temperament, thereby simultaneously elaborating musical theory and mathematics. It is advisable to specify that what interested the Greeks was not pitch in itself but the concept of interval and *tone*, in its original sense, which includes the idea of tension. The invention of interval and tone lays the metaphysics of musical sound, which has led to certain specialists such as J. Lohmann (1970: 38) stating that the Greeks *invented* music – just as certain philosophers were able to say that the Greeks invented philosophy. These assertions are difficult to uphold today. Although music theorists do their utmost to clear the universe of noises, it is obvious that, in the other history of music – that of musical practice – noise preserves its full place: can one imagine the cult of Dionysus being celebrated without crotales and other *bruiteux* (percussion) instruments?

The Middle Ages pursued the construction of the concepts of interval and tone, focussing on the notions of note and pitch (see M.É. Duchez, 1983). However, being unable to exclude noise from musical practices, theorists associate it, because of theology, with evil: 'innumerable images in manuscripts show us [the] division between celestial music – in general, angelic singing accompanied by the harp or stringed instruments – and infernal music – most often noisy, with pipes, drum, and trumpet' (N. Wilkins, 1999: 28; our translation). It is from this era that the French word synonymous with loud noise dates, '*charivari*', derived from the Greek *karêbária*, 'headache'. In the famous *Roman de Fauvel* (1310–1314), on the wedding night of Fauvel and Vainglory, a great charivari begins in town, accompanied by deafening noise, symbolising the folly of unlikely unions (see **Example 2.2 online**). Moreover, in the Middle Ages, the 'high' sound (loud volume), synonymous with noise, was associated with impiety, the devil, witches, death, eroticism, hell, and the confusion of senses (see L. Charles-Dominique, 2008).

50 *On noise*

In Baroque music, where pitch dominates more than ever, the instruments themselves are bearers of noise. Giovanni Antonini (in F. Delalande, ed., 2001: 121), founder of the ensemble Il Giardino Armonico, which became known through an interpretation of Vivaldi's *Four Seasons,* bringing the universe of noises back into favour, quotes the Frenchman Charles de Brosses who, in his Italy journal, complains about Italian double basses 'because he said they only made noise'. Moreover, we are familiar with the criticisms of contemporaries accusing Rameau's operas of being noisy, this time not owing to the tonal imperfection of the instruments but the very dense writing: 'It is a horrible racket, it is only noise, one is deafened by it', 'Much noise, much humming, a din', 'A noise that astounds the ear' (quoted by O. Pot in J.-J. Rousseau, 1995: 1435). But Baroque music tolerates numerous noises: this is particularly the case with descriptive sounds – storms, wars… – which are delightfully staged. In Act IV of Rameau's *Hippolyte et Aricie* (1733), the score indicates a 'noise of sea and winds' (see **Example 2.3**), which will accompany the cries of the chorus: 'Quel bruit! Quels vents!' (What noise! What winds!), before 'a horrible monster' suddenly appears and which Hippolyte will confront. We will also think of sonic depictions of the original chaos: the last work by Jean-Féry Rebel, *Les éléments* (1738), made up of a suite of dances, is preceded by the famous *Chaos*, which begins with a chord containing all the notes of the key of D minor (see **Example 2.4 online**). Other less stylised noises call for more secret listening: as Michel Chion writes (2016: 63–64):

> The role of noise does not start, as is often thought, with contemporary music. It is already important in the seventeenth century and pertains not only to imitative musical effects. The repeated notes and trills in Scarlatti's harpsichord sonatas are notated such that creakings and cracklings might be heard…. What hides this role of noise from the ear – and from the eye and mind – of classical musicologists… is the fact that in the score those effects intended to produce it are marked using the same symbols as the 'notes'.

In the theoretical domain, the Classical and Romantic eras pursued the exclusion of noises. In fact, musical theory finished the edifice constituted by harmony: tonality achieved its level of balance, pitch became king. Coinciding with that, an acoustic developed, centred on the so-called periodic sounds. It was Helmholtz, in the latter half of the 19th century, who constituted the culmination:

> The first and main difference between various sounds experienced by our ear is that between *noises* and *musical tones*. The sighing, howling, and whistling of the wind, the splashing of water, the rolling and rumbling of carriages are examples of the first kind, and the tones of all musical instruments of the second […] When the wind howls the alternation is slow, the sound slowly and gradually rises and then falls again […] On the other hand, a musical tone strikes the ear as a perfectly undisturbed, uniform sound, which remains unaltered as long as it exists, and it presents no alternation of various kinds

Example 2.3 Jean-Philippe Rameau, *Hippolyte et Aricie*, Act IV, sc.3: 'Bruit de mer et vents'.

of constituents [...] On what difference in the external means of excitement does the difference between noise and musical tone depend? [...] The irregularly alternating sensation of the ear in the case of noises leads us to conclude that for these the vibration of the air must also change irregularly. For musical tones on the other hand we anticipate a regular motion of the air, continuing uniformly, and in its turn excited by an equally regular motion of the sonorous body, whose impulses were led to the ear by the air. Those regular motions which produce musical tones [...] are *oscillations, vibrations*, or

52 *On noise*

swings, that is, up-and-down, or to-and-fro motions of sonorous bodies, and it is necessary that these oscillations be regularly *periodic* [...] Our definition of periodic motion then enables us to answer the question proposed as follows: *The sensation of a musical tone is due to a rapid periodic motion of the sonorous body; the sensation of a noise to non-periodic motions.*

(Helmholtz, 1895: 7–8)

'A musical tone strikes the ear as a perfectly undisturbed, uniform sound': here is an acoustic that eliminates (the evolution of sounds in) *time*. This acoustic put the finishing touches to the metaphysics of harmony, from an ordered, static universe that can only be deaf to noises. However, at the same time, musicians appreciated them more and more. And so it was that percussion instruments – and especially those not producing a fixed tone – made great advances with Romantic music. It would be impossible in these summary notes to mention all the percussion instruments as well as noise-producing (and noisy) accessories that served in 19th-century operas and symphonic music. We are familiar, for example, with the real or symbolic use of the cannon: symbolic with Berlioz (caricature depicting him conducting an orchestra in which a cannon is shown: see **Example 2.5**), real in Tchaikovsky's *1812 Overture*.

Example 2.5 A concert in 1846!: caricature by Andreas Geiger (1846) showing Hector Berlioz conducting.

Dissonance

So, we have two parallel histories: one that keeps only sounds of fixed tone (the 'notes' of music); and the other, of musical noises. Beginning in the late 19th century, these two histories started to converge thanks to an element that, coming from the first of the two histories, tends towards the second: dissonance. By definition, dissonance exists only in the first of the two histories, since it constitutes fixed tones. However, its progression, which ended up exploding tonality, was experienced as the progression of noise.

Dissonance could be apprehended as the 'noise of emotions'.[1] In fact, its progression made music increasingly expressive. This heightened expressiveness would take on dark colours, ending up with Mahler, then German Expressionism and musical works speaking of suffering. Adorno powerfully developed this interpretation of dissonance. Writing about the Schoenberg of free atonality – in which dissonance becomes the rule – he explains that dissonance, whilst having become material, keeps the trace of its origins:

> Dissonances arose as the expression of tension, contradiction and pain. They deposited sediment and became 'material'. They were no longer media of subjective expression. Still, they did not thus disavow their origin. They became characters of objective protest. It is precisely the enigmatic happiness of these sounds that, as a result of their transformation into material, dominates the suffering they once announced, and does so by holding it fast. Their negativity remains loyal to utopia: It contains in itself the concealed consonance – hence new music's passionate intolerance of everything reminiscent of consonance.
> (T.W. Adorno, 2006: 68)

Bernard Herrmann would take the use of dissonance for expressive ends to its apotheosis – for numerous music lovers, the composer of *Psycho* (Hitchcock) perhaps definitively associated fear with dissonance. However, the emancipation of dissonance can have other significations. With Stravinsky's *Rite of Spring* (1911–1913), Prokofiev's *Scythian Suite* (1914) or even Milhaud's *Création du monde* (1923), it is no longer about suffering – be it protestation against society or the expression of personal pain. Resorting to the primitivist aesthetic, these works play with the temptation of challenging civilisation: here, dissonance represents primitive barbarism. So it goes with the beginning of 'Augures printaniers' (see **Example 2.6**), where Stravinsky superimposes two chords a semitone apart, F flat major and E flat, dominant seventh, repeating them in a 'barbarous manner'.

During the same period, dissonance also spread thanks to the American 'ultra-moderns' and their taste for sound experimentation (see D. Nicholls, 1990). With some of them – described as 'bad boys' – we find a penchant that would be the equivalent of Stravinskian primitivism: such is the case of Leo Ornstein, author of a *Wild Men's Dance* (1914). With others, it is significant to take note of their political involvement: Henry Cowell, Ruth Crawford and Charles Seeger were militants in the Composer's Collective, a progressive association. Cowell also

54 *On noise*

Example 2.6 Igor Stravinsky, *The Rite of Spring*, 'Augures printaniers', measures 1–7: reduction.

Example 2.7 Henry Cowell, clusters from *New Musical Resources*.

earned a place in the history books for his famous book *New Music Resources*. Published in 1930, but begun as far back as 1914, it invents the notion of 'cluster' (a chord made up of adjacent keys on a keyboard) and proposes a theorisation. To his mind, clusters represented an enlargement of the material and did not necessarily call tonality into question, as can be judged from **Example 2.7**.

The most famous of these Americans who made dissonance proliferate – along with polytonality and cross rhythms – was Charles Ives. In his *Concord Sonata* for piano (1909–1915), we find many of the ways with which he introduces dissonances. We must also add that Ives was in the habit of going back to his pieces, adding dissonances[2] – did the taste for dissonance increase with age or else was it the desire to seem like a prophet?

Bruitisms

The 1910s and 1920s marked the era of avant-gardes. With them, the second musical history, that of actual noises (freed from pitch) took a giant step forward. The reasons for this are manifold. There was a minimal common denominator: the desire to break with tradition. Thus, one would endeavour to integrate into music the noises of industrial society, which, at the time, constituted the symbol of modernity. We are familiar with the fascination that trains exerted: Honegger's *Pacific 231* (1923) is the best-known example of this – the fascination lasting until the post-war period with, for example, the 'Étude aux chemins de fer' (the first of Schaeffer's *5 Études de bruit*, 1948), or even Kraftwerk's album *Trans-Europe Express* (1977). Also admired were factory noises, especially during the construction of the Soviet Union, which aestheticised industrialisation to an extreme: representative examples are Prokofiev's *Le Pas d'acier* (1924) and, above all, *Zavod* (or *Iron Foundry*, 1927) by Mossolov, a composer who would be banned during Stalin's great purges.

The bruitist *dilemma*

But these works from the 1920s are for orchestra: although they integrate noises (primarily through the use of percussion), they remain 'musical' – we do not hear a real factory in Mossolov. One of these avant-garde trends would make the leap, as its name indicate: *bruitism*. Here, let us follow one of its promoters, Luigi Russolo, author of the Futurist manifesto of 1913, *L'arte dei rumori* (*The Art of Noises*). Russolo was, with Pratella, one of the important musicians of the group of Italian Futurists. In 1913–1914, he made a name for himself in concerts with instruments he had just made: the *intonarumori* (the noise instruments) – a mixture of *intonare* (to sing or play) and *rumori* (noises) (see **Example 2.8 online**). At the end of the 1910s, his creations enjoyed a certain success as far afield as revolutionary Russia (see G. Lista, 1975: 30). Antifascist, unlike other Italian Futurists, he exiled himself to Paris in 1927, where he sank into oblivion until his recent rediscovery.

For a long time, musicians hardly appreciated Russolo, and rightly so: it was believed that he wanted to *get away from* music. Thus, we can read in the 1913 manifesto:

> We futurists have all deeply loved and enjoyed the harmonies of the great masters. Beethoven and Wagner stirred our nerves and hearts for many years.

> Now we have had enough of them, *and we delight much more in combining in our thoughts the noises of trams, of automobile engines, of carriages and brawling crowds, than in hearing again the* Eroica *or the* Pastorale.
>
> (L. Russolo, 1986: 25)

He defended the idea of a history of music leading to what he calls 'noise-sound':

> From the beginning, musical art sought out and obtained purity and sweetness of sound [...] As it grows ever more complicated today, musical art seeks out combinations more dissonant, stranger, and harsher for the ear. Thus, it comes ever closer to the *noise-sound. This evolution of music is comparable to the multiplication of machines*, which everywhere collaborate with man.
>
> (Ibid: 24)

Thus, his plan was to broaden the material of the so-called musical sound:

> Musical sound is too limited in its variety of timbres. The most complicated orchestras can be reduced to four or five classes of instruments different in timbres of sound.... Thus modern music flounders within this tiny circle, vainly striving to create new varieties of timbre. *We must break out of this limited circle of sounds and conquer the infinite variety of noise-sounds.*
>
> (Ibid: 24–25)

It is true that the addition of texts when the manifesto was republished in 1916 contributed to the idea that Russolo wanted to get out of music. In those additions, he studied noises that do not belong to the latter. First of all, 'The Noises of Nature and Life': thunder, wind, tramway, accelerations of engines (electric, internal combustion, etc.), factory noises, etc. Then, 'The Noises of War', with detailed descriptions such as: 'The Austrian rifle – heard from our trenches (I do not know how it sounds to those who are shooting) – has a curious noise of two beats: *teak-poom*. Ours has a single, dry report that becomes muffled at a certain distance' (Ibid: 52). Finally come 'The Noises of Language (Consonants)'. Of course, these are especially his new instruments, the *intonarumori*, which contributed even more to this idea, instruments whose description makes us wonder; for example: 'The howler is a mysterious, suggestive instrument that takes on an intense expressiveness in various enharmonic passages and offers many resources, being capable of the most perfect intonation' (Ibid: 78).

Let us repeat that: 'capable of the most perfect intonation'. Amazing! Russolo has just invented magnificent new sounds, very rich (noises), acoustically speaking, but what interests him is the fact that they are capable of playing musical *notes*... In sum, he inscribes his noise-makers in the first of the two histories of music, the one dealing with the so-called musical sounds, where pitch dominates. Thus, we will not be surprised that, in the 1913 text, Russolo writes: 'We want to assign pitches to these diverse noises, regulating them harmonically and rhythmically [...] Every noise has a pitch, some even a chord, which predominates among the whole of its irregular vibrations' (Ibid: 27).

The 1916 edition proposes a chapter on 'The Conquest of Enharmonicism'. Russolo criticises equal temperament and observes that, in Nature, sounds do not change by whole-tone leaps but by enharmonic gradations. Stating that the human ear is sensitive to small intervals, quartertones as well as eighth-tones, he concludes: 'Thanks to the noise instruments, [...] enharmonicism is today a reality' (Ibid: 64). To convince his reader, he offers an excerpt from his score *Il risveglio di una città* (The Awakening of a City), noted on *musical staves* (see **Example 2.9**). Russolo's manifesto constitutes one of the first attempts at introducing micro-intervals in music.

Russolo thus opened the door to noise but ended up closing it again: whilst introducing real noises into the universe, he endeavoured to harness them – as often during that period, avant-garde gestures were accompanied by neoclassical aesthetics. Its history is the prisoner of the dilemma: leave music or not. When pretending to leave, it was by staging real noises such as they were, but without drawing musical conclusions. Conversely, when he chose to enter it was, to the contrary, by harnessing noises to make them conform to the so-called musical sounds. This is perhaps why his adventure had no future. For the history of integrating noises into music would go by way of the acceptance of their true nature, in particular because they evolve in time: if we accept noise as such, we will be sensitive to its evolution and not seek to circumscribe it in abstract, supposedly timeless forms – notes of music. In the long run, once noises are accepted in the sphere of music, the musical field will end up being reunified, at which time it will quite simply be a matter of *sound*.

'Organised sound'

Varèse did not fall into this dilemma. He knew Russolo and his *bruitist* concerts, and they were even friends. But he quickly sought to distinguish himself from bruitism (see J. Stenzl, 2006), writing a highly critical text against him in 1917. The accusation of imitation has sometimes been remembered: 'Why, Italian futurists, do you slavishly reproduce the trepidation of our daily life only in what is superficial and annoying in it?' (E. Varèse, 1983: 24; our translation). But his primary criticism was even more stinging and perhaps also aimed at other composers:

> Whatever is not a synthesis of intelligence and will is inorganic. Certain composers, in their work, have only a succession and a light touch of sound aggregates in mind.... I dream of instruments obeying thought – and which, with the contribution of a flowering of unsuspected timbres, lend themselves to combinations that I will enjoy imposing on them and bending to the demands of my inner rhythm.
>
> (Ibid: 23–24)

Varèse would research these new instruments for decades. In 1933, he presented a laboratory project to the Guggenheim Foundation to explore the possibilities of electric instruments and 'pure fundamental sounds' (Ibid: 68–69), without success.

58 *On noise*

Example 2.9 Luigi Russolo, *Il risveglio di una città:* beginning (for *ululatori, rombatori, crepitatori, stropicciatori, scoppiatori, ronratori, gorgogliatori, sibilatori*).

However, during the same period, he composed *Ionisation* (1930–1931), a piece for solo percussion (and, what is more, without keyboards, except in the final section where they play clusters or fixed polychords), which, consequently, radically opens to noises not subjugated to pitch. Chapter 5 will propose an analysis of the piece.

Moreover, Varèse invented a new appellation for music: 'As the term "music" seems to me to have increasingly lost its meaning, I would prefer using the expression "organised sound" and avoiding the monotonous question: "But is it music?"' (Ibid: 56). The expression's primary function is to put an end to the debate waged by conservatives who contested the quality of 'music' with works making dissonance and even more, noise, widespread. Varèse rejected the musical sound/noise cleavage and postulated that all sound, all noise can be used (in music), on the condition that it be 'organised'. The expression also perfectly applies to the new sounds that Varèse was one of the very first to use: 'concrete' sounds, stemming from recordings and which, for a large part, constitute noises in the literal sense (sounds without fixed pitch). Varèse's most explosive work on the subject is incontestably *Déserts* (1950–1954), one of the first mixed (instrumental and electronics) works in the history of electroacoustic music: it alternates movements (called 'episodes') played by an instrumental ensemble on stage, and 'interpolations', made up of parts on tape. The latter, containing factory noises and urban sounds, primarily recorded in the United States and reworked in the *musique concrète* studio that Pierre Schaeffer had just opened in Paris, sound like a hymn to noises of the industrial society and, even today, despite the *Noise* new wave, remain quite fresh and pioneering. The percussion, played onstage (episodes) or present in the 'organised sound' parts, often serves as a binder between the latter and the orchestral parts. Thus, the episode that follows the last interpolation is introduced by six measures of solo percussion (see **Example 2.10 online**). In his interviews with Georges Charbonnier (1970: 43–44; our translation), Varèse proclaimed the non-distinction between noise and sound and explained the role he gives to percussion:

> The rhythmical percussion works are rid of the anecdotal elements that we find so easily in our music. As soon as melody dominates, the music becomes soporific [...] I do not distinguish between sound and noise. When someone says noise (to contrast with musical sound), there is a refusal of a psychological order: the refusal of everything that diverts from droning, 'pleasing', 'lulling'. It is a refusal that expresses a preference. The listener who states his refusal affirms that he prefers what diminishes him to what stimulates him.

The incredible noises of *Déserts* explain why, at its premiere in December 1954 (see the recording of this concert in Varèse, 2009), at the Théâtre des Champs-Elysées in Paris, the work – shoehorned between Mozart's *Overture in B flat* and Tchaikovsky's *'Pathétique' Symphony* – provoked a memorable scandal: 'The audience contributed generously to the event', the critic of *Le Monde* wrote. 'Murmurs at first, then, crescendo, waves of vociferous protest mingled with wavering applause, baritones and tenors hurling shouts of "That's enough!", "Shame, shame," etc. The seats in the Théâtre des Champs-Élysées are, thanks be to heaven, solidly screwed to the floor' (quoted in F. Ouellette, 1968: 185–186).

Musiques concrètes

In the post-war period, the integration of noises in the musical sphere progressed. With avant-garde music, dissonance was brought into general use, as was the case with serialism. In avant-garde music competing with serialism, one finds gigantic clusters that go radically beyond the consonance/dissonance conflict, subsuming it in the sonority of the cluster: in the clusters of *Metastaseis* (I. Xenakis, 1953–1954) or *Atmosphères* (G. Ligeti, 1963 [composed in 1961]), we are quite far from Cowell's philosophy. Those works call for totally individualised orchestrations (each instrument of the orchestra playing its own part), the intervallic function disappears, and the overall colour emerges, produced by the accumulation of notes, a colour that varies according to the density of this occupation, of the register occupied or of the instruments. All these phenomena converge, with the first of the two histories of music, the one based on all musical sounds, leaning towards the second.

In the second of these two histories, which is centred on noises, sound sources not producing a fixed pitch invaded avant-garde music in the 1950s and 1960s. Here we could mention the increasingly intensive use of percussion or '*bruiteux*' playing methods of traditional instruments – not to overlook Cage's 'prepared' piano, invented in 1938. But the major emergence of noise is the result of one of the era's two technological revolutions: *musique 'concrète'*. First appearing 1948 and based on radio practices, *musique concrete is* focussed on sounds in the natural state, with those of fixed pitch constituting only a very small part: noise is its central element, and that is why the very first *concrète* work was called *Five Studies of Noise* (P. Schaeffer, 1948).

Making noise musical

There is an argument regarding the birth of *musique concrète*: namely, what its inventor, Pierre Schaeffer, owed to Russolo and whom he allegedly did not recognise. In the introduction to his French translation of *L'arte dei rumori*, published in 1954, the lettrist Maurice Lemaître (1954: 15–16; our translation) accuses Schaeffer of being 'dishonest with Russolo. He quotes him only once and then reluctantly [...] This cannot be ascribed to a lack of culture, as Schaeffer was surely familiar with this manifesto'. This argument is important not only for the human facts but also for the musical facts, since we can support the hypothesis that Schaeffer replayed the *bruitist dilemma* of whether or not to leave music, and that he responds to this, like Russolo, with an attempt at the *musicalisation of noise*.

To leave music or not? Like Russolo, Schaeffer seems to have hesitated, this being attested to by the fact that he named his invention '*musique concrète*'. In 1953, on the occasion of a symposium he organised (see P. Schaeffer, ed., 1957), he cautiously advanced the more general term 'experimental music' to include in it the developments of electronic music as well as serial music. Some of his successors, such as François Bayle (1993: 52), who brought the expression 'acousmatic music' into widespread use in the mid-1970s, would clarify the dilemma. But the debate was closely argued, for we know that, with certain historical supporters of *musique concrète*, the temptation to leave music was strong. In 1950, Schaeffer's very young companion, Pierre Henry, a recent graduate of the Paris Conservatoire, proclaimed: 'We must destroy music' (P. Henry in P. Schaeffer, 2002: 143). Michel Chion, who might be presented as an heir to both Schaeffer and Henry, but with a preference for the latter, would write in the mid-1970s:

> It is certain that electroacoustic research would have taken another course if, as for the cinematograph, an original name had been created for it and if the quality of 'music' had not been bequeathed to it as a title of nobility to be deserved, a law to achieve.
> (M. Chion, 1982: 12; our translation)

Limiting ourselves to Schaeffer – who was not a musician but a graduate of the École Polytechnique – let us note that he finally made the decision to remain in music. Knowing when this decision was made is a delicate issue. In any case, his historic book *La musique concrète* (P. Schaeffer, 1967) lets no ambiguity subsist, since he would go so far as to revise his own history to show that there was no ambiguity from the start: Chapter 2, entitled 'Les trouvailles de 1948', is written in the present tense to explain how he went from radio research to music:

> The brainwaves of 1948 surprise me alone. Having come to the studio to 'make noises speak' and get the most out of a 'dramatic sound décor', I started in music. By accumulating sounds having the value of a *clue*, these clues end up cancelling each other out, no longer evoking the décor or events of an action but articulating themselves for *themselves*.
> (P. Schaeffer, 1967: 18; our translation)

The famous *Treatise on Music Objects* (*Traité des objets musicaux*) bears witness to this ambition of integrating music. The slow gestation of this *Treatise*, published in 1966, could be apprehended as the way to resolve the conflict between the two positions, getting out of music or integrating it, in favour of the latter. We might advance the hypothesis that this resolution came about thanks to the mediation of the notion of 'musical research' – a very restrictive notion for the young musicians working at the studio founded by Schaeffer[3] (that is why Pierre Henry left the studio in 1958). But this notion enabled Schaeffer to integrate the universe of noises into music.

To rejoin music, Schaeffer started from the principle that there is no difference between musical sounds and noises: he universalised the notion of sound, postulating that all sound material can serve music. The words 'noise' and 'musical sound' are abandoned in favour of the sole word 'sound'. However, he introduced a difference, which he therefore did not situate in the material itself but in its *significance*. The leitmotiv of the *Treatise* is that, in order for a sound to serve music, it must refer to no exterior meaning, which implies that we have forgotten its origin and are focusing on its morphology. This sound, cut off from its cause, provides the definition of the famous 'sound object' concept:

> When I listen to a galloping noise on the gramophone, the object I target [...] is the horse galloping, just as the South American Indian in the Pampa does. It is in relation to this that I hear the sound as an *indicator* and around that intentional unity that my various auditory impressions organize themselves.
>
> When I listen to a speech, I target concepts, which are transmitted to me by this medium. In relation to this concepts, *signifieds*, the sounds I hear are *signifiers*.
>
> In both cases there is no sound object: there is a perception, an auditory experience, through which I target *another object*.
>
> There is sound object when I have achieved, both materially and mentally, an even more rigorous reduction than the acousmatic reduction: not only do I keep to the information given by my ear (physically, Pythagoras's veil would be enough to force me to do this); but this information now only concerns the sound event itself: I no longer try, through it, to get information about something else (the speaker or his thought). It is the sound itself that I target and identify).
>
> (P. Schaeffer, 2017: 210)

Starting from there, the 'research' can begin. His first step, to which he devoted a very large part of the *Treatise*, consists of defining the criteria that will allow for the classification of all possible sounds. Russolo (1986: 28) envisaged, in a synthetic way, six sound categories:

> 1) Roars, thunderings, explosions, hissing roars, bangs, booms; 2) Whistling, hissing, puffing; 3) Whispers, murmurs, mumbling, muttering, gurgling; 4) Screeching, creaking, rustling, humming, crackling, rubbing; 5) Noises obtained by beating on metals, woods, skins, stones, pottery, etc. 6) Voices of animals and people, shouts, screams, shrieks, wails, hoots, death rattles, sobs.

The Schaefferian typology is not only extremely refined but, above all, does not classify sounds according to their origin. Cut off from their cause, Schaefferian sounds submit to a very elaborate abstract classification, based on the morphology of sound as such.[4] It being impossible to analyse the criteria of this typology here, let us simply say that, after several successive approaches, the *Treatise* resulted in a 'summary diagram' (P. Schaeffer, 2017: 467). This chart consists, horizontally, of seven 'criteria of musical perception' (mass, dynamic, harmonic timbre, melodic profile, mass profile, grain and allure) that several columns fill with 'descriptions' and 'evaluations'. For example, regarding the criterion of 'mass' – a term that corresponds, roughly speaking, to an approach to sound according to its spectral dimension, or a generalisation of the notion of pitch – we have several 'types': 'tonic (type N), complex (X), variable (Y) and some or other (W, K, T)'. Another example: the dynamics criterion has several 'classes', which distinguish sounds according to their 'profile' (cresc., decresc., etc.) whether they are lifeless or in anamorphosis (shocks and resonance). Final example: grain – which constitutes one of the most original criteria and denotes the variations in microstructure of a homogeneous sound – has several 'genres': 'harmonic, compact-harmonic, compact, compact-discontinuous, discontinuous, discontinuous harmonic'.

One might think that, after having de-contextualised and classified the sounds, Schaeffer would go on to the next step: envisaging their use in a musical work, i.e., their musical use, precisely in order to go towards music. It is still a well-travelled path: like a language, music would not be so much a matter of materials (musical sounds or noises) as of their organisation. However, in the *Treatise*, Schaeffer does not need this step: in truth, the musical aspect *has already slipped* into the typology of sounds that he has just carried out. In fact, to borrow Anne Veitl's terms, Schaeffer aims at the 'foundations of music itself, regardless of what type' (A. Veitl, 1993: 43; our translation). Where do these foundations lie? Schaeffer's discovery was that of the plurality of sounds and not of the plurality of types of music – he did not start from the experience of an ethnomusicologist but from that of a recording engineer. Also, it is *in the sounds* that these foundations must lie.

In the excerpt of the overall chart of the classification of sounds, one will have noticed that Schaeffer speaks of 'musical perception' and not simply of 'perception'. This chart is located in the part of the *Treatise* that discusses *musical* objects: classification has, in a rather surreptitious way, allowed for going from *sound* objects to the latter. This is why that part is entitled '*Solfège* of musical objects'. Schaeffer's intention is thus not to write a treatise on the 'harmony' or 'counterpoint' (or even 'composition') of *musique concrète*. Modestly, he limits himself to the foundations, the primary elements of music, which music theory (*solfège*) customarily deals with. But it is indeed a matter of music theory (*solfège*) and not a treatise on instrument-making or the way of tuning instruments, to continue the parallel with traditional music. With *solfège*, we are *already* in music. But how did we go from sound objects to musical objects and from the pure classification of sounds to music theory?

The operation is simple, as attests a paragraph from the beginning of the part devoted to the *solfège* of musical objects, emphasizing one phrase:

> We must emphasize yet again: the most important part remains to be done, to move from the sound object to the musical object or, again, to find out from *suitable sound* objects what the repertoire of possible musical signals is.
>
> (Ibid, our italics)

In the previous pages of the *Treatise*, Schaeffer had already given signs of this focus on 'suitable' sound objects. We learned that there are 'eccentric sounds' (Ibid: 360), which are 'on the outer edges of the musical domain' (Idem). These are sounds 'where the balance is upset by an excess of *originality*' (Idem):

> If, in fact, one of these sounds happens to appear in a work, it is likely to grab the listener's attention, for, too structured, too unpredictable, and generally

too bulky, but always striking, it imposes itself at the risk of destroying any 'form' other than its own.

(P. Schaeffer, 2017: idem)

These sounds are produced when, for example, the physical cause of the sound is maintained permanently, as in the case of a sound produced by a child who, 'touching a violin string with his finger while his bow wanders clumsily all over the place, produces us a sound as incongruous as it is interminable' (Ibid); or else, in the opposite case, in the accumulation of sporadic sounds – 'a shower of pebbles pours out of a truck, or a flight of birds twitters, or Xenakis's orchestra' (Ibid).

About *suitable* sounds, we could more simply say 'musical sounds'. In short, the opposition between musical sound and noise – i.e., a sound propitious to music and sound theoretically excluded from music – is in no way abolished. Schaeffer opens himself up to the generality of sounds but in order to sort them. Certainly, the sounds selected can henceforth be noises. However, in our two histories of music, the second, centred on musical noises, must always be subject to the first, focussed on musical sounds. Unlike Varèse, who juxtaposed musical sounds and noises in the hope that, one day, the two histories would merge, Schaeffer sought to subject noises to musical sounds.

The musical potential of noise

For Schaeffer noises must be modelled on the so-called musical sounds; they must be 'suitable'. But, just as Varèse, by differentiating himself from Russolo, had developed the project of liberating noises, i.e., an emancipation of their *own musical potential*, the first generation of *concrète* musicians would include numerous composers fond of 'eccentric' or 'non-suitable' sounds. One could mention the trend in the 1960s consisting of using *musique concrète* for its realistic potential. With *Hétérozygote* (1963), Luc Ferrari developed a sort of 'sound cinematography' in which diverse anecdotal sounds blend, in particular in soundscapes and words. In *Rituel d'oubli* (1969), François-Bernard Mâche develops an art of 'phonography'. Moreover, numerous composers did not follow Schaeffer but integrated noise without seeking to make it musical. There was a large number of pieces focussing on noises as such – and concealing their origin or not – applying a musical logic to them that was not external to them but, to the contrary, deduced from their own nature. Pierre Henry's *Le Voile d'Orphée* (1953) is doubtless one of the very first. It opens (see **Example 2.11 online**) with the 'tearing of the veil of Orpheus, an excessively slow tearing from which arises a noise that constitutes the principal component' of the first sequence (P. Henry in M. Chion, 2003: 39; our translation), a noise which is admittedly symbolic, but manifested by a series of abrupt attacks forming one of Pierre Henry's characteristic sounds. Limiting ourselves to the 1950s and 1960s, we might also mention Stockhausen's *Gesang der Jünglinge* (1955–1956), Berio's *Thema. Omaggio a Joyce* (1958),

Malec's *Reflets* (1961), Nono's *La Fabbrica illuminata* (1964), Bayle's *Espaces inhabitables* (1967)...

Xenakis's *Diamorphoses* (1957) is one of the works of the time that attest to this desire of showing the musical character peculiar to noises. The composer of *Metastaseis* explains that, in this piece, he uses

> noises that were not considered musical and which, I believe, no one had used in this way before me. I took the shocks of skips [...], earthquake recorded quickly, and then I put them together to try to understand equally well their internal nature, by contrast or by similarity, and make them evolve and go from one to the other.
>
> (Xenakis in F. Delalande, 1997: 39; our translation)

Diamorphoses can be apprehended as an etude on the diverse qualities of noises as well as on their gradation with the help of the densification process. In his sketches, Xenakis mentions 18 concrete sounds of which the names are sometimes obscure ('aircraft, jet plane, thunder, dustcart shocks, crushers, pebbles, bomb explosions, drills, ionosphere, saw, wind, earthquake, meteor [?], gunshots, coitus [?], earth alone, background noise, whistling'), alongside in-depth work on bells. If you listen to the piece without seeking the origin of the sounds, you will distinguish fifteen types of them that can be classified in five families as shows the graphic transcription (**Example 2.12 online**): continuous noises (sounds $a.1$-$a.4$); percussive sounds ($b.1$, $b.2$); pure sounds, either with *glissando* (c) or static in a continuous way ($d.1$) or interrupted with silences ($d.2$); quasi-sinusoidal sounds organised in small static or sliding fields (e, f) or in masses of shrill *glissandi* (g); sporadic sounds, isolated or in small masses ($h.1$, $h.2$, i) (see M. Solomos, 2011).

How does Xenakis manage to convince as to the musical quality of these sounds and noises? With a well-known dramatic process by leading us to immerse ourselves in the work. As the latter then becomes the overall framework, the origin of the noises – which, in certain cases, can easily be identified – is integrated into the aesthetic project itself: recognising the cause of a noise does not make us leave the work. *Diamorphoses* virtuosically stages Xenakis's *Dionysian* aesthetic, in which the artist seeks a fusion with Nature. Noises are the world of Nature; owing to this aesthetic project, their musical quality lies precisely in their own quality as noises, which bears the trace of their natural origin.

Revolt, protest and social criticism

In the 1960s and 1970s, the progression of noise also became noticeable in musical practices other than electroacoustic, including free jazz, rock and avant-garde instrumental music. Moreover, it is significant to point out that, during this period, a few boundaries that were thought to be solid – between rock and jazz, between avant-garde music and jazz and/or rock – were transgressed. This progression of noise in such varied musical practices can be put in parallel with the multiplication

Free jazz

Blending art and life: this anti-establishment attitude, espoused by certain artistic avant-gardes in the early 20th century, again became topical with free jazz, which developed at the beginning of the 1960s, advancing the cause of noise in an important way. The terrain was prepared by the adventure of bebop, which made widespread complex harmonies and their rapid progressions, dissonances as well as the liberation of the rhythm section. With it, jazz musicians proclaimed, both in their art and their life, free practices: an emancipated art and a life in which the musician is no longer the slave who entertains. The birth of bebop would be stigmatised by critics as 'intellectual' and accused of not being a *black* music, for only music that made one dance could be black, not music that made one think.[5] Thelonious Monk 'carried the art of dissonance to the highest degree – but not just any dissonance, interrupting, for example, a recording by pretending that he made a "wrong mistake"!' (P. Baudouin, 1992).

Free jazz appeared at the same time as a clear radicalisation of the political struggles of Afro-Americans: it would even become one of its major spokespeople. *Blues People* by LeRoi Jones (1963) was one of the first works putting American black music into close relation with Afro-American history. Numerous free jazz musicians would assimilate their musical revolution not only with the latter's struggle for emancipation, but also with all the struggles underway. Thus, in 1966, Archie Shepp declared:

> We see jazz as one of the most meaningful social, aesthetic contributions to America. It is that certain people accept it for what it is, that it is a meaningful profound contribution to America – it is anti-war, it is opposed to the U.S. involvement in Vietnam, it is for Cuba; it is for the liberation of all people. That is the nature of jazz. [...] Why is that so? Because jazz is a music itself born out of oppression, born out of the enslavement of my people.
> (in P. Carles, J.L. Comolli, 2015)

The noises that free jazz incorporates belong to this nature of noises – 'cacophony' – that, for a reticent listener, makes insupportable those sounds of which he does not, however, deny the adjective 'musical', since it concerns instrumental music. The first factor is the type of improvisation implemented by free. Initially there is a deliberate absence of the most obvious reference point: the theme tends to disappear, and everything seems carried away by improvisation. Equally, improvisation frees itself from the harmonic grid and it is, moreover, the very notion of harmony that liquefies, due to flirting with atonality and generalised free polyphony. Finally, we take up collective improvisation again, often without a common beat or even without any beat. The transcription by Ekkehard Jost of the beginning of 'Enter, Evening' from Cecil Taylor's album *Unit Structures* (1966) (**Example 2.13**) fully illustrates the principles of such an improvisation. Moreover, if one focusses on rhythm, the stability of which guaranteed the

Example 2.13 Cecil Taylor: 'Enter, Evening' (*Unit Structures*, 1966): transcription by Ekkehard Jost (1994: 73). © By kind permission of Helgi Jost. Cecil Taylor (piano), Eddie Gale Stevens (trumpet), Jimmy Lyons (alto saxophone), Ken McIntyre (oboe).

essence of jazz for some people, we observe that, alongside the instability or disappearance of the beat and, at the same time the generalisation of cross rhythms and polymeter – which was already taking shape in bebop, and which LeRoi Jones (1963: 206–207) interpreted as a rejuvenation in Africa – the drums were liberated as drummer Milford Graves said in a 1969 interview (in P. Carles, J.L. Comolli, 2015):

> Until now the drummer's job was to keep the beat. He did nothing else, even if sometimes he took off in a solo. Now, he has to create sounds according to what he plays and his means of expression. You can use any part of your drums, in any way, at any time. Now drums have become an instrument; you have to use it to make music, not to connect other instruments together.

The fact that drums became an 'instrument', with specific timbres, signifies that they would be listened to for themselves and not for their rhythmic function. Yet, these sounds are *bruiteux* in the acoustic sense of the term: continuous cymbals, tom rolls or bass drum irruptions, which are adored in free jazz, are sounds without fixed tone. The same is true for the other instruments. Freed from their melodic or harmonic function and improvising freely, they readily explore the limits of their playing methods: very wide dynamic variations, very high registers, multiphonics, breathing noises, noises of keys, whistling of reeds, etc.

Rock

Recent studies have gone back over the 'naively romantic view that simply assumes that rock was and is supposed to be resistant, oppositional, or somehow situated outside the political mainstream of American culture' (L. Grossberg, 1993: 201). However, it remains undeniable that a part of rock was anti-establishment even albeit in a heterogeneous way. In the 1960s, it was borne by various forms of subversion, ranging from real questioning of the family model to the most abstract criticism of uniform society as theorised by Marcuse in 1964 (*The One-Dimensional Man*), not to overlook the more clearly political struggles against the Vietnam war, which managed to federate protest. In the 1970s, we witnessed an attempt at establishing a counterculture. Although the episode soon ended, the *bruiteux* questioning resumed in the second half of the decade with the punks, who had to confront the economic crisis and English Puritanism.[6]

Almost from the beginning, rock has been noise in a literal sense: the amplification of sounds, from which it is indissociable, flirts, in some of its manifestations (concerts in closed places), with noise nuisance. It has often been found that the sound level of rock groups approaches the pain threshold: the image of the cannons with which Berlioz's contemporaries caricatured his music also applies to rock. However, in the mid-1960s, other, hardly harmful, noises came on stage. The last song of the Beatles' album *Revolver* (1966), 'Tomorrow Never Knows', one of the first electroacoustic elaborations in the rock sphere, goes in this direction. This song is immediately related to Lennon's LSD experience, in which, it would seem, he initiated himself alone from the 1964 book – which was going to become quite notorious – by the former Harvard psychologists Timothy Leary and Richard Alpet, *The Psychedelic Experience* (see I. MacDonald, 1994: 268). The song substantiated the quest for depersonalisation by its continuous buzzing – the noise in question – realised thanks to the mixing of five loops:

> (1) a 'seagull'/'Red Indian' effect (actually McCartney laughing) made, like most of the other loops, by superimposition and acceleration (0:07); (2) an orchestral chord of B flat major (0:19); (3) a Mellotron played on its flute setting (0:22); (4) another Mellotron oscillating in 6/8 from B flat to C on its string setting (0:38); and (5) a rising scalar phrase on a sitar, recorded with heavy saturation and acceleration (0:56). The most salient of these are (5), which forms the first four bars of the central instrumental break and subsequently dominates the rest of the track, and (3) which, working in cross rhythm, invites the audience to lose its time-sense in a brilliantly authentic evocation of the LSD experience.
>
> (Ibid: 274)

By means of sound interference, noise introduces itself in a much more pronounced way with Velvet Underground, for example in the album *White Light/ White Heat* (1968). As John Cale would write (in B. Blum, 2008: 121):

> *White Light* is the product of our experiments on stage. As we were on the road, we quickly realized that people were there to dance, so we began to play rock'n'roll. But no one had the patience to look for arrangements, and that was obvious. We went to the studio, we turned on the amps as loud as possible and we blew up everything. Everyone's nerves were flat, we were enraged. That's when I decided to leave.

A few years later, Lou Reed would make a very 'noise' solo album, *Metal Machine Music* (1975), entirely made up of guitar feedback. As concerns noises introduced by electric guitar, we would, of course, have to devote in-depth analyses to Jimi Hendrix, who explored saturation and distortion, as well as all the other techniques transforming and enriching the instrument's spectrum. The 1960s end with the live recording at Woodstock (1969) of 'Star-Spangled Banner', in which the interference of the American national anthem marks all the complexity that rock acquired by the end of that decade. It is perhaps more an act of revolt (the sound equivalent of burning the flag), but it is also possible to establish a parallel here with Coltrane's last period and his mystical flight.

At the end of the 1960s and during the 1970s, the development of progressive rock, synonymous with the counterculture, introduced a musical complexity that some would deem cacophonic: dissonance, harmonic complexity sometimes evolving towards a certain atonality and rhythmic complexity, as can be judged in listening to *In The Court of the Crimson King* (1969) by King Crimson (Robert Fripp) or *The Lamb Lies Down on Broadway* (1974) by Genesis. At the same time, the development of hard rock and its derivatives would lead to an immersion in intense noise. In hard rock, the musical structures are simple, those of the minimal baggage of tonal music; but this tonal minimum is passed through the prism of a distorting mirror, which becomes the essential thing to listen to: sound interference, which, one customarily tried not to hear, became the thing to hear. Hard rock bet on the dead ends of the language and marked the moment when protest retreated into the psychological realm. In the latter half of the 1970s, the punk movement took up with radical protest and was accompanied by music (the Sex Pistols' *Anarchy in the U.K.*, 1975) in which ugliness and amateurism are proclaimed and where interference and other forms of noise are omnipresent. For example, Greil Marcus (1989: 39) hears 'squeaks, squeals, snarls, and whines, unmediated female noises never before heard as pop music' in the sole disc recorded by the female group, The Slits.

'Touching a sound'

Another sphere where, during the 1960s and 1970s, noise became widespread: the instrumental production of contemporary music, which set in after World War II. The use of clusters was pushed to its extremes in Penderecki's *Threnody for the Victims of Hiroshima* (1959–1961) and Christou's *Praxis for 12* (1966–1969). Moreover, pieces for solo percussion proliferated increasingly, and we witnessed the creation of specialised ensembles such as Les Percussions de Strasbourg (founded in 1962), which contributed powerfully to the creation of a repertoire. In addition, the infinite variety of playing and singing methods began to be exploited, in which 'normal' playing or singing, producing a pitch, determined and stable, was no longer just a particular case. In this extraordinary search for new timbres, the share of noise (in the sense of a sound whose morphology is more important than pitch) is quite important. From Berio's *Sequenza III* (1965) to Aperghis's *Récitations* (1978), by way of Cage's *Song Books* (1970), there are numerous vocal pieces that go in this direction. And we could mention numerous singer-performers who are sometimes on the dividing line of musical genres: Cathy Berberian and her famous *Stripsody* (1966); Demetrio Stratos who sometimes draws his techniques from ethnic music; Joana La Barbara and her extended vocal techniques... Concerning instruments, starting at the end of the 1960s and throughout the 1970s, a plethora of playing methods on the clarinet, flute, saxophone and other winds were 'discovered' – in fact, known in the past but as defects to be eliminated. Instrumentalists, who inspired numerous creations, specified in detail these new, globally *bruiteux* playing methods (muddling or erasing pitch), in treatises: Bruno Bartolozzi (1967), Phillip Rehfeldt (1976), Pierre-Yves Artaud (1980) or Daniel Kientzy (1990). With them and pieces like *Discours II* (1967–1968, for five trombones) by Globokar or *Unity Capsule* (1976, for flute) by Ferneyhough, words like 'split sounds', 'multiphonics', *bisbigliando*, 'key percussion', 'tongue ram', 'Aeolian sounds' or 'whistle-tone' entered the musical language.

Most of these musical developments did not stem from political protest. One might, however, note, with Hugues Dufourt (1999: 9; our translation), that 'the growing share that noise takes in art music attests to the emergence of a repressed plebeian element and reveals the guilty conscience of the symbolic authorities', a thesis developed by Pierre Albert Castanet (1999). In a more Adornian sense, one can also consider that, in the 1960s and 1970s, noise substituted for dissonance – henceforth banal in avant-garde music – as a musical element of social criticism. One composer would make this thesis his own and develop it in his music: Helmut Lachenmann, in his *'musique concrète instrumentale'*. Lachenmann starts from the Adornian observation that musical material is not neutral but is already in conflict with reality:

> Musical material is something other than simple, docile raw matter waiting uniquely for the composer to fill it with expression and thereby give it life within such and such a set of relations: it is itself already inscribed in relations and marked expressively, even before the composer approaches it. These features that have engraved themselves in the material come from the same reality, which has marked us ourselves, composers and listeners.
> (H. Lachenmann, 1991: 262–263; our translation)

Against an authoritarian domination of the material, which empties it of its concrete qualities – of its share of reality – by transforming it into something neutral, and that regardless of its nature (tonal material, dissonances, noises), Lachenmann develops, to use Adornian language, a veritable mastery, enabling it to preserve these qualities. To do so, he advances the idea that composing means 'building an instrument': composition is not an abstract task (a blind domination), but a confrontation with matter, like the musician's confrontation with his or her instrument. In sum, it is a matter of 'touching a sound' (see H. Lachenmann, 1993: 233; our translation). 'Touching' a *note* has never really been possible: with a pitch or an interval, one can only 'vibrate'. Only the sounds closest to concrete life can arouse

On noise 71

the impression that we rub them or touch them. A slow, methodical rubbing of the bow, the grating of a string procures the sensation of a contact with the matter, with something concrete. Hence the choice to meticulously explore the delicate, infinite world of noises that can be produced with musical instruments.

With his '*musique concrète instrumentale*', Lachenmann composes pieces that constantly *rub* with the matter. Moreover, the literal action of rubbing is quite important in his works, as we can observe in the opening of *Pression* ('Pressure', 1969), a piece for cello (see **Example 2.14**). The score,[7] which constitutes a tablature – Lachenmann indicates the action to carry out and not the sound result – indicates the bow's motion (up) and the fingers' on the strings (down); the vertical divisions of each system correspond to a crotchet = 66 MM. In the beginning,

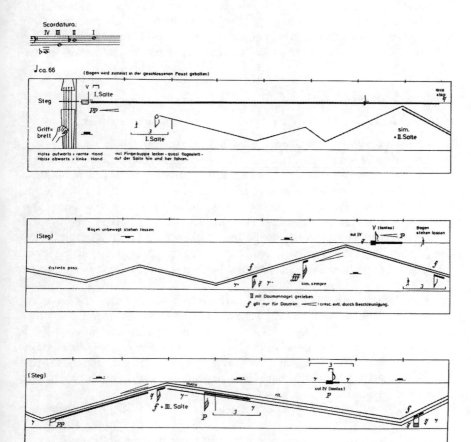

Example 2.14 Helmut Lachenmann, *Pression*: beginning (H. Lachenmann, 1972).
© By kind permission of Musikverlag Hans Gerig, Köln, 1980 assigned to Breitkopf & Härtel, Wiesbaden.

the bow rubs the first string *pianissimo*, while the left hand 'enters', sliding the fingertip very loosely on the same string in order to produce quasi-harmonics. Then, the gliding occurs on the first two strings whereas the bow stops (end of the first system). Thumbnail hits on the second string intervene, *forte* or *fortississimo*, the bow's movement resumes briefly on the fourth string but without producing a pitch (end of the second system), and the sliding conquers the third string (third system). Generally speaking, in *Pression*, Lachenmann rejects operations concerning the notion of note, for it can be obtained only by abstraction: the musical material is made up uniquely of the cello's concrete sounds and the actions for obtaining them.

By putting the accent on the matter, the concrete, the living and the sensitive, Lachenmann's music makes us aware that the domination of Nature leads to its disappearance. It is in this sense that, with him, noise constitutes the musical sign of social criticism. In a musical way, Lachenmann prolongs the criticism of the 'instrumental' reason that Horkheimer and Adorno (1944) had carried out in their *Dialectic of Enlightenment*, which tends towards the blind domination of Nature.

Noise and sound

Industrial music, metal, rap, New York Noise, radical improvisation...

Beginning in the 1980s, noise propagated in other musical trends, whether or not in relation to an anti-authority inclination. In the sphere of rock, we might cite certain albums by Frank Zappa such as *You Are What You Is* (1981). One of his most politicised albums – in it he criticised the 'conservative revolution' that brought Reagan to power – it can be described, on the musical level, as noise due to the very extensive use of overdubbing. The group Sonic Youth went even further, using prepared guitars, especially in its album *Confusion is Sex* (1983). We should also mention 'industrial music', a trend that, with its 'sound aggressions', goes in the direction of 'anti-music', i.e., the refusal of pretty sound:

> The Germans Einstürzende Neubauten destroy stages with jackhammers, whereas Test Dept, SPK or Z'ev use metal percussion and staging that looks like a worksite, plunging the spectator into a purely industrial universe. [...] Violence is an integral part of the concerts but is rarely gratuitous and can serve a rich, fascinating aim as with Etant Donnés. The principal quality of the industrial groups is to have gone beyond the sound barrier and turned noise into music.
>
> (M. Lachaud, 2007: 163–164; our translation)

Other derivatives of rock also made widespread use of noise in diverse forms: hard, metal, gothic rock... Thus, heavy metal, with groups like Iron Maiden, Judas Priest and Mötley Crüe, went in this direction with very energetic rhythmic drumming patterns, guitars of extreme distortion (creating a powerful, heavy sound) – this evolution went towards a raw sound counterbalanced by virtuosic guitar solos – and, perhaps even more, its extreme loudness. In 1994, at the occasion of a concert in Hanover, the group Manowar was listed in the *Guinness Book of Records* as the world's loudest group, with 129.5 decibels registered. Knowing whether, in the heavy-metal context, noise has a protest virtue is no small affair. A group like Metallica was able to compose songs with critical lyrics (for example in the album *And Justice For All*, 1988), but somewhat episodically. Concerning less media-conscious groups, one could read, in the advances of noise proposed by heavy metal, rather its social origin, namely the proletariat, which, in the 1980s and early 1990s, was subjected to the vagaries of deindustrialisation (see R. Moore, 2009 and G. Bayer, 2009).

Starting in the 1990s, we observe a certain quietening down in rock, doubtless because a much more individualistic generation appeared, centred on narcissistic problems of the individual in post-industrial society. It is possible to analyse the social content of a group like Radiohead speaking about the 'improbability of resistance' (C.W. Jones, 2005). Earlier groups also evolved in this direction. Thus, in 2000, Einstürzende Neubauten released an album entitled *Silence is Sexy*, characterised by introspection, calm atmospheres and silence. During that period, it was rap that took over in the combination of more or less advanced content and social protest. This was the case, for example, with Public Enemy, of which we shall mention 'Louder Than a Bomb' from the album *It Takes a Nation of Millions to Hold Us Back* (1988), a piece whose sound is quite compact owing to overdubbing. Generally speaking, rap is closely linked to the social violence of the underprivileged backgrounds from which it comes. In part uniquely festive music at its beginnings, it became social conscience – according to an aesthetic that could be described as realistic – with *The Message* (1982) by Grandmaster Flash and the Furious Five in which the first verse, 'Broken glass everywhere, / people pissing on the stairs, / you know they just don't care, / can't take the smell, can't take the noise, / got no money to move out, / guess I got no choice', is accompanied by a sound sampling of the noise of broken glass.

In the sphere of jazz, free jazz has left lasting traces liable to be updated at any moment, for example with the movement straightforwardly named 'New York Noise'. Born in the 1980s, this movement developed with musicians such as John Zorn, Anthony Coleman or Joey Baron. The guitarist Marc Ribot (2000: 233) provided thinking on the relation between pain – due to the very high volume – and music:

> I'm a guitarist who points extremely loud amplifiers directly at his head. […] Doctors say this could […] create an uncomfortable sensation of density in one's head and eventually make it impossible to hear human conversation. Yet I persist – why? It's true most amps sound better at volumes enough to fray the edge of notes with the subtle distortion that is to electric guitars what make-up is to a drag queen of a certain age. […] We seem to love broken voices in general: vocal chords eroded by whiskey and screaming […]. Maybe it means something that representation of the struggle (once shown by the trembling effect called *vibrato*) to maintain the distance necessary to hold

an instrument or sing a note in the face of overwhelming emotion is signified in our time by a direct attack on the equipment itself.

To evoke another guitarist of the same musical movement, Fred Frith, his work on prepared guitars – beginning with the album *Guitar Solos* (1974) – is often mentioned as an immersion in the universe of noise with the help of *objets trouvés* or finely controlled electronic effects (see **Example 2.15 online**).

A radical trend has appeared more recently, focussing on research that can also be compared with free jazz, as well as with trends stemming from rock, post-punk or experimental music, a trend in which the federating point is 'radical improvisation' thought of as a total alternative and therefore a radical criticism of capitalism. The book *Noise and Capitalism* (Mattin, A. Iles, 2009) federates some of this research. The British drummer and percussionist Edwin Prévost writes:

> If we – as musicians and listeners – have any choice when confronting the morality of capitalism, then it must be to do rather than to be done to. We must decide who we are rather than be given an identity. In our freely improvised music there is the opportunity to apply a continual stream of examination. We search for sounds. We look for the meanings that become attached to sounds. […] The search is surely for self-invention and social-invention. This is an opportunity to make our world. If we do not act to make our world then somebody else will invent a world for us.
>
> (Ibid: 58)

Radical improvisation is often associated with political activism in other milieus as well. We will, for example, mention Richard Barrett who, in addition to free improvisation activity (duo FURT with Paul Obermayer), composes works catalogued rather as 'contemporary music' (see B. Gilmore, undated). Barrett was, for quite some time, a member of the British Socialist Workers Party. One of the major historical references in this field is the Scratch Orchestra, founded in 1969 by Cornelius Cardew, Michael Parsons and Howard Skempton, which developed free improvisation as well as composition based on graphic scores. We are familiar with Cardew's Maoist political involvement, which led him to abandon experimental music (regarding free improvisation at the turn of the 1960s and his relation to politics, see M. Saladin, 2014).

Noise and construction

As of the 1980s, in the sphere of contemporary music, research on timbre (playing methods) and/or – in the same vein as a Lachenmann – on *musique concrète instrumentale*, considerably reduced the gap between 'musical' sound and noise: the refined work on qualities of sound other than pitch ends up convincing the listener that the relative disappearance of the latter does not necessarily mean that one is in the presence of a 'noise' in the sense of nuisance. Here we can mention the work of German composer Carola Bauckholt. **Example 2.16 (online)** gives an excerpt of *Treibstoff* (1995), in which we see all the instruments produce noises that could be described as 'soft' – *Geräusch* in German, i.e., noise in the sense of sound quality and not *Lärm*, noise in the sense of very loud sound – thanks to various processes: preparation of the instrument (strings and piano), *pizzicato* sounds made with the tongue (bass flute), 'tongue ram' (clarinet played without embouchure).

The work of the Russian composer Dmitri Kurljandski (Kourliandsky) could enlighten us on some of the stakes of the noise wave that unfolded – beginning in the 2000–2010 period. In his pieces *Four States of Same* (2005) or *White Concerto* (2006) (see **Examples 2.17** and **2.18 online**), we find no stave even though the score is instrumental – the sole stave in *Four States of Same* has no clef: all the musicians produce sounds without fixed tone. Despite the historical distance and return to the instrumental, this type of noise shares with historical *bruitism* the position in relation to reality, proposing, in a way, to integrate the latter in the musical work. Several of his works constitute sorts of transcription of real sound situations. As regards... *pas d'action* (2003), the composer states:

> One day as I was sitting in a cafe with my wife, I heard noises from a building site, made by, among other things, a pneumatic drill that sounded like an Alpenhorn. I there and then decided that this would be the pièce for Aleph [the ensemble which created the piece]!
>
> (D. Kurljandski, 2004: 69)

Thus, music would integrate the real or, conversely, would be a fragment of reality. However, the composer's historical reference is not *bruitism*, but Russian Constructivism, which was contemporary to it. And with him, one often finds the most characteristic materialisation of the Constructivist idea: mechanism. He recognises that he is fascinated by 'the periodic process' and mechanicity in all its aspects' (D. Kurljandski, 2010a: 18; our translation). As today's Constructivism can not be the same as the Constructivism of the beginnings of the Soviet Union – we must be more modest, definitely less confident in the future! –, Kurljandski's mechanisms will be a sort of broken machineries owing to constraints that oblige the performers not to repeat themselves exactly:

> I strive to integrate constraints into the musical text so that the performer cannot play it exactly. For example, in *Broken Memory*, the musicians repeat the same movements, but the sonorities are a bit different each time, and it is this impossibility of exact repetition that often constitutes the 'meta-language' of my works: it does not appear in the score but appears in performance.
>
> (D. Kurljandski, 2010b: 50; our translation)

Perhaps to show both the proximity and distance between his aesthetic and that of historical Constructivism, Dmitri Kurljandski came up with the notion of 'objective music'. 'The essence of my approach to sound is that sound as such does not interest me; it is the conditions of the appearance of sonority that interest me:

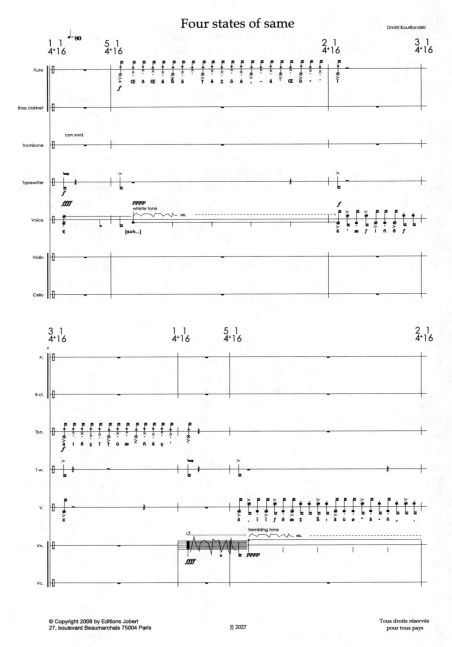

Example 2.17 Dmitri Kurljandski, *Four States of Same*: 1 (D. Kurljandski, 2005a). © By kind permission of Editions Jobert.

the natural physical data, coordination, i.e., the physiology of the musician, the construction, material and physical characteristics of the instrument; the character and intensity of the musicians' gestuality. Sonority is the projection, the outcome of these conditions' (D. Kurljandski, 2010a: 18; our translation). Here, we again find Lachenmann of course: 'As for me, I want to violate sound, "de-musicalise" it by presenting it as the direct or indirect result of actions and mechanical processes, in order to lay the foundations of a new comprehension', wrote the German composer (quoted in M. Kaltenecker, 2001: 45–46; our translation). But other composers share this point of view: one will think, in particular, of Agostino Di Scipio, who is interested in music as the composition of interactions, the sound result being only an 'epiphenomenon' (see R. Meric et al., 2009). In sum, it is not noise as such that counts: noise is only the sonic symptom of a construction.

Electronic noises and Noise

In the field of electroacoustic music, we have seen that *musique concrète* was born from its musical exploration of noises. On the other hand, electronic music would take its time in appropriating the universe of noises: at its beginnings, given the limited means at the disposal of sound synthesis, it could not produce rich sounds and therefore no noises in the acoustical sense of the term. But there were a few important exceptions. One of the first pieces going in this direction was James Tenney's *Analog #1* (subtitled 'Noise Study', 1961). The composer explains the idea behind the piece:

> For several months I had been driving to New York City in the evening, returning to the Labs [the Bell Laboratories] the next morning by way of the heavily travelled Route 22 and the Holland Tunnel. [...] The sounds of the traffic – especially in the tunnel – were usually so loud and continuous that, for example, it was impossible to maintain a conversation with a companion. [...] One day I found myself listening to these sounds, instead of trying to ignore them as usual. [...] When I did, finally, begin to listen, the sounds of the traffic became so interesting that the trip was no longer a thing to be dreaded and gotten through as quickly as possible. [...] From this image, then, of traffic noises – and especially those heard in the tunnel, where the overall sonority is richer, denser, and the changes are mostly very gradual – I began to conceive a musical composition that not only used sound elements similar to these, but manifested similarly gradual changes in sonority.
>
> (J. Tenney, undated)

To carry out his idea, Tenney wrote an algorithmic piece – one of the first works of sound synthesis entirely generated by computer – in which sound is synthesised in a stochastic (probabilistic) manner. In fact, to generate noise in continuous variation, he created an 'instrument' (in the sense of the program of the MUSIC family, which he used) producing 'noise-bands' by random amplitude-modulation of a sinusoidal carrier, of which one will find the outline, in the composer's hand, in **Example 2.19 (online)**. As Larry Polansky points out, it is interesting to note that the 'instrument' that 'Tenney built at Bell Laboratories represented what electronic music was looking for before eliminating everything: a complex noise generator' (L. Polansky, 1983).

In the period from the 1970s to 1990s, some of the most experimental research regarding computer-generated noises was carried out, in several stages, by Xenakis. Towards the end of the 1960s, in Bloomington (Indiana), Xenakis finally had computers at his disposal such as he had dreamt of since the 1950s. Even though technical resources remained limited, he imagined a principle of sound synthesis that contrasted radically with harmonic-type methods: 'the stochastic variations of the sound pressure curve' (see I. Xenakis, 1992: 242–254). To do so, he compared the curves he sought to obtain with 'Brownian movements' (small, chaotic movements of molecules suspended in a liquid or a gas, which result from their collision with the surrounding molecules) and used probabilistic functions generating 'random walks'. **Example 2.20 (online)** shows the drawing of such a curve.

At the time, due to lack of technical resources, Xenakis was unable to test this method on a whole piece. Thus, he decided to *transpose* it to instrumental music (see M. Solomos, 2001b). To do so, it sufficed to change the two coordinates of the sound's pressure curve (amplitude and micro-time) and preserve the same graphs. One thereby obtains curves with the two well-known axes of instrumental music (pitch and macro-time), which Xenakis transcribed on staves: this was the technique of what he called 'Brownian movements' and which he applied for the first time in *Mikka* (1971 for solo violin, of which **Example 2.21 (online)** gives the beginning of the score).

In two polytopes from the 1970s, *Polytope de Cluny* (1972–1974) and *Diatope* (of which the music is entitled *La Légende d'Eer*, 1978), the music combines transformations of concrete sounds and sound synthesis, the latter including, for the first time, long stochastic passages. These passages were realised with the help of mathematical functions on the computer and converted from digital to analogue at CEMAMu, the research centre founded by Xenakis. The functions used are, 'essentially Cauchy functions ($t/(t^2+x^2)\pi$) and the famous "logistic" $\alpha \cdot \exp(-\alpha x-\beta)/(1+\exp(-\alpha x-\beta))$, as well as functions of these functions. It is therefore a means of controlling Brownian movement (random walks)' (I. Xenakis, 2008: 262–263). These functions produce highly elaborate noises and, having a sort of melodic profile (see **Example 2.22 online**), evoke the instrumental 'Brownian movements'.

The last step in Xenakis's work was the GENDYN (for 'dynamic generation') software, with which he made two pieces, *Gendy 3* (1991) and *S.709* (1994) (see P. Hoffmann, 2001). Developed in the late 1980s, it exploits dynamic stochastic synthesis thanks to 'polygonal variations': the wave form, simplified with a polygonal line of points, is constantly modified by random steps (see **Example 2.23**). Therefore, one no longer synthesises a single sound but, having provided a few data to start with, the computer produces an entire work, i.e., a state where the division between micro-composition (sound synthesis) and macro-composition (composition strictly speaking) is no longer pertinent.

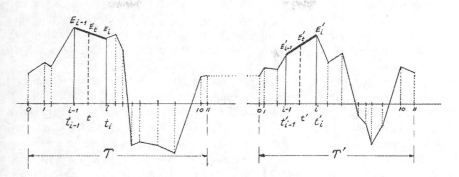

Example 2.23 Iannis Xenakis (1992: 290), GENDYN program: polygonal stochastic variations (Archives Xenakis). © By kind permission of Mâkhi Xenakis.

The work on noise is also the result of certain experimental trends in popular types of electronic music that developed in the 1990s and for which a – somewhat catchall – label could be created: 'Noise' or 'Noise music'. A sub-trend, sometimes described as 'post-industrial' or 'post-digital' and sometimes as 'glitch' (see C. Kelly, 2009; on the notion of 'glitch', see M. Nunes, ed., 2011), includes musicians as varied as Nicolas Collins, William Basinski, The Haters, Boyd Rice, Pole, Stephen Vitiello, PBK, Howard Stelzer, Chris Douglas (aka O.S.T.), Aube (Akifumi Nakajima), Andrew Deutsch, Leif Elggren, Robin Rimbaud (aka Scanner), Alva Noto (Carsten Nicolai), Oval, Boards of Canada, DJ Spooky (Paul D. Miller), Florian Hecker, Farmers Manual, Solypsis (James Miller), Thanasis Kaproulias (aka Novi_sad), Christian Fennesz, Pan Sonic, Yasunao Tone, Arcane Device (David Lee Myers) or Francisco López. These musicians integrate the defects of the digital universe: 'Glitches, bugs, application errors, system crashes, clipping, aliasing, distortion, quantization noise, and even the noise floor of computer sound cards' (K. Cascone, 2000: 16), as can be heard in Markus Popp's (Oval) album *Ovalprocess* (2000). This album can be compared to a musical theatre work from the same year: Aperghis's *Machinations* (2000), which explores ugly sounds, the sound 'defects' of the computer. In both cases, the use of noise refers to a criticism of the sanitised sounds of the computing universe and the strange silence in which it plunges us.

A particular trend of *Noise* is called 'Japanoise', for it includes Japanese artists, quite radical in their use of noise. The best known of them is the very prolific Masami Akita, who writes under the pseudonym of Merzbow, borrowed from *Merzbau*, an enormous, provocative construction by the Dadaist Kurt Schwitters. Merzbow's music is characterised by extreme noises, often very loud and of quite varied nature: feedback, explosions, saturations, coloured noises of all kinds, superimposed layers, high densities, static noises of high or low frequencies, noises with or without beats… This music has often been compared to sound barriers, difficult to cross but which, when one succeeds, give a glimpse of rich, interesting universes. In fact, if one manages to 'penetrate' this music, one begins to hear very fine, permanent variations of noises. This is the case, for example, with 'Elephant Memory', from the album *Another Merzbow Records* (2010), of which **Example 2.24 (online)** gives the spectrogram of the beginning: we see that this very compact noise is run through by changes (at 2.5" and 5").

Merzbow's music is often characterised as 'extreme' – and it is true that he often publishes on a label called 'Extreme'... One might also speak of 'excess' (P. Hegarty, 2007: 155). In it one could see a relation to sexuality and pornography. Here is what he says about this: 'If music was sex, then Merzbow would be pornography. [...] I mean that pornography is the unconsciousness of sex. So, Noise is the unconsciousness of music' (Merzbow, 2006: 60). We must also emphasise the link with the BDSM culture, which the Japanese musician has studied at length. Among other things, he is the author of two CDs entitled *Music for Bondage Performance*.

Noise and sound

Thus, noise is increasingly a part of music, and it is probable that the two histories of music mentioned at the beginning of this chapter will end up coming together. The metaphysics of sound that the Greeks constructed around the notion of harmony postulated an essence of sound that was progressively decanted in the construction of the notion of pitch and note. This construction is metaphysical in the literal sense: here, the note refers to something other than itself. Helmholtzian acoustics constituted the final culmination of this construction: in postulating that the musical sound is based on identity (repetition, periodicity). Therefore, by excluding evolution in time, Helmholtz tried to harmonise a physical existence with a mathematical abstraction.

Twentieth-century acoustics has taken it upon itself to dismantle this construction. To tell the truth, the very first acoustic works on timbre, beginning in the early 19th century, were set to go off on a different path. In his *Treatise on Acoustics* (1809), Ernst Chladni, proposing one of the earliest reflections on timbre, explained that the difference of timbre between sounds of which the 'manner of vibration, the speed and force are the same' 'seems to be caused by a bit of noise mixed with appreciable sound; for example, in singing, in addition to the vibrations of air, we hear the rubbing of this fluid on the organs of the voice; on the violin, in addition to the vibrations of the strings, we hear the rubbing of the bow on the strings, etc.' (Chladni quoted *in* F.-J. Fétis, 1833: 194; our translation). However, it would not be before the development of instruments (such as the sonagraph, which came out in the 1940s) enabling the measurement of the evolution of sound in time to back up this hypothesis. Modern acoustics will then be able to again question this mechanist-type model: 'rather than stabilise sound in a form and divide it into distinct, quite separate categories, the contemporary acoustic comes to recognise the intrinsic value if the transitive states of sound as well as the intelligibility of the dynamic processes' (H. Dufourt, 1991: 271;

our translation). As soon as we integrate the dimension of *time*, the difference between noise and musical sound tends to blur.

It is of this vision of sound about which recent music convinces us by the progressive convergence of its two histories: it is not so much a matter of introducing noise as recognising that, without it, music does not exist. 'Rather than bringing noise into music, noise music is thought of as amplifying, extending and foregrounding the noise that is always already within the techno-musical system. This approach, I assert, allows for a broader range of artistic practices and aesthetics – from the 'full noise' of Merzbow and Incapacitants to the subtle 'crackle dub' of German electronic music producer Pole', writes Marie Thompson (2017: 11), in a book that develops an 'ethical-affective' approach to noise.

That music, to accentuate the demonstration (owing to the fact that it has always been on the side of noise), has become more '*bruiteux*', is perhaps a secondary issue – henceforth, nothing prevents us from hearing, in music that is supposed to be non-noisy, its implicit share of noise. In sum, it is appropriate to abandon not only the noise/sound opposition but also the very notion of noise, be it musical or non-musical – we must, of course, preserve it for harmful noises.

This evolution was made possible because the musical civilisation that is in the process of establishing itself is centred on the *sonorous*. If it proves to be increasingly difficult to distinguish between musical sound and noise, it is because we are progressively entering a universe where only a single category now exists: *sound*. As was the case with timbre, noise is one of the elements leading to this new civilisation. However, the dissolution of timbre and noise into the sonorous comes about only if one really wants to hear it: this shows that the next history leading to sound will be the history of *listening*.

Chapter 2 online examples

Example 2.2 *Le Roman de Fauvel*: detail of Charivari.
Example 2.4 Jean-Féry Rebel, *Le Chaos:* first chord.
Example 2.8 Luigi Russolo with his assistant Ugo Piatti and their *intonarumori*.
Example 2.10 Edgar Varèse, *Déserts:* measures 264–269 (E. Varèse, 1953–1954). © By kind permission of Editions Ricordi.
Example 2.11 Pierre Henry, *Voile d'Orphée*, 0'00"–0'09": spectrogram.
Example 2.12 Iannis Xenakis, *Diamorphoses*: graphic transcription.
Example 2.15 Fred Frith concert, April 2009 (photograph by Aaron).
Example 2.16 Carola Bauckholt, *Treibstoff*: p. 3 (C. Bauckholt, 1995). © By kind permission of Thürmchen Verlag.
Example 2.18 Dmitri Kurljandski, *White Concerto:* 1 (D. Kurljandski, 2005b). © By kind permission of Editions Jobert.
Example 2.19 James Tenney: 'Instrument' from *Analog #1* ('Noise Study') (J. Tenney, undated). © By kind permission of John Tenney.
Example 2.20 Iannis Xenakis (1992: 253): stochastic pressure curve. Duration: 8 milliseconds (Archives Xenakis). © By kind permission of Mâkhi Xenakis.

Example 2.21 Iannis Xenakis, *Mikka* (I. Xenakis, 1971). Notice on the score: 'glissando everywhere'. © By kind permission of Editions Salabert.
Example 2.22 Iannis Xenakis, *La Légende d'Eer*, 14'27''-14'41'': spectrogram.
Example 2.24 Merzbow, *Elephant Memory*, 0'00''-0'06'': spectrogram.

Notes

1 I borrow this expression from Milan Kundera (1981: 21–24; our translation) who, in a nice text on Xenakis, explains that he found a 'relief' in the 'objective', 'unsentimental' noises of the latter's music (he thinks of Xenakis's references to mathematics and physics): 'Music has participated decisively in [the] progressive "sentimentalisation" of Man. But the moment may come [...] when sentimentality [...] is straightaway revealed as the "superstructure of brutality". It was at that time that I came to see music as the *deafening noise of emotions,* whereas the world of noises in Xenakis's compositions became, for me, *beauty*, beauty cleansed of affective filth, stripped of sentimental barbarism'.
2 Thus, in 1947, Ives published with Arrow Music Press a version of the *Concord Sonata* with 'substantially richer writing: [he] added inner voices, modified the harmony in a way both richer and more dissonant, and gave more differentiated dynamic and agogic indications [...]' (G. Schubert, 1986: 114; our translation).
3 One composed 'without Expressionism or gags, music that was sombre, objective, based on patient research starting from simple sound bodies from which one draws sounds that are assembled in modest *Études*. The chief set the example with his *Études aux sons animés, aux allures, aux objects*'. (M. Chion, 1982: 80; our translation).
4 Here, the words 'typology' and 'morphology' are not used in their Schaefferian sense. For Schaeffer, typology is linked to *listening* to a sound and morphology to its *making*. Chapter 3 will deal with the importance of listening in the *Traité des objets musicaux*.
5 See the writings of the French music critic Hugues Panassié (1965) who, in the 1940s, on the pretext of enhancing the status of jazz, had linked it to such notions as 'authenticity', 'race' or 'essence' in an ideological context close to the National Revolution of Vichy (see L. Tournès, 2001: 324–325).
6 It would be impossible here to mention the innumerable studies dealing with the political protest led by rock and sometimes combining it with noise. Let us refer to *There's a Riot Going On* by Peter Doggett (2007), which, in the chapter devoted to 1968, subtitled 'Radical Noise', partly deals with anti-authority musicians such as Phil Ochs or Country Joe McDonald (Country Joe and the Fish), whose music is, however, quite tame. To the degree that, precisely, political contestation is not necessarily synonymous with noise in the musical sense of the term – it suffices to think of Joan Baez – one might prefer talking about the 'savage' nature of rock. This seems more logically linked to noise in the musical sense (for an analysis of the 'dirty, savage sound' of the emblematic song *Ramble* (1958) – which numerous American radios stations banned – by the Amerindian guitarist Link Wray, see G. Gilles (2018).
7 The example reproduces the first edition of the piece. There exists a revised edition 'which is not a compositional revision of my work, but rather a new design of the notation, one which takes into consideration the knowledge and experience gained in regards to the performance of the work and reading of the score since its first publication' (H. Lachenmann, 2010).

3 Listening (sounds)

Liberating listening

Happy new ears

Cage never liked notes, fixed pitches or the supreme musical art that teaches you to associate them: harmony. That was not due to lack of musical culture or education, since he studied with the modern master of harmony, Schoenberg. The inventor of dodecaphonism introduced atonality whilst remaining attached to notes and tones; that is why he did not like the term 'atonal', writing that 'a piece of music will necessarily always be tonal in so far as a relation exists from tone to tone, whereby tones, placed next to or above one another, result in a perceptible succession' (A. Schoenberg, 1984: 283). As for Cage, he was always fascinated by sounds taken *individually*. In spite of all his goodwill, he remained alien to harmony and to its art of establishing relations between sounds. As he liked to say:

> When Schoenberg asked me whether I would devote my life to music, I said, 'Of course'. After I had been studying with him for two years, Schoenberg said, 'In order to write music, you must have a feeling for harmony'. I explained to him that I had no feeling for harmony. He then said that I would always encounter an obstacle, that it would be as though I came to a wall through which I could not pass. I said, 'In that case I will devote my life to beating my head against that wall'.
>
> (J. Cage, 1961: 261)

The absence of relations constitutes a means for avoiding imposed, restrictive relations, which do not stem from sounds themselves: intervals

> are not just sounds but they imply in their progressions a sound not actually present to the ear. [...] For instance: there are some progressions called deceptive cadences. The idea is this: progress in such a way as to imply the presence of a tone not actually present; then fool everyone by not landing on it – land somewhere else. What is being fooled? Not the ear but the mind. The whole question is very intellectual,
>
> (Ibid: 116)

wrote Cage in his famous 'Lecture on Nothing'. That is why he gave up notes, which automatically bring with them a set of relations that we have not chosen. To do so, he turned to *noises*: 'I began to see that the separation of mind and ear had spoiled the sounds, that a clean slate was necessary. […] I used noises. They had not been intellectualized; the ear could hear them directly and didn't have to go through any abstraction about them' (Ibid: 116). Cage's earliest music would therefore be *bruiteux*. Percussion became his favourite vehicle, in keeping with the model of Varèse's *Ionisation*. In his *First Construction (In Metal)* of 1939 for six percussionists and an assistant, metallic sounds predominate, the most vivid being provided by different-sized plates of sheet metal: an infinity of sounds were extracted from them, almost already as in Stockhausen's *Mikrophonie I* (1964), which explores all the sounds that can be produced with a tam-tam.

But noise could only be a step in Cage's research: as he explained in his first major lecture, in a very Varésian tone, 'The Future of Music: Credo' (1937), music for percussion should constitute the transition between 'keyboard-influenced music to the all-sound music of the future' (J. Cage, 1961: 5). Hence the invention of the prepared piano in 1940, which provided a plethora of sounds emanating from a keyboard. During the same period, Cage also tried a few other tricks to create an 'all-sound music': turntables of variable speed and frequency oscillators (*Imaginary Landscape No.1*, 1939), radio sounds (*Imaginary Landscape No.4*, 1951), etc.

Cage could have continued in this way – he would do so – and increased the various strokes of inspiration and tinkering to invent new sounds. To be exact, 'he is not a composer but a brilliant inventor', Schoenberg would say (in J. Cage, 1961: IV). However, his greatest invention was *large new ears*. Indeed, to be able to accept the opening up of music to all possible sounds, he tells us, it suffices to *listen differently*. Listen differently: let us not try to save music at all costs by taming new sounds; let us only learn to listen to them: they are *already* music. So the essential thing is not to articulate these sounds but to prick up one's ears and accept them as they are, without asking questions. 'I simply keep my ears open', Cage would say (1981: 77). Every sound deserves to be heard: 'I never heard a sound I didn't like: the only problem with sounds is music' (J. Cage, 1994: 21). Because they are already music, sounds are enough for us on condition that we are aware of them i.e., that we know how to listen (to them).

Refocussing on listening

From this, there results a refocussing on listening. Learning to listen differently means quite simply learning to listen. Putting listening at the heart of musical activity and learning to listen constitutes a change of musical paradigm, a new conception of music, which modifies it in its entirety. One could mention the Husserlian *épochè* and infer that, by refocussing on listening, Cage insists on the very condition of the existence of music. In the language of Daniel Charles (2001: 248; our translation):

> It is a matter […] of attaining, with the composer as with the listener, a *receptiveness to the event* that *precedes any position of a principle of acting;* and to refute any hasty opposition between creative activity and the perception that reaps the result.

Starting from there, all possibilities are open.

Listening is, above all, making oneself available. In his 'Lecture on Nothing', John Cage (1961: 109–110) began thus: 'I am here, and there is nothing to say [...] I have nothing to say and I'm saying it. [...] We need not fear these silences – we may love them'. However, he added: 'Most speeches are full of ideas. This one doesn't have to have any. But at any moment an idea may come along. Then we may enjoy it' (Ibid: 113). On this point, the influence of Zen Buddhism on Cage was important.

Listening is also listening to others. Cage was always very concerned with that, as attests a very fine political text, 'Other People Think', which he wrote at the age of 15 (1927) for an oratorical competition (which he won). Here are a few excerpts:

> Today the United States is a world power. [...] It is the popular belief that we have promoted friendly relations with all Latin America. [...]
>
> Why, then, is there any misunderstanding between the Latins and the Anglo-Saxons of this continent?
>
> There are two sides to every question. For other people think otherwise. Concerning the question of American Intervention in Latin America, many people are thinking otherwise. [...] This thought, that has penetrated the intellectual life of the Latin Republics so effectively, has been influenced by the actions of certain citizens of the United States. The great majority of these are capitalists who have zealously invested money in the Southern Republics and eagerly exploited them. [...] It was to protect the 'Lives and Property' of just such money-grasping men [...] that the United States Marines entered Nicaragua fifteen years ago. [...] Other people began to think that no government could exist in Central America without the sanction of the United States. [...] Many have feared our interference in the past. Many will hate our intervention in the future. [...]
>
> What are we going to do? What ought we to do?
>
> One of the greatest blessings that the United States could receive in the near future would be to have her industries halted, her business discontinued, her people speechless, a great pause in her world of affairs created, and finally to have everything stopped that runs, until everyone should hear the last wheel go around and the last echo fade away... [...] Then we should be capable of answering the question, 'What ought we to do?' For we should be hushed and silent, and we should have the opportunity to learn that other people think.
>
> (J. Cage in R. Kostelanetz, 1991: 45–48)

Listening means many other things: being attentive, collecting one's thoughts, meditating, etc. It is also a matter of forgetting – 'To start listening to sound, one must forget the names, relations, limits, prejudices and inferences by which thought guides sound' (C. Pardo Salgado, 2007: 24; our translation). And, finally, listening means being silent. Learning to listen involves experiencing silence, which already shows up in *Sonatas and Interludes* and which would become, in the early 1950s, beginning with *Music of Changes* (1951), the centre of Cage's musical practice. The decisive experience was that of the anechoic chamber:

> I had honestly and naïvely thought that some actual silence existed. [...] So when I went into that sound-proof room, I really expected to hear nothing. [...] The instant I heard myself producing two sounds, my blood circulating and my nervous system in operation, I was stupefied. For me, that was the turning point.
>
> (J. Cage, 1981: 115–116)

If silence does not exist, it is because there is always something to listen to. It suffices that *I*, listener or composer, be quiet to be aware of this. Silence is therefore all the sounds that I do not determine, whether they come from me – I do not control the pulsating of my blood – or from someone else. These are all unintentional sounds that do not depend on my intention.

The famous *4'33"* (see **Example 3.1**) takes into account, musically, this experiment in which, through the intermediary of silence thus defined, listening is what allows for receiving all possible sounds. The piece had been thought out by 1948 with the title *Silent Prayer* but, at the time, the idea of silence stemmed from a desire for asceticism or meditation (see J. Pritchett, 1993: 59). The *4'33"* we know is completely different for, in the meantime, the anechoic chamber experience occurred. Able to be played by 'any instrument or combination of instruments' (J. Cage, 1960), the work is made up of three parts (movements). During the first performance, on 29 August 1952, the pianist David Tudor indicated the beginnings of parts by closing, the endings by opening, the Keyboard; the parts lasted 33", 2'40" and 1'20" (Ibid). A second version proposes 30", 2'23" and 1'40" (Ibid). Finally, the third indicates only 'I', 'II' and 'III'.[1] Cage's desire was to include in the musical performance the various noises of the audience, who progressively realises what is happening – namely that the musician on stage will not 'play' – as well as the other noises of the environment, inside or outside the concert hall.

I

TACET

II

TACET

III

TACET

Example 3.1 John Cage, *4'33"*: reduction.

During the first performance, 'you could hear the wind stirring outside during the first movement. During the second, raindrops began pattering on the roof, and during the third, the people themselves made all kinds of interesting sounds as they talked or walked out' (J. Cage in R. Kostelanetz, 1988: 65).

Free listening

The listening that Cage invented is poles apart from traditional listening. In musical tradition, the work is supposed to convey a meaning that the listener must 'understand': he must vibrate to its crescendos, shiver at its dissonances, feel that he is approaching the end. In Cagean listening, such as emanates from *4'33"*, we have an 'unfocused perception' (J. Branden, 2016: 92). However, it is not a matter of taking the opposite position of tradition and making believe that the listener holds the sense. If the work does not hold sense, neither does the listener: the sense is produced at the moment of listening. This is why it is so important to note that Cage, whilst spurning social conventions inherited from Romanticism (and in particular the deification of the Artist and Composer), did not seek to convince us that art does not exist, that we could do without works of art, that only that which exists would count. In teaching us to listen, Cage – whilst renouncing this 'other world' that was supposed to bring us a work to which we were to submit the orientation of our listening – sought to go beyond the terrible force of inertia of reality.

For Cage, this inertia was due to the restrictive set of determinations that the individual has acquired. It therefore does not suffice to free oneself from external things; one must also free oneself from oneself, otherwise listening risks being a tautology where one listens only to what one is willing to listen to. On this point, Zen Buddhism, in which Daisetz Teitaro Suzuki initiated Cage in the early 1950s, played an important role. It taught him to tone down the *ego* and free it from its determinations, i.e., from its tastes, emotions, etc. Only in that way can one be free, truly listen and be sensitive and open to what surrounds us:

> We made the *ego* into a wall, and the wall does not even have a door through which the interior and exterior could communicate! Suzuki taught me to destroy that wall. What is important is to insert the individual into the current, the flux of everything that happens. And to do that, the wall has to be demolished: tastes, memory and emotions have to be weakened; all the ramparts have to be razed.
>
> (J. Cage, 1981: 48)

Cage set the example himself, through his practice as a composer, producing impersonal works, undetermined by his will. At the beginning of the 1950s, he invented composition processes going through indeterminacy and focussing on chance. In the first two movements of the *Concerto for Prepared Piano*

(1950–1951), the piano 'remains romantic, expressive', i.e., composed according to the composer's tastes (see J. Pritchett, 1993: 62); on the other hand, the orchestral parts are composed according to the 'diagrams' technique; the third movement ends up also imposing indeterminacy on the soloist. Then, Cage would universalise and use the processes of chance in composition, in particular using the *I Ching*. Indeterminacy was also soon introduced by the non-fixation of sounds. Thus, in *Imaginary Landscape No.5* (1952), the result is not predictable: the score invites creating a tape using 'any 42 phonograph recordings', and indicates the precise moments when discs are to be changed as well as variations of intensity to carry out. Finally, at the end of the 1950s, Cage also introduced indeterminacy in performance. The scores themselves become indeterminate: the performer must choose between several options and 'interpret' instructions. The *Concert for Piano* (1957–1958) – 'concert' and not 'concerto', for this is not meant as a precise piece, but a total moment of music, a concert – can last as long as the musicians wish; not all the instrumentalists are obliged to play, the conductor only indicates durations, and the performers have, in truth, only a reservoir of materials. There is no overall score, so the result will never be the same. '[…] It is not the results that interest us. The results are like death. What interests us are things that move, that they change and do not remain set', says Cage (in R. Kostelanetz, 1988: 150).

In becoming process, music no longer imposes constraints on things: they can be themselves. Evoking his initiation into Zen Buddhism, Cage (in R. Kostelanetz, 1988: 77) tells us that, thanks to it:

> I saw art not as something that consisted of a communication from the artist to an audience but rather as an activity of sounds in which the artist found a way to let the sounds be themselves. And, in being themselves, to open the minds of people who made them or listened to them to other possibilities than they had previously considered.

Listening freely comes down, in the final analysis, to being oneself and letting sounds be themselves. From that point on, we can envisage the practice of free listening as a practice of freedom itself. The whole conception of music brought by Cage can be read like the metaphor of a better life. But it also entails putting this into practice, as is true with the *Musicircuses*. Cage called *Musicircus* the reunion, in the same venue, of musicians all practising, simultaneously and for a given duration, their own music – Cage himself executing his own works – with the audience circulating freely. The first *Musicircus* took place in 1967, and Cage organised several others. With the *Musicircuses*, he established a non-hierarchical space (all types of music and all musicians – amateur or professional – are of equal worth), decentred, where no authority imposes itself. As for listening, Cage's aim was precisely that the listener not end up mixing all types of music or that the musicians, who play their own music, end up playing together. On the occasion of a debate following the last *Musicircus*, which took place in 1992, a few months before Cage's death, an enthusiastic listener told him: 'I noticed last night at the

Musicircus that the musicians listened to each other playing, and often joined in, finding spontaneous harmony where it was least expected'. Cage replied: 'I think instead of believing they've reached something positive by "fitting in" with each other, that they should remain separate' (in C. Junkerman, 1994: 57).

For Cage, men, like instruments, do not need to tune up: they can coexist as they are, they hardly need harmony (of an imposed order) to *hear each other*[2]...

Phenomenology of listening

A treatise of listening

The refocussing on listening is also due to Pierre Schaeffer: in many respects, the *Treatise on Musical Objects* is, first of all, to borrow its author's terms, 'a treatise on listening' (P. Schaeffer, 2017: 539) (**Example 3.2 online**). The starting point is the same as for Cage: the opening up of music to all possible sounds, to the generality of sound. Faced with his vast *terra incognita*, Schaeffer, just like Cage, conceptualised not the manner of producing its innumerable regions but the *curiosity* they arouse, i.e., the fascination they generate for every well-intentioned ear. For, even more than Cage, Schaeffer was placed straightaway on the listener's terrain. A man of the radio (manager, designer and host of radio programmes, recording engineer: see M. Robert, 1999), he knew the private life of sounds exclusively by listening to them. As for the 'invention' of *musique concrète*, it first constituted a revolution in listening. It is indeed a change of perspective (in listening) that enabled Schaeffer to consider this brainwave an art – hence the necessity of 'making noises musical', which was discussed in the previous chapter. Like Cage, but in a totally different register, Schaeffer would tell us: *let us learn to listen*, that is the essential thing for founding an art based on all possible sounds.

However, Schaeffer's and Cage's perspectives are different. Cage concluded with the refocussing on listening *without opposing it to what* the instrumentalist or composer is *doing*. With him, listening happens everywhere, it is just a matter of becoming aware of it. 'I simply keep my ears open', he told us (J. Cage, 1981: 77). Schaeffer discovered listening in opposition to musical practice (playing music). On this point, his experience as a soundman was decisive and doubtless what led him to problematise listening: by discovering that, through recording, sound is listened to in a completely different way. As he said in one of his first texts (dating from 1946), which we quoted in the introduction:

> The microphone gives events [...] a *purely sound* version. Without transforming sound, it transforms listening. [...] The microphone can confer the same importance then, if it pushes the magnification further, the same dimension of strangeness to a whisper, a heartbeat, the ticking of a watch.
>
> (P. Schaeffer, 2002: 82–84; our translation)

Starting from there, Schaeffer would hesitate, for this situation can lead to two different positions. One can choose to put the accent on the new listening with a prosthesis (microphone), on the details that it allows for grasping, and to wager on the fact that, once rid of the visual cause of sound, it will focus on the 'purely sonorous'. But one can also choose to insist on the possibility of transforming this auditory prosthesis into an instrument that, without producing sound, transforms it and ends up achieving a different sound. This hesitation and this duality are at the heart of *musique concrète* and even constitute its principal characteristic: *musique concrète* is both a new way of listening and a new (compositional) musical practice. But Schaeffer insisted on the opposition and although, in the *Treatise on Musical Objects*, he chose to focus on listening, it is because he presented it as 'the most general musical situation possible', where, in a way, the ear is substituted for the instrument.

For a phenomenology of listening

Another reason led Schaeffer to focus on listening: his philosophical readings. Alongside physics and acoustics, as well as linguistics, the *Treatise on Musical Objects* turns to philosophy in order to *fill the gap between acoustics and music*. This is, doubtless, the explanation as to why what Schaeffer called on was phenomenology. Husserl's ambition to bridge the gap between subjective experience and the objectivity of knowledge, between psychologism and realism, finally, between subject and object (see J. Patocka, 1992: 119), is taken up by Schaeffer through the theme of listening, and through Merleau-Ponty's *Phenomenology of Perception* (M. Merleau-Ponty, 1945). After the quoted phrase 'the *Treatise on Musical Objects* is first and foremost a treatise on listening', Schaeffer (2017: 539) added: 'Is it so surprising that we should wish to recall what is always forgotten? The object implies the conscious subject; the activity of the conscious subject confronted by any object is the bedrock of the musical'.

This contribution of Schaeffer is important because, as he stressed, listening is not primordial in the experience such as it is shaped by our culture, which puts the accent on 'doing': musicians abide by this priority. Owing to this, thinking about music – be it called music theory, musicology or philosophy of music – has examined listening very little. To remedy this situation, Schaeffer would go so far as to say that the 'acousmatician' works on his ear as the instrumentalist worked on his instrument (Ibid: 270) – which, as has been said, constitutes a way of removing the hesitation as regards the microphone, conceived as an auditory prosthesis or a new (musical) instrument.

In an article written after the *Treatise on Musical Objects*, Schaeffer explained how he came to the theme of listening:

> So I was led to reinvent an authentic, adequate approach to the object of our listening and to help me with correlations between measurable (i.e., physical) and perceptible (psychological) phenomena. Although I first thought to work on *external* objects (even they were 'objects of our listening'), I had to agree that they were, above all, marked by the activities of perception and the intentions of the *subject*.
>
> (P. Schaeffer, 1971: 8 our translation)

It is thus clear that the interest in listening is linked to that in phenomenology. *Entendre* (to hear) indeed means *tendre vers* (lean towards) even though, as Schaeffer emphasised (2017: 99), the word has emptied its etymological content. Hearing and listening do not constitute a passive act: they call on our consciousness – all physicalist, positivist theory of musical perception, which postulates a non-mediatised chain between the object of perception and its mental image, fails. In other words, to use a technical word, hearing always presupposes an 'intention'.

On this point, it is suitable to distinguish between perception and sensation. '"Phenomenology", fifty years ago, in particular with Husserl, endeavoured to do justice to falsely scientific counting. Indeed, the phenomenological discipline teaches us that there is no question of confusing *sensation* and *perception*', wrote Schaeffer (1967: 35) in a book contemporary with the *Treatise on Musical Objects*, which constitutes the first book tracing the history of *musique concrète*. In the *Treatise on Musical Objects*, he quotes Merleau-Ponty to prove that sensation, contrary to common belief, is not prior to perception (P. Schaeffer, 2017: 104). Basing himself on Merleau-Ponty – who wrote: 'to perceive is not to experience a host of impressions [*sensations*] [...]; it is to see, standing forth from a cluster of data, an immanent significance' (M. Merleau-Ponty, 1945: 26) – Schaeffer attacks the physicalist *credo* of electronic music of the time and distinguishes between frequency and pitch, level and intensity, time and duration, spectrum and timbre. The first term of each pair describes the acoustic phenomenon but cannot account for perception: if one is interested in the latter, then other concepts must be used, which correspond to the second term in the pairs. In sum, Schaeffer can be considered one of the founders of psychoacoustics.

The four ways of listening

Schaeffer did not settle for distinguishing between the sensation of perception and analysing the intentionality of hearing. Giving another sense to this verb, he included it in a tetra-partition that redefined four verbs in the current French language, *écouter, ouïr, entendre, comprendre* – translated, by Christine North and John Dack, in the recent English version of the *Treatise* by 'listen', 'perceive aurally', 'hear' and 'understand' – classifying them in a grid (**Example 3.3**). We might say that it is a matter of isolating the two types of listening favoured by our culture and enhancing two others. The first two are at the top of the chart. To 'listen' (*écouter*) relates to our way of apprehending a sound as a result, caused by something (whether it be a musical instrument or any sound source); the sound then identifies with an 'event', and I perceive it as a 'clue' (it informs me about its source). To 'understand' (*comprendre*) indicates the moment when the sound is taken as an element of what musical tradition calls 'language'. Sounds, put in relation with one another, have 'values' attributed to them by a musical code and, in relation to it, I perceive them as 'signs'. These two types of hearing are placed at the extremes (numbers 1 and 4), for 'listening' refers to the most 'concrete', and 'understanding' to the most 'abstract'. But they are located at the top of the chart for they submit to an 'objectivity' of listening: one 'listens to' the cause of the sound, one 'understands' its sense. The other two types are

92 *Listening (sounds)*

4. To UNDERSTAND (*comprendre*) -for me: signs -in front of me: values (meaning-language) Emergence of a sound content and *reference to, encounters with,* extra-sound concepts	1. To LISTEN (*écouter*) -for me: clues -in front of me: external events (agent-instrument) Sound *production*	objective
3. To HEAR (*entendre*) -for me: qualified perceptions -in front of me: qualified sound object *Selection* of certain specific aspects of the sound	2. To PERCEIVE AURALLY (*ouïr*) -for me: raw perceptions, vague idea of the object -in front of me: raw sound object *Reception* of the son	subjective
abstract	concrete	

Example 3.3 The four types of listening from the *Treatise on Musical Objects* in their first presentation (after P. Schaeffer, 2017: 83).

'subjective', one being 'concrete' and the other 'abstract'. The first, to 'perceive aurally' (*ouïr*), presupposes that I have before me a sound whose nature I have not yet analysed and that I am settling for rough perceptions; it is the moment of its 'reception'. The second, to 'hear' (*entendre*), starts from this step and proceeds to a determination of the nature of the sound (for itself). I therefore 'selected' some of its aspects.

Let us simplify: to 'listen' means focussing on the cause of the sound; to 'understand' is compared with traditional musical listening; to 'perceive aurally' is identified with an overall perception; to 'hear' is the moment of analytical perception. In this sense, to perceive aurally and to hear constitute a 'narrowing on the object', 'contemplated for itself at the price of an "époché" of which Husserl remains the master' (P. Schaeffer, 1976: 71). It is therefore not insignificant that they be placed at the bottom of the chart: they correspond to the two types of listening that culture has buried and which must be rediscovered. 'We have to make a special effort to put aside these ordinary aims' constituted by listening and understanding and to learn to perceive aurally and to hear, notes Schaeffer (2017: 540) in the addition to the second edition of the *Treatise on Musical Objects*.

Reduced listening and the sound object

'Narrowing on the object', '*époché*': to perceive aurally and to hear lead to the last borrowing from Husserl in the *Treatise on Musical Objects*, what he calls 'reduced listening', defined in Chapter 15 and refined in Chapter 20.

His definition is henceforth obvious: reduced listening relates to listening that loses interest in both the cause of the sound and the meaning it takes on in a musical context; these two ways of listening being those to which our cultural conditioning predisposes us, only their bracketing, *épochè*, and reduction enable us to achieve reduced listening (to perceive aurally and to hear). It is thanks to this reduced listening that we grasp what Schaeffer calls a 'sound object'.

But when Schaeffer gives a definition of the sound object for itself, the parallel with phenomenology stops. Certainly, he relies on Husserl to define objectivity and the object (P. Schaeffer, 2017: 205–210), but Books V and VI, which are devoted to sound (and musical) objects, fall short of these definitions. They do not analyse them according to the Husserlian principle that the object is constituted through knowledge and is therefore relative to experience, but as if the object constituted a reality independent of my consciousness. For in Schaeffer's intellectual development, the notion of sound-object predates his phenomenological thinking. His model remains the 'closed groove', an object in the non-phenomenological sense of the term: which is already there, pre-constituted. This reading of Schaeffer does not cancel out everything that has been said about him and phenomenology: it only underscores the initial contradiction. Starting from his radio experience, Schaeffer did not manage to clear up the contradiction between two ways of apprehending the microphone: auditory prosthesis or, indeed, a new (musical) instrument? At present, the contradiction can be stated in the following manner: must one treat fixed sounds (the sound objects) as materials, which, owing to their complexity, allow for going beyond the idea of music as language, or else as materials that can be reduced to units starting from which one listens to and composes music as before? When Schaeffer puts the accent on listening, he seems to be opting for the first possibility; elsewhere, it is the second that wins.[3]

A multiplicity of ways to listen

Acousmatic

Some of Schaeffer's heirs would choose to substitute the expression 'acousmatic (music)' to '*musique concrète*' (or 'electroacoustic') – Schaeffer himself was already using the term. It has become customary to use this expression for composers who are affiliated with *musique concrète* and, perhaps, more generally, electroacoustic music, from 1970 up to the present day. Limiting ourselves here to the strict relation with *musique concrète*, let us mention only François Bayle, Michel Chion, Francis Dhomont, Denis Dufour, Luc Ferrari, Beatriz Ferreyra, Christine Groul, Robert Normandeau, Bernard Parmegiani, Ake Parmerud, Guy Reibel, Denis Smalley, Annette Vande Gorne, Daniel Teruggi and Christian Zanési. François Bayle, Schaeffer's successor as head of the GRM, is perhaps the one who has theorised most on the notion of acousmatic. He gave an in-depth reflection on what he calls 'i-sound' (for 'image-of-sound'), a concept that, with him, tends to replace the sound-object concept:

> The image for the gaze is defined starting from the trace on a support of the light energy coming from an object. I-sound is similarly defined for hearing, in an isomorphic appearance to the sound source (i.e., identically transmitted to the auditory system by air).
>
> But like the image, i-sound is distinguished from the sound source by a double disjunction – physical, coming from a substitution of space of causes, and psychological, from a displacement of air of effects: awareness of a simulacrum, an interpretation, a sign.
>
> (F. Bayle, 1993: 186; our translation)

I-sound 'is not a sound in the same way as others', he added (Ibid: 134): it is *like* a sound but is the 'sound of nothing'. This is why Bayle insisted on the fact that i-sound could also be described as absence, or even as 'lack' (Ibid: 30). Bayle continues: 'I-sound constitutes […] a *figural object* including the coded marks of its production of listening, unlike the natural sound for which these codes and marks refer to an external system' (Ibid: 186). This is why 'acousmatic appears […] as *listening to listening*' (F. Bayle, 2007: 16). It constitutes an immersion in 'perceptive thought' so that the sonorous becomes 'a manageable object on which experience can practise' (F. Bayle, 1993: 17). That is perhaps the most important reason he speaks about 'images': the musician's work, as much as the listener's, must be carried out in us, in our imagination. Thus,

> there is not one single space peculiar to the movements of acousmatic sounds, which would be the tri-dimensional physical space […] It will be understood that it is a 'journey to the centre of the head', and that *the space remains to describe just as well by the mind*, like a *cosa mentale*, especially in the world of i-sounds, since these are spaces of representation.[4]
>
> (Ibid.: 137–138)

Bayle originated a software allowing for visualising our listening: the Acousmographe (developed by Olivier Koechlin and Hugues Vinet). The '*acousmogrammes*' (products of the Acousmographe) allow for refining the 'listening scores' that were previously carried out by hand.[5] They can also help in the performance of an acousmatic work, i.e., in its being played in the concert space, and contribute to musicological analysis. **Example 3.4** shows an *acousmogramme* realised by the composer himself for the beginning (first 38 seconds) of 'Transit 1' from the cycle *Tremblement de terre très doux* (1978, part of *Érosphère*).

A second composer-theorist who is fundamentally renewing Schaeffer's heritage, Michel Chion, chose to extend acousmatic in '*acoulogy*', in order to enlarge the field of analysis to all possible sounds and all possible listening situations. In the introduction to his book *Le promeneur écoutant. Essais d'acoulogie*, he writes

> As I envisage it, acoulogy will therefore be the discipline that, in rigorous words, deals with sounds, with what we hear, in all its aspects, which neither acoustics [...] nor the ill-named psycho-acoustics [...] do.
>
> (M. Chion, 1993: 11; our translation)

The book includes an index of 148 words or groups of words such as

> barking, cheering in the concert hall, musical chord [...] waterfall (murmur), [...] bird, ondes Martenot, storm [...]; steps (noise of: in dead leaves, crunching in the snow, on the planks, of Yahweh, scurrying of mice), [...] signal (of locomotives, of boats), silence [...].
>
> (M. Chion, 1993: 189–192)

With Bayle or Chion, as with all musicians coming from *musique concrète*, it is indeed the refocussing on listening that allows for being interested in original sounds and the general nature of sound: the pleasure of new sensations, ambiguities of listening, sweet straying of 'understanding' and 'listening' (in the Schaefferian sense of the terms), which, for a moment, authorises talking nonsense...

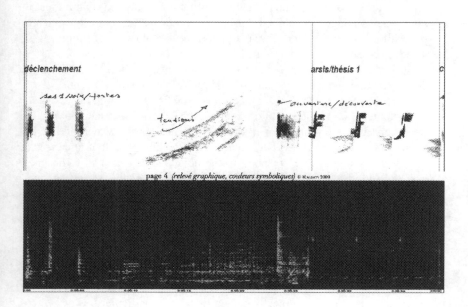

Example 3.4 François Bayle, *Érosphère, Tremblement de terre très doux*, 'Transit 1': *acousmogramme* realised by the composer. © By kind permission of François Bayle. The original is in colour.

Composing from what one perceives

Up until now, it was essentially a matter of 'listening'. But another term has also participated in this interrelation between openness to sound and focussing on the ear: *perception*. It was previously used in following Schaeffer (and Merleau-Ponty), to distinguish it from 'sensation' and to note that, in this regard, Schaeffer could be considered one of the founding fathers of psychoacoustics, which concentrates precisely on the mechanisms of perception. Yet, the recent history of psychoacoustics is parallel to a history of musicians who have tried to *compose from what our ear perceives*. In Chapter 1, it was said that this idea was not new: Rimsky-Korsakov's (1964: 116) treatise on orchestration already mentions 'orchestral operations which are based on certain defects of hearing and faculty of perception'. But it is true that, up until the work of psychoacousticians, musicians had only empirical knowledge of such phenomena, which prevented them from exploiting them in a systematic, programmatic way.

One of the first musicians to have simultaneously advanced psychoacoustics and composition was Jean-Claude Risset, whom we mentioned in the first chapter. Here, we quote at length from his article 'Perception, environnement, musique':

> The reader can think that the idiosyncrasies of perception, peculiarities, insufficiencies or illusions are of hardly any interest or significance for music. [...]
>
> As for me, I could not forget this intermediary of perception, for it was on my musical paths and unavoidable [...] Of course, in learning an instrument then writing, I developed this 'inner ear' which allows a musician to predict the auditory effect of a given chord or combination of timbres. [...] The instruments are familiar to us [...]
>
> With 'electric sound', the notion of instrument is woollier. [...] With the computer, one can build a sound of arbitrary physical structure, but what is important is its perceptible effect. As one of the first to explore the resources of computer sound synthesis, I often found the experience disappointing: the operations that are stipulated in physical terms do not always modify the sound in the expected way. The sound effect obtained is often unexpected, not always seeming to correspond to the objective arrangement. The inner ear is of little use here, unless limiting itself to sounds close to instrumental sounds. Hearing has very specific modalities: the 'psychoacoustic' relation between physical structure and perceived structure is much more complex than is thought, and sometimes even counterintuitive. If one wants to put the computer's resources to good use, the particularities of perception must be taken into account.
>
> (J.C. Risset, 1988: 11–12; our translation)

As a composer, Risset, sometimes wrote starting from 'particularities of perception'. In his *Computer Suite from Little Boy* (1968), he stages the famous 'acoustic illusions' (or 'acoustic paradoxes'). This suite comes from the incidental music for the eponymous play by Pierre Halet, which evokes the bombing of Hiroshima through the fantasies of the pilot, Eartherly. The second movement, entitled 'Fall', is famous: '[Here], amidst diverse rockets, sound runs through the large circles of an endless descent: indeed, the pilot identifies with the bomb, code-named 'Little Boy', and the fall is imaginary, in a bottomless psychical space' (J.C. Risset, 1990; our translation: 125–126). Robert Cogan was the first analyst to give the spectral image of 'Fall' (see **Example 3.5**). In the first part (upper line), we see that Risset achieves the illusion of the endless fall by the following procedure: a glissando begins in register 6 and, at the moment it reaches register 5, a second glissando begins in register 5 – the entrance of each glissando rises in crescendo and is thereafter barely perceptible; similarly for what follows. It will be noted that, in contrast with these glissandi, Risset, inscribes, in the upper register, glissandi that are clearly finished. In the second part (second line), the glissando giving the illusion of the endless descent becomes slower, then progressively fades. 'Before the development of spectral photos, it was difficult to describe and understand this type of spatial, temporal and sonic – in a word, structural – relations, which are now visible in *Fall*', noted Cogan (1984: 111).

At the end of the 1970s, the spectral composers developed an intense relation to psychoacoustics. Seeking to break with the structuralism of serialism and compose music that 'perceives itself', i.e., of which the listener can understand the processes, they would use laws of perception that psychoacousticians had formulated. Some of these psychoacousticians were in their close entourage, especially in the 1980s, within IRCAM. And we should not overlook the role played by the acoustician Émile Leipp, several spectral composers having taken his courses or read his book *Acoustique et musique* (E. Leipp, 1971). Tristan Murail wrote:

> The sounds and, even more, the relations between sounds, have an acoustic reality and a perceptive reality that are not necessarily equivalent; the study of this 'sentiment' is the object of psychoacoustics and the psychology of perception, which cannot be ignored.
> (T. Murail, 2004: 148; our translation)

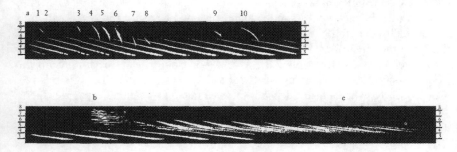

Example 3.5 Jean-Claude Risset, *Computer Suite from Little Boy*, 'Fall': spectrogram by R. Cogan (1984: 109). © By kind permission of Robert Cogan.

In his music, he sometimes uses logarithmic curves of durations, curves that are found in several perceptual processes and which thus sound more 'natural'. In the first part (measures 17–70) of *Ethers* (1978), which is presented as a series of 'waves', he organised an overall acceleration, each wave being shorter than the previous one: the first lasts 20.2 seconds, the last 0.6 second. 'This acceleration was calculated like a logarithmic curve, a curve that, however, has undergone slight deformations, for practical reasons, in the course of the transcription work' (J. Anderson, 1989: 128) as is shown in **Example 3.6 (online)**. In other works, the reference to psychoacoustics is metaphorical. For example, *Mémoire/Érosion* (1975–1975) imitates certain phenomena peculiar to memory, calling on classic writing techniques.

With Gérard Grisey, we find these two types of reference to psychoacoustics. He, too, used logarithmic curves to build the evolutions in some of his processes. Moreover, his thinking about musical time – which accompanies *Tempus ex machina* (1979) – is full of remarks of a prospective nature: talking about rhythmic symmetries over long sequences, he notes:

> Since the musical work and the listener are two entities in motion, we would need to imagine an *anamorphosis that would distort the symmetrical structures in such a way that their blurring in memory be rebalanced*. (Unfortunately, we are far from having the psychoacoustic data of such an operation, but it is not unthinkable that we shall succeed).
>
> (G. Grisey, 2008: 84; our translation)

Above all, Grisey was interested in thresholds of perception, all those highly particular moments from which the fusion of musical dimensions (especially timbre and harmony) occurs. The dream of alchemy is omnipresent with him, for he was revitalised by the discovery that the ear is much more fluctuating than the physical reality of sounds.

Getting back to electronics, another interesting moment concerning this research on the possibility of composing from what one perceives (or does not perceive) is constituted by certain experimental musicians of *electronica*. This was the case with Ryoji Ikeda and his +/- (1997), a set of seven pieces. The sixth, entitled '-..,' begins with a simple sound repeated at regular intervals, up until the arrival (just before the 45th second) of a denser sound (**Example 3.7 online**). Between the repetitions, silence seems to dominate. Yet the spectrogram of the first seven seconds (**Example 3.8**), which goes from the first occurrence of the simple sound to the beginning of its second, shows that the silence is relative. Consequently, what is heard depends on *each* person's listening capacities (here, in terms of intensity): for example, an elderly man will hear silence unlike a cat. In this piece, as in others, Ikeda practices the same 'test' as to frequencies by playing on our ability to perceive.

It is likely that the master of the art of working on perception, and in particular acoustic illusions, will remain, for the 20th century, Ligeti. One of his first masterpieces in this sphere was the piece for solo harpsichord *Continuum* (1968), in

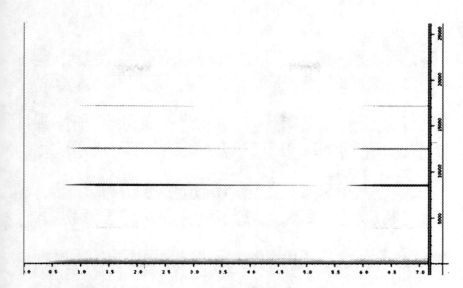

Example 3.8 Ryoji Ikeda, +/-: -.., 00"-07": spectrogram.

which the performer plays equal rhythmic values without discontinuity for nearly four minutes, 'as fast as possible, so that the individual notes are difficult to perceive, as in a continuum' (G. Ligeti, 1968: 1). Yet this continuum is highly differentiated, in a very subtle way (see J. Delaplace, 2007: 121ss). Indeed, Ligeti created a virtual polyphony, somewhat as Bach did in his *Sonatas and Partitas for Solo Violin* or his *Suites for Solo Cello*, the difference here being that the polyphony concerns rhythm. To quote Ligeti (2007, II: 130; our translation) himself, it is a matter of 'multidimensional rhythmic patterns':

> What I mean here by 'multidimensional' is not at all abstract, it is simply a matter of simulation of a depth of space that does not exist objectively in the musical piece but which is produced in our perception like a stereoscopic image. It is in [...] *Continuum* [...] that, for the first time, I achieved such acoustic illusions, under the influence of Maurits Escher's graphics.

Like Escher, Ligeti uses the technique of progressive transformation. In *Continuum* (**Example 3.9**), in α, a transformation, begun previously, gradually eliminates notes: periods of 3 then of 2 for the right hand, periods of 5, 4 and finally 3 for the left. During this evolution, the ear perceives the F sharp (and perhaps also the G sharp) as belonging to an autonomous voice, which repeats this note faster and faster. In β, the piece freezes on a major second. The transformation resumes in γ, where, in principle, the lowest note, the D sharp, would become for our perception the autonomous voice with, first of all, an impression of acceleration then slowing down, impressions resulting from the appearance of the D sharp in the two hands

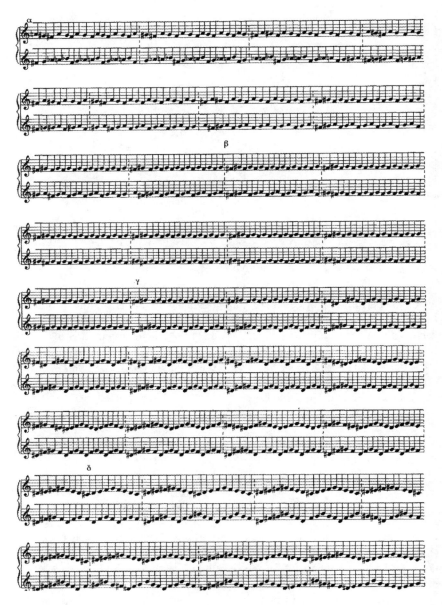

Example 3.9 György Ligeti, *Continuum:* page 2, 4th system – page 3, 4th system.
© By kind permission of SCHOTT MUSIC, Mainz.

and the transformation of the length of the periods. Finally, in δ, listening would tend to distinguish in the continuous flux the two outer notes, the C sharp and the B sharp, as an autonomous voice with rhythmic fluctuations (that it could also interpret as tempo fluctuations).

Listening and time

Ligeti or Ikeda, in the aforementioned pieces, implement a minimalist aesthetic in the broad sense of the term. Historic musical minimalism, i.e., that of the American composers La Monte Young, Terry Riley, Steve Reich or Philip Glass – which spread rapidly with Louis Andriessen, Tom Johnson, Julius Eastman, Michael Nyman, Gavin Bryars and John Adams, to mention only a few names – also appreciates auditory paradoxes. One of the most curious books on this trend is *Minimalism and the Baroque* (C. Swan, 1997). The comparison is not all that out of place: Baroque and Minimalist aesthetics share a taste for illusion, albeit embodied quite differently. In his book *Gödel, Escher, Bach*, Douglas Hofstadter (1979) often quotes Bach – for example, the 'endlessly rising canon' (or canon *per tonus*) of *The Musical Offering* – to illustrate the idea of 'strange loops', which he compares to Escher's optical illusions, in order to illustrate Gödel's 'Incompleteness Theorem'. But an even more pertinent example would have been early Steve Reich (*It's Gonna Rain*, 1965, *Drumming*, 1970–1971, *Music for Eighteen Musicians*, 1974–1976) or, better yet, La Monte Young's universe of 'hieratic minimalism' (J. Rockwell, 1983: 114).

Minimalist art 'no longer calls for contemplation but, rather, arouses a reaction touching on the experience of its perception' (C. Swan, 1997: 35). Thus, with La Monte Young, the listener shapes the music for, during the listening's process, he becomes aware of the elements that constitute it. But what 'experience of its perception' is concerned when it comes to listening? La Monte Young's answer is: musical listening is an experience *of time*. Everything happens as if music were rediscovering the Hegelian aesthetic that magnified the art of sounds because it is an art of time, but relieving it of the characteristic notions of German idealism. In *Composition 1960 #7*, of which the score consists simply of a B-F sharp fifth in semibreves with a legato mark (prolongation) accompanied by the note 'to be held for a long time',

> the link with the composer's concern with sustained sounds is obvious, right down to the choice of a 'pure' interval which allows the listener to focus on aspects otherwise unnoticed. More clearly, because even more reductively, than any of Young's earlier Works, *#7* opens up with the world of psycho-acoustic events behind a simple acoustic phenomenon: combination tones, for instance, and the possibility of hearing the balance of partials within each note of the interval quite differently in different parts of the room.
>
> (K. Potter, 2000: 51–52)

Later on, La Monte Young would come to pure sines. In a text concerning the composition entitled *Map of 49's Dream The Two Systems of Eleven Sets of*

Galactic Intervals Ornamental Lightyears Tracery, he explains that this piece is based on sinusoidal sounds according to precise relations. The sounds must be held for a long time. He adds: 'To my knowledge, there have been no previous studies of the long-term effects on continuous periodic composite sound waveforms on people. (Long-term is defined to be longer than a few hours in this case)' (La Monte Young, M. Zazeela, 2004 6). And further on, 'The sets of frequency ratios listened to are often played continuously 24 hours a day for several weeks or months. Marian Zazeela and I have worked and lived in this environment, and various groups of people have been invited to listen and report their reactions to the frequencies' (Ibid: 7).

Another American composer who also wove time and listening together was Morton Feldman. His music is poles apart from the Structuralist tradition. Whereas for the latter, each note calls for another, each chord brings another in keeping with a profound logic, Feldman celebrated sound for itself and for its infinite resonances: 'From practice, we quickly learn that all elements of differentiation already exist by themselves in the sound phenomenon' (M. Feldman, 2000: 135). While the constructivists focussed on the sound's onset, Feldman composed (with) the sound's decay portion where things vanish, where usually nothing is perceived as a sign pointing to something else: 'The attack of a sound is not its character. Actually, what we hear is the attack and not the sound. Decay, however, this departing landscape, *this* expresses where the sound exists in our hearing – leaving us rather than coming towards us' (M. Feldman, 2000: 25). Feldman constitutes the antithesis of the Xenakis of the 1960s, who wanted to favour timeless structures (see his article 'Towards a Metamusic', in I. Xenakis, 1992). With him, to the contrary, the 'in-time' seems to dominate totally. Here is what Thomas DeLio, had to say in the conclusion of his analysis of the third of the *Last Pieces* for piano (1959) (see **Example 3.10 online**):

> The composition's first part begins with a series of what appear to be separate, isolated sounds. Gradually, underlying similarities emerge and a simple hierarchy is established. [...] Thus, from isolated events, relationships are formed and a language emerges. In a sense, the subject of this composition is the evolution of language itself. [...] Feldman's is a music in which there is no apparent structuring of sound prior to its actual unfolding in time. [...] Thus [Feldman] creates structures in which order never seems imposed by the will of the composer, but rather, evolves within the perceiver's own awakening consciousness.
>
> (T. DeLio, 1996: 65–67)

Rock of the mid-1960s and 1970s also practised refocussing on listening, in relation to the emergence of sound. We will think of the long layers and drawn-out bands that certain musicians realised using synthesisers or this stretching of time that is often related to the particular listening (full of imagery and quite detailed) procured by LSD. Thus, in the last track of the LP *Stratosfear* (1976) by Tangerine Dream – which spans more than 11 minutes – the first third is made up of what customarily constitutes the accompaniment, the background sound: layers, an ostinato bass, and a guitar with wah-wah pedal. The listener is, in a way, dragged down, immersed in this background sound, and sees (hears?) himself listening. Such a beginning would never have been possible without the new sounds exploited by Tangerine Dream. The second, more conventional third proposes a repetitive melody. Then comes an exceptional passage: the melody again dissolves into the background, this time made up of electronic transformations and very rich synthesised sounds. The conclusion prolongs the atmosphere designated by the title, 'Invisible Limits'. Another example shows how the issue can shift emphasis. In the song 'Set the Controls for the Heart of the Sun' from Pink Floyd's album *Ummagumma* (1969), a dilated time is achieved due to the fact that the song calls for continuous transformations by the form that leads one to believe in the myth of the eternal return, its orientalising, incantatory melody and the suspension of the beat in certain passages, or the section with psychedelic sounds. Yet here, this stretching of time is synonymous rather with its dissolution and the opening towards space, as analysed by Erik Christensen (1996: 125–127).

Authentic listening

The emergence of sound does not necessarily call for a new way of listening. It can be linked to the *rediscovery* of listening. According to this point of view, it is inferred that the listening which is the issue would be an *authentic* listening. Re-appropriating authentic listening in contact with types of music that would have reinvented the essential, i.e., their sound-being: numerous musicians and thinkers have worked in this sense. We shall confine ourselves here to commenting on two writings, an article by the philosopher Jean-François Lyotard and an interview with Luigi Nono who, starting from the same premises, end up at different positions.

In his essay entitled 'Obedience', Lyotard (1991: 167) centred his thinking on two areas:

> One is called *Tonkunst*, the art of sound and/or tone, the old Germanic word for music, and the other, also German, is called *Gehorsam*, translated as *obéissance* [Translator's note: here Lyotard exploits the French distinction between *obéissance*, which corresponds to the most common sense of the English 'obedience', and *obédience*, which implies ecclesiastical jurisdiction], but thereby losing the *hören*, the *listening* containing in it, and which should rather be transcribed as *obédience*, in which the Latin *audire* can be heard more clearly, something like *lending one's ear to*, and also *having the ear of*, an *audience* brought or accorded to something that sounds, makes a sound or a tone, *tönt*, and which obliges, has itself obeyed.
>
> Everything I have to show is quite simple: first, that what we call music never stops becoming, or becoming again, an art of sound, a competence *to* sound [...]; and secondly, that in becoming, becoming again, this competence and this address in sounds [...], music reveals [...] a destination of

104   *Listening (sounds)*

> listening to listening, an 'obedience' that should perhaps be termed absolute, lending the ear an ear [...].

The first part of the demonstration was carried out in the same terms as the demonstrations of the present book, aside from one – major – detail: here what is called 'emergence' or 're-focussing' on sound constitutes for Lyotard an 'anamnesis': 'It looks as though the task of composers was to go through an anamnesis of what was given them in the name of music', he notes (Ibid: 168). An anamnesis that can have several meanings: for example, in the parallel with painting, which concentrates on colour, for music, by focussing on sound, it would be a matter of pointing to a sort of residue: 'In painting, after the exploration of the constraints bearing on the chromatic organization of surfaces, only colour remains (Delaunay's first *Windows* dates from 1911). Similarly in music, the analysis of the regulation of pitch eventually leaves as its remainder only the material, the enigmatic presence of vibration' (Ibid: 171).

If, to simplify, music proceeded to a rediscovery (or reinvention) of sound, we then understand that the same is true of listening: for Lyotard, the musical anamnesis that makes sound re-emerge (and takes music back to its primary definition: a *Tonkunst*) is synonymous with the rediscovery of listening. Lyotard takes care to specify that the listening we are talking about here is not a 'natural' kind of listening:

> [...] Obedience, if it is indeed with this that we are dealing, is not given, it is to be unveiled in hearing. Deconstructing hearing in no way means returning to some natural state of listening that musical culture has allegedly caused as to lose. But constructing a knowledgeable culture of hearing can have a 'musical' value (in the sense of *Tonkunst*) only if the sound-machines and the exact structurations they demand eventually destine the work to the marvel of the sound-event alone.
>
> (Ibid: 177)

But what does 'the marvel of the sound-event' that leads to obedience consist of? And above all, what is 'obedience'? Here, Lyotard opens Pandora's box, by quoting Emanuel Swedenborg, an 18th-century theosophist and founder of the Church of the New Jerusalem, who wrote:

> The Spirits which correspond to Hearing, or which constitute the province of the Ear, are those which are in simple Obedience; that is those which do not reason to see if a thing is thus, but which, because it is said to be thus by others, believe that it is thus: whence they can be called Obediences. If these spirits are like this, this is because the relation of hearing to language is like that of passive to active, as like the relation of him who hears speech and acquiesces to him who speaks: whence too in common language, 'to listen to someone' is to be obedient: and to 'listen to the voice' is to obey.
>
> (in Ibid: 178)

'It is possible to read this text, [...] laughing at a man who "hears voices", i.e., when no-one is talking', commented Lyotard.

> On the other hand one can understand him to be designating precisely the essential features of what there is to be 'liberated' in sound, and in particular the essential features of what music, aided by contemporary technologies, is trying to free in sound, its authority, the belonging of the spirit to the temporal blowing-up involved in the 'being-now' of the heard sound.
>
> (Ibid: 179)

Certainly, for Lyotard – and for a whole movement of thinking that flourished in the 1970s and 1980s – it was a matter of reasserting the value of 'passivity', the attention paid to things, to oppose blind domination (to instrumental reason). But why should music – *via* the power of sound – be the absolute model of passivity? Why does one continue to oppose sight and hearing according to the active/passive pair? Do we not have a long tradition that, in turning 'theory' into 'contemplation', also made sight a model of passivity? Above all, to go beyond blind domination, is it not suitable to go beyond opposition itself rather than take a stand for passivity and obedience? Regardless, Lyotard's position is embarrassing because it sends the listening liberated by the emergence of sound back to submission and to the mystical religious tradition.

Late Nono, he of *Prometeo* (1981-85), subtitled *'tragedia dell'ascolto'* (tragedy of listening) – composed for the space of the Venetian church of San Lorenzo – also asks the question of authentic listening in relation to the refocussing of music on sound. Here are a few chosen excerpts from his fine interview with Michele Bertaggia and the philosopher Massimo Cacciari (who assembled the texts for the libretto of *Prometeo*), given during the composition of the piece:

> NONO. [...We can] localise in the history of music the genesis of this process of effacing the original dimension of listening. It is most likely situated in the 18th [century], in the return, carried out under the impetus of Rameau, to the classical-Platonic classification of the Greek modes – based on the identification of describable feelings –, and of which his *Traité d'harmonie* is the outcome: thus the definition, for example, of the major and minor chord, through 'L'Héroïque, le Furieux, le Faible, le Plaintif' [...] This is also the pitfall of Italian opera theatre or Italian-style theatre, which produces a *total neutralisation of space*... whereas, for me, the relation uniting sounds and spaces is fundamental: how the sound combines with other sounds in space, how they re-compose in it... In other words: how the sound *reads* the space, and how the space discovers and reveals the sound.
>
> CACCIARI. *Ecco*, that's it... space... [...] The concentration and homogenisation of space, the disappearance of the possible multi-spatiality of the musical fact are closely linked to the flagrant reduction of possible polyvocity, multivocity of the 'senses' of listening. [...] Sound thus finds

itself irremediably visualised... rather than listening, vision and image are preferred... [...]

BERTAGGIA. [...] There has been allusion on several occasions to an original, authentic dimension of listening and, more globally, of the musical *thing*, but there has not yet been explicit mention of the 'natural condition' of the experience. Could you specify, Luigi, whether the problem of 'natural' intervenes in your research and, if so, how? Above all, would it not be precisely a 'natural' space that should be listened to according to the approaches mentioned?

NONO. Absolutely!... And this place is, for me, essentially Venice... [...] Venice is a complex system, which offers exactly this pluridirectional dimension we've been talking about... The sounds of bells are diffused in different directions: some add up, carried by the water, transmitted along the canals... Others vanish almost completely, yet others link up in various ways to other signals of the lagoon and the city. Venice is an acoustical *multi*-universe, the absolute opposite of the tyrannical system of transmission and listening to sound to which we have been accustomed for centuries. [...]

CACCIARI. I think I'm interpreting the current state of Gigi's research correctly in saying, on the basis of our discussions, that his writing is becoming ever more the space of this listening. His writing *demands* this listening, needs it. [...]

NONO. Indeed, I currently find myself, in my work on *Prometeo*, in a very particular situation... It is said that the composer writes music because he *hears* it, but it's obvious that the composer always hears on the basis of certain notions and information he possesses... As far as I'm concerned, at this time, I feel as if my head *was* San Lorenzo... I have the impression of occupying the space and silences of the church of San Lorenzo – and I'm also doing my best to let myself be totally occupied by them... [...] The fact is that today, my head no longer belongs to me: it lives with this problem, and the work, which does not yet exist, of which the sounds and writing are absent, already lives, *is already the work of this listening*! [...]

My current condition, vis-à-vis *Prometeo*, is exactly that of the person who wonders: 'How do you achieve in San Lorenzo the infinite possibilities of San Lorenzo, those possibilities that are, precisely, unrealisable...?'

CACCIARI. The 'work' which is done as 'compossible' in a multiple universe, a multi-universe of innumerable other possibilities. [...]

NONO. [...] The 'eventual' of the work: this 'compossible' [...], this comparticipation in silence... is already open, here and now! San Lorenzo has doors and windows clear and open....

(in L. Nono, 1993: 487–511; our translation)

Sound and space: we shall come back to them. Let us simply observe here that the authentic listening about which Nono was speaking is that which focusses on sound by defying the tradition that makes the latter a simple means of representation.

Thus liberated, sound is also freed of its authority: it is linked to silence. And listening has nothing to do with an obedience: it is the opening-up to possibilities.[6]

Amplified listening

Whether it be new or rediscovery, listening that immerses itself in sound has benefitted – as has already been observed with Schaeffer – from this extraordinary technological invention that is amplification. Amplification has two opposing traits. The first generates the illusion that the artist is everywhere at once – that is the auratic version. Beginning in the late 1930s, crooners realised that, thanks to the microphone, the artist's 'personality' became very important (see C. Chocron, 1994: 121). The beginnings of rock'n'roll confirmed this use of amplification of the voice and its 'reduction' by artificial reverberation: as Richard Middleton noted (1990: 89):

> Elvis Presley's early records, with their novel use of echo, may have represented a watershed in the abandoning of attempts to reproduce live performance in favour of a specifically studio sound; but the effect is used largely to intensify an *old* pop characteristic –'star presence': Elvis becomes 'larger than life'. Similarly, multi-tracking of vocals, which can be used in such a way that it 'destroys' or 'universalises' personality, is in fact widely used to *amplifying* a star singer's persona, 'aura' or 'presence'.

In the 1960s, doubtless as a reaction to this auratisation of the artist, rock began to amplify, no longer the smooth faces and voices but the defects and flaws. The puny voices (think of Lou Reed of Velvet Underground) or rasping the voice of a Janis Joplin, discussed in Chapter 2, go beyond the realist aesthetic; by concentrating on the nicks and cracks, they no longer come from the aesthetic of representation. In parallel, in the late 1960s and early 1970s, live American electronic music took over this use of electric amplification, poles apart from its auratic use. With *0'00"* (1962), Cage was one of the pioneers of this trend, in the same way as David Tudor and Robert Ashley.

An emblematic work of this musical trend was Alvin Lucier's *I am Sitting in a Room* (1969). This piece, which calls for one microphone, two tape recorders, amplifier and one loudspeaker, has instructions for scores. In it, Lucier asks to 'choose a room, the musical qualities of which you would like to evoke', read and record a text on the first tape recorder, then play this recording on the second tape recorder (connected to the amplifier and loudspeaker) and record the result on the first tape recorder and so on and so forth, several times; finally these recordings are put end to end. The read (Lucier, 1995) explains precisely everything that is going to occur:

> I am sitting in a room different from the one you are in now.
> I am recording the sound of my speaking voice and I am going to play it back into the room again and again until the resonant frequencies of the room

> reinforce themselves so that any semblance of my speech, with perhaps the exception of rhythm, is destroyed.
>
> What you will hear, then, are the natural resonant frequencies of the room articulated by speech.
>
> I regard this activity not so much as a demonstration of a physical fact, but more as a way to smooth out any irregularities my speech might have.

This text – it would be appropriate to mention that Lucier stammers, which allows for understanding the importance of the last phrase read – is also representative of the very American tradition of what, in philosophy, is called 'performativity', the essence of which is clearly defined by the title of philosopher, John Austin's book *How to Do Things with Words*: in a way, it is a matter of putting the accent on everything that, in language, does not only *say* things but *makes* them. Moreover, as the composer himself stressed, the idea of process is a fundamental given of this piece's aesthetic:

> If I had consulted an engineer, he or she would probably have found a way to get the end result in one process, one fast process, or one generation. There are ways to bypass erase heads on tape recorders or make large loops which could get the end result very quickly, but I was interested in the process, the step-by-step, slow process of the disintegration of the speech and the reinforcement of the resonant frequencies.
>
> (A. Lucier, 1995: 94)

In the final analysis, the place is determining:

> I made a preliminary version of *I'm sitting in a room* in the Brandeis University Electronic Music studio, a small, bright, somewhat antiseptic room in which I never enjoyed very much. [...] The resonant frequencies got reinforced very quickly after the fifth or sixth generation, resulting in harsh, strident sounds. But the version I did at 454 High Street, in Middletown, took a longer time because it was a softer, friendlier room with a wall-to-wall carpet and drapes on the windows. When I first moved into the apartment, I never dreamed that I would come to enjoy wall-to-wall carpeting, but I soon learned that if you have it, people enjoy sitting on the floor.
>
> (Ibid: 98)

In using his own flat to record the piece, Lucier emphasised the importance of place. Connecting the sound to the space (the physical place): Nono and Lucier pursued the same objective, which they interpreted differently: with the former, it was a matter of opening up to what was possible; for the latter, the challenge was the real presence. Similarly, for Nono, this importance of place came back to putting the accent on listening. One of Lucier's articles, 'Careful Listening is More Important Than Making Sounds Happen' (A. Lucier, 1995: 430–439), is subtitled 'The propagation of sound in space'.

Listening (sounds) 109

The use of amplification to arouse careful listening to the real – i.e., sensitive – presence is not limited to voices, as attests Pascale Criton's instrumental music. This must be listened to 'up close', i.e., if it is in a concert situation, with very sensitive microphones because she works with the minuscule variations of sound matter. A student of Ivan Wyschnegradsky's, who was the first theorist of the musical continuum (see I. Wyschnegradsky, 1996), she works with solutions of continuity particularly apparent in the use of micro-intervals, as is the case in *Territoires imperceptibles* (1997) for bass flute, cello and guitar. In this piece, the guitar is tuned in sixteenths of tones: on the one hand, it is equipped with barrettes that divide the fingerboard in quartertones rather than semitones; on the other, the customary set of strings is replaced by six of the same string, a low E, the first four being tuned a sixteenth of a tone apart, the last two doubling the chord of the two middle strings. This tuning of the guitar in itself provokes an exquisite, unexpected sensation, which has to be listened to as closely as possible, scrutinised as if from the inside. More generally, these are sensations that stem from the minuscule variations of matter that interest Pascale Criton:

> In *Territoires imperceptibles*, I sought to provoke sensations of transformation and mobility, to approach variations in matters and energies on the threshold of the imperceptible. [...] The micro-tempered universe enables me to drag perception beyond its habits, penetrate the minute variations of time and motion, and express sensations of mutation.
>
> (P. Criton, 1998b: our translation)

In her music, the minute variations also affect dimensions other than pitches: intensities, playing methods, 'grain', etc. This can be observed in this excerpt from *Territoires imperceptibles* (**Example 3.11**), which brings into play long crescendos and diminuendos, variations in the pressure of the cello's bow (in the second 10/4: 'without pressure' then 'accentuate in the sound') and fine variations in the speed of the guitar's *rasgueádo* (rolling all the fingers of the right hand, a playing method much used in flamenco: in the second 10/4, two vertical traits, then three above the stave). The microvariations of sound constantly produce situations of imbalance in the sound production, which can be described as threshold effects. The work on the continuum makes the elusive experience of liminal zones of sound production, all of which, in physical playing, provoke transitory states owing to the resistance of the materials (strings, pipes, blades) or the conjunction of conflictual gestures. Marked by the teaching of Gilles Deleuze, Pascale Criton has always insisted on the necessity of concentrating on 'perception' (in the Deleuzean sense, what is called 'sensitive' here), which she constantly conceives for experimenting:

> Is perception given or can we extend it, project it, experiment with it...? If perceiving can be considered an open field, which modifies itself as dispositions go along and according to different points of view, we are in a position to make audible an almost infinite diversity of sensitive surfaces.
>
> (P. Criton, 1997: 166; our translation)[7]

110 *Listening (sounds)*

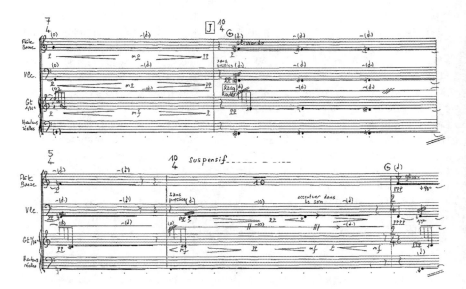

Example 3.11 Pascale Criton, *Territoires imperceptibles:* systems 18–19 (P. Criton, 1998b). © By kind permission of Editions Jobert. In the guitar part, the lower stave indicates the result ('real notes'), the upper giving the fingerings (tablature).

Equipped listening

In this history that refocusses music jointly on sound and listening, technology plays a major role. Amplification, which has just been discussed, is only one of the states of listening that is increasingly 'equipped'. This is also attested to by the history of recording. With the birth of recording, a new figure appeared: the record lover or 'discophile' who maintains a particular relation with his instrument, the phonograph, with which he 'plays' music:

> Equipped with his phonograph, the listener can believe himself a musician, as attests the appearance, in the course of the between-the-wars period, of the expression 'play a record' to designate the operation consisting of putting it on the machine for listening.
>
> (L. Tournès, 2008: 62; our translation)

In this new listening, the role of technique is determining. Discophiles of the 1920s and 1930s, who witnessed the electric revolution, 'by their experience and the aesthetic competence they progressively elaborated, […] made technology (objects – needles, diaphragms – gestures and material adjustments) a resource of their emotion: far from being an obstacle to listening (or to music), technology becomes a mediation' (S. Maisonneuve: 140; our translation). The debate on needles was quite intense at the time (see **Example 3.12 online**), as can be seen in this 'confession' of an enthusiast:

> There are times, I confess, when I enjoy playing romantic or sentimental tricks with it [gramophone], when I can persuade myself that by playing some orchestral record with the thinnest possible needle I have produced a delicate, distant kind of fairy music, something not at all like the actual orchestra but with an original quality of its own. This can best be done with good but imperfect records, such as the Columbia version of *L'après-midi*, which crackles and is much cut down, yet makes a faint and beautiful *concours* of sounds with a very thin needle. Most people, I am sure, play their gramophones too loud and I have been astonished at the undiscriminating use of needles in shops where they try records for you; they will put on the ordinary thick needle for everything, when it is fit for little except fox-trots. Of course, there is a larger public that demands noise and nothing else; and it is this public which maintains the prejudice against gramophone. Any piece played with too loud a needle has more gramophone-noise than music in it.
> (A. Clutton-Brock, 1924: 151)

This quotation might also have warranted appearing in Chapter 2, regarding noise. Here, one will note that our enthusiast, however centred on a reproduction apparatus, ends up reckoning that he is *producing* music. This turning point is associated with the fact that, in recording, sound becomes the central category:

> It is both in the production of an object, a sound, and technical categories that companies are participating, in a close interaction with amateurs. In so doing, they also participate in the development of a particular ear [...]. We [...] are progressively witnessing the development of aural listening in which sound becomes a central component of emotion.
> (S. Maisonneuve, 2009: 147–148; our translation)

One of the musicians who grasped the possibilities of this new listening was Glenn Gould, who decided to no longer play in concert, preferring recording. His masterful essay of 1966, 'The Prospects of Recording', summarises his position. In it, he asserts that, with the concert's extinction, music will be able to provide a more cogent experience: 'The more intimate terms of our experience with recordings have [...] suggested to us an acoustic with a direct and impartial presence, on with which we can live in our homes on rather casual terms audio culture' (G. Gould, 1966: 116). A large part of his essay is entitled 'The participant listener'. Here, he hypothesises that, thanks to recording, a new type of listener is being born, who participates increasingly in the musical experience, a listener who is no longer given over to passive listening but who acts on the music, thanks to the technology at his disposal:

> Dial twiddling is in its limited way an interpretative act. [...] And these controls are but primitive, regulatory devices compared to those participational

possibilities which the listener will enjoy once current laboratory have been appropriated by home playback devices.

It would be relatively simple matter, for instance, to grant the listener tape-edit options which he could exercise at his discretion. Indeed, a significant step in this direction might well result from that process by which it is now possible to disassociate the ratio of speed to pitch and in so doing (albeit with some deterioration in the quality of sound as a current liability), truncate splice-segments of the same work performed by different artists and recorded at different tempos.

(Ibid: 122)

Recent research goes in the direction wished for by Glenn Gould. Thus, IRCAM, between 2003 and 2006, developed a project entitled '*écoutes signées*' (signed listenings), in which 'investigation bears on singular ways of listening, situated technically, dynamic, and able to give rise to clarifying. […] This listening would be called "signed", in the sense that the listener is, in a way, the author of his listening' (APM; our translation). Moreover, IRCAM's director of scientific research, Hugues Vinet, evokes the upheavals in the system of musical diffusion brought about by the appearance of new formats and networks, which are going to progress faster, in relation to the other mutations of the musical system (instrument making, production, distribution, access, listening, playing…). He mentions a European project prefiguring tomorrow's hi-fi system, with which one could envisage 'access potentially given to the music lover, through new material artefacts […], to materials constitutive of the works, authorising him to manipulate them individually, thus extracting them temporarily from their musical context to better identify and interiorise them', an access that 'would stem from an interactive production process, with an aim of favouring the comprehension of the work' (H. Vinet, 2005: 54; our translation). And we could quote many other contributions to 'equipped' listening.[8]

 Chapter 3 online examples

Example 3.2 Pierre Schaeffer (1966), *Treatise on Musical Objects*: cover page. © By kind permission of Editions Seuil.

Example 3.6 Tristan Murail, *Ethers*, part 1: analysis of the durations of the 'waves' by Julian Anderson (1989: 129). © By kind permission of Julian Andreson. The dotted line indicates durations played according to the tempi of the score, which are derived from the logarithmic curve (continuous line).

Example 3.7 Ryoji Ikeda, +/-: -.. , 00"-46": analysis of the wave form.

Example 3.10 Morton Feldman, *Last Pieces:* third piece (M. Feldman, 1959). © By kind permission of Peters Editions.

Example 3.12 Phonograph needles.

Notes

1 The second version, performed in 1953 by Irwin Kreme, corresponds to the 1993 edition, the last to the 1960 edition. See also K. Gann (2010).
2 Translator's note: the French verb *s'entendre* – to get along – literally means to hear one another.
3 To prolong this development, see M. Solomos (1999) and B. Kane (2014), who gives a critical reading of Schaeffer's relations with phenomenology and, more generally, his theorisations of acousmatic listening and the sound object.
4 To theorise this 'journey to the centre of the head' and these 'spaces of representation', Bayle would call on the semiotics of Charles Sanders Peirce, distinguishing between 'icon', 'index' and 'symbol' (see M. Solomos, 2012).
5 It was such a 'score' that I provided in the Chapter 2 regarding Xenakis's *Diamorphoses*.
6 Among the numerous other musicians who claim to represent listening that could also be described as 'authentic', let us mention Pauline Oliveros (2005), who developed the concept of 'profound listening'. In a different register, we could mention Peter Ablinger's *Hörstücke* (*Listening Pieces*) in which what is important is not the heard thing but the listening itself.
7 For further details, see C. Delume et al., 2002.
8 On the general idea of 'signing' one's listening, see P. Szendy (2008). On the 'signed listening' project, see N. Donin (2004). The European project mentioned by H. Vinet, entitled SemanticHIFI, is documented on http://shf.ircam.fr. As for other equipped-listening projects making the listener 'active', this is what Jean-Claude Risset wrote to me upon reading these lines: 'Beginning in the 1970s, [we knew] the vinyl discs specially realised by Martin Davorin-Jagodić and Costin Miereanu so that listeners modify them in their own way – well before DJs. Also, in the early 1970s, the experiments of Max Mathews (with various musicians such as Pierre Boulez, Gerald Schwartz and Paul Zukofsky), on the hybrid real-time system Groove, which he implemented with F. Richard Moore, led to a range of possibilities for controlling the musical result, blurring the borderline between composer, performer and listener. I had taken up this idea, with the notion of matrix-work – not fully realised but proposing materials to shape, vary, arrange – and that of musical creation tool-workshop, for example in issue 4 (1993) of the *Cahiers de l'IRCAM* (Recherche et musique) devoted to utopias ('Fragments d'un discours utopique'): "If I had to defend utopian projects, what would they be? First of all, the Babelian project of a *musical creation tool*, which would be more than an instrument, more than a technological machine: a music *workshop*, material as much as intellectual, gestural and formal, theoretical and practical, which would accumulate memory, knowledge and know-how. Which could help in composition, performance and listening – but not a unique, stereotyped way: it would allow everyone to 'build his own house', to build his own tools. Thus, listening would not be purely passive: the listener could act to sculpt, give rhythm, measure out, transform, or elaborate according to multiple modalities by choosing the degree of his intervention."' (J-C. Risset, personal communication, February 2012; our translation).

Finally, numerous studies have focussed on the influence that technology exerts on listening, for example with the mp3 format, headphone listening and cell phone listening, etc.: see, amongst others, A. Williams, 2007; M. Bull, 2007; J. Sterne, 2013; S. Niklas, 2014.

4 Immersion in sound

The 'inner' life of sound

'I tried to get as close as possible to a sort of microscopic, inner life such as is found in certain chemical solutions, or through filtered light'. Thus did Varèse express himself (1983: 184; our translation) in one of his last interviews, regarding a section of strings in *divisi* from *Bourgogne*, a work that has disappeared.[1] *Inner life:* whoever focusses on sound itself may be tempted to apprehend it as a 'subject'. It would not be an *ob-ject*, a closed entity that would stand facing us, manipulated from the outside; we would be worked on by *it*. In this sense, focussing on sound prolongs the organicist metaphor – music as a growing plant – which dominated part of the 19th century, and gave it an unexpected outcome: sound would have an 'interiority'. Being *in* the sound, *immersing oneself* in sound, being *enveloped* by sound, travelling *to the heart* of sound, sinking into *the abyss* of sound... thus become new metaphors, capable of inspiring composers and listeners alike. Let us begin with the initial expression: there are numerous types of music which evoke, in one way or another, the 'inner life' of sounds. Here is a small anthology of them.

Although *Bourgogne* has disappeared, perhaps we can nonetheless see in it a prefiguring of the masses of *divisi* strings in early Xenakis. In *Pithoprakta* (1955–1956), the strings play up to 46 real parts, forming gigantic overall sounds in which the listener is invited to immerse him- or herself to observe its inner life. Thus, in measures 122–171, the strings are divided into six groups of timbre: brief *arco*, struck *col legno*, rubbed *col legno* in *glissando*, *arco* in *glissando*, *pizzicati* and noises of the hand striking the instrument's body. **Example 4.1** shows the beginning of this section, in which one can hear a microscopic swarming, a surprising universe of bubbling details, if we may borrow Varèse's 'chemical solution' metaphor. Xenakis himself went by another metaphor. In specific places in this section, he asks the conductor to bring out one of the six groups: 'In this nebula of sounds, bring out the galactic configurations of the instruments playing *normal arco*', he indicates for measures 125–127 (I. Xenakis, 1967: 17). One might also hear this passage like an entomologist: 'It is as though the insect kingdom were at war. There is a buzzing, whirring, droning, humming, shot through with pointed screams [...] of busy intense movement on a minuscule scale' (N. Matossian, 2005: 107–111).

Example 4.1 Iannis Xenakis, *Pithoprakta:* measures 122–125 (I. Xenakis, 1967).
© By kind permission of Boosey & Hawkes.

116 *Immersion in sound*

In our little anthology, early Stockhausen would also have a place of choice. In *Punkte* (1952), all the music constitutes a background, but 'if it's only background, it's not background any more – it's a textural music, and you listen into the sound. It's not that there's something put on top which immediately removes all the rest to a secondary function in order to give an atmosphere' (K. Stockhausen in J. Cott, 1974: 35). At the time, the German musician was quite interested in the interiority of sound for in it he found a sound world already organised:

> The basic principle underlying my whole attitude when I compose is the following: What occurs within single sounds in the micro-musical region is enlarged. *Piano Piece XI* is nothing but a sound in which certain partials, components are behaving statistically.
>
> (Ibid: 70)

Let us concentrate on the 'structure' XIA to XIF of the electronic part of *Kontakte* (1958–1960). **Example 4.2** shows its schematic representation, which is to be

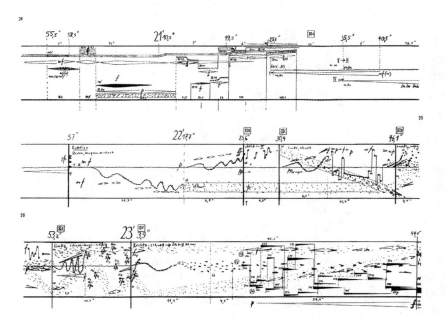

Example 4.2 Karlheinz Stockhausen, *Kontakte:* pp. 24–26 of the handwritten score (electronic part). © By kind permission of Stockhausen Foundation for Music, Kürten, Germany, www.stockhausen.org. The sound layers are designated by Arabic numerals. Roman numerals above each system: timing. Figures in brackets: intensity in decibels – ∞ means inaudible. Roman numerals within a system: loudspeakers (I to the left, II in front, III to the right, IV rear) – 'rotation' designates sounds turning towards the right (*rechts*) or left (*links*) at the indicated speed (*langsam:* slow; *schnell:* fast; *mäßig:* moderato).

found in the score. This excerpt includes six sound layers, designated by Arabic numerals. Shortly before XIA, at 21'25.5", the six layers are superimposed on the same pitch, forming a complex, almost harmonic, static sound as to its pitch and timbre: the ear perceives it clearly as *one* sound. Then each layer progressively begins to diverge, first with a glissando, then by changing timbre. Shortly after 21'57", the first effects a glissando curving towards the low register then becomes successively 1b (22'17.7"), 1c (22'46.1"), 1d (22'53.2") and 1e (23'3.9"). At 22'17.7", the second diverges towards the high end to then become 2b (22'25.6") and 2c (22'30.4") and so on. At 23'3.9", the last remaining layer (6) also begins to slide and ends up at a different timbre (6b). In short, everything happens as if, by differentiating the sound layers one by one, Stockhausen lets us hear the inner life of the sole sound from the outset.

The metaphor of inner life has been able to flourish due to the attention to detail and its microscopic observation, which characterise modernity in general: as Pierre Francastel (1956: 178; our translation) wrote, in modern art the 'near-hallucinatory enlargement of details' occurs. At least since Debussy, with whom 'the method of organisation of sequences was much less important than their internal construction', as Célestin Deliège (1989: 36; our translation) asserts, the musical instant opened up to infinity and revealed its slightest details. In instrumental music, the interest in timbre is synonymous with the 'microscopic' observation of sound, since one works on phenomena that tend towards micro-time. This is why the metaphors evoking 'the interior' of sound are frequent. In his *Traité d'orchestration*, even though written before the explosion of new playing techniques, Charles Koechlin (1944: 183; our translation), commenting on the use of *col legno* in Berg's *Lyric Suite* (1925–1926), wrote that, 'with his atonal, undecided music, it is of hallucinating movement, and the *pianissimo* dynamic is like a whirlwind of atoms'. In the post-war era, our anthology could be composed almost at random of intentions. Thus, György Ligeti (1983: 33), evoking the vision of a 'static' music that he had back in the early 1950s (and which would finally materialise in *Apparitions*, 1958–1959 and *Atmospheres*, 1961), spoke of a 'music that would change through a gradual transformation almost as if it were changing colour from the inside'. Grisey (2008: 77; our translation) evoked a 'zoom effect that brings us closer to the internal structure of sounds', putting it in an inverse relation to time: 'The more we dilate our auditory acuity to perceive the microphone world, the more we shrink our temporal acuity, to the point of needing fairly long durations'. Alberto Posadas (2005: 43; our translation) who, like Grisey, is interested in the transfer from micro-time (sound as physical phenomenon) to macro-time (form of the work), wrote for his work *Oscuro de llanto y de ternura* (2005) – a piece that carries out this transfer using fractals – that he endeavoured to 'create a form that would reflect the internal structure of sound'. Let us also quote Pascale Criton (2005: 133), who developed the idea of 'penetrating' the material while describing the latter's 'molecularisation' – an expression borrowed from Deleuze and Guattari.

With electroacoustic music, the impression of plunging into the sound to listen to its inner life is perhaps even more intense. It is born of amplified listening, about which we have already spoken, made possible by the microphone. Schaeffer (1967: 44; our translation), commenting on the art of recording, noted:

> If more than one beginner, still full of the traditional spirit of fidelity to acoustic sound, records, preferably at a normal distance, he will quickly become accustomed [...] to bringing the mikes closer to the sound bodies [...] to grasp mellowness, granulations, fine high-pitched resonances, glitterings.

He added that one thereby develops a new sphere defined by an 'intimacy with the matter' (Idem). Pierre Henry (1996: 56) always insisted on the possibility of 'making sounds grow'. His *Tam Tam I* to *IV* (reprised in *Le Microphone bien tempéré*, 1950–1952) stage a tam-tam 'enlarged and multiplied by manipulation and turning into a gigantic sound factory' (M. Chion, 2003: 31; our translation). An even more famous tam-tam is used in Stockhausen's *Mikrophonie I* (1964–1965), one of the first pieces of live electronic music. Whilst two musicians produce sound in several ways (rubbing, scratching, etc.), two others play the microphone (the score indicates where on the tam-tam the mike is to be placed, the speed of its displacement, etc.) and the last two transform the sound result with filters and potentiometers. The tam-tam was not chosen by chance: with its size (Stockhausen carried out his experiments on an instrument 1.55m in diameter: see **Example 4.3 online**) and connotations (Far East, meditation), it opened this famous interiority of sound.

Another 'huge' instrument, the large tenor bell of Winchester Cathedral, was sounded from the inside in Jonathan Harvey's *Mortuos Plango, Vivos Voco* (1980), for computer-processed concrete sounds. In addition to the bell, Harvey recorded the voice of a young chorister, his son. In the composition, these two sources are associated with synthesized sounds, produced according to acoustic models 'deduced from their own nature' (J. Harvey et al., 1984: 117), i.e., from their spectral analysis (in **Example 4.4 online** one will find the analysis of the bell sound). *Mortuos Plango, Vivos Voco* has a very clear form in eight sections, each based on the domination of a partial of the bell; the passage from one section to the next occurs with *glissandi* (see **Example 4.5 online**). The piece's most fascinating sounds plunge us into the aesthetic of hybridisation, which, in the early 1980s, seemed like a promising path. On multiple occasions, the sound of the bell and that of the young boy are 'crossed'. For example, one can have an aggregate (chord) of which the notes correspond to the frequencies of the bell's partials – we thus hear overall a bell sound – but are sung by the chorister. At the beginning of section 4 (3'30"-3'46"), of which **Example 4.6** gives the spectrogram, it is difficult to say what belongs to the bell and what belongs to the boy. Generally speaking, in this work, everything happens as if, by decomposing the bell, Harvey were making us discover its inner life, hybridised or not. As for the concert: 'The walls of the concert hall are conceived as the sides of the bell inside which is the audience, and around which (especially in the original 8-channel version) flies the free spirit of the boy' (J. Harvey, 1980) (see the analyses by A. Georgaki, 1998; B. Bossis, 2004; M. Clarke, 2006).

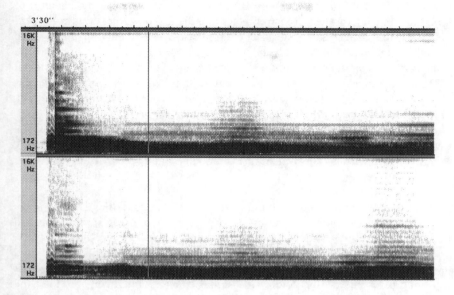

Example 4.6 Jonathan Harvey, *Mortuos Plango, Vivos Voco*, 3'30"-3'46": spectrogram (realised with Audacity).

It is important to note that, in electroacoustic music, the acoustic model chosen is determining for the metaphor that interests us here: to be specific, the spectral model on which Harvey worked, because he postulated that a sound 'decomposes' in partials, authorises, in a way, apprehending the latter as witnesses to the 'inner' life of the sound – it is, of course, the same model that led Grisey or Murail to speak about the 'internal structure' of the sound. On the other hand, if one works directly on the wave form, it is difficult to extend the metaphor, since the sound is then envisaged as a variation of air pressure, a curve mathematically without 'thickness' – without an 'interior' or an 'exterior'. Moreover, since we have the possibility of 'zooming', thanks to editing software (see **Examples 4.7 online** and **4.8 online**), the metaphor of observation under the microscope seems to have become reality: there exists an inner life in the sound, will tell us he who thinks 'to descend', plunge, immerse himself, etc. in the thousandth of the second.

To continue our anthology with 'large' sound bodies, we could mention Christian Zanési's *Grand bruit* (1991, for tape), which uses a single 21-minute recording of a sound of the express train the composer took to go from his studio to his home:

> Large mobile sound bodies have the banal yet astonishing property of placing the listener-traveller inside, as if he found himself in a gigantic double bass, which, in the case of the train, is rubbed by a double bow: the rails and the air.
> (C. Zanési, 2002; our translation)

Travelling Still (1997, for tape), by Paul Fretwell is a piece based on sounds of the London Underground. Regarding the title, the author wrote: '*Travelling Still* plays on this idea, leading the listener from real-world sounds of travel to an interior sound world of symbols and references' (P. Fretwell, 2001). For from the 'interior' of sounds to simple interiority, the distance is crossed relatively quickly: 'These landscapes, of course, are inner journeys, to which acousmatic art essentially refers', noted Jean-François Minjard (1998: 4; our translation) concerning his piece *Paysages* (1998, for tape).

In addition, in electroacoustic music – as well as in instrumental music – the work on space, which often goes hand in hand with the exploration of sound, reinforces the sensation of 'penetrating' the sound. François Bayle (1997: 24; our translation) tells us:

> The spatial projection of sound introduces a staging, which is quite interesting because it can function according to several registers (close and far, what moves and what is immobile, the 'big' and the 'little' sounds, etc.). In the traditional concert, the music stands in a clearly circumscribed area [...]. Completely different is the situation of acousmatic music where one [...] 'enters' the sound (the sound event is much 'bigger' than the listener and has no precise outlines), as in a 'penetrable sculpture', a 'Big Sound, within which one must reconstruct his capacity for observation and interest.

About 'immersion'

Immersive sound–space

The question of the 'inner' life of sound is inextricably linked to another question, which, over the past several decades, has risen to the level of a central issue of music: space. The notion of space in music is of an incredible polysemy – we shall come back to it in Chapter 6. One will distinguish between its literal use, which is sometimes called 'spatialisation of sound' (distribution of instruments or loudspeakers in the hall, sound 'journeys' from one localised point to another), and its figurative use, which refers to the idea of a spatialisation of the music itself, often synonymous with an affirmed static nature. Whether used figuratively or literally, the word 'space' has two opposite meanings: a protean totality of type, representing the original chaos, intensely close receptacle and matrix; and, quite the contrary, a substratum serving as differentiation (space as 'spacing'). The impression that sound be endowed with an inner life comes in part from the emergence of space, figurative or literal, according to the former of these two meanings: an amorphous place, without reference points, without evolution or indeed with a perpetual evolution that refers back only to itself. There, music becomes a static sound–space that abolishes 'external' multiplicity (that of the evolution) to reveal its 'inner' multiplicity: an enveloping sound–space, in which it feels good to *immerse oneself*.

In its literal sense, this space can take the sphere as a model. One will think of the auditorium of the German pavilion at Expo '70 in Osaka, where the totality of Stockhausen's music was performed for 183 days. The architect of this auditorium, Fritz Bornemann, had initially planned to build an amphitheatre, with a central stage for the orchestra surrounded by the audience. Stockhausen had him change ideas and build a sphere (see **Example 4.9 online**), in which the audience, in the centre, is surrounded by loudspeakers spread over the interior walls. At the console, Stockhausen projected the sounds using, in particular, small rotation mills, which he had built and thanks to which it was possible to 'imagine any configuration whatsoever, whether in a circle or spiral, having angles, to transport the singers' voices or the sound of the instruments. The audience thus had the possibility of following the movement of sounds' (K. Stockhausen in T. Horodyski, 1998: 354, our translation; for the description of these rotation mills, see K. Stockhausen, 1978: 381–382).

Another pioneer in sound spatialisation, Xenakis, proposed – as if in echo, 20 years later, at the famous Philips Pavilion of the Brussels World's Fair – in the *Diatope*, which sat imposingly several months in 1978 before the Centre Georges Pompidou (see **Example 4.10 online**), an architectural form 'which is a sphere in its principles, yet open to the world by the convergence of its geometrical construction, using hyperbolic paraboloids' (I. Xenakis, 2008: 262). Inside, laser beams and light flashes – producing images that were sometimes concrete, sometimes abstract – plunged the listener in a sensorial immersion. The sound component consisted of a fully fledged musical work with the autonomous title *La Légende d'Eer*, and which, after starting slowly, reached peaks of sound and density that continued until the very end. Composed on seven tracks, it was reproduced by eleven loudspeakers covering the architectural canvas (see **Example 4.11 online**) and drowning the listener in strange, sometimes bewitching, sounds (see M. Solomos, 2006).

Since these historic experiments, immersive-type spatialisation has become widespread, and we shall come back to it. As regards space in the figurative sense, immersive sound–space can be associated with these innumerable musical works of the 20th century, which, challenging the logic of development, seem to constitute an 'endless succession of instants', to use Boucourechliev's term (quoted in E. Lockspeiser et al., 1980: 678) regarding Debussy's *La Mer*. Adorno, one of the first to study this phenomenon, evoked in his *Philosophy of Modern Music* a 'pseudomorphosis on painting' (T. W. Adorno, 2006: 141), which leads to the spatialisation of music itself. Condemning this phenomenon, he made it a characteristic common to the two composers whom, however, he contrasted: Schoenberg and Stravinsky: 'In both, music threatens to congeal as space', he wrote (T. W. Adorno, 2006: 56).

In the 1950s and 1960s, Ligeti (1960) developed the idea of a musical form conceived as an imaginary space: in tonal music, he tells us, form followed a linear temporal development; today, music works with simultaneity, it convokes a continuum that transforms the temporal flow into space. *Apparitions* and *Atmospheres* embodied his vision of a 'static' music. In the same period, Scelsi deployed his music, conceived as a single sound, according to an 'oriental' conception. In the 1960s and 1970s, American minimalism put the accent on this illusory staticity (or illusory mobility?) characteristic of Reich's *Piano Phase* (1967) and *Music for Eighteen Musicians* (1974–1976) – not to mention the immobility of the works by La Monte Young. Almost at the same time, psychedelic rock gave way to the mind-blowing rock of Pink Floyd and their album *The Dark Side of the Moon* (1973). *Saturne* (1979) by Hugues Dufourt seems to inherit this same aspect and contributed to the birth of spectral music, which, in the 1970s and 1980s, participated in the immersive sound–space adventure. For his part, Jonathan Harvey (1984: 86) would not hesitate to write that his music 'is more concerned with space than with time'.

Immersion and 'oceanic feeling'

Another example of static music, which invites immersion: ambient and its 'spacey, immersive textures' (S. Cooper in V. Bogdanov et al., 2001: 261, regarding *Shades of Orion* by Tetsu Inoue and Pete Namlook). The theme of immersion flourished in a good number of 'fin-de-siècle' – or even millenarian – speeches accompanying the emergence of this musical trend as well as certain related trends of *electronica* in the 1990s. David Toop's book, precisely entitled *Ocean of Sound* (1995), offers a good example of this. In the customary New Age context (shamanism, mantras, Zen…), Toop grasped, in a single movement, Ambient, Debussy, American minimalism, the music of Bali, Sun Ra, Cage, acid house, Charlie Parker, Futurism, Tangerine Dream, Yoko Ono, Satie, Kraftwerk, Aphex Twin, Pauline Oliveros, The Cocteau Twins, Suicide, Saw Throat, Eric B. and Rakim, Phill Niblock:

> Much of the music I discuss could be characterised as drifting or simply existing in stasis rather than developing in any dramatic fashion. Structure emerges slowly, minimally or apparently not at all, encouraging states of reverie and receptivity in the listener that suggest (on the good side of boredom) a very positive rootlessness […] This past hundred years of expansiveness in music, a predominantly fluid, non-verbal, non-linear medium, has been preparing us for the electronic ocean of the next century.
> (D. Toop, 1995: prologue)

'Immersion is one of the key words of the late twentieth century', David Toop tells us. 'Bass is immersive, echoes are immersive, noise is immersive. […] Music is felt at its vibrational level, permeating every cell, shaking every bone, derailing the conscious, analytical mind' (D. Toop, 1995: 273). One paragraph of the book speaks of a Japanese satellite radio conceived in 1990, St GIGA, whose programming was governed by 'cyclical motifs' such as the rising and setting of the sun, or the different phases of the moon so that, its designer tells us, the listeners 'experience the sweet beginnings of life itself, reminiscent of the start of existence, as an embryo within amniotic fluids' (D. Toop, 1995: 154).

One of the tutelary figures of these discourses was Brian Eno, the inventor of Ambient Music with his *Music for Airports* (1978). In his 1978 manifesto, he wrote:

> To create a distinction between my own experiments in this area and the products of the various purveyors of canned music [Eno evoked Muzak] I have begun using the term Ambient Music. [...] Whereas the extant canned music companies proceed from the basis of regularizing environments by blanketing their acoustic and atmospheric idiosyncrasies, Ambient Music is intended to enhance these. Whereas conventional background music is produced by stripping away all sense of doubt and uncertainty (and thus all genuine interest) from the music, Ambient Music retains these qualities. And whereas their intention is to 'brighten' the environment by adding stimulus to it [...] Ambient Music is intended to induce calm and a space to think.
>
> (B. Eno in C. Cox et al., 2004: 97)

Remembering the beginnings of Ambient, Eno noted: 'And immersion is really the point: we were making music to swim in, to float in, to get lost inside' (B. Eno in C. Cox et al., 2004: 95). 'To swim in, to float in, to get lost inside': the 'states of reverie and receptivity in the listener', the reminiscence 'of the start of existence as an embryo within amniotic fluids' indicate that the immersive sound–space which we are dealing with here perhaps stemmed from the desire for a gentle *annihilation*...

One might venture a parallel between this type of immersive sound–space and late Wagner, he of *Parsifal* (1882). In Act I, just before the 'transformation music', Parsifal and Gurnemanz 'seem to walk', accompanied by the 'bells' of Montsalvat motif, in a tonal journey evoking an ascension (passage from A major to E flat then E). The neophyte exclaims: 'I am barely walking and already I feel so far'. His guide then pronounces the most commented-on words in the whole opera: 'You see, my son: here time becomes space' (see **Example 4.12 online**). *Zum Raum wird hier die Zeit:* this phrase also takes into account what is happening in the music.

We shall underscore the extreme slowness of the prelude that is prolonged throughout the opera. *Langsam, sehr langsam, noch langsamer, sehr ruhig, zurückhaltend* (slow, very slow, even slower, very calm, restrained) are the dominant tempi here, especially in the two outer acts – in his series of articles *German Art and German Politics,* Wagner maintained that *andante* is the German rhythm *par excellence*. This slowness has an equivalent only in the extreme staticity of the music. The technique of derivation of the leitmotifs in *Parsifal* is pushed so far that, on the surface, in the music's temporal unfolding, Wagner is not concerned with their dynamic progression: development work has been replaced by a dream-like type of progression, which proceeds by associations of ideas. Similarly, the harmony evolves by constantly falling back on itself, often making cyclic trajectories. This is attested to by these 'ecstatic' progressions of major thirds, which, at the end of three progressions, reproduce the initial chord. Space can be revealed as the standard by which Wagnerian time is measured: not only because it is at the origin of the idea of symmetry but also because it offers the model *par excellence* of infinity as continuity without tie.

Moreover, we witness the abolition, except in quite particular moments, of the beat, which allows for discretising time. This becomes smooth, without ridges and cannot be measured or quantified. It is set forth as pure experience and is no longer apprehended as a tool for advancing things. With *Parsifal*, the need for making things advance disappears: we must listen to them from the inside, letting ourselves branch out, becoming a thing amongst other things. Wagnerian space is truly of the immersive type. Thus it is that the feeling of well-being is sometimes confused with hypnosis. Baudelaire had already described this feeling, well before the composition of *Parsifal*, in a letter he sent to Wagner in 1860 following the Parisian performance of excerpts from *The Flying Dutchman, Tannhäuser, Tristan* and *Lohengrin*: 'I experienced a sentiment of a bizarre nature, it is the pride and enjoyment of understanding, of letting myself be penetrated and invaded, a truly sensual delight, like rising in the air or tossing upon the sea' (Baudelaire quoted by A. Cœuroy, 1965: 198; our translation).

'Tossing upon the sea' or, in the language that Romain Rolland would subsequently use in a December 1927 letter to Freud to name the source of all religiosity: the headiness of the 'oceanic feeling'. Freud responded publicly by writing *Civilisation and its Discontents* (1929), which he would send to the French writer with the following dedication: 'To his great oceanic friend, the terrestrial animal Sigmund Freud'. According to Freud, who doubted the existence of such a feeling and, in particular, its relation to religiosity, the oceanic sentiment stemmed from the child's distress (*Hilflosigkeit*) and aspired to the 're-establishment of unlimited narcissism': the 'fusion with the whole' that this feeling evokes comes back at the closing of 'pure pleasure-ego'. Yet the latter rejects everything that seems alien and hostile to it. Also, under the appearance of universal love, the oceanic sentiment bears the seeds of the destruction instinct or death drive to which *Civilisation and its Discontents* is devoted in large part (S. Freud, 1962).

Dionysian immersion

Not all sound immersion backs up Freudian pessimism. Taking the example of the *Diatope*, what interested Xenakis in unleashing sounds in *La Légende d'Eer*, the *Diatope*'s music, as well as the flashes and laser beams, was not the annihilation of the listener–spectator, but the physical and psychic pleasure he could draw from it. Stretched out on the ground, as was already the case with the *Polytope de Cluny* (1972–1973: see **Example 4.13**), this spectator–listener, unlike typical listeners of Beethoven (see **Example 4.14**), who seek a transcendental kind of communication, saw himself merging with his environment and enjoyed an immersion that could be described as Dionysian.

Example 4.13 Spectators at the *Polytope de Cluny* (Archives Xenakis). © By kind permission of Mâkhi Xenakis.

Example 4.14 Albert Graefle, 'Ludwig van Beethoven with close friends listening to him playing'.

The Dionysian type of immersion was perhaps the most important characteristic of rave parties (see **Example 4.15 online**). In the 1980s and 1990s, raves, vast gatherings, sometimes clandestine or, more generally, cultivating the 'underground' spirit, were known for their drug consumption and especially the famous (and very dangerous) ecstasy, which lowers inhibitions and makes everyone likeable. Sociologists (following Michel Maffesoli, 1988) tried to read into raves parties survivals of primitive rites. However, fans of raves sought, above all, an 'elsewhere' in them, a flight characterised by depersonalisation, which is perhaps not without similarities with the quest for annihilation underlying the oceanic sentiment. Might Freud have been right all the way: might Dionysian immersion be but one more mask? Let us listen to the narrative of a 19-year-old woman:

> After long hours of an infernal trip to get to the meeting place, dashing for the shuttle then driving an hour, we finally arrived in front of a sinister hangar miles from any inhabitation. [...] After being frisked and paying 100 francs, I went through the door to enter the hangar bathed in coloured lights but, above all, completely filled with music. [...] I timidly followed the others who were already all smiling, to the rear of the hangar. One of them solemnly gave me a pill and a bottle of water. [...]
> From time to time, I clearly felt the effect of the drug, which seemed to follow the music in its spirals, its risings, its tunnels. I got more and more into the rhythm and evolution of this music. [...] Without realising it, I got closer to the speakers, and the sound penetrated me a bit more. At the climax, it seemed like my body was lifted by the music. My mind no longer controlled it. It was a sort of abandonment, giving the body over to the vibrations provoked especially by the bass notes.
>
> (in A. Fontaine et al., 1996: 16–17; our translation)

At present, the expression 'sound immersion' tends to designate either loudspeaker technology or a relaxation technique. In the former case, one also speaks of audio in 3D, the intention being to give the illusion of sound in relief; rather a Dionysian type of immersion is therefore sought, exploiting the listener's senses, the pleasure of sound. In the second case (see **Example 4.16 online**: an advertisement for a website proposing relaxation), the accent is on depersonalisation. Sound immersion will therefore never be a simple thing: sometimes physical pleasure, sometimes 'oceanic' sentiment, sometimes a fluctuation between the two.

The 'depth' of sound

Let us immerse ourselves in Scelsi's *Fourth String Quartet* (1964). Here is a work in a single movement lasting 9′51″ – in the version by the Arditti Quartet (1995), which will serve as a reference – that is extremely fluid. Not only do I hear different things each time I listen, in addition, it is always difficult for me to know whether what I hear (or think I hear) is 'there' (in the score or in the recording) or whether my mind is inventing it. Owing to the near-absolute continuity, everything there is ephemeral as well as transitory and, in a way, eludes memory. This is music in the image of sound. And, in fact, I can quite hear the quartet in its totality as a single sound: an entity, which, from start to finish, deploys a unique, complex gesture, consisting of the progressive thickening of a single note, ending up by grabbing the listener in his 'interiority'.

The first two-thirds of the work (up to measure 157, at 6'37″) present a very continuous evolution whose nature is three-fold (see **Example 4.17 online**, where the temporal references are quite relative, given the very fluid nature of the music): a) a progressive rise, in steps, with intermittent flashbacks. At every moment, a new pitch seems to dominate, while it is wreathed in a halo, a dust of notes surrounding it in a cluster, or fleetingly creating a separate line that can be heard almost as a higher or lower formant; b) a thickening of this halo, even more progressive than the rise of pitches and much less perceptible. On the one hand, it affects the density, i.e., the number of different notes (one could also take the unisons into account) and, on the other, the increase in registers played; c) a crescendo fully written, also by stages.

The rise will continue to the end of the work, almost in keeping with the logic of the auditory illusion of a perpetual ascension. On the other hand, the double thickening (seconded by the crescendo) leads to a break. Given the very progressive, hesitant nature of the thickening, the break is not at all violent. To tell the truth, one can decide not to hear it. If we accept it, we will take it as a gesture full of gentleness, an invitation to travel: a journey to the 'centre of sound', an expression of which Scelsi was quite fond. In fact, everything happens as if a dimensionless entity, a point (the note of the very beginning of the work) were progressively acquiring dimensions to become a sphere: the break marks the moment when we immerse ourselves in the sphere.

Musically speaking, in the quartet, if the point is a note, the sphere is a chord. Whereas the long beginning of the work sounds like a monody (rise of a note that progressively thickens), in measure 158 (6'38″) a sensation of harmony sets in. In both senses of the term, harmonic and harmonious: the chord that dominates is a D minor; one can, moreover, speak of 'new consonance' with regard to the quartet, for there are other consonant passages. However, this is hardly a functional harmony, i.e., evolving, modulating, etc.: the chord of D seems to be set for eternity. But this is a light eternity, as if hanging: some ears will never hear this chord, for it is constantly interfered with, worked on by inharmonic notes, and dominated by an upper line that, continuing its ascension, draws attention. In addition, it is presented on a first inversion (F), then lets a fundamental, often open, emerge before coming back to the first inversion and finally disappearing totally and imperceptibly. Starting from measure 208 (8'45″), the sensation of harmony disappears, and the work concludes quickly.

The sphere is hollowed out from the inside, as shown in **Example 4.18** (measures 167–170: 7'01″-7'10″). Scelsi works variations of timbre in detail: *arco tenuto*, *pizzicato*, *flautando*, *sul tasto*, harmonic, *col legno*, change of string for the same note. We go from one note to another via a *glissando-portamento*. A note can thicken momentarily with a trill or tremolo. And, of course, intensities are extremely elaborate.

Example 4.18 Giacinto Scelsi, *Fourth String Quartet:* measures 167–170 (G. Scelsi, 1964). © By kind permission of Editions Salabert. Each stave indicates a single string. Top to bottom: violin I (3 staves), violin II (4 staves), viola (3 staves), cello (3 staves).

According to Scelsi himself, the 'spherical' passage, which has just been commented on, contains the work's key moment. Franco Sciannameo, violinist of the Quartetto di Nuova Musica, which premiered the work, evokes the rehearsals: whereas the musicians strove to get over the piece's great technical difficulties, the composer

> keeping himself out of sight, was mostly concerned with the overall aesthetics of the piece. I remember him saying, 'There is an arch somewhere in the piece which I want you to reach to; it should sound like the culmination of a chorale'. But he was never clear where in the piece it was going to occur, and the notation in the score seemed unable to identify it. One evening the search for the elusive chorale leading to the quartet's 'golden' moment finally revealed it, as Scelsi exclaimed from the other room, '*È qui, è qui!*'. It was there all along, in bar 167, triggered by a low pedal note in the cello, played *fortissimo*. We just were not getting enough into the centre of the sound to strike the right note – we had not yet entered into the illusive third sonic dimension about which Scelsi was so adamant. That was indeed a moment of discovery which unlocked, for the four of us, the door to this complex man's poetic.
> (F. Sciannameo, 2001)

The 'third dimension' in question is *depth*. In a text that is very important for understanding his aesthetic, 'Sound and Music' Scelsi wrote:

> Sound is spherical even if, when listening to it, it appears to us to have only two dimensions: pitch and duration; as for the third, depth, we know that it exists but, in a certain sense, it eludes us. Higher and lower harmonics (the latter less so) sometimes give us the impression of a sound more vast and complex than that suggested by the duration or the pitch, but it is difficult for us to grasp its complexity. Besides, one would not know how to notate it musically. In painting, perspective was discovered, giving an impression of depth, but in music, despite all the stereophonic experiments and successive attempts of all kinds, we have so far been unable to escape the two dimensions […].
> I am convinced that this will be possible in one way or another before the end of the century, especially by acquiring a subtler faculty for perception or a state of awareness that permits a greater approximation of reality.
> (G. Scelsi, 2006: 126–127; our translation)

We can add, with Tristan Murail (2004: 82; our translation) – one of the composers who participated in the 'rediscovery' of Scelsi – that the Italian composer 'exploits, probably unconsciously, acoustic phenomena such as the transients, the beats, the notion of breadth of critical band, etc… The notion of "critical band" (very close frequencies which engender beats) is, to a certain degree, the theoretical justification of the intuitive idea of "depth" of sound' (Idem).

The 'abyss' of sound

With Scelsi, sound is thought of as a framework in which the listener will immerse himself. As he himself tells us: 'It is by playing a note a long time that it becomes large. It becomes so large that we hear much more harmony, and it grows within. In sound, we discover an entire universe with harmonics which are never heard. Sound fills the room you are in, it encircles you. We swim inside' (G. Scelsi, 2006: 77; our translation). Sound would be 'living' in a way. More than a subject in the philosophical sense of the term, it would be a 'being'.

> *Sono-Suono*: the Italian language almost brings together homophonically 'I am' and 'sound'. That would merely be a banal pun, like 'I sound, therefore I am' if it did not open on this, of which Scelsi's life and work are the powerful testimony: being and sound are both consubstantial.
> (J-P Dessy, 2008: 121; our translation)

Dessy's writing opened the best route to a discussion on Scelsian *mysticism* and his 'floating religion' (see P.A. Castanet, 2008a: 84; see also L.V. Arena, 2016, for the relations between Scelsi and oriental philosophies).

Scelsi never hid his fondness for spiritualism, as his numerous writings bear eloquent witness. It is often difficult to distinguish his music from these penchants. If we eliminate the latter, there would be a large risk of the former's being 'uniquely' sound, i.e., pure matter, then illustrating the dead ends in the evolution of music towards sound. Scelsi is not a particular case: numerous other composers combine esotericism and sound emergence: thought of as a framework, as music in itself, sound, as has been said, can be hypostatised and taken for a 'being'. In 1923, Rudolf Steiner was able to prophesise:

> In the future, we shall no longer recognise the individual sound only in its relation to other sounds [...], but we will apprehend it in its depth. [...] In modern musical art, there is a desire to understand sound in its spiritual depth and a wish – as in other arts – to go from the naturalist element to the spiritual.
> (quoted in J. Harvey, 1984: 85)

Amongst the composers of the early 20th century who were carried towards sound, Scriabin perfectly illustrates the esoteric trend. His theosophy culminated with the idea that the substance of states of mind is vibration (see M. Kelkel, 1984, vol. II: 48). *Prometheus or The Poem of Fire*, Op. 60 (1908–1910, for large orchestra and piano with organ, chorus and light organ) 'is the most densely Theosophical piece of music ever written' (F. Bowers, 1979: III). To finish the mystical totality of which he dreamt, Scriabin had thought up a keyboard of lights, indicated '*luce*' on the score (see **Example 4.19 online**), and based on light-notes (see **Example 4.20 online**). The score begins with the famous 'synthetic' chord made up of diverse types of fourth (perfect, augmented and diminished): A-D#, *G-C#, F#-B*.

One of the pioneering composers of sound, Varèse is not known for having developed a musical mystique but, however, he enjoyed quoting Joseph-Marie-Hoene Wronski and, in particular, his definition of music as 'the embodiment of the intelligence which is in sounds' (E. Varèse, 1983: 153; our translation). Mathematician, engineer and theosophist among other things, Wronski left writings on music, which are known, thanks to his disciple, Camille Durutte. In them, he developed a rational pythagorism and the idea – which could have greatly interested Varèse – that music is both science and art (see J. Godwin, 1991: 11–144).

In the post-war era, one of the most interesting cases would be that of Stockhausen. His evolution is instructive: the mystical turning point that he carried out in the late 1960s resulted not from a conversion but, precisely, from the very rational analysis of the material, which he was one of the first to do (see his article '...wie die Zeit vergeht...': K. Stockhausen, 1963: 99–139), and his realisation of the importance of sound. The 'void' of positivism can easily be turned upside down in the 'surplus' of mysticism – and that is why Hugues Dufourt (1991: 312; our translation) could write that 'Stockhausen's technological authoritarianism turned mystical, the ineffable foundered in hypnosis'.

In the following generation, musical esotericism, worked to varying degrees, was current among the composers who contributed to putting sound at the centre of musical preoccupations. In a 1960 lecture, La Monte Young stated:

> The trouble with most of the music of the past is that man has tried to make the sounds do what he wants them to do. If we are really interested in Learning about sounds, it seems to me that we should allow the sounds to be sounds instead of trying to force them to do things that are mainly pertinent to human existence. [...] When we go into the world of a sound, it is new. When we prepare to leave the world of a sound, we expect to return to the world we previously left. We find, however, that when the sound stops, or we leave the area in which the sound is being made, or we just plain leave the world of the sound to some degree, that the world into which we enter is not the old world we left but another new one.
> (La Monte Young, M. Zazeela, 2004: 73–75)

With spectral musicians, the mystical attitude is also an integral part of Horațiu Rădulescu's approach. Regarding *infinite to be cannot be infinite, infinite anti-be could be infinite* (1976, for string quartet and imaginary 128-string viola da gamba), he wrote: 'Whilst being infinite in its aspects, our being, our earthly existence, cannot be truly infinite, but our non-being, our eternal, cosmic existence – projecting us like a vibration towards life and death – could last infinitely' (H. Radulescu, 1996; our translation). As for the French composers – by definition more 'rational', at least in their discourse – only Grisey sometimes let himself go to declarations able to open the doors of certain forms of spiritualism. Thus he liked to mention 'the splendour of the ONE', evoked by Deleuze (regarding Samuel Butler's *Erewhon*):

> Composition of process stands out from the everyday gesture and by that very fact frightens us. It is inhuman, cosmic and provokes the fascination of the Sacred and the Unknown, joining what Deleuze defines as the splendour of the ONE: a mode of impersonal individuations and pre-individual singularities.
> (G. Grisey, 2008: 84; our translation)

In addition, the doubt cast by his 'liminal' writing on what can be defined as a sound has sometimes led him to hypostatise the latter. Certainly, he did so less than Scelsi, settling for referring to a biomorphic conception: 'With a birth, a life and a death, sound resembles an animal; time is both its atmosphere and territory. Treating sounds outside of time, outside the air they breathe, would amount to dissecting cadavers', said he (Ibid: 52).

Of the composers associated with spectralism, it is certainly Jonathan Harvey – having a particular interest in oriental religions (see M. Downes, 2009) – who maintained the links between music centred on sound and spiritualism. Starting from the idea that the '"timbral experience" is fundamentally one of shifting identities' (J. Harvey, 1986: 179; our translation), the British composer generalises and takes the plunge: he demands to leave our narrow ego to immerse ourselves in a new world full of spirituality:

> Serialism and electronic music, with its ability to get into unknown sorts of sounds, both suggest a new world which could be called spiritual; or one might speak of a greater awareness of what is. It's a matter of the expansion of the narrow self. [...] It's the function of art to make one expand our one's consciousness so that the narrow, insecure, individual self disappears and a larger self, the absolute is broth to consciousness.
> (quoted in P. Smith, 1989: 11)

We might also mention the New Age spiritualism of the 1980s and 1990s which was often accompanied by an accent on sound. That is the case with composers as different as Arvo Pärt, Philip Glass, John Taverner and Glenn Branca. The latter's *Symphony No. 9*, presented as a single overall sound, even though the texture is fairly traditional, is subtitled '*l'eve future*' and leads to the following commentary: '*Symphony No.9* is the most drastic work in the Branca canon. [... It is] the most mystical of symphonies, the one that foretells death. [...] After a lot of Glenn's performances, people report various kinds of Gnostic sonic visitations' (T. Holmes, 1995). For Arvo Pärt, the most widespread commentaries are of this type:

> Fervour and fidelity pervade his work, which reincarnates spirituality in music. Appeased himself, he pours for us a huge relief that flows beyond time. Humble, radiant with the enchantment of the simple, he holds out an offering to us of a music tending towards rarefaction but going to the very string of the soul [...] In a disoriented world in search of transcendental values, his 'simplistic' music will have been a profound consolation.
> (G. Pressnitzer, 2010; our translation)

Finally, we should study the relation between Coltrane's spiritualism and his music, which, in *Love Supreme* (1964) or *Meditation* (1965), is entirely centred on sound. Let us quote just part of the original notes he wrote for the album *Love Supreme:*

> Dear Listener, [...] During the year 1957, I experienced, by the grace of God, a spiritual awakening which was to lead me to a richer, fuller, more productive life. At that time, in gratitude, I humbly asked to be given the means and

privilege to make others happy through music. I feel this has been granted through His grace. ALL PRAISE GOD. [...]

This album is a humble offering to Him. An Attempt to say 'Thank you god' through our work, even as we do in our hearts and with our tongues. May He help and strengthen all men in every good endeavor.

(J. Coltrane, 1964)

We can read this text as a profession of faith in the literal sense, which has little to do with music. However, it is appropriate to note that the god in question is a god turned entirely towards love. If you read this text whilst listening to the music at the same time, nothing prevents you from thinking that its 'liquid', immersive nature constitutes an expression of this love: one can easily imagine that the composed sound offered by Coltrane and his musicians would be a metaphor of god-love in which the mystical is blended. Here we join other strictly sonic experimentations of the 1960s, like those of Stockhausen's 'meditative' music, for example in *Aus den sieben Tagen* (1968). In that work, the German composer gives texts in place of a score. That of the piece 'Set Sail for the Sun' (dated 9 May 1968) is thoroughly indicative of the spiritual potentialities contained in music entirely centred on sound: 'play a tone for so long / until you hear its individual vibrations / hold the note / and listen to the tones of the others / –to all of them together, not to individual ones – / and slowly move your tone / until you arrive at complete harmony / and the whole sound turns to gold / to pure, gently shimmering fire'.

Immersion in sound can take on the ways of the famous oceanic merging or, when the intention is spiritualistic, a merging of a mystical nature. More generally, through this vision of the emergence of sound, we take up again with the ancestral theme of the power of music and the effect it can have on the human being, a very important theme with the Pythagoreans, Damon and Plato, Augustine of Hippo... Its return in the 20th century, thanks to the refocussing on sound, is linked to the hope that music might again take up with this extraordinary force. Thus, Scelsi (2006: 131; our translation) noted:

> Western classical music has devoted nearly all its attention to the musical framework, to what is called musical form. It has forgotten to study the laws of sonic energy and to think music in terms of energy, i.e., life, and thus, it has produced thousands of magnificent frameworks, which are often fairly empty, because they were merely the product of a constructive imagination, which is quite different from a creative imagination. The melodies themselves go from sounds to sounds, but the intervals are empty abysses for the notes are lacking in sound energy. The inner space is empty.

He added: 'Do you want me to tell you that the music of Bach and Mozart could not have brought down the walls of Jericho? Yes, it's a bit that' (Ibid: 131, 133).[2] We can also quote Stockhausen (in J. Cott, 1974: 81): 'Sounds can do anything. They can kill. The whole Indian mantric tradition knows that with sounds you can

134 *Immersion in sound*

concentrate on any part of the body and calm it down, excite it, even hurt it in the extreme'.

It is advisable to emphasise that not all the musicians for whom sound has become the central point of music share this spiritualistic vision. In fact, this vision presupposes, as Michel Chion (2016: 124) stressed, faith in a 'cosmic vibratory unity':

> The myth of sound as a continuum that links us via sensory perception to the imperceptible world remains to this day completely alive, and it is perpetuated by the fact that we retain – against all logic – the term 'sound' to designate vibratory phenomena that are beyond auditory perception: 'infrasound', 'ultrasound', and even 'hypersound' (waves the frequency of which is 10^9 Hertz or higher; they no longer having anything to do with audibility). The idea that everything would be reducible to sound – a pseudoscientific expression of the transmutation into energy perhaps? – is the absolute form of this myth. We even come across those who would depict audible sounds as the tip of a vibratory iceberg. This tip would be the least interesting part, albeit serving to certify the rest, made up of more beautiful vibrations. Sound is in many respects mythologized as the representative of another vibratory reality that would be much loftier, of a music without sound and beyond sounds, of a voice without a voice and beyond voices.

This faith alone allows for envisaging sound as the equivalent of the unity lost during the accession to language and, as such, granting it all the powers that legend attributes to it.

 ## Chapter 4 online examples

Example 4.3 The tam-tam used by Stockhausen for *Mikrophonie I*. © By kind permission of Stockhausen Foundation for Music, Kürten, Germany, www.stockhausen.org.

Example 4.4 Jonathan Harvey, *Mortuos Plango, Vivos Voco*: analysis of the bell sound (the first 24 partials) (after B. Bossis, 2004: 123). © By kind permission of Bruno Bossis. The fractions above the stave indicate an approximation in quarter- or eighths of tones that must be added to or taken away from the pitch indicated on the stave to obtain the frequency. Below the stave are indicated: the number of the partial; the frequency in Hz; the amplitude.

Example 4.5 Jonathan Harvey, *Mortuos Plango, Vivos Voco*: transition between sections 2 and 3 (M. Clarke, 2006: 125). © By kind permission of Michael Clarke. A. Spectrogram B. Pitch structure: a) partials of the voices; b) bell on C (260Hz): partials 2, 5, 8, 10, 17, 19, 21, 23; c) bell on C (260Hz): partials 5–10; d) bell on F (347Hz): partials 3–8; e) bell strike on F (347Hz): beginning of section 3.

Example 4.7 Spectrogram (realised with Audacity) of the first two chords of the first movement of Beethoven's *Third Symphony* in a recording by Karajan (1977).

Example 4.8 Successive zooms (realised with Audacity) of the first chord (above, the time in seconds).
Example 4.9 The auditorium of the Osaka World's Fair. © By kind permission of Stockhausen Foundation for Music, Kürten, Germany, www.stockhausen.org.
Example 4.10 The *Diatope* in front of the Centre Georges Pompidou, Paris (Archives Xenakis). © By kind permission of Mâkhi Xenakis.
Example 4.11 Display of the loudspeakers in the architecture of the *Diatope* (Archives Xenakis). © By kind permission of Mâkhi Xenakis.
Example 4.12 Richard Wagner, *Parsifal:* Act I (Gurnemanz: 'Zum Raum wird hier die Zeit').
Example 4.15 Rave in Vienna, 2005.
Example 4.16 Ad for a website proposing relaxation.
Example 4.17 Giacinto Scelsi, *Fourth String Quartet*, measures 1–157: analysis. -1/4, -3/4, +1/4, +3/4 indicate respectively a quartertone and three-quarters of a tone lower, a quartertone and three-quarters of a tone higher.
Example 4.19 Alexander Scriabin, *Prometheus or The Poem of Fire*: 1.
Example 4.20 Alexander Scriabin, *Prometheus or The Poem of Fire*: light-note correspondences.

Notes

1 The works that Varèse composed before 1918 have been lost, with the exception of *Un grand sommeil noir* and *Bourgogne*. However, the composer destroyed the latter around 1962 (see F. Ouellette, *Edgar Varèse*, 1968: 52). It had been performed in Berlin, in 1910, and provoked the first of the Varèse scandals: the critic Bruno Schrader 'announced that it was an infernal din, mere caterwauling' (quoted by F. Ouellette, 1968: 35).
2 Scelsi referred to the Old Testament, Joshua 6, where is related how the god of the Hebrews helped them conquer the city of Jericho: when seven trumpets were blown and the Hebrews pushed a 'great cry', the city wall collapsed.

5 Composing sound

The question of material

The historicity of material and the notion of material

The period during which tonality emerged went through a revolution on the level of musical grammar, owing to the establishment of a new functionality. To assert itself, it restrained the material: the musical material of the era when tonality was particularly stable, the Classical era, was less rich than the material of earlier periods. Inversely, post-tonality spread like an emancipation of the material and a decline of functionality. This occurred, first of all, with the progression of chromaticism and dissonance the proliferation, which culminated with the 'new music' (Vienna School). Certainly, Schoenberg tried to introduce a new functionality by setting forth the laws of dodecaphony, but the post-war era pursued the liberation of material, as much with the empowerment of new 'parameters' as with the birth of electroacoustic music. And the movement did not stop there: every time new laws were established, which were supposed to re-establish order in the anarchic abundance of material, the latter began to proliferate again, destroying them. The history of musical modernity could be written as the succession of increasingly closer revolutions of materials, going from the emancipation of dissonance up to granular synthesis.

Thus modernity put forward the *historicity* of the musical material. Marie-Élisabeth Duchez (1991: 54) wrote:

> This historicity concerns the conception of sound as a natural phenomenon (physical structure and psychoacoustic reception of which the knowledge is evolving), as much as a cultural phenomenon (means of production, aesthetic nature, philosophical valorisation). That sound be a 'fact of culture', a 'phenomenon of civilisation', has become a trivial idea.

To impose this recognition of the historic nature of musical material, it would have been necessary to convince that tonal material is in no way 'natural', that it too constitutes a fact of culture. Indeed, historical adversaries of atonality such as Ernest Ansermet (1961) or Claude Lévi-Strauss (1964) always advanced the argument that tonality is based in Nature, owing to the principle of resonance.

But anyone who has studied the question of temperament knows that the perfect chord of equal temperament is not more natural than a chromatic chord, this being, in truth, only the (historic) consequence of the former. In addition, defenders of the supposedly natural character of tonal material have been short-circuited by composers such as John Cage or François-Bernard Mâche who, introducing into music sounds drawn directly from Nature, proclaimed a return to Nature, or by composers such as Harry Partch who tried to come back to natural temperament.

But it is not only the historicity of the materials that is put forward, but also the historical character of the very *notion* of material itself. Indeed, we know that the notion of musical material is recent. Certainly, it underlies western music theory from at least the birth of polyphony but, up until the 20th century, it remained diffuse and was not encountered as such. It was in the 1920s and 1930s, in atonal music circles, that it began to be clarified, especially in the debates between Krenek and Adorno, which culminated, in the early 1940s, with the latter's *Philosophy of New Music*. Then, in the post-war period, everything happened as if this notion was becoming central to music, even going so far as to prevail over other notions.

Refocussing on material

What is the meaning of the emancipation of material in atonal music, i.e., its ongoing proliferation? In many respects, tonality could be viewed as a chain of mediations – thus by appealing to organicist philosophy – linking different levels. It would be possible to apprehend a large part of tonal music as an edifice of three storeys communicating with each other thanks to this chain: material, functionality (often also called 'language' or 'syntax') and form (linear construction from the level of the theme up to the overall form). With modernity, the need to strive towards the work's absolute singularity seems to have given considerable importance to the level of the material, to the detriment of the other two levels. In sum, the primary characteristic of modernity is the *refocussing* on the level of material, which overrides the other two levels, language and form. This is why we can say that the tonal edifice has *collapsed*.

Indeed, it might have been supposed that, once its materialogical revolution was achieved, musical modernity would have created languages, syntaxes providing pertinent rules of combination of the new materials, as well as adequate forms. However, history thwarted this expectation. The case of the serial generation, which had set itself the task of elaborating superstructures in accordance with the new material (atonal material), is quite instructive. In his famous article of 1952, 'Schoenberg is dead' (in P. Boulez, 1966: 255–261), in which he criticised the inventor of dodecaphony for his treatment of the row that he deemed inconsequent (treatment in which tonal forms were superimposed on it), Pierre Boulez summed up the pressing needs of a large portion of his contemporaries, searching for a new universal language, sensed as the generalisation of the serial principle. Twenty years later, he acknowledged the utopian aspect of a search for a 'collective style' or 'common language' (P. Boulez, 1974: 125–126; our translation), for 'the evolution of musical material tended to break down *the very idea that one could make of language*' (Ibid: 126, our italics).

Is this to say that the anarchic exploration of materials, their extraordinary abundance, in short, the refocussing on the level of the material would be synonymous with the disappearance of the other two levels, language and form? In certain cases, one will tend towards this solution (once again, we think of John Cage). Elsewhere, the situation is more complex. In this chapter, we shall speak of situations where these levels, far from having disappeared, have been revitalised, but on the basis of this refocussing on material. To again refer to the early 1950s, an idea concerning language (or 'structure') had spread: extracting it from material. Thus, Boulez wrote: 'Perhaps one could look for [...] sound EVIDENCE by trying one's hand at the fathering of the structure from the material' (P. Boulez, 1966: 271; our translation). A few years later, the musicologist Massimo Mila (1960, 56–57; our translation), friend of Nono, criticises this idea by saying that it is 'as if music should be reduced to being nothing more than the necessary product, the chemical secretion, so to speak, of a determinist structure of sound matter'.

Composing the material

This criticism is, of course, measured by the standard of the most automatic, most mechanical and therefore most depersonalised kinds of music of the 1950s. However, even in relation to those pieces, the notion of 'sound matter' about which Mila spoke is problematic. In truth, the refocussing, the immersion in the material in question in no way signifies the advancing of a *pure* sound matter.

In fact, in its evolution throughout the 20th century, material is presented less and less as 'sound matter': it has a tendency to *dissolve*. In other words, it is characterised by extreme fluidity, at least since the Impressionistic 'blur'. If one likes metaphors, one might say, concerning Debussy, for whom we know the importance of the theme of water (see in particular V. Jankélévitch, 1976: *passim*), that it was *liquefied*. Subsequently, with the 'clouds of sounds' of a Xenakis, it went to the *gaseous* state. With the spectral revolution, it was *sublimated* – 'the material no longer exists as an autonomous quantity, but is sublimated in a pure, constantly changing evolution', wrote Grisey (2008: 27; our translation). In a way, it offloads its quality of object and tends to contain an important share of spirit: as Adorno (1997: 141) wrote in his *Aesthetic Theory*, the mastery of the material constitutes a 'predominant process of spiritualisation'. Hence the spiritualist tendencies that were evoked in the previous chapter regarding 'immersion' in sound – another way of referring to the dissolution of the material – which can be confused with an inner (spiritual) 'life' of the matter.

Influenced by Max Weber, Adorno focussed on a concept that can explain this 'dematerialisation' of material: its progressive *rationalisation*; in other words, an increase in its *mastery*. Adorno distinguished between blind domination and mastery. The former sets itself up as an end in itself, whereas the latter is only a means, precisely the best means for letting the material reveal its own potentialities.

Then, the material is not treated like 'matter' that would be combined with other matter. It is in this sense that mastering material comes down to focussing on it: freeing dissonance, noise or, more generally, sound does not mean perpetually searching, according to a logic of headlong rush, for new, unusual objects that would continue to be treated from afar but, on the contrary, inscribe the unusual at the heart of the compositional approach, placing sound itself in its general nature at the centre of interest. This is why material proliferates or, more exactly, everything tends to become material. 'The possibility of technical control of the material developed together with its emancipation', wrote Adorno (2006: 44).

The refocussing on material, in the case of the kinds of music concerned in this chapter, is therefore synonymous with its dissolution, i.e., its rationalisation, and this is why, when all is said and done, material is no longer 'sound matter': it is no longer given by Nature; it tends to be *integrally composed, constructed*. This is, of course, the case with electronic music calling on sound synthesis. But it is also the case with advanced instrumental music in which the sound 'matter' (natural, acoustic) produced by instruments does not constitute material but is simply a starting point that is transmuted by the latter. The material also eludes the idea of second nature, i.e., constructions – like those of tonality – which strove to pass off as natural: it is no longer based on a pre-established, inherited typology.

In fact, the material is no longer the 'base' of the musical edifice. Fully composed, it is no longer necessarily distinguished from the other 'stages', language or form, in which tonal music recognised a character of construction. Hence, ultimately, for all these types of music that have worked towards a mastery of material, a tendency to destroy the musical edifice: refocussing it on material and its proliferation do not mean that language or form disappear but that one has more and more trouble distinguishing them from the level of material. Henceforth, stemming just as much from the principle of construction, the latter no longer has any reason to differentiate itself from them.

Composed resonances

Change in listening

Let us plunge into a historical moment stemming from this principle of integral construction, wherein the material is constructed just as much as form: the first movement of Webern's *Symphony* (1928), *Op. 21*, of which **Example 5.1** proposes a four-part reduction. The extraordinary economy of means that this work summons attests to the composer's concern for coherence where, according to his own terms, it is a matter of making appear 'as clear as possible the relationships between the parts of the unity; in short, to show how one thing leads to another' (A. Webern, 1963: 42). This concern, which constitutes one of the peaks of his organicistic view of music, begins with the series: this series – the form of the original is given here starting from the second movement: F, Ab, G, F#, Bb, A, Eb, E, C, C#, D, B – is composed like a microcosm and has internal symmetries. The most obvious, which will have a considerable influence on the macroform,

Example 5.1 Anton Webern, *Symphony, Op. 21*, first movement: four-part reduction.

Example 5.1 Continued.

Example 5.1 Continued.

Example 5.1 Continued.

Example 5.1 Continued.

divides it into two groups of six notes, the last six constituting the recurrence, transposed to the tritone, of the first six. In that way, the serial material is half as much: one can generate only twenty-four (instead of forty-eight) serial forms. Other symmetries, more hidden, also characterise it (among many analyses, see K. Bailey, 1991).

Concerning the macroform, although the second (and last) movement of the *Symphony* is classic in appearance (a theme and variations), the first, untitled (tempo: *ruhig schreitend*, at a calm pace), is revolutionary: it offers a first materialisation of this 'chemical secretion, so to speak, of a determinist structure of sound matter', which Massimo Mila spoke about as regards music of the 1950s. The deduction of the macroform starting from the material (series) is based on a wilful gesture even though the process is mechanical: Webern calls on the most determinist technique of music of the past: the canon. A first section (measures 1–25a and 1–26) constitutes a double canon (staves 1–2 and 3–4 in the reduction). The voices imitate the rhythms and timbres (within sections) – the canon is retrograde for parts 1–2 as for the timbres. In relation to the series of pitches, the two parts proceed by inversion. As for the serial superstructure, Webern creates superseries by linking series that fit into each other (common notes between the ends and beginnings of series). Second section: with measure 25b begins the most fascinating passage of this first movement: a four-part canon, fully retrograde, as much for the pitches as for timbres, intensities and rhythms. In fact, the music 'reverses' starting in measure 35. A third section[1] re-establishes the initial double canon with the same serial material.[2]

The analysis that has just been sketched shows the almost fully constructed character both of the microform (material) and macroform of this first movement. Now we must answer the classic question, which every listener asks of serial music: *But is all that heard?* Does the listener hear the internal symmetries of the series? Does he hear the double canon, the retrograde motion of the central section, as well as the final re-establishment of the initial double canon?[3]

To this question, which is crucial for a large part of atonal music, we can provide two answers. First of all, we could begin with the remarks of René Leibowitz (1949: 212–213) who, in his first introduction to dodecaphony, wrote:

> Certain listeners, who come to appreciate [Webern's] works up to and including Opus 20, admit to being completely disconcerted when hearing most of the following scores. [...] A few notes seem to have been tossed here and there with no apparent reason. [...] The whole produces the effect of chaos, where the most complete arbitrariness reigns.

Recognising the listener's confusion in the face of the first movement of *Opus 21*, Leibowitz was acting as a pedagogue, explaining the piece's compositional mechanisms, hoping to make our listener hear the canons, serial symmetries, etc. Defenders of contemporary music reasoned thus for a long time.

It was then that the idea was born that new music could not be appreciated like the old and that it necessitated a *change in listening*. So, faced with our classic question, a second response consists of saying that Webernian construction is not heard on the surface but at a deeper level. According to this perspective, the listener does not perceive *consciously* – he does not 'understand' – but that does not mean the piece has no sense for him. This, on condition that he opens himself up to another kind of listening, a listening that could be modelled on 'unconscious', 'undifferentiated' or 'syncretic' perception about which Anton Ehrenzweig spoke, in his famous book *The Hidden Order of Art*, regarding modern art, a perception that allows for 'overcom[ing] the superficial impression of chaos and disruption and appreciat[ing] the stringent formal discipline underneath' (A. Ehrenzweig, 1967: 67). As concerns the macroform of the first movement of the Symphony, only the second section could be the object of customary, i.e., analytical, listening for it is the only one where the listener can hope to understand the structures composed by Webern: in measure forty, we clearly hear the inversion of the initial figure (clarinet, measures 25b–26) made up of an assemblage of notes, which, by its rhythm, melodic contour and envelope, constitutes the first figure that we perceive as such in this first movement, which, up until then, was composed rather of scattered notes forming a mosaic. The canons of the first and last sections would act through syncretic type perception.

What does this syncretic perception consist of, procuring a latent sensation of order under the appearance of debris? I would maintain that this hidden order is situated at a musical level where traditional means (pitches, forms in the classic sense, etc.) become means for composing *entities* of a new type, which syncretic listening can appreciate perfectly. These entities, *emerging* in a way, are what can already be described as 'sounds', specifying that these are *composed* sounds. The term that best suits them, in Webern's case, is: *composed resonances*. It is such entities that constitute the object of syncretic listening.

In fact, one might posit that the listener perceives the evolution of the macroform in the introduction of *Opus 21* like a *succession of three composed resonances,* three sound states corresponding to the three sections of the work. According to this kind of listening, the repetition of the serial material in the third section would not be heard (at all), and the outline would be ABC (AABCBC if the repeats are counted) – and not ABA' – where the letters do not symbolise 'sections' but overall sound states.

Composed resonances or overall sound states: numerous analysts have pointed out the 'hypnotic magic' that emanates from the *ruhig schreitend*. Henri-Louis Matter (1981: 85–86; our translation) writes:

> For, although we are not concerned (or just barely) by the relations between the parts, we are more so by the flimsy relations related to isolated sounds: echo [...] and *Klangfarbenmelodie* effects, secret affinities that gradually impose their hypnotic magic.

He observes that, even 'in full knowledge of the facts', we do not perceive the canonic structure. Gisèle Brelet (1968: 260; our translation) underscored the

Composing sound 147

affinities between Webern and Debussy, both carrying out a pulverisation of time and material to glorify the present and 'sound':

> Becoming enclosed in an indivisible present, sound, which organises time, is complete music by itself. It suffices that it be confined in its 'solitude' for it to reveal its autonomy and sufficiency, not only its structuring powers but also its qualitative magics: hence the 'glittering' with which, in Webern, each note is adorned, and the incantation that emanates, in Debussy, from a single sound.

'Hypnotic magic' or 'glittering': these expressions attest to the intense impression of presence and absolute focus on the instant, due to the *refocussing on sound*. However, we must insist on the fact that the 'sound' we are talking about here does not identify with the note, the isolated sound: with Webern, it concerns an entire section. Hence the idea of an *overall sound state*, a *composed resonance*.

To support the hypothesis of composed resonances, we must now mention a capital element in the first movement of *Opus 21*, an element that the listener perceives immediately in the framework of syncretic listening: the absolute *fixity* of notes in the register. In each of the three sections, a sole distribution of pitches in relation to the register is brought into play (**Example 5.2**). The first section occupies a register of thirty-eight semitones with only thirteen notes (the twelve chromatic pitches with a doubling at the octave of the E flat). This arrangement is symmetrical: from the low register to the central A and from the upper register to the same note, the intervals are the same. The register of the second section (measures 25b-44) is much broader (nearly five octaves), and its occupation, with twenty-seven notes, denser. Finally, the last section deploys a register of which the dimension (forty-four semitones) and density (fourteen notes) are close to the first, but which is carried towards the upper register and, above all, structured differently. Here, too, a symmetry prevails: we have the same arrangement of

Example 5.2 Anton Webern, *Symphony, Op. 21*, first movement: distribution of pitches in the register.

intervals from the low register to the D in the middle and from the upper register to the E that is close to the latter. Given this fixity, this particular writing could be likened to sound synthesis on the instrumental level, every pitch equivalent to the frequency of a spectrum. In sum, the three sections of the first movement of *Opus 21* provide overall 'colours'.

In addition, each of these sections has a set of its own characteristics, which are not given progressively, according to a logic of development but, in a way, of a bloc, like the characteristics of a sound state. Thus, on the level of intensities, each section has an overall 'envelope'. The first functions in a static manner around *pp, p* and *mp*, undergoing a brief crescendo, followed by an equally brief diminuendo at the end. The second works constantly on brief, sporadic crescendos and diminuendos around *pp*, but has a hollow in its centre (the point of recurrence: measures 34–35) with a *ppp*. Finally, the last soars towards higher dynamics, even reaching *f*, then, after a period of diminuendo, ends *pp*. Rhythmic writing also characterises each section. The beginning is marked by sporadic durations (no *tenuti*); the interlocking of the instruments first generates an extreme regularity. Then we reach regular crotchet beats; the section ends with a rarefaction. In the second section, the regularly striated tempo disappears in favour of a smooth tempo made up of numerous *tenuti*. The last proposes a compromise between the other two. Last characteristic: the repetition of notes (on the same register) from instrument to instrument. The register's low occupation density in the two outer sections explains their overabundance of repetitions, unlike the middle section. However, here the repetitions are done differently: in the first, they are above all perceived as echoes, whereas in the last, this is, in a way, a matter of fixations.

It goes without saying that this interpretation is not univocal: certain characteristics (in particular, the melodic figures, which have not been mentioned, with the exception of the one in the second section) continue to proclaim an analytical perception. In truth, *Opus 21* is at the turning point of two conceptions of music, one as the art of composing *with sounds*, the other the art of composing *sound*, 'sound' which materialises here through what is called 'composed resonances'. Amongst the characteristics described, only the register clearly goes in the direction of an overall sound state. To this, it would be necessary to add the role of silences, which so disconcerted the work's first listeners. The pointillism resulting from their reduction gives birth to the famous 'diagonal dimension' (the expression is from P. Boulez, 1966: 372), exploited and pushed to its climax by the serial works of the early 1950s, a dimension that generates a unified sound space.

Éclats

Composed resonances: prior to Webern – as regards the idea of a fully constructed work – one will find numerous works. We could refer to the history of timbre. The prelude to Wagner's *Das Rheingold* unfolds like a gigantic resonance, the same chord for 137 measures. Some of Debussy's chord-timbres (for example, in *La Cathédrale engloutie* from Book I of the *Preludes* for piano) or Messiaen's are even more representative. One composer after Webern, lying in

Composing sound 149

the Debussyst lineage and who was not mentioned in the chapter on timbre, could be apprehended as a master of composed resonances: Maurice Ohana, an aficionado of natural resonances, which are doubtless related to his quest for a primitive incantatory magic, a mythical time and space, amplified them by composing them (see C. Rae, 2000). Moreover, nothing prevents us from speaking about composed resonances regarding certain New Age works of the 1970s and 1980s, the most perfect example being represented by the first movement, 'Ludus', of *Tabula rasa* (1977) by Arvo Pärt. **Example 5.3** shows the beginning of the score, where we see the attack of the two solo violins on a single note, the tonic A, followed by a long silence, then arpeggios of the A minor chord in the strings and soloists; the process recommences seven times, the silences diminishing as they go (see the analysis of P. Hiller, 1997: 114–118). Another interesting example – this time coming from the beginnings of minimalism and British experimental music as defended by Michael Nyman's henceforth classic book *Experimental Music: Cage and Beyond* (1974) – would be Gavin Bryars's *The Sinking of the Titanic* (1969, a work in progress, with a first version recorded in 1975), of which the very pretext (the inspiration for the work came from a report that the wireless operator, Harold Bride, on the Titanic had witnessed the house band continuing to perform as the ship sank), allows for composed resonances.

Coming after the model proposed by Webern's *Opus 21*, we find the integral serialism and post-serialism of the 1950s and 1960s. Coming after, for integral serialism claims to represent artefact and construction. Nonetheless, a 'natural' model endures with it: the attack/resonance acoustic model. Based on the physics of sound, this model advances our history of the emergence of sound. With composers such as Boulez, Berio, Nono, Stockhausen, Barraqué, Nunes and others, one often encounters passages that transpose, on the instrumental level and in a more or less conscious way, the model in question. Limiting ourselves to the orchestra, with Berio we could mention, amongst others, *Allelujah I* (1956), *Quaderni I* (1959) or the orchestration of 'O King' in the *Sinfonia* (1968). The work of Boulez – a composer who was always charmed by natural resonance[4] – teems with such composed sounds. *Éclat* (1964–1965, for ensemble)

Example 5.3 Arvo Pärt, *Tabula rasa*, 'Ludus': beginning. © By kind permission of Universal Editions.

is built almost solely around two types of figures, which Boulez (quoted in J.-P. Derrien, 1970: 122) called 'movements of action' and of 'contemplation', the second type corresponding to what is called 'composed resonances' here. The piece's atypical instrumentarium is based on the choice of solo instruments with an almost percussive attack and resonants (piano, harp, celesta, glockenspiel, vibraphone, mandolin, guitar, cimbalom, chimes, tubes). Thanks to the heterogeneity of these percussive/resonant instruments, Boulez managed to 'compose profiles of singular resonance' (P. Schoeller, 1986: 199). Moreover, thanks to these two types of figure, he invented, to use his own terms, music 'written on rubber', 'It's a non-directional conception of time, one does not go towards a goal but lives in the compressed instant' (P. Boulez in J.-P. Derrien, 1970: 122; our translation).

It is true to say that when resonances are composed and thus not natural, 'contemplation' (to borrow Boulez's word), the 'hypnotic magic', the 'glittering' (to come back to Webern) suddenly appear, owing to the fact that one is working on a flexible, elastic tempo (the 'duration', to use Bergsonian vocabulary). Here is a common point between the structuralist tradition, to which serialism belongs, and a composer like Feldman who, as we said in Chapter 3, was interested in the extinction of sound. What is the extinction of sound, if not the moment when the resonance of a weak sound is on the point of vacillating? One of Feldman's last works, *Coptic Light* (1986, for orchestra) sounds like a gigantic resonating extinction continuously (re)composed. As Feldman (2000: 201) explained, 'an important technical aspect of the composition was prompted by Sibelius's observation that the orchestra differed mainly from the piano in that it has no pedal. With this in mind, I set to work to create an orchestral pedal, continually varying in nuance. This *chiaroscuro* is both the compositional and the instrumental focus of *Coptic Light*'.

To come back to serialism, let us pause on *Le Marteau sans maître* (1953–1955). In this work, Boulez developed a very complex serialism, and at the same time what he called a 'local indiscipline': it is a fearsome piece for the analyst (see L. Koblyakov, 1990; U. Mosch, 2004; P. Boulez, 2005). And yet, the charm works. Sometimes, to quote Pousseur (1972: 78–79; our translation) talking about Book I of *Structures*,

> we hear sorts of sound cohorts, statistical and of variable density [...]. Although the charm of this piece is however incontestable, it is less a matter of the charm of a perfectly clear and translucent 'geometry' than a more mysterious charm, exercised by many distributive forms encountered in Nature, like the slow moving of clouds in shreds, the scattering of gravel at the bottom of a mountain stream or the gush of a wave breaking on some rocky strand.

This 'charm' refers back to the undifferentiated, syncretic perception, mentioned for Webern's *Opus 21*. Moreover, Boulez is one of the very rare musicians quoted in Ehrenzweig's book (1967: 111–112): in Boulez's music,

> any continuity of melodic line or harmonic progression seems missing; the instrumental sounds tumble like the tinkles of an Aeolian harp responding

to irregular gusts of the wind. [...] We must listen to this music without trying to connect the present sound with the past and future; [...] after a while the sounds will come with the feeling of inevitable necessity, obeying an unconscious submerged coherence of a different order that defies conscious analysis.

As with Webern, the object of this undifferentiated perception is made up of fully constructed totalities, which are presented like *surplus*. In fact, *Le Marteau sans maître* is composed with the help of traditional dimensions (pitch, harmony, rhythm, polyphony, etc.), but those dimensions have lost their pertinence and autonomy. In truth, they constitute the means for ramifying from the inside a totality that, alone, would be 'audible' as such. This totality is given to us by the '*éclats*', resonances and sound surfaces so characteristic of Boulez.

To support this hypothesis, let us analyse the first part of the fourth piece (the beginning of which is shown in **Example 5.4**), 'Commentaire II de "Bourreaux de Solitude"', based on a succession of attacks/resonances. 'Accompaniment with nothing to accompany' (D. Jameux, 1984: 360), background without figure, the instrumental ensemble (xylorimba, vibraphone, two cymbals, guitar and viola in pizzicato) called for in this passage invites us to an *immersion*, the sounds merging almost perfectly to generate an overall space. This space is heard from different angles, for it consists of a succession of thirty-seven brief sections (from four measures to a simple semiquaver) separated by *fermate*,[5] each of these sections corresponding to an attack/resonance, a composed *éclat*.

Example 5.5 proposes a transcription of measures 1–18 (or the first thirteen sections) evoking a spectrum. This transcription does not give an account of the serial relations but perhaps succeeds in schematising what our ear perceives. On the one hand, each section is listened to as a whole, modelled from the inside by three factors: the disposition of pitches in the register (and not the intervallic relations); their evolution in time (rather than of hierarchies of 12 or *n* durations); their more or less large pregnance (intensity). In this sense, the series of the three dimensions in question (pitch, duration, intensity) play a major role for listening, however not as an end in itself but as a means for sculpting each section from the inside. On the other hand, relations between sonorities (the sections) are clearly shown in this transcription. For example, the first sonority, which includes only two notes played *ff* on the guitar, becomes an integral part of the following sonority: these two notes (in the same register) will be repeated (by other instruments) with the same intensity whilst being drowned in a very rich context. Conversely, it appears quite clearly that the ninth section is only a brief, filtered resonance of the eighth, whilst anticipating the tenth. On the other hand, the thirteenth sonority, with its heightened intensities as well as its high density that goes hand in hand with a large fragmentation (very brief durations), seems to contrast quite strongly with the preceding. However, their tonal composition is close: the twelfth section has eleven different notes, and the following twenty-six (for repetition again, the register is taken into account); but eight are common.

152 *Composing sound*

Example 5.4 Pierre Boulez, *Le Marteau sans maître*, 4. 'Commentaire II de "Bourreaux de Solitude"': measures 1–7 (P. Boulez, 1965b). © By kind permission of Universal Editions.

As for the internal composition of sonorities, the example of the register shows the refinement of Boulez's work. To be convinced of this, we need only examine sonority-sections 2–4 of this excerpt (see **Example 5.6**), the first lasting – if we take into account the tempo variations – 2.13", the second less than 0.9" owing to an *accel.*, and the third more than 1.38" because of a *rit*. The occupation of the

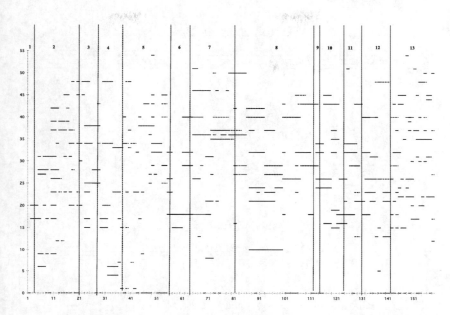

Example 5.5 Pierre Boulez, *Le Marteau sans maître*, 4. 'Commentaire II de "Bourreaux de Solitude"', measures 1–18: transcription. The ordinates represent the pitches, form the low E of the guitar (ordinate 1) to the high A (54) of the xylophone (the bells are noted in ordinate 0). The abscissas represent the time, their unit being the semiquaver; not taken into account are the frequent tempo changes or their progressive variations; the *fermate*, which separate the 13 sections, are indicated by the vertical dots. The thickness of the strokes suggests six different intensities; --pp – p - -mp — mf – – f — ff.[6]

register is constantly renewed in extreme concision (small duration), which reinforces the idea of a section as synonymous with a composed sound. The second section includes sixty different attacks, which can be doubly reduced: at forty-three, if we suppose that a note immediately going from one instrument to another is attacked only once (the transcription is constructed according to this hypothesis), and, at seventeen, if we retain only the different notes. It goes without saying that these seventeen pitches encompass the chromatic total; however, the resulting sonority is 'softened' by the fact that the disposition proceeds according to a quasi-symmetry: in relation to the middle F sharp, the seven pitches in the lower register and the nine in the upper register form an almost perfect mirror. In addition, the three low notes are doubled at the octave, the first even being tripled. We could therefore speak of an inharmonic spectrum. The third section plays on only fourteen attacks, ten of which have different notes: here, the disposition is regular (five low notes and five high), but the distribution is random. Finally, the fourth sonority (seventeen attacks), which has twelve notes (including a doubling of one of the low notes, the G), is totally asymmetrical: if we divide the register in two,

154 *Composing sound*

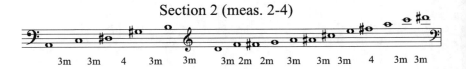

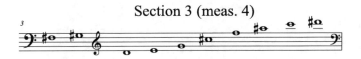

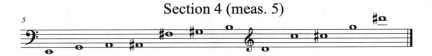

Example 5.6 Pierre Boulez, *Le Marteau sans maître*, 'Commentaire II de "Bourreaux de Solitude"', measures 2–4, 4 and 5: registers.

there are twice as many pitches in the low register as in the high; similarly, the distribution is quite irregular.

Of course, this interpretation, which evokes attacks/composed resonances is something of a metaphor – doubtless a bit less than for Webern's *Opus 21*. But it perhaps explains the charm of this beginning of the fourth piece of *Le Marteau sans maître*, the syncretic perception being able to appreciate these composed sounds for their morphological variety, and their dynamic or melodic (in a broad sense of the term) profile – not to mention the 'African' charm of the timbres.

Electroacoustic resonances

The model of composed resonance also allows for understanding how electroacoustic music, at its beginnings, also opened up the path leading to a work conceived fully as composed sound. The idea of resonance, taken in a very general, metaphorical sense – for example, a simple continuum – or in a literal sense, incites composers to think entire sections of the work on the model of sound composed on a vast scale, i.e., according to the logic of the fusion of form and material. Here, we could again mention the beginnings of electronic music with Stockhausen's *Elektronische Studie I*. It is also the case, in the 1960s and 1970s with several electroacoustic, live electronics or mixed (instruments and tape) works, composed in the various studios that came into being at the time. Let us comment on three pieces.

Amongst the musical works related mainly to *musique concrète*, Pierre Henry's *Le Voyage* (1962) is in a position to illustrate this paradigm of composed resonance. Originally conceived for a ballet by Maurice Béjart, the work is based on *The Tibetan Book of the Dead*, which indicates how to accompany the dead person during the 'in-between' period when he has the possibility of freeing himself from the infernal cycle of reincarnations. A long (50 minutes) work, *Le Voyage* is made up of seven movements. The movements that best embody the model of composed resonance are *Souffle 1*, *Divinités paisibles* and *Le couple*, in particular because they are constructed in an almost total continuum. *Souffle 1* 'is constituted from a single flow of breath, which goes through three states' (M. Chion, 2003: 90; our translation): a first part in which the breath is calm; a second (beginning at 1'22") where, with the human element intervening, the sound is uneven; and a third (beginning at 4'24") where, after an explosion, sound becomes smooth again (the timings are given by P. Henry, 1992). The fourth movement, *Divinités paisibles*, which constitutes the centre of the work, is 'conceived on "delta" form, as concerns the overall form, as well as in relation to the sounds that compose it. Like hearing a train pass [...], it begins in the distance, passes at top speed, and dies out' (M. Chion, 2003: 93). This form, whether for the entire work or each sound taken separately, contributes to creating the sensation of a resonance finely composed for this movement. But the very nature of the sounds makes it even more so: it is a matter of sounds of 'vibrating stems', realised in the 1950s (at the time when Henry was still working for French Radio), i.e., 'metal stems stuck at one end, which we make oscillate or which we rub [... and which] will be heard again abundantly in works of the 1990s' (M. Chion, 2003: 87). As for the movement entitled *Le couple*, made up of Larsen sound effects and rough electronic sounds, it proposes 'a closed, dramatic form, that of an implacable crescendo, burning and accumulating a tension that rises to the unbearable' (M. Chion, 2003: 95).

One mixed work would be quite representative of the idea of composing sound materialised by what is called here electric resonance: Luigi Nono's *...sofferte onde serene...* (1976), for piano and tape (see **Example 5.7 online,** which gives the end of the score – the part that is played). The untranslatable title (literally: 'suffered, serene waves') is linked to tragic deaths that bound the Italian composer to his pianist friend who gave the first performance, Maurizio Pollini. The resonant character doubtless comes from the image of Venice: 'At home in Venice, on the isle of the Giudecca, various bell sounds, of different provenances and meanings come to me continually, by day and by night, through the fog and with the sun', wrote Nono (2007: 662; our translation). The tape part is entirely elaborated, like a gigantic composed resonance in the form of a mirror, from reworked piano recordings:

> Recordings by Pollini, made in the studio, especially attacks of sounds, his extremely articulated way of hitting the keys, different fields of intervals, were then composed on tape, always at the RAI Studio di Fonologia Musicale in Milan, with the assistance of Marino Zuccheri. From this result two acoustic planes that often 'merge', frequently cancelling out the mechanical strangeness of the tape. Between these two planes, what was studied

were the relations of sound formation, particularly the use of vibrations of pedal blows, which are perhaps particular resonances 'from the depths of our being'. These are not 'episodes' that are exhausted in succession, but 'memoirs' and 'presences' that superimpose and which, as memoirs and presences, also merge with the serene waves [reference to the title: 'suffered, serene waves'].

(L. Nono, 2007: 662; our translation)

In the field of real-time processing, we could mention the work of Gordon Mumma, pioneer of both live electronic music and computer music. As concerns live electronic music, he also innovated by inventing the concept of 'cybersonics', which designates:

a situation in which the electronic processing of sound activities is determined (or influenced) by the interactions of the sounds with themselves – that interaction itself being 'collaborative'. As both a composer and a sound designer with analog-electronic technology, I have experienced no separation between the collaborative processes of composing and instrument-building.

(G. Mumma, 2005)

This concept, which can also include interaction with the audience and the acoustics of the performance venue, thereby prefigures the sound installations in the form of the 'audible ecosystems' of an Agostino Di Scipio. The CD version of *Cybersonic Cantilevers* (1973) stems from a performance given in a New York museum. Visitors were invited to produce sounds serving as material for the piece, and these sounds were then treated by the 'cybersonic' processors developed by Mumma. The result was transmitted back through loudspeakers in the museum. Visitors could again reinject material or else transform this initial result. Throughout the day, as the material and transformations accumulated, the result became richer and richer. During the final hour, the audience concentrated on the fine-tuning of the existing material. In the result preserved on CD, the second and final part of the piece, a very long track (from 7'50" to the end, or 19'16" in all) constitutes, in a way, a finely worked resonance, stemming from the work carried out during this last hour.

From rock to disco: the studio as site for the composition of sound

Again going back to the 1960s, let us now broach popular music. Here we might also use the notion of (composed) 'resonance' in a metaphorical way, to designate the fact that 'sound', having become increasingly important, encompasses, in a way, 'music'. To tell the truth, the notion of 'arrangement' would also be suitable: there is a classic skeleton (melody, harmony and rhythm), which, through arrangement, takes on a new carnal envelope: sound. The principal tool of arrangement is henceforth the *studio*. Indeed, although this was long conceived primarily as a place devoted to recording and the most faithful reproduction of 'live', starting in the late 1950s, it freed itself. As Virgil Moorefield (2005: XIII) wrote:

> Over the last fifty years, the philosophy and technique of music production have undergone a major transformation. As the activity of recording has widened in scope from a primarily technical matter to a conceptual and artistic one as well, it has assumed a central role in areas such as instrumental arrangement and the sculpting and placement of audio samples. The concept of a *sound* in the sense of stylistic choice, and the ability to capture and mold it, have grown in importance as recording technology has become increasingly complex.

Phil Spector is customarily mentioned as one of the first producers to contribute to this evolution, and his name will remain associated with the 'wall of sound'. This model consisted of having several similar instruments play in the studio. Musicians recognised Phil Spector as one of their own, capable of enriching their music with studio innovations and considerable imagination that was specifically musical. Brian Wilson (quoted in V. Moorefield, 2005: 16–17), in a late interview, would distinguish his aesthetic of 'instrumental clarity' from the wall of sound aesthetic but acknowledge that Spector 'knew in his head what he wanted before he got to studio. [... One learned from him] that if you had a piano and a guitar and combined them together that created a third sound. You get a different sound'.

In the mid-1960s, one title made studio work progress: the Beach Boys' *Good Vibrations* (1966). The leader of the group, Brian Wilson, whom we have just quoted, was composer, singer and bass player, as well as producer. It is perhaps to this latter capacity that we owe the originality of this song. Wilson invented the modular method, consisting of doing several takes and carrying out a final mixing of the passages selected from the different takes (the song apparently necessitated seventeen sessions in four different studios and used a total of 90 hours of tape). The refrain will remain as a highpoint of sensuality and 'good vibes' with its Theremin or cello playing triplets.

The album that marked the history of rock as an almost total studio product is *Sgt. Pepper's Lonely Hearts Club Band* (1967) by The Beatles, and especially 'A Day in the Life'. 'Made in a total of around thirty-four hours, "A Day in the Life" represents the peak of The Beatles' achievement. With one of their most controlled and convincing lyrics, its musical expression is breathtaking, its structure at once utterly original and completely natural', wrote Ian MacDonald (1994: 231). Last track on the album, even though composed at the beginning of the recording, this song – as is the case with 'Tomorrow Never Knows' (commented on in Chapter 2) – probably refers to LSD: the sung verses 1, 2 and 4 doubtless attest to the absurdity of the world and 'the alienating effect of "the media"' (Ibid: 230); life would be but disillusion, where LSD invites you to 'turn' – the second and fourth verses end with the phrase 'I'd love to turn you on', introducing the two famous sequences in *glissandi*.

158 Composing sound

These three verses, sung by John Lennon, even though masterfully arranged, recorded and reworked with studio effects, derive from classic song peculiar to pop music. The same is true of the third – even though it introduces a break – sung by Paul McCartney who, in it, relates his awakenings during his school years. Legend has it that, between the second (Lennon) and third (McCartney) verses, which have nothing in common, the Beatles left 24 measures of silence 'counted by road manager Mal Evans, whose reverbed voice remains on the finished' (Ibid: 231) (at 1'41" and 3'46"), waiting to know how they would connect them. At a party at the Abbey Road studio, where the recording took place, the Beatles heard an orchestra. McCartney, who had already listened to avant-garde orchestral works (by, amongst others, Stockhausen, whose photo appears on the album cover), then thought of linking these parts with an orchestral interlude, played by a 'symphony orchestra going from its lowest to its highest note in an unsynchronised slide: a "freak out" or aural "happening"' (I. MacDonald, 1994: 231). It was George Martin who organised this orchestral interlude; during the recording, 'Geoff [Geoff Emerick, recording engineer] was tweaking away at the studio's built-in "ambiophony" system, which instantly fed the music back through the hundred speakers spaced around the studio walls to create a customized – and highly amplified – sound' (V. Moorefield, 2005: 33).

During the second orchestral glissando, after the last verse, George Martin asked the orchestral musicians to make their way towards an E major chord. Then, without transition, a passage is mounted where this chord is attacked on three pianos (played by Lennon, McCartney, Ringo Starr, Evans and Martin) and doubled four times. Here we have a veritable composed resonance (see **Example 5.8**). In fact, the resonance of this chord is prolonged (it lasts nearly 43") by manually augmenting the volume on the potentiometers – which is why we end up hearing sounds of people in the studio (around 4'50"). Moreover, one will notice on the spectrogram, after a brief silence, the famous frequency too high to be truly audible (at 5'06" in the song) (to extend the analysis, see A.F. Moore, 1997).

In 1973, another album heightened the importance of sound with studio work: *The Dark Side of the Moon* by Pink Floyd, also produced in the Abbey

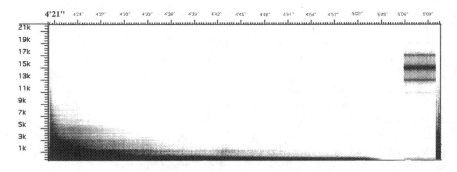

Example 5.8 Beatles, *Sgt. Pepper's Lonely Hearts Club Band*, 'A Day in the Life': 4'21"-5'12": spectrogram (realised on Audacity).

Road studios. Thanks to the mastery of stereo and reverberation, Pink Floyd put the finishing touches to the construction of a sound in which the listener is totally immersed, and which procures a feeling of well-being. The arrival of the first song, 'Breathe' is significant in this regard: it emerges from the overture, 'Speak to Me', with a spectacular fade-in, which results in a sensual sound enveloping the listener from all sides. Another revolution: the use of concrete sounds. The album opens ('Speak to Me') with a mixing of voices, sounds of slot machines, laughter, helicopters, cries – not to overlook the bass drum played so as to simulate a heartbeat. 'On the Run', which follows 'Breathe', imitates a pursuit, with drums played continuously in an oppressive way, synthesisers producing whirling effects, running noises, airport announcements, helicopters turning or 'crossing' the loudspeakers, voices and ironic laughter, and anguished cries, ending up in the final explosion, leading to the alarm clocks on the following track, 'Time'. The beginning of 'Money' is equally famous, with Roger Waters constructing loops of diverse sounds produced by coins. We will also emphasise the use of synthesisers, often in a veritable logic of sound synthesis, at least production of sounds escaping the 'instrument' category. This is the case with the EMS VCS 3 (see **Example 5.9 online**), built in 1969, which marks the songs 'Any Colour You Like' and 'Brain Damage'. One will notice that the recording used sixteen-track tape recorders, whereas *Sgt. Pepper's* was obliged to settle for four tracks. Finally, what is interesting, and which marked a turning point in the history of relations between musicians and producers, is that Pink Floyd also acted as producers.

To pursue this brief history of composed sound in the framework of popular music, one of the important names to mention is Brian Eno. The former musician of the glam rock group Roxy Music theorised about the evolution that allowed for the transition from the studio conceived as a recording venue to the studio conceived as a veritable place of composition. In a 1979 reading with the title 'The studio as compositional tool', he wrote:

> Till about the late '40s, recording was simply regarded as a device for transmitting a performance to an unknown audience, and the whole accent of recording technique was on making what was called a 'more faithful' transmission of that experience. [...] Now this is a significant step, I think; it's the first time it was acknowledged that the performance isn't the finished item, and that the work can be added to in the control room or in the studio itself. For the first time composers [...] were thinking, 'Well, this is the music. What can I do with it? I've got this extra facility of one track'. [...] Then it went to four-track [...] After four-track it moved to eight track – this was in '68, I guess – then very quickly escalated: eight-track till '70, 16-track from '70 to '74, 24-track to now when you can easily work on 48-track, for instance, and there are such things as 64-track machines. [...] From that impulse two things happened: you got an additive approach to recording, the idea that composition is the process of adding more [...]; it also gave rise to the particular area that I'm involved in: in-studio composition, where you no longer come to the studio with a conception of the finished piece. Instead, you come with

160   *Composing sound*

actually rather a bare skeleton of the piece, or perhaps with nothing at all. I often start working with no starting point.

(B. Eno, 1983: 50–52)

If we must mention Eno as a composer developing this idea, an important reference would be his first *ambient* album, which we have already mentioned in Chapter 4: *Music for Airports* (1978). The disc's four tracks are based on an assemblage of loops put together entirely in the studio from musicians' recordings. For the first, '1/1', Eno tells us:

I had four musicians in the studio, and we were doing some improvising exercises that I'd suggested. I couldn't hear the musicians very well at the time, and I'm sure they couldn't hear each other, but listening back, later, I found this very short section of tape where two pianos, unbeknownst to each other, played melodic lines that interlocked in an interesting way. To make a piece of music out of it, I cut that part out, made a stereo loop on the 24-track, then I discovered I liked it best at half speed, so the instruments sounded very soft, and the whole movement was very slow. I didn't want the bass and guitar – they weren't necessary for the piece – but there was a bit of Fred Frith's guitar breaking through the acoustic piano mic, a kind of scrape […] I had to find a way of dealing with that scrape, and I had the idea of putting in variable orchestration each time the loop repeated. You only hear Fred's scrape the first time the loop goes around.

(B. Eno, 1983: 50–52)

To conclude, we shall mention the emergence of disco, in which this compositional work in studio is perhaps even more flagrant: it is a musical genre in which the producer is quite often the central figure, alongside, of course, the singer. Let us mention Giorgio Moroder, to whom we owe the production of 'Love to Love You Baby' (1975), which magnifies the voice and sensuality of Donna Summer, the 'lady of the thousand orgasms', so nicknamed because, in the song, she moans, pants and simulates love-making. There are two versions of this song: the first lasts some three minutes, the second (produced for the homonymous album) more than sixteen. This second version begins and ends with the original version. The ten-minute middle part juxtaposes several variations, with and without voice, which attest to the mastery of the cumulative process realised in the studio. Quoting the analysis of Robert Fink (2005) – whose book establishes a daring parallelism (!) between 'Love to Love You Baby' and Steve Reich's *Music for Eighteen Musicians* (1974–1976) –**Example 5.10 (online)** transcribes on staves the loops progressively added to the second variation, which begins at 7'15".

Electronic auras

Coming back to contemporary music, the composed resonance aesthetic seems to find a culmination, in the period from the 1980s to the 2000s, in mixed music, where the instrumental coexists with electronic parts. One will think in particular of a repertoire that developed at IRCAM, as well as in other studios, including works such as Pierre Boulez's *Répons* (1981–1984), where the electronics often sound like a 'double' of the instrumental, or its amplification *via* the creation of a halo or its artificial prolongation, giving the sensation of an *aura*, or even an immersion – a feeling heightened in particular when there is elaborate spatialisation work.

Sometimes, this 'aura' feeling is created by the fact that the electronics are worked so that the frequential components sound like an echo in the instrumental part. This is especially the case with music stemming from Spectralism, like Kaija Saariaho's earliest works, centred on the timbre-harmony relation. In *Amers* (1992), for solo cello, instrumental ensemble and electronics, the material is 'deduced' from a cello sound, thanks to several spectral analyses of a trill by varying the pressure and position of the bow. **Examples 5.11** and **5.12 (online)** provides the analytical data of two cello trills, the first with normal pressure and position of the bow, the second with greater pressure of the bow and *sul ponticello* position. As for the procedural aspect so characteristic of spectral scores, in each part of the work we witness evolutions that are sometimes imperceptible – or, at least, quite progressive – as attests, for example, the evolution of pitches at the beginning of the work, where a single spectrum seems to unfold, becoming richer or poorer at times (see **Example 5.13 online** which shows a reduction of it). The electronic transformations, which affect the cello, use the Iana,

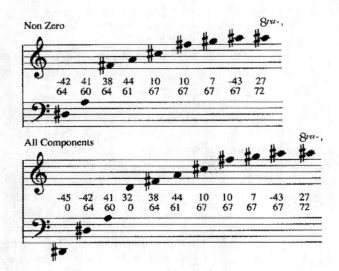

Example 5.11 Kaija Saariaho, *Amers:* spectral analysis of the trill with normal pressure and positions of the bow (I. Stoïanova, 1994: 54). © By kind permission of Ivanka Stoïanova. The first series of figures indicates the relative amplitudes, the second, the perceptual weight; on the second staves are seen all the frequencies and on the first, those having a pertinent perceptual weight.

CHANT programmes, the Phase Vocoder SVP and IRCAM's Mosaïc (renamed Modalys) physical modelling synthesis programme (see M. Battier, ed., 1994 and I. Stoïanova, 1994). They aim at generating a sound halo that sometimes tends to merge with the instrumental, as in letters GG-HH.

A second example of 'electronic aura' is provided by Fausto Romitelli, a composer who died prematurely. Heir of Spectralism, which he enriched and took in new directions, Romitelli realised several works at IRCAM in which the aura favours dirt. He liked to refer to Bacon and rock, asserting, as regards the latter:

> Sound in contemporary music is 'castrated' by formalism and dogmas on the purity of musical material: a cerebral, body-less sound, without flesh or blood. Personally, I like the dirty sound, distorted, violent, and visionary, that pop music sometimes manages to express and which I strive to integrate in my writing.
>
> (in A. Arbo, ed., 2005b: 143; our translation)

The saturated energy of his music gives rise to an intense, perturbing feeling of sound 'presence', which the composer expresses verbally regarding *EnTrance* (1995–1996, for soprano, ensemble and electronics), saying that, in it, he wanted to abandon 'any dialogic, discursive, dialectic and purely formal desire, in favour of a desire for sound presence, immobile and continuous, hypnotic, spherical and rolling in time and space' (F. Romitelli, 1996). Alessandro Arbo (2005a: 43) summed up Romitelli's aesthetic well: 'The aesthetic category that this music most often puts into play is the sublime dynamic: the paradoxical pleasure felt before a sudden unleashing of forces'.

His *Professor Bad Trip* (1998–2000) cycle, made up of three pieces, illustrates perfectly the idea of composed resonance according to a logic of shaded aura. In his notes for the full cycle he wrote:

> What prevails in *Professor Bad Trip* is the hypnotic and ritual aspect, the taste for deformity and the artificial; haunting repetitions, continuous, insistent accelerations of materials and time subjected to torsions and distortions to the point of saturation, white noise, and catastrophe, a constant drift towards chaos, objects named and already liquefied; unbearable speed and density; itineraries aborted, interrupted, or else brutally predictable, like a missile's trajectory.
>
> (F. Romitelli in A. Arbo, ed., 2005b: 55; our translation)

The first of the three works, *Professor Bad Trip. Lesson I* (1998), is written for an ensemble of eight instrumentalists (flute and bass flute, bass clarinet, electric guitar, piano and electronic keyboards, percussion, violin, viola, cello) and electronics. The piece begins with a part that confirms the composer's taste for 'haunting repetitions'. This part, which could be described as a 'phenomenon of accumulated energy' (P. Michel, 2005: 67), is finely composed from the inside in keeping with the idea of a total *fusion* of the elements (including the electronics): it will be understood that it is this fusion that generates the aura feeling. **Example 5.14 (online)** provides an excerpt from one of the 'fusional' highpoints of this part. It consists of several overlapping layers supplementing each other: winds, guitar, electric keyboard, vibraphone and strings, electronic sounds, the overall result being 'a rich, particularly continuous texture, in motion, where it is difficult to isolate one element or another' (Ibid: 71).

Composed sonorities

'Sonority'

In 20th-century instrumental (and mixed) music, the idea of composed resonance can be thought as part of a more general tendency to compose the material. To give a name to the more general case, I shall speak of *sonority*. This notion designates an overall entity, fully constructed and composed from the inside, stemming from the dissolution of classic dimensions of sound (pitch, rhythm, timbre...), i.e., the loss of their autonomy. The recomposition and fusion of these dimensions generates sonority as a surplus, an emerging quality. It also ensues from the merger of form and material.

The choice of the term 'sonority' indicates that we are close to the notion of 'sound', but it is a matter of composed sound, articulated, built, i.e., an artefact and not natural sound – even less 'timbre'. Moreover, in instrumental music, it designates the merger of sounds of instruments in vaster overall natures. As sonority emerges in different ways, let us examine a few of them.

Organised sound (2)

Resolutely modern in an historical context – pre-1945 – where neo-classicism dominated, Varèse looks like a precursor in many domains converging on sound: the aforementioned use of noise, composition by volumes and masses, the quest for new instruments. In Chapter 2, we said that Varèse proposed a new appellation for music, 'organised sound', which allows for going beyond the split between noise and musical sound. Varèse himself would tend to reserve the expression for the tape part of *Déserts* (1950–1954, for instrumental ensemble and tape) and for *Poème électronique* (1957–1958, tape alone), i.e., in reference to new sounds (sounds recorded and transformed, electric sounds) that he had for the first time the occasion to develop in the 1950s. But we can also apply it to his instrumental music, which can be analysed using the notion of sonority, as attests *Ionisation*.

Composed in Paris in 1929–1931 and first performed in New York in 1933, *Ionisation* is written for thirteen percussionists, practically a first in the universe of western music. With percussion, Varèse carried out a triple movement: he moved away from instruments of the traditional orchestra at a time still too linked to the Romantic universe; he simultaneously abandoned the universe of pitches and opened up the universe of complex sounds (noises). To understand their use, it is important to classify all the percussion instruments used in *Ionisation* in seven categories (see C. Wen-Chung, 1979: 28–29), within which the instruments are named according to their register (from high to low): 1. metals: triangle, two anvils, cencerro, cymbal, large Chinese cymbal, suspended cymbal, gong, two tam-tams, large tam-tam; 2. untuned skins: bongos, snare drum, tenor drum, two bass drums, very low bass drum; 3. tuned skins: tarole, side drum, military drum; 4. wooden: claves, three Chinese wood blocks, whip; 5. instruments that are scraped or shaken: (small) bells, castanets, tambourine, maracas, güiro; 6. wind or friction instruments: two sirens, 'lion's roar'; 7. keyboards: glockenspiel, chimes, piano.

Several analysts who have studied *Ionisation*, whilst stressing the extraordinary novelty of its sound material, describe the work according to traditional listening, giving a *thematic* reading of it – it is the case with Nicolas Slonimsky, the famous conductor and friend of Varèse. 'One might believe [...] an acoustic "experiment" inspired by the theory of electrolytic dissociation; one discovers a sort of sonata', Marc Bredel wrote (1984: 143; our translation). It is true that the famous phrase of the military drum in measure 9 functions as a theme (see Example 5.16). This reading of *Ionisation* is relevant, but only in part: a more detailed analysis reveals its limits. Thus, it is difficult to find another phrase as meaningful, which would serve as a second theme, especially if we think in terms of sonata form: significantly, Nicolas Slonimsky, who evoked a 'sonata-overture', hesitated over the choice of a phrase as second theme – his first analysis (in E. Varèse, 1967) hears it in measure 44, whereas his second (in O. Vivier, 1973: 99) localises it in the Chinese wood blocks beginning in measure 18. Above all, 'if one seeks to make a thematic analysis, one immediately runs up against the absence of development, variation, or accompaniment' (F.-B. Mâche, 1983: 113–114; our translation). It is possible to enumerate the ensemble of rhythmic cells used in *Ionisation* and show that the work does not ensue from development[7]: 'It is derived exclusively from the context of the conditions of [...] literal repetition of the motivic-timbric identities, control of the length of the instrumental interventions and polyphonic superpositions' (J.-C. François, 1991: 60).

This is why, as with Webern, another kind of listening must be solicited. We will have to have waited for Chou Wen-Chung's analysis (1979) for musicologists to emphasise this other listening that goes via the notion which Wen-Chung calls 'texture', and which, here, we call 'sonority'. It is the work's particular charm, which can be followed according to traditional, thematic listening – with the limits that have just been underscored – as well as according to the new listening centred on sound. However, as soon as the ear subscribes to the notion of sonority, not only does it immediately hear the sonorities of *Ionisation* but also hears them in the whole piece. In fact, the entire work can be analysed with the notion of sonority, a sonority consisting of a totality resulting from the convergence of all the dimensions of sound operative in *Ionisation*: rhythm, timbre, register, density, space (role of sirens), articulation – only intensity seems organised autonomously.

The work is based on three sonorities and begins with their exposition. The first appears at the beginning, in measures 1–8. **Example 5.15** provides a reduction of measures 1–4. The reduction constitutes in itself the start of an analysis:

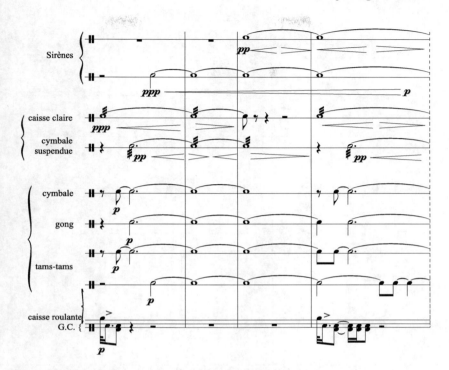

Example 5.15 Edgar Varèse, *Ionisation*, measures 1–4: reduction.

in the organisation of the rhythmic lines, it takes into account both the nature of each sonority, the seven categories of percussion and the register. This first sonority can be listened to like a gong sound transposed to the macroscopic: a very muffled attack in the low register (measure 1: tenor and bass drums) is followed by the progressive appearance of 'harmonics' (according to their order of appearance, measures 1–3: side drum, cymbal and high tam-tam, suspended cymbal and gong, low tam-tam and low siren, high siren). These 'harmonics' can be unvarying in intensity, with small crescendos followed by diminuendos or else with large crescendos. The whole starts over twice (measures 4–5 and 5–8) with very rich variations and ending with an overall crescendo; the ensemble of measures 1–8 can thereby also be considered a unique 'gong sound'. This sonority is the result of precise values taken by each of the dimensions mentioned: long *tenuti* or very brief attacks for the rhythm; combination of low skins, metallic sounds and sirens for timbre, low or middle register, low density, spatial sensation (sirens). To the degree that the four groups of sounds making it up (from bottom to top in our reduction: attack, *tenuti*, *tenuti* with rolls and slight variations in intensity, sirens) merge perfectly, this sonority, unlike the other two, is noticeably on the side of overall sound ('gong sound') and that is why, to the ear of the thematic reading, it can only appear as an 'introduction'.

166 *Composing sound*

Example 5.16 Edgar Varèse, *Ionisation*, measures 9–12: reduction.

The second occurs in measures 9–12 (**Example 5.16**). The groups of sounds making it up do not merge but are superimposed. This sonority is most closely related to traditional writing, hence the thematic reading, which, precisely, recognises the main 'theme' of *Ionisation* in this passage: a 'main line' (military drum) is played in counterpoint to a 'secondary line' (bongos), the whole being 'accompanied' (maracas, cymbals and very low bass drum, whip). However, here too, when we step back, we can clearly speak of sonority. Despite the relative independence of these three layers – accentuated by the structural difference between the first (twice eight crotchets) and the other two (twice three-three-two crotchets) – there is indeed an overall result with all the dimensions taking particular values: precise rhythm deriving from the very possibilities of the instruments (for the three layers), timbre dominated by the skins, register higher than the first sonority, density noticeably greater.

After a brief return of sonorities 1 and 2, the third suddenly appears in measures 18–20 (**Example 5.17 online**). On the level of the relation between detail and global nature, this sonority is located exactly between the other two. It borrows the merging of the constituent elements of the first for one of its three components, in the upper register (instruments that are shaken: bells, castanets and tambourine). But its second component, based on the succession of lines of the tarole and Chinese wood blocks, can also pass for the 'main line', which would be 'accompanied' by the first, as well as the third (bass drums which allow for tying this sonority to the second). Here are the values that the various dimensions

Composing sound 167

take to configure this sonority from the inside: rhythm partially derived by the diminution of the previous phrase of the military drum (tarole), the combination of two other cells (Chinese wood blocks) or a third (instruments that are shaken); complex timbre (low skins, skins with snare, woods and shaken instruments); high register; greatest density of the three sonorities.

It has been said that the entire work can be analysed with the notion of sonority. In fact, all of *Ionisation* can be apprehended as the elaboration of the three sonorities according to three procedures: superposition, fusion and envelopment. A first part introduces the three sonorities: sonority 1, then 2 (measure 9), 1 (measure 13) and 2 (measure 17) once again and finally 3 (measure 18). In a second part, which begins at measure 21 with sonority 2, we have superimpositions: 1/2/3 (measure 23), 1/2/3 (measure 28) and 1/2/3 (measure 31) again, then 2/3 (measure 33) and 1/2/3 (measure 35) again. The third part gives rise to fusions: 1+2+3/2/3 (measure 38) and 1+2+3 (measure 44). The fifth part, after sonority 1 alone (measure 51), alternates superimpositions and fusions: 1/2/3 (measure 56), 1+2+3 (measure 66), 1/2/3 (measure 67), 1+2+3 (measure 68), 1/2/3 (measure 69), 3 alone (measure 72), 1+2+3 (measure 73). In the last part, which begins at measure 75, sonority 1 envelops the other two.

Example 5.18 (measures 23–26) illustrates the superposition process, which dominates in the second large part of *Ionisation*. The first sonority is reduced to one of its components, the *tenuti*, moreover, entrusted to a single instrument. Sonorities 2 and 3 are treated equally. The second is based on the superposition of a main line (bongos), a secondary line (military drum and tenor drum) – exchange of timbres in relation to the first exposition of this sonority – and of an accompaniment here reduced to punctuations (rim shots and whip). The third sonority, in the upper register, is quite similar to its first occurrence. This example also illustrates the most important procedure implemented by Varèse to proceed to the superposition of sonorities, namely, the creation of intermediary lines, which allow for making the connection between the sonorities dominating in the superposition, in this case, 2 and 3 in this passage: the 'accompaniment' of the very low bass drum (and large cymbal) belong, as has been said, just as much to sonority 2 as to 3; the maracas and güiro are rhythmically close to the second but, as to their timbre (instruments that are shaken or scraped), are akin to one of the timbres making up the third.

The third large part of *Ionisation* is dominated by processes of sonority fusion. Abruptly, at measure 38, the work is reduced in a succession of two overall gestures, decomposable in numerous quasi-repetitive small gestures. Up to measure 44, the fusion is not total, leaving aside certain aspects of sonorities 2 and 3, which are superimposed on it. On the other hand, from measure 44 to measure 50, only the fusion subsists, during the second overall gesture. **Example 5.19 (online)** reduces its beginning,[8] which is broken down into three gestures: two almost identical, each based on the triplet-quintuplet-triplet succession (in the second gesture, the end of the quintuplet and the beginning of the second triplet differ in register and thus in instruments due to the introduction of a rest in the quintuplet) and one which doubly prolongs the middle of this gesture (quintuplet). The fusion is total, for the values taken by the rhythm and density – different for the three

168 *Composing sound*

Example 5.18 Edgar Varèse, *Ionisation*, measures 23–26: reduction.

sonorities in their exposition or superposition – are common to them here. Only the values of timbre and register allow for dissociating them: metallic sounds, friction instruments or low skins for the first (cencerro, cymbal, tenor drum and bass drums, lion's roar and very low bass drum), skins with or without snare for the second (bongos, military drum and tenor drum), skins with snare, woods or shaken instruments for the third (castanets, tambourine, maracas, Chinese wood blocks, tarole and side drum). As for register, our reduction shows its importance: on the one hand, contrary to what might be believed, this passage is not a succession of timbres but a movement of (relative) pitch; on the other, we note that the two triplets envelop (as for their register) the central quintuplet. Although the third sonority remains the highest, and the second is still confined in the middle register, the first (which concludes the second triplet, first with the cencerros in the highest register then with the bass drum in the extreme low register) tends to extend over the whole register, which already announces the process of envelopment characterising the work's final measures.

Composing sound 169

The final example (**Example 5.20**) comes from the last part of *Ionisation*, called 'coda' by nearly all the commentators, a term overly rooted in thematic reading to be able to be used here. It is possible to see a part in itself here, wherein the third procedure intervenes for the first time: the first sonority *envelops* the other two. On the one hand, this sonority has increased from the keyboards, which our example reduces to their rhythmic play, for their sound aggregates (of which the pitches, frozen in the register, amount to what can already be considered a 'spectrum' in the sense of music called 'spectral') do not vary. On the other hand,

Example 5.20 Edgar Varèse, *Ionisation*, measures 75–82: reduction.

170 *Composing sound*

sonorities 2 and 3 have been absorbed and no longer exist except in the form of residue: residues of the principal and secondary lines (extended here over five relative pitches) for the second; residues of the alternation of Chinese wood blocks and tarole combined with the side drum for the third. Diluted, these two sonorities are enveloped by the first, which turns out to be a true 'oceanic' sonority, in which everything ends up being immersed.

Continua

Research on the continuum has also contributed to the emergence of sonority. Continuum is on the side of morphology, thus of sound, where discrete division implies combinatorics and lends itself more to the notion of note. It can affect several dimensions of musical construction: pitch, form, timbre. If we think of pitch, it can materialise either with the help of a very small basic interval (infrachromaticism), or with the *glissando*. In the first case – for example, we can imagine a basic interval of a sixteenth-tone – we continue to perceive pitches, however, the difference between neighbouring pitches barely being perceptible as an interval (of pitches), we are in the presence of a *sound* variation. As for the *glissando*, it breaks down the notion of note and constitutes a sonority in itself. As we know, Xenakis was the first composer to have put the *glissando* into widespread use. Not hesitating to write about *Pithoprakta* (1955–1956) that 'sound-points, or granular sounds […] are in reality a particular case of sounds of continuous variation' (I. Xenakis, 1992: 13), he likened the *glissando* to a 'speed', which would enable him, in certain pieces, to calculate the 'slope' of the *glissando* (the interval covered, divided by the duration). Elsewhere, he would use graph paper to construct his *glissandi* (see later examples in this chapter as well as the beginning of *Mikka*, shown in Chapter 2). Even if they are related to pitches, *glissandi* belong clearly to the universe of sound morphologies. It is also often the case with later composers who, in the lineage of Xenakis, used various forms of *glissando*, such as Francisco Guerrero, Julio Estrada and Alberto Posadas, or who were interested in *glissando* via other paths, as is the case with Chaya Czernowin or Clara Maïda (see **Example 5.21 online:** excerpt from ...*who holds the strings*..., 2003, for string quartet). We should also mention the Chinese and Far-Eastern composers for whom the *glissando* constitutes a natural figure, given that they practise it in the language:

> 'It is impossible for us to write straight things; that comes from how we speak', asserts Leilei Tian. There are quite numerous examples of this, and the *glissando* can be at the very basis of the structuring of certain pieces as, for example, in Tan Dun's (1986–88) Second String Quartet or Zhou Long's *The Immortal*.
>
> (M.H. Bernard, 2011: 282–283; our translation)

Research on continuum on the level of timbre was already at work in the Schoenbergian notion of melody of timbre (see Chapter 1). It proliferated starting in the 1950s: from Stockhausen's *Kontakte* (see Chapter 4) to spectral music

Composing sound 171

and 'timbre maps' (see Chapter 1), a number of research projects on sound endeavoured to define a continuum on this dimension. On the level of form, the notion of process, which will be discussed further on and which is encountered as of the 1960s with the minimalists or with Ligeti's *Continuum* (see Chapter 3), often aims at creating a temporal sound continuum. One could also mention a particular musical genre, which developed in the late 1990s: drone music, characterised by stable sounds, *tenuti* of all sorts of drones, which established stationary continua – one group of drone music even bore the name Continuum. Astonishingly pioneering in this field is the work of Éliane Radigue from the late 1960s, starting with systems of feedback and desynchronised tapes then, as of the early 1970s, with the ARP 2500 synthesiser. One could just as easily mention ambient, and its quest for immersion, which was discussed in Chapter 4. Finally, research on the Continuum works on the 'detail of sound' (C. Szlavnics, 2006: 39) in order to open an infinitesimal perception. Let us mention Chiyoko Szlavnics's music, who composes using drawings: **Example 5.22** shows the whole drawing

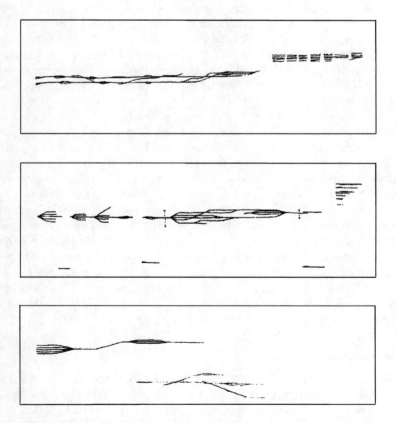

Example 5.22 Chiyoko Szlavnics, *Gradients of Detail:* drawing of the whole piece (C. Szlavnics, 2006b). © By kind permission of Chiyoko Szlavnics.

172 *Composing sound*

that served for the composition of *Gradients of Detail* (string quartet, 2005–2006), of which **Example 5.23 (online)** shows the beginning.

Pierre Boulez (1989: 366; our translation) wrote that 'the continuum is a borderline case, representing indifferentiation, the most general matrix possible, of which the qualities are thus quite limited, given that the characteristics, literally speaking, are absent'. But, precisely, as Francis Bayer (1981: 132; our translation) wrote:

> the particular power that is given off by musical works that swear allegiance to this aesthetic of continuity, stems, it seems to us, from the fact that their significance, since it is immanent to the sensitive, immediately imposes itself on us in favour of a sort of wild perception of our whole body, prior to any analytical approach to our understanding.

The same Boulez (1975: 89; our translation), when treating the continuum in the field of rhythm, tended to enhance its status by evoking 'a music that can do completely without beats; a music that floats'. And it is starting from the Boulezian notion of 'smooth' space that Deleuze and Guattari (1987: 474ss) developed their concept of 'nomadic' art concluding *Mille plateaux*.

One of the pioneers of the notion of continuum was Ivan Wyschnegradsky. The Russian composer's thinking developed with the birth of atonal music in the 1910s and 1920s, after freeing himself from the influence of Scriabin. Having elaborated an extended principle of spatiality, generalised to all audible sounds, he conceived, wrote Pascale Criton (1998a: 79; our translation), the sound continuum as 'plan of establishing thought starting from which new spaces would be able to open out, updating themselves in a diversity of partial continua like so many original cuts or differential positions obtained by the play of spacings of an arithmetisation of sound matter'. Moreover, as for his harmonic system, called 'ultrachromaticism' – which also has its rhythmic equivalent – it goes as far as using twelfths of tones. Thus, in *Arc-en-ciel*, Op. 37 (1956, premiered after the composer's death, in 1988, for six pianos, conceived and realised in the twelfth-tone scale, a sound milieu of density 72: see **Example 5.24 online**), piano 1 is tuned to the conventional diapason, piano 2, 1/12 a tone higher, piano 3, 1/6 higher, piano 4, a quartertone lower, piano 5, 1/6 lower, and piano 6, 1/12 lower – 'the six different degrees of ultrachromatic alteration corresponding to the six colours of the rainbow' (I. Wyschnegradsky, 1956; on the sound/colour relations in Wyschnegradsky, see B. Barthelmes, 1995).

Textures, surfaces, masses

A concept that emerged in the 1960s and 1970s is close to the idea of sonority as developed here: sound 'texture', a concept to which can be linked the notions of sound 'surface' and 'mass'. In musicology, this word has a sense both very vague and precise: we encounter it with Robert Erickson (1975), where he designates a work on timbre in the broad sense of the term, with Wallace Barry (1976), who gives a very general definition, or with Charles Rosen (1975: 36), who wrote, for example, that Schoenberg was the first to perceive that 'timbre, tone color, and texture were not merely accessories but could be as fundamental to music as pitch'. In music itself, one can designate as 'music of texture' the sound masses of a Xenakis, the large surfaces finely composed from the inside by the Ligeti of the 1960s (see the example of *Continuum* in Chapter 3) or the works of the Penderecki of that period (see the example of *De natura sonoris No. 2*, 1971, in Chapter 1).

Xenakis is perhaps the composer who best condensed all the questions linked to the emergence of sonority as composed textures, masses or surfaces. In direct relation with Varèse (see M. Solomos, 2008), following the latter's death, he would say: Varèse was 'the first to "compose" sounds rather than write notes of music' (I. Xenakis, 1965: 38; our translation). He himself did not theorise this new conception of composition – we know that the essential part of his theoretical discourse concerns the question of the formalisation of music. However, there exist a few important passages in his writings that refer to refocussing on sound.

One such passage is to be found in one of his very first articles, 'Problems of Greek musical composition' (I. Xenakis, 1955), written at a very important time of transition: with the composition of *The Sacrifice* (1953) and *Metastaseis* (1953–1954), he went from his youthful works, in which an issue *à la* Bartók dominates (see F.B. Mâche, 2000: 302–321; M. Solomos, 2001), in musical questionings – notion of continuity (*glissandi*), mass, etc. – which would bring him fame. During that period, he hesitated between several paths. Even though already settled in France, he continued to be torn between the Greek musical tradition (he referred primarily to demotic music, i.e., the rural tradition) and western music. But he also had to confront the gap separating western music of the past and that of the avant-garde. In addition, the avant-garde had just split in two: the serial movement (which Xenakis still called 'dodecaphonic') clashed with *musique concrète* ('electronic', in his terms). Finally, he seemed fascinated by the rhythmic qualities of jazz. In a simple, direct language, he posed the question of choice between all these paths: 'What then is the right path? What is the true music? European traditional music, dodecaphonic, electronic, jazz, demotic music?' (I. Xenakis, 1955: 12; our translation).

To answer this question, Xenakis formulated a new one: 'Is there a link between [these types of music]?' (Idem). This question is fundamental and its answer even more so:

> The connection exists. It is the very foundation, the content of sound and the musical art that uses it. [...] Sound in acoustics is analysed in physical-mathematical equations (it is an elastic vibration of matter), which are measured: intensity, colour, time. [...] But as soon as the threshold of the ear is crossed, it becomes impression, sense, and consequently qualitative size. The psychophysiology of music is not yet a science. The good composer will be able to express the meanings he desires.

(Idem)

One might find this response banal. However, here Xenakis did not propose the customary approach, which, rooted in a linguistic conception of music, begins by defining sound, to then go on to music, the 'art of sounds'. He did not contrast a first level of articulation (sound) with a second (music). For this pairing, he substitutes the quantitative/qualitative dichotomy. The qualitative aspect remains somewhat imprecise in his remark as he includes both 'impression' and 'sense'. On the other hand, the quantitative aspect is quite clearly delimited: it is sound. This is therefore no longer defined as a simple level of articulation, a neutral material. Placed as a link between all types of music, for Xenakis it constituted the 'very heart' of music – its *foundation*, we might add.

Setting sound as 'foundation' comes down, in a way, to overturning the traditional outline: sound is no longer treated as the starting point of musical composition but as its endpoint. One could establish a parallel between the debate on the 'crisis of foundations', which went through mathematics in the last century and avant-garde musical research during the same period. Like mathematicians and epistemologists who tried to 'found' mathematics, musicians experimented with several paths to bring out sound as the foundation of music. From Schoenberg's *Klangfarbenmelodie* to the mysticism of Scelsi, there were numerous paths that concentrated, more or less explicitly, on the sound phenomenon itself. They can be grouped in two, taking up the terminology from the debate of the epistemologists: the 'intuitionist' path and the 'axiomatic'.[9] In the former case, it is a matter of 'letting sounds be themselves', according to Cage's famous phrase; in the latter, of *composing sound*.

Xenakis was one of the most important representatives of the second path. A very large part of his music, instrumental as much as electronic, can be analysed and listened to as composed sound, or sound synthesis transposed to the work's temporal scale. Some of his pieces are quite explicit on this point. Such is the case with his last two electronic pieces, composed with the GENDYN program: *Gendy3* (1991) and *S.709* (1994). In Chapter 2, we said that, with this software, an algorithm continuously synthesises the sound starting from probabilist variations of its pressure curve. So, strictly speaking, there is no difference between the synthesis (of sound) and composition (in the traditional sense): in theory, the latter is the immediate result of the former – in Xenakis's conceptual language, 'macrocomposition' results from 'microcomposition' (see I. Xenakis, 1994: 21). The granular conception of sound that Xenakis developed in the late 1950s is also quite revealing: this hypothesis implies that composition (of the entire work) is a synthesis (of sound) on a higher scale.

The compositions that have just been commented on constitute exceptions with Xenakis. The general case is not that of a macrocomposition deduced without mediations of microcomposition, of a composition that would be just a transposed synthesis, were it only because the most important corpus (on the quantitative level) of his production is instrumental and therefore does not call for synthesis or microcomposition. However, it can be shown that a large part of his music can easily be analysed as composed sound. To do so, it suffices to replace the word 'sound' by 'sonority', in order to indicate that the composed object in question is not sound in the physical sense of the term but a more complex entity, for example the entire section of an orchestral work.

Let us take as an example the beginning of *Jonchaies* (1977), starting from measure 10 up to measure 62, which features the strings (as well as a few percussions). This passage constitutes a very long, almost monolithic, section with a progressive, very clear inner evolution like the evolution of a single sound. The strings are divided in eighteen parts, which are coupled or become more individual. The section begins with a unison line in the upper register, following a sinuous itinerary, descending irregularly into the low register. Progressively, other lines enter, with the same itinerary according to a technique that evokes a canon or, more exactly, a heterophonic discourse. In measures 24–29, the whole reaches the low register, then begins an ascension according to the same sinuous, heterophonic logic. In measure 43, one of the lines reaches the highest note, followed progressively by the others. The melodic trajectory then marks time in the upper register before a few lines finally descend again into the low register. Despite its large spreading in time, the very continuous trajectory is sufficiently schematic for the ear to follow from start to finish, as would the eye with an outline (see the graphic transcription provided by J. Harley, 2001: 41). Moreover, this whole passage is based on a single sieve (scale) given in **Example 5.25 online** – a sieve which, according to Xenakis (in B.A. Varga, 1996: 162), would be close to the scale of the *pelog*. But the intention is not the sieve itself, as a succession of pitches. Here, pitch is not a primary characteristic: owing to the fact that it is spread over a fairly long duration, patiently explored over its whole range in so linear a way, and treated in the gigantic halo of sound provoked by the technique of heterophony, one would say that this sieve is used for its colour. In sum, this passage can be perceived as a single sound that is progressively deployed and of which one explores, as under a microscope and with a slow-motion effect, the inner composition as well as the temporal evolution.

In the 'axiomatic' tradition that leads to conceiving the work as composed sound, Xenakis occupied a place that was not only major but also particular. With him, composing sound meant working it like a *sculptor*. Let us examine the graph with which he composed measures 52–59 of *Pithoprakta*[10] (**Example 5.26**). For these few measures, he calculated more than a thousand *glissandi*,[11] using a Gaussian distribution. However, the latter are spread over time thanks to the graph. Also, the overall result – sonority – is, according to the remarks of Xenakis (1956: 31; our tranlsation) himself, 'a plastic modulation of sound matter'. Let us now observe this latter closely. One notes 'holes', voids in entire regions (registers), in the low, high or middle. The work carried out might be compared to a filtering. But one could also evoke the action of the sculptor cutting his block of stone. The block of stone would be the type of sonority that this passage implements: a very dense mass of *pizzicati-glissandi*. The graph, with the intentional gesture that gives it its sharp contours, would then be the equivalent of the work on this block.

Xenakis often composed with graphs, at least up until the late 1970s. Numerous sonorities that he was the first to experiment with and which gave him such a

176 *Composing sound*

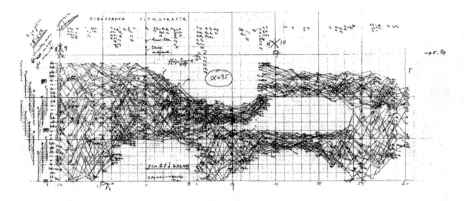

Example 5.26 Iannis Xenakis, *Pithoprakta*, measures 52–59: composer's graph (Archives Xenakis). © By kind permission of Mâkhi Xenakis.

straightforward originality, were imagined thanks to outlines traced on graph paper. The invention of the *glissando*, the Xenakian signature par excellence, was possible thanks to this method. For *Syrmos* (1959: **Example 5.27 online**), which, in a way, constitutes a study on *glissandi*, we have several categories: ascending, descending, crossed, convergent, divergent, in curved surfaces. 'Arborescences' and 'Brownian movements', which dominate the works of the 1970s, also ensue from graphic forms (**Example 5.28 online:** arborescences in *Erikhthon*, 1974). Moreover, in return, one can visually schematise Xenakian sonorities. Several commentators have used graphs as an analytical tool. One will find in **Example 5.29 (online)** my transcription of measures 291–303 of *Terretektorh* (1965–1966), which brings out the extraordinary 'tresses' that characterise numerous passages in this piece.

Composed with or without a graph, Xenakis's music is poles apart from the tradition that makes music an art of time. With it, it tends to become, in a way, an art of space. In a text on time, Xenakis (1994: 94; our translation) asks: 'Is time not simply an epiphenomenon-notion of a more profound reality?'; after having mentioned theories and experiments, sometimes paradoxical, of modern physics, he came to placing space, 'freed of the supervision of time', as a more substantial phenomenon (I. Xenakis, 1994: 96). Because it intends to sculpt sound rather than develop some primary element (theme, cell, etc.) in time, his music perhaps illustrates this hypothesis.

Process

Sometimes, Xenakis's composed sonorities are made up of *progressive transformations*. Like certain realisations of Op Art or etchings by Escher, they start from a state of sound matter and result, almost imperceptibly, in another as if by magic: the first state is transformed bit by bit, its characteristics gradually making way for those of the second. In *Formalized Music* (I. Xenakis, 1992: 9), Xenakis speaks about continuous or discontinuous transformation, realized with the use of stochastics (probabilities), but his work abounds in continuous transformations of all sorts, most often realised 'by hand', i.e., without calculations, frequently with the help of graphs. *Pithoprakta* constitutes a model of the diverse techniques applied to particular sections and affecting either particular characteristics of the sound (register, density, spatial movement, 'filtering', etc.) or the sound state in its overall nature. Thus, in measures 172–179, the graphic transcription (**Example 5.30 online**) brings out a transformation of register: starting from a register entirely remote, the 46 strings in *col legno* are oriented in a very continuous way towards a compact cluster with the range of a major ninth.[12] Within this transformation, each instrument has its own melodic pattern.[13] It would seem that Xenakis realised the forty-six melodic curves according to three basic outlines: one line descending on the whole, one ascending and a path that proceeds by compression. **Example 5.31 (online)** presents three exemplary curves.

In addition, *Pithoprakta* is one of the few Xenakis works that seems to espouse the model of physical sound: its entire form goes from noise (blows on the soundbox of the strings with which the piece begins) to pure sound (final harmonics at the very end). But this work is not immediately perceptible, for Xenakis realised it through interpolations, with frequent returns to states already passed as for the degree of noise. To summarise the process: 1. Noises with continuous transformation of density and spatialisation and progressive emergence of *pizzicati* and *arco* (measures 0–51); 2. Overall transformation through 'filtering' of a 'cloud of sounds' (measures 52–59); 3. *Tenuti* with progressive emergence of *pizzicati* then *glissandi* (measures 60–104); 4. Discontinuous transformations of a field of *glissandi* (measures 105–121); 5. *Bruiteux* superposition of six timbre groups with sporadic 'views under the microscope' (measures 122–171); 6. Continuous transformation of the register of sounds in *battuto col legno* (measures 172–179); 7. Discontinuous transformations through 'filtering' of a cluster (measures 180–207); 8. Fields of *glissandi* with irregular then linear transformation of register (measures 208–231); 9. Large cluster that 'evaporates' progressively in the high register (measures 231–250); 10. Harmonics in discontinuous spatial transformations (measures 250–268). One will note that all the sections are in progressive transformation, with the exception of measures 122–171, which offer a static superposition – these are the measures that served as an example in Chapter 4 to evoke the 'immersion' in sound (for a detailed analysis of the beginning, see A. Antonopoulos, 2008).

Other musicians of Xenakis's generation also took an interest in the composition of progressive transformations. Thus, evoking the works he composed beginning with *Atmosphères*, Ligeti (1974: 110; our translation) wrote:

> This is a music that awakens the impression of continuous flowing, as if it had neither beginning nor end. Typical of all these pieces: there are very few caesuras, so the music really continues to flow. Its formal characteristic is being static: it gives the impression of stagnating. It is only an impression.

Inside this stagnation, this static state, there are progressive transformations. Here I will think of a surface of water on which an image is reflected. This surface gradually ripples, and the image disappears, but quite gradually. The water becomes smooth again, and we see another image.

In the following generation, the issue of progressive transformation takes on a more general nature and goes as far as characterising entire musical trends. Henceforth, it would be a matter of *process*. In what follows, let us focus on two musical trends to be entirely designated as art of composing processes, as music made of the *composed process*.

First of all, there is American minimalism, born in the mid-1960s. If we limit it to the question of composed processes, one will, of course, think of the work of Steve Reich. In *It's Gonna Rain* (1965), for tape, Reich introduces a particular type of process: progressive phase shifts. The tape mixes the product of two tape recorders, which reproduce the same sermon given by a black preacher; starting simultaneously, they desynchronise progressively, thereby generating a phase shift producing virtual relations of pitches, rhythms and even timbre, i.e., which are not 'on' the tape but result from the phasing process. Reich (in J. Cott, 1997: 5) likes to say that he discovered this technique by chance:

> I discovered the phasing process by accident. I had two identical loops of a Pentecostal preacher, Brother Walter, whom I recorded in San Francisco's Union Square, saying 'It's gonna rain'. I was playing with two inexpensive tape recorders – one mono jack of my stereo headphones plugged into tape recorder A, the other into tape recorder B. And I had intended to make a specific relationship: 'It's gonna' on one loop, against 'rain' on the other. Instead, the two recorders just happened to be lined up in unison, and one of them gradually started getting ahead of the other. The sensation I had in my head was that the sound moved over to my left ear, moved down to my left shoulder, down my left arm, down my leg, out across the floor to the left, and finally began to reverberate and shake and become the relationship I was looking for– 'It's gonna/It's gonna, rain/rain'–and then started going in retrograde until it came back together in the center of my head.

After *Come Out* (1966), also for tape, Reich applied the procedure to instrumental music, in particular in *Piano Phase* (1967) and *Violin Phase* (1967). The latter can be played by four violinists or by one violinist and a tape recording of the other three parts. The phasing process is written for and, this time, affects four voices. At the beginning of the piece, the violin (the one on stage in the second version or 'violin 2' in the first) plays the same thing as another violin, 'violin 1' (recorded in the second version). Both repeat the same measure, which itself repeats a motif of five attacks. At the end of the first line, the score asks the onstage violin to accelerate very slightly, enabling it, at figure 3, to be out of phase by one note in relation to the tape (violin 2). The process continues with the further addition of the other two violins. Then the onstage violin stops playing the motif and plays *resultant* motifs.

Composing sound 179

In fact, during the resulting phasing polyphony, Reich notes that the ear begins to hear melodies that are not played by an instrument but result from the phase shift; to be specific: the ear connects adjacent sounds in the register to make a virtual melodic line from them – this phenomenon is well known in Bach's *Sonatas and Partitas for solo violin*, in which he composes a virtual polyphony. To come back to *Violin Phase*, **Example 5.32** provides a later excerpt from the score, which gives, from top to bottom, the parts of three violins (recorded or played on stage), a part which is not played and which simply provides the superposition of the previous three parts, then the part of the onstage violin, which plays one of the resulting motifs for the ear, composed only of the lowest note.

In 1968, Steve Reich published an article entitled 'Music as a Gradual Process', which shows that his intention was fairly close to that of minimalist visual artists, in search of a sort of desubjectivation through emphasis put on very attentive perception:

> While performing and listening to gradual musical processes one can participate in a particular liberating and impersonal kind of ritual. Focusing in on the musical process makes possible that shift of attention away from he and she and you and me outwards towards it.
>
> (S. Reich, 2002: 34–35)

At the beginning of the 1970s, Reich decided to try something new by leaving for Ghana to study percussion with a master-drummer from the Ewe tribe. Upon returning, he composed *Drumming* (1971, a demanding piece for bongos, three marimbas, glockenspiels, woman's voice, whistling and piccolo): the technique of the process applies henceforth on several levels and in the framework of a composition lasting nearly 90 minutes.

Example 5.32 Steve Reich, *Violin Phase*: figures 20–20a (S. Reich, 1979). © By kind permission of Universal Editions.

The masterpiece in terms of process that Steve Reich's minimalism would produce was composed in the mid-1970s: *Music for 18 Musicians* (1974–1976), for amplified instrumental ensemble (clarinets, pianos, marimbas, xylophone, violin, cello, women's voices), marked by the Balinese gamelan, which Reich had had the opportunity of studying without leaving the United States (see L. Denave, 2007). The work lasts just under an hour and is made up of several sections linked without transition. In the first, *Pulse*, eleven chords follow one another very slowly (**Example 5.33 online**). Then the following sections are constructed on just one of the eleven chords. Reich (2002: 89) wrote:

> This means that each chord that might have taken 15 or 20 seconds to play in the opening section is then stretched out as the basic pulsing harmony for a five-minute piece, very much as a single note in a cantus firmus or chant melody of a twelfth-century organum by Perotin might be stretched out for several minutes as the harmonic center for a section of the organum.

Each section uses its own procedural techniques, and the whole constitutes almost an 'illustration' of process composition (see the analyses of J. Bodon-Clair, 2008 or R. Fink, 2005: 47–55).

The second trend that carried the art of composed processes to full fruition was born in the early 1970s: spectral music. The question of progressive transformation was broached implicitly in the frameworks of the harmony-timbre issue, i.e., the threshold between timbre and harmony and, consequently, of a 'liminal' type of writing, to use Gérard Grisey's expression (see Chapter 1). It was the same as regards the research of the spectral composers on perception, where their interest was noted for logarithmic-type curves that present, precisely, progressive evolutions (see Chapter 3). This interest is proportional to their organicist penchant. Thus, Tristan Murail 'compared the composer's role to that of a gardener: it would quite simply be a matter of planting a musical seed and watching it grow. In other words, music would be a natural process that the composer would settle for engendering by selecting the initial material' (J. Anderson, 1989: 135; our translation).

Grisey is doubtless the spectral musician who worked process composition the most, owing to this link with the organicist aesthetic as well as the fact that he thought of himself as a composer of time. In one of his first published texts, 'Devenir du son', he wrote:

> It is henceforth impossible for me to consider sounds as defined objects that can be swapped between each other. Rather, they appear to me like beams of forces oriented in time. These forces – I purposely use this word and not the word 'form' – are infinitely mobile and fluctuating; they live like cells, with a birth and a death and, above all, tend to a continuous transformation of their energy. The immobile sound, the frozen sound does not exist, anymore than the rocky strata of mountains are immobile.
>
> (G. Grisey, 2008: 28; our translation)

Spectral music quickly came to think of process composition as the merger of material and form in favour of a totally articulated entity. In Grisey's language, this meant the interchangeability of the object and the process. In a text extending 'Devenir du son', he wrote: 'Since sound is transitory, let us go further: *object and process are analogous. The sound object is only a contracted process, the process is only a dilated object*' (Ibid: 84). As for Hugues Dufourt (1991: 284; our translation), he wrote that spectral music is characterised by 'a style made up of openness and refusal of assignation', and he goes so far as to use an expression from the 1960s: 'informal art' (Ibid: 285). In sum, we are dealing with the liquefaction of form, which goes hand in hand with a dissolution of material. It is as such that we can talk about form/material fusion: 'Above all, the difference between the material and form of the piece is progressively blurred: Murail discovered that sounds go through evolutions of such complexity that they already constitute a sequence of music by themselves' (J. Anderson, 1989: 125). Spectral music carries out the form/material fusion through the simulation of sound, an idea that was also found in Scelsi: the form of the work is only the deployment of the structure of sound – which, of course, presupposes a change of scale. But this fusion takes on true meaning with the process technique.

In Chapter 3, an example of process in Murail was mentioned: in *Ethers*, a progressive acceleration follows a logarithmic curve. As concerns Grisey, Jérôme Baillet (2000: 48–64) listed the types of process he used in six main categories: continuous metamorphosis of sound textures; discontinuous evolution in successive phases; transition from one type of perception to another; progressive phasing of a polyrhythmic superposition; transformation of two objects; and evolution of an alternation of objects. This just shows that the process is omnipresent and decisive in Grisey's work, at least as much as in minimalist music. A borderline case is provided by *Jour, Contre-Jour* (1979, for ensemble), in which the overall form is defined entirely by a single process summarised in two diagrams, borrowed from Jérôme Baillet. The first (**Example 5.34 online**) shows the succession of durations of the phases, 'each one determined by a new chord, and divided into two opposite parts A and B, one being more *bruiteux* than the other' (J. Baillet, 2000: 72–73; our translation). The second (**Example 5.35 online**) describes the overall evolution of frequencies and dynamics, 'which is symmetrical in all its aspects except for the frequential register' (Ibid: 73). We must point out that the two outlines are modelled on each other, even though they do not have the same axes.

Micro-composition

Sound syntheses

In instrumental music, the idea of a work entirely composed from the level of material has a limit: sound itself. Of course, thanks to the very elaborate work on timbre and on playing methods, sound has also become a compositional challenge. Nonetheless, below the threshold of the note, control – via the writing, the

182 Composing sound

tool of composition par excellence – is difficult here. Thus, the perspective of composing sound in the literal sense, i.e., constructing *microtime*, really becomes possible only with electroacoustic music. *Musique concrète* opened up this perspective, thanks to the process of editing, as was seen in Chapter 2. However, the composition of microtime can truly be carried out only with the other component of electroacoustic music: electronic music, in which sound synthesis unfolds. In fact, only a synthesised sound – thus a total artefact – can be said to be fully composed. (It will be noted that *com-position* is the Latin translation of the Greek *syn-thesis*.)

After the Paris studio founded by Schaeffer, the second site where electroacoustic music developed was devoted precisely to electronic. Founded in 1951 by the physicist specialising in information theory, Werner Meyer-Eppler, and by the musicologist-composer Herbert Eimert (assisted by recording engineer Robert Beyer) (see E. Ungeheuer, 1992), this studio was based at the (N)WDR (Nordwestdeutscher Rundfunk, part of which, later on, would remain the studio, becoming the Westdeutscher Rundfunk), in Cologne, and quickly welcomed Stockhausen, who would compose important works there such as *Hymnen* (1966–1967: see **Example 5.36 online**). At the studio's beginnings, serialism was quite important, which explains the patient elaboration of pieces of music from practically nothing – a minimal definition of sound synthesis. The first works – such as *Klang im unbegrenzten Raum* (1951–52), *Klangstudie I* (1952) and *Klangstudie II* (1952–1953) by Eimert and Beyer, or Stockhausen's two electronic studies (1953 and 1954) – are sober (see Chapter 1 for Stockhausens's *Elektronische Studie I*.) Stockhausen's next two works, *Gesang der Jünglinge* (1955–1956) and *Kontakte* (1959–1960), distinctly richer, have earned a place in history as musical, and not only technological, successes. Numerous other composers would pass through this studio, but limiting ourselves to the early years, we shall mention only Ligeti (*Artikulation*, 1958), Cardew (*1st* and *2nd Exercises*, 1958) and Kagel (*Transición I*, 1958–1960).

The third European studio to be inaugurated was the Studio di Fonologia Musicale, founded by Luciano Berio and Bruno Maderna at the RAI (Radio Audizioni Italiane) in Milan in 1955. The two young composers, already known for their involvement in serialism, were open-minded and sought to combine *musique concrète* (or American tape music, which Berio knew from his 1952 trip to Tanglewood) and electronic music, as demonstrated by the equipment in their studio: in 1962, one found sound generators (of sinusoidal waves, white noise and impulsion), apparatuses for transforming sound (echo chambers, filters, ring modulators…) and devices for recording and reproducing sound (see GRM, 1962). In the beginning, the two friends undertook numerous experiments. For both of them, their first real works dated from 1956, with *Mutazioni* (Berio) and *Notturno* (Maderna). The second, as shown by the analysis of Nicola Scaldaferri (2009), is a touching piece: despite limited means, Maderna succeeded in delivering an ample musicality. Thus, during the first four seconds of the work, we have a sort of slow tremolo, in an interval of a fifth, between two filtered sounds. The lowest sound, around 900 Hz, is in truth made up of six filtered sounds on narrow band having their own dynamic, recorded on bits of tape. They then went into an echo chamber and recorded on another tape. The resulting six bits of tape – each one including the original sound and its reverberation – were then assembled on a tape with angled cuts (in order to limit the effect of editing). A second tape was composed identically with four bits of tape, from filtering of the high sound (approximately 1400 Hz). Finally, these two tapes (the second beginning with a bit of blank tape) were launched simultaneously on two tape recorders, with a third machine recording the result, which is the tremolo in question: a highly musical figure and constituting the main element of the *Notturno*. In the RAI's phonology studio pieces were then composed that would mark the history of electroacoustic music such as Pousseur's *Scambi* (1957), Berio's *Thema (Omaggio a Joyce)* (1958), Nono's *Intolleranza 1960* (1960–1961)...

In the United States, Louis and Bebe Barron were doubtless the first to have begun musical experiments with a tape recorder in *Heavenly Menagerie* that, in an interview with Thom Holmes (2008: 80), Bebe Barron dated from 1950. The couple is often cited for having assisted Cage in *Williams Mix* (1952–1953) – which, in a way, constitutes a sort of sampling sound synthesis via sampling before that existed: the piece assembles more than 500 bits of tape consisting of recordings of sounds – but they would also be among the first to make electronic music on the occasion of the soundtrack of the science-fiction film *Forbidden Planet* (1956), which they created with circuits they built themselves:

> We never considered what we did at that point, [to be] composing music. It really wasn't at all like music because we were not concerned with note-by-note composition. What we did was build certain kinds of simple circuits that had a peculiar sort of nervous system, shall we say. They had characteristics that would keep repeating themselves.
>
> (Ibid: 81)

In 1951, again in the United States, composers Otto Luening and Vladimir Ussachevsky founded the Columbia Tape Music Center, which would become the Columbia-Princeton Electronic Music Center in 1958. At the beginning, they only did tape manipulations (in sum, *musique concrète*), inventing American tape music with pieces such as *Fantasy in Space* (1952, Luening) or *Sonic Contours* (1952, Ussachevsky). Then they became interested in the work of Harry F. Olson and Herbert F. Belar, engineers at the Princeton laboratories of the Radio Corporation of America (RCA), who had elaborated a kind of rudimentary composing machine. In 1955, they created the RCA Electronic Music Synthesizer (also called Mark I, an improved version of which, Mark II, dated from 1958), the first synthesiser commissioned using a computer, but producing analogue sound. Around this apparatus and their own equipment, Luening and Ussachevsky built a project that would receive considerable institutional help, thereby creating the first American electronic music studio. Milton Babbitt (**Example 5.37 online**) was the first important composer to experiment with the RCA synthesiser, beginning in 1957. However, he would wait several

184 *Composing sound*

years before producing finished works. One of them, *Philomel* (1963–1964, for soprano, recorded soprano and synthesiser) was an important success, doubtless because the 'coldness' of the machine here is tempered by the use of the voice (recorded and onstage). Amongst other composers having used the RCA synthesiser, let us mention Charles Wuorinen (*Time's Encomium*, 1968–1969). Moreover, numerous composers used the Columbia-Princeton Electronic Music Center studio without using the RCA synthesiser, its use being quite delicate: Mario Davidovsky (*Electronic Study*, 1960), Michiko Toyama, Varèse (who revised the tape part of *Déserts* in 1960–1961, with the help of Max Mathews and Bulent Arel), Halim El-Dabh (*Leiyla and the Poet*, 1961)...

Numerous other studios were created in the late 1950s and early 1960s: in the Japanese Radio (1954), in Gravesano (1954, founded by Hermann Scherchen), Ontario (1955, Elmus Lab), Eindhoven (1956, the Philips Studio, where Varèse composed his *Poème électronique*, which was to move to Utrecht and become the Institute of Sonology), Munich (1957, Siemens-Studio für elektronische Musik), in the Polish Radio (1957), in Stockholm (1957), Buenos Aires (1958), Ann Arbor (1958, Gordon Mumma and Robert Ashley's studio), Toronto (1960), Moscow (1961), San Francisco (1961), Ghent (1962) ... Starting in the mid-1960s, studio proliferated. At the end of the first decade of the new millennium, according to Paul Doornbusch (2009: 582), 'there exist at least 1,000 musical studios in universities and institutions in the world, several of which are involved in research'.

In 1957, the first entirely digital sound syntheses[14] were developed at the Bell Telephone Laboratories in Murray Hill (New Jersey, United States), thanks to Max Mathews, who elaborated the MUSIC N family of programmes. Mathews introduced ideas that have had considerable influence on the logic of musical programming up to the present day (see G. Wang, 2007: 59). The programming centred on the unit generator concept, meeting elementary functions: oscillators, filters, envelopes, etc. By connecting these unit generators, one obtains an 'instrument'. A collection of instruments forms an 'orchestra'. To finish, an orchestra is run by a 'score'. Thus, in **Example 5.38**, in MUSIC V program, excerpted from Mathews's historic book (1969), we have, at upper left, a functional diagram showing the connections between the unit generators that create the sound; at upper right, are two 'functions' (*diminuendo* and *crescendo*); on the stave is the music that will be synthesised on a square wave; at the bottom, the 'score' of MUSIC V, which contains the definition of the 'instrument' (lines 1–7), the definition of the function tables (lines 8–10) and the list of notes (lines 11–12). The MUSIC V software (1967–1969) constituted an important step since, written in FORTRAN, it could be implemented on any computer using that language. The few pieces realized on the MUSIC N programs were primarily demonstrations (*In the Silver Scale*, 1957, Newman Guttman; *Frère Jacques*, 1961, Mathews: *Bicycle Built for Two*, 1961, John Kelly, Carol Lochbaum, Max Mathews...). It would not be until the arrival of James Tenney at the Bell Laboratories for truly compositional attempts, described in Chapter 2. In the mid-1960s, Jean-Claude Risset conducted research at Bell Laboratories and, in 1969, published his famous catalogue of synthesized sounds (see Risset, 1969), which takes up the 'instruments' used in

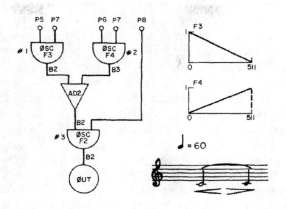

```
 1   INS 0 3 ;
 2   ØSC P5 P7 B2 F3 P30 ;
 3   ØSC P6 P7 B3 F4 P29 ;
 4   AD2 B2 B3 B2 ;
 5   ØSC B2 P8 B2 F2 V1 ;
 6   ØUT B2 B1 ;
 7   END ;
 8   GEN 0 1 3 .999 0 0 511 ;
 9   GEN 0 1 4 0 0 .999 511 ;
10   GEN 0 1 2 0 0 .99 50 .99 205 −.99 306 −.99 461 0 511 ;
11   NØT 0 3 2 0 2000 .0128 6.70 ;
12   NØT 2 3 1 2000 0 .0256 6.70 ;
13   TER 3 ;
```

Example 5.38 Example of programming in MUSIC V: 'Instrument with crescendo and diminuendo' (M. Mathews, 1969: 59). © By kind permission of Peter Mathews.

his two pieces of 1969, *Computer Suite for Little Boy* and *Mutations*, commented on in Chapters 1 and 3. Risset was one of the first composers to have said and demonstrated through his compositions that, henceforth, the composition *of* sound replaced composition *with* sounds, an affirmation to be taken literally if, by 'composition', one means 'sound synthesis' and thinks of additive synthesis methods.

In the mid-1960s the first commercial analogue synthesizers appeared (see J. Chadabe, 1997: chapter 6). In 1964, Robert Moog developed his first synthesiser. Made famous by Wendy Carlos's *Switched-On Bach* (1968), the Moog (see **Example 5.39 online**) was popularised by rock – among the first to use it were The Doors, in the first track of the album *Strange Days* (1967), played by Jim Morrison, or the album *The Notorious Byrd Brothers* (1968) by The Byrds. At the same time as Moog, Donald Buchla was also trying modular synthesis and produced his first instrument in 1965, at the San Francisco Tape Music Center; Morton Subotnik's *Silver Apples of the Moon* (1967), composed for the Buchla synthesiser, would enjoy widespread public success. Moreover, Pauline Oliveros deserves to be mentioned for two 1966 works written, respectively, for the Moog and the Buchla: *A Little Noise in the System* and *Once Again*. The history of analogue synthesisers would continue into the 1980s, with firms such as EMS, Korg, Roland…

In the 1970s, new software applications methods, digital instruments and devices for sound synthesis saw the day: GROOVE (1968–1970, Max Mathews and F. Richard Moore, Bell Telephone Laboratories), hybrid synthesis in real-time (analogue sound controlled by computer); SSP (1971, Gottfried Michael Koenig, Institute of Sonology), Sawdust (1972, Herbert Brün, University of Illinois) and Auditu (1972, Pierre Barbaud, Frank Brown, Geneviève Klein, CENT/IRIA), synthesis software; Synkeyboard I (1975, Sydney Alonso, Cameron Jones, Jon Appleton, Dartmouth College), digital synthesiser; 4A real-time digital sound processor (1976, Giuseppe Di Giugno, IRCAM; then 4C, 1978 and finally, 4X, 1981) … (see P. Doornbusch, 2009: 557–584). We should also mention two important contributions of Xenakis's: one, stochastic synthesis in the late 1960s, discussed in Chapter 2, would give rise to the GENDYN program in the late 1980s; the other was the invention, at CEMAMu (Centre d'Études de Mathématique et Automatique Musicale, a studio founded in Paris in 1966 and which first name was EMAMu) in 1977, of the UPIC (Unité polyagogique informatique du CEMAMu) system, a synthesiser that Xenakis's whole oeuvre awaited since *Metastaseis*. This was a draughting table connected to an analogue-digital converter on which one draws successively, using an electromagnetic pencil, the pressure curve of the sound and the 'score'. In the first case, we are in microtime, and the UPIC synthesised a sound; in the second, we are in macrotime, and one draws the whole work (in this second stage, one indicates on the 'score', by a particular code, the chosen sounds that were already constructed in the first stage – not to mention the envelopes of intensity that the machine also enables drawing): see **Example 5.40 (online)** for an excerpt of the 'score' of *Mycènes alpha* (1978).

Another important innovation of the 1970s was FM (frequency modulation) synthesis. The FM applications had been known for quite some time, but it was John Chowning who – after a visit to the Bell Telephone Laboratories, where he learned about Risset's work and the MUSIC IV source code – began to explore FM for sound synthesis around 1971. It was while exploring very rapid vibratos that he invented the method (see C. Roads, 1996: 193). Once the method was perfected, he registered a patent that Yamaha began to exploit in 1975, arriving at the famous DX synthesisers. *Turenas* (1972), produced on a computer at Stanford University, was the first piece in which Chowning systematically explored FM synthesis – after having already used it in *Sabelithe* (1971) – created with a version of the MUSIC IV program. Herein, he generated diverse types of sounds: percussive highs, low *tenuti* (which would be highly prized by users of the DX7), bell- or gong-type inharmonic spectra… To obtain the latter, Chowning used a relation between the carrier frequency and the modulating frequency equal to the square root of two, or 1.414…, an irrational number. Just as with Risset (beginning of *Mutations*), the bell sounds can be heard as both chords and synthesised sounds, as attested by **Example 5.41 (online)**. A later piece by Chowning, *Stria* (1977), for which **Example 5.42** gives the FM synthesis algorithm, has become a

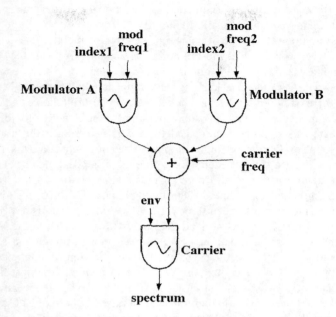

Example 5.42 John Chowning, *Stria*: FM synthesis algorithm. © By kind permission of John Chowning.

classic: it has been abundantly analysed and given rise to several reconstructions (see J. Chowning, 2007; O. Baudouin, 2007; K. Dahan, 2007; M. Meneghini, 2007; L. Zattra, 2007).

Starting in the late 1970s and early 1980s, micro-computers arrived (David Behrman's *Figure in a Clearing*, 1977, using a KIM-1 computer: see **Example 5.43 online**; Laurie Spiegel's *A Harmonic Algorithm*, 1981, created on an Apple II computer; *Little Spiders*, 1982, by Nicolas Collins, for two keyboard players and two micro-computers equipped with programs analysing the gestures of the latter…), is adopted to the MIDI norm (1983), digital synthesisers developed (the aforementioned Synkeyboard I, 1975; Casio VL-Tone, 1980; Crumar Synergy, 1982; Kurzweil K250, 1983; DX7, 1983, which we just discussed; Roland Compu Music CMU-800R, 1984; Korg DS-8, 1987; Roland JV-1080, 1994; Kurzweil K2600, 1999…) as well as new types or new sound synthesis methods.

As concerns synthesis methods that interest the current chapter, making a detailed history starting in the late 1970s – i.e., as the heroic pioneering phase of the early times was drawing to a close – would be totally irrelevant in the context of this book. Let us point out that there are several ways of apprehending this history (see J. Dack, 2002). Some reason by families; thus, Curtis Roads (1996) proposes distinct chapters on sampling, additive, multiple wavetable, wave terrain, granular (of which he was one of the pioneers), subtractive, modulation, physical modelling, formant, waveform segment, graphic and stochastic synthesis. Other approaches are more historic (see P. Manning, 2009).

By crossing these two types of approach,[15] let us first mention the derivatives of the MUSIC N software. The most important is Csound (**Example 5.44 online**), a program that was developed beginning in 1986, when Barry Vercoe realised a version of MUSIC 11 using C language. Its logic stemmed from the MUSIC N family, for here one finds the distinction between 'orchestra' (choice and configuration of components of synthesis sub-programmes) and 'score' (list of parameters and data). Csound has been considerably enriched from its birth up to the present day, one of the reasons for this important development being that this software was shareware and then became free. Amongst other descendants of MUSIC N, we can mention F. Richard Moore's Cmusic (University of California, San Diego) and Cmix, developed in the 1980s by Paul Lansky (Princeton University).

Let us next mention the spectral models, which had a royal history. Here we find additive synthesis and its derivatives: analysis/resynthesis, Phase Vocoder, synthesis by spectral interpolation... We also encounter subtractive synthesis (vocoder, linear predictive coding...). We can also mention formantic synthesis (CHANT program, resonance models, VOSIM program...). Amongst the innumerable examples, we shall mention the work of two other pioneers, Charles Dodge and Paul Lansky who, in their musical works, took hold of LPC synthesis (see M. Byrne, 1999). Thus, the former used it to transform a recording of Caruso in *Any Resemblance is Purely Coincidental* (1978, for piano and tape).

A third category, with various kinds of sampling synthesis, also activates the whole history of synthesis, but in a more discontinuous, heterogeneous way. Here we can cautiously include *musique concrète* (it is, in fact, the process of editing on tape and not *musique concrète* in the strict musical sense), wavetable synthesis in the temporal dimension, methods using sampling strictly speaking... These have been widely developed, for example with waveform segment techniques or granular synthesis, which will be discussed in the final section of this chapter.

Another, more homogeneous category, groups together methods of physical modelling synthesis. They are based on the study of instrumental acoustic modelling, starting not from sound but from the way in which an instrument produces it. Born in the late 1960s with the works of Lejaren Hiller and Pierre Ruiz (University of Illinois), physical modelling syntheses developed in the 1970s, when Kevin Karplus and Alex Strong studied the model of plucked strings, and Claude Cadoz founded ACROE (1977, Association pour la Création et la Recherche sur les Outils d'Expression, Grenoble), which would carry out pioneering work in this field. Several other works developed next: the programs CHANT (Xavier Rodet, Yves Potard and Jean-Baptiste Barrière, IRCAM, 1979); Mosaïc (IRCAM, 1991) which became Modalys or Cordis-Anima (ACROE). Modalys allows for constructing virtual instruments starting from the analysis of physical objects, whether simple (strings, plates, tubes, membranes, plectra, bows...) or more complex (see **Example 5.45 online**). As for Cordis-Anima, its designers developed adapted apprenticeship tools based on an 'ontology of musical models' (O. Tache et al., 2009).

Composing sound 189

In this brief look, the Max/MSP program would require an independent development: this software progressively became one of the dominant programs. Thoughtout from the beginning in the 1980s with the research of Miller Puckette (first at MIT then at IRCAM) on the development of graphic interfaces, it was created in 1988 (and took the name 'Max' in homage to Max Mathews) and marketed in 1991. In 1993, MSP (Max Signal Processing) was added. Subsequently, Puckette, who had left for the University of California, San Diego, developed Pure Data (Pd), an open source program. Its beginnings were carried out in close relation with composition and especially with a composer, Philippe Manoury, and a flautist, Lawrence (Larry) Beauregard. At that time, Manoury began a cycle of compositions entitled *Sonus ex Machina*, its theme being the dialogue between instruments and computer (the 4X signal processor), of which *Jupiter* (1987, revised in 1992), for flute and computer, was the first piece, composed in collaboration with Miller Puckette, Cort Lippe, Marc Battier, Olivier Koechlin and Thierry Lancino (see M. Battier et al., 2003).[16] The Max program was realised in part to meet compositional necessities as they appeared in the course of various stages in the cycle's composition. In fact, 'the history of the cycle could [...] be summed up by the genealogy of a sole computer score – called "patch" – taken up and developed from one piece to the next' (P. Odiard, 1995: 42; our translation), Max being completed only for the second piece in the cycle, *Pluton* (1988–1989, for piano MIDI and 4X computer). **Example 5.46 (online)** shows the 'large central patch' of *Jupiter* in Pure Data.[17] Each box represents a sub-patch with a particular function. In the excerpt of the score given in **Example 5.47**, the following functions intervene: *Harmonizer* ('Harm.'), which allows for transposing without changing the duration (here, a chord is obtained from a single note of the flute); *infinite reverb* ('Rev. ∞'), providing a reverberation that can be prolonged at will by looping the sound on itself (a sort of selective piano pedal is obtained, taking only certain notes); *Frequency shifter* ('Freq. sh.'), which transforms the sound

Example 5.47 Philippe Manoury, *Jupiter:* first page (P. Manoury, 1987). © By kind permission of Editions Amphion.

spectrum by introducing inharmonicity (for an analysis of the piece, see Bonardi, 2003; A. May, 2006; M. Larrieu, 2018).

This very synoptic panorama is, of course, incomplete: it offers no place to the history of real-time synthesis (which developed, beginning in the late 1970s, and was a very important challenge for, amongst others, IRCAM), to synthesis by modulation, convolution (or crossed synthesis), to important software such as the object-oriented SuperCollider program. Moreover, this brief overview has put the accent on software syntheses, but we must not neglect the history of material syntheses, i.e., DSP (digital sound processing) units, which, appearing at the end of the 1970s, permitted the first real-time syntheses, as well as digital audio workstations (DAW)[18]: Syter DSP real-time system developed by the GRM beginning in 1975, Digidesign Turbosynth and Sound Tools (1989, first DAW), Capybara (1990, a DSP unit on which the Kyma software functions), SoundHack DSP unit (1991), Lemur DSP unit (1992), Loris DSP unit (2000), SoundHack Spectral Shapers DSP unit (2004)... (see P. Doornbusch, 2004).

The granular paradigm

One particular method of sound synthesis perfects the idea of total construction, articulation and composition: granular synthesis. Relying on a particular conception of sound, it corresponds to its *corpuscular* description at variance with its description as a wave form. Synthesising a sound according to this approach consists of juxtaposing, in a very short lapse of time, a very high number of grains (samplings). There is a threshold of perception on the level of density, situated between 50 and 100 milliseconds, below which *microtime* begins: with less than 10 to 20 sounds per second, the ear perceives grains as entities; with more, it perceives them as being part of an overall texture: synthesised sound. According to this view of sound synthesis, the very notion of sound tends to move more freely. On the microtime level, the limit between recognisable entities, which we call 'sounds' and grains, is difficult to establish. As for macrotime, the limit between these entities perceived as sound, i.e., as *material*, and whole sections of the work perceived as parts or sections of the work, i.e., as *form*, is equally difficult to determine. *What is a sound?* one might wonder with the granular conception (see R. Meric, 2008). Is it a grain? A heap of grains? Is it part of a granular work? Or even the entire work? From the microstructure to the macrostructure of the work, from micro- to macrotime, from sound in the physical sense (material) to the entire work (form), a continuum is born. Granular synthesis invites us to think of a musical composition as an entity built totally from grains. That is why its logic, whilst being linked to a technology (a type of sound synthesis), is more than a technology: it relies on a way of thinking music; one might speak of a granular *paradigm* or *sensitivity*.

The granular paradigm has numerous theoretical and musical antecedents. From the theoretical point of view, we could mention the wave/particle debate, waged since Antiquity, or else Einstein's hypothesis on the existence of 'phonons' (the equivalent of 'photons' for light). But it was the physicist Dennis Gabor who, in the late 1940s, developed the idea that 'any sound can be decomposed into an appropriate combination of thousands of elementary grains' (C. Roads, 2001: 57). From the musical point of view, it would be difficult to find distant antecedents, but one could go back to the musical tachisme developed by Debussy in *Jeux*, where sometimes smooth sound surfaces are constructed from very brief motifs. We should also mention Varèse, who approached the granular through the purely sonic aspect, for example in the third sonority of *Ionisation* (stated in measures 18–20: see *supra*). As pure sonority, the granular became an implicit model in serial pointillism of the 1950s. For example, in Stockhausen's *Gruppen* (1955–1957), certain rhythmic 'formants' (see K. Stochausen, 1957) display sufficient density that, in theory, the ear carries out the synthesis and perceives an overall structure.

During the same period, Xenakis was the first composer to develop theoretical hypotheses inaugurating the granular paradigm. Here is the formulation he proposed, in a text that would become famous, thanks to its being taken up again in his book *Formalized Music*:

> All sounds represent an integration of corpuscles [grains], of elementary acoustic particles, of sound quanta. Each of these elementary particles possesses a double nature: the frequency and the intensity (the life-time of each corpuscle being minimum and invariable) [Each of these elementary grains has a threefold nature: duration, frequency, and intensity]. Every sound, every even continuous variation of sound is to be understood as an assembly of a sufficient number [of a large number] of elementary particles [grains] being disposed adequately within the time level. Hecatombs of pure sounds are necessary for the creation of a complex sound. This one should be imagined as to be a display of fireworks sparkling in all colours.
> (I. Xenakis, 1960: 86–87 / In square brackets:
> I. Xenakis, 1992: 43–44)

Concret PH (1958, tape) is Xenakis' first granular composition. It was played during the interludes of the multimedia performance in the famous Philips Pavilion at the Brussels World's Fair (1958), and it is a brief composition, almost without beginning or end, conceived as a sole sound made up of thousands of grains. The grains in question are sounds of burning embers assembled in a very large number, transposed and mixed. Next there was the mixed piece *Analogique A* (1958, for nine strings, which produce brief sounds: *pizzicati*, brief *arcos*, *col legno*: see **Example 5.48 online**) and *B* (1959, for tape, made up of very short sinusoidal sounds). It is likely that Xenakis conceived this piece as an experiment, for, regarding piece *A*, he wrote in *Formalized Music*: 'This hypothesis of a second order sonority [the fusion of grains into a complex sound] cannot […] be confirmed or invalidated' (I. Xenakis, 1992: 103). Doubtless owing to this conclusion, he did not repeat the experiment and thus abandoned the granular paradigm that he had just inaugurated.[19] But it remained in his instrumental pieces, whereever he uses masses of brief sounds (see the excerpt from *Eridanos*, for orchestra, 1972, in **Example 5.49 online**).

After Xenakis, the granular paradigm first went through a few isolated realisations – with Horacio Vaggione (*Modelos de Universo*, 1971) and Bernard Parmegiani ('Matières induites', one of the movements from *De natura sonorum*, 1975). It became sound synthesis in the late 1970s with Curtis Roads, who developed an algorithm for granular synthesis, first at the University of California, San Diego, then at MIT (see C. Roads, 1978: 61–62), as well as with Barry Truax, who developed real-time granular synthesis, first at the Institute of Sonology in Utrecht, then at Simon Fraser University in Vancouver (Canada) (see B Truax, 1988). In the 1980s and 1990s, granular was worked by composers as diverse as Agostino Di Scipio, Ludger Brümmer, Manuel Rocha, Ramón González-Arroyo, Eduardo R. Miranda, Damian Keller or Mara Helmuth. Today, one could say that, as a means of producing particular sonorities, it ended up becoming banal; however, as a paradigm (in which the idea of a fully composable work, from micro- to macrotime, dominates), it necessitates a more advanced involvement.

Amongst the composers mentioned, Horacio Vaggione, known as much for his electroacoustic or mixed music as for his theoretical thinking, is an excellent case study allowing for further detailing the logic and richness of the granular paradigm. A group of questions raised by his writings deal with time. Amongst the most important, one will first note that his music, following Xenakis and in parallel with the spectral musicians, integrates the modern idea of time, thought to be irreversible. In this context, sound is no longer conceived in terms of periodicity, repetition, according to Helmholtz's model of acoustics but as a dynamic phenomenon of energy. One of the important references of Vaggione, the theorist, is represented by the works of physicist Ilya Prigogine, inventor of the 'theory of dissipative structures'. It is to this theory that he refers when describing sound structures as 'dissipative structures of sound energy' (H. Vaggione, 2003: 102; our translation).

Moreover, Vaggione is interested in diving into the infinitely small, i.e., into what is often presented as the 'inner life' of sound (see Chapter 4). Vaggione's originality was in posing the question in terms of *articulation*, of how to *compose* these phenomena (see H. Vaggione, 1996). Moreover, whereas, in the issue of 'inner life', it is frequently a matter of a fascination for a supposed original matrix, a Unit – hence the mystical penchants of a Scelsi, a Stockhausen, a Harvey or even a Grisey – Vaggione, on the contrary, sees that as the occasion for discovering *pluralism*:

> For a musician, going down to micro-time is the means for discovering phenomena that he does not know about […] As Bachelard said: 'Our temporal intuitions are still quite poor, summed up in our intuitions of absolute beginning and continuous duration'. We must therefore 'find pluralism under identity' and 'break the identity beyond the immediate experience too soon summed up in an aspect of a whole'.
>
> (H. Vaggione, 1998; our translation)

Hence his interest in granular synthesis: it is precisely a matter of finding 'pluralism' (the grains) under the 'identity' (the resulting sound). Moreover, he emphasises that the corpuscular description, unlike that of the wave type, refers by principle to irreversible time: the granular approach 'enables us to work with complex morphologies in a space-time where irreversibility reigns: "dissipative" structures that emerge within a directional space-time, rather than in symmetrical, smooth continuities' (H. Vaggione, 2005: 314). This is why, in Vaggione's music, the granular approach is much more than a synthesis technique.

Vaggione's writings develop the idea of a *multi-scale* approach to time. He starts from the pragmatic observation that there exists, as much on the level of musical tradition as of human perception, a threshold from which one can delimit two orders of level: micro- and macrotime. On the level of musical tradition, it concerns the note: macrotime 'encompasses all possible scales' above, and microtime all those below (H. Vaggione, 1998b: 172; our translation). Apprehended from this angle, the gap between instrumental music and electroacoustic music lies not in a difference of 'nature' (of material, for example) but consists of a change of scale (temporal). One may then think of the two sides of the threshold, micro- and macrotime, as under the common sign of the composable, the articulable, without, for all that, *abolishing* the threshold, since there is a change of scale. On the perception level, the threshold is situated, as it was said, between 50 and 100 milliseconds. The application of this model to synthesis as much as to instrumental thus allows for unifying them without, however, abolishing their difference. In the case of synthesis, one perceives the granular nature of the resulting sound – which, precisely, is not exactly *a* sound. Conversely, with the instrumental, even when the threshold to microtime tends to be crossed – as is often the case in Vaggione's scores, where the musicians are called on to play demisemiquavers, and sometimes even more, with the crotchet equalling 100 MM: see **Example 5.50 (online)**, which gives an excerpt from *Phases* (2001, for clarinet, piano and electronics) – we remain in the framework of a segregative flux. That is why granulation must not be taken literally when applied to instrumental music: Vaggione does not seek an 'instrumental' granular synthesis.

Pieces such as *Tar* (1987, for bass clarinet and tape), *Ash* (1990, electroacoustic), *Till* (for piano and tape-computer), *Atem* (2002, for horn, bass clarinet, double bass, piano and electroacoustics) and *Gymel* (2003, electroacoustic) are quite representative of the idea of time scales (for *Till*, see the analysis by M. Laliberté, 2007, and for *Gymel*, that of R. Meric, 2009: 465ss). Thus, *Schall* (1994, electroacoustic) constitutes

> a pure electroacoustic work utilizing exclusively some sampled piano sounds, processed by means of digital techniques [...] The work plays essentially with tiny textures of feeble intensity, composed of multiple strata, which contrast with some stronger objects of different sizes [...] — as an expression of a concern with a detailed articulation of sound objects at different time scales.
> (H. Vaggione, 1995)

194 Composing sound

It has been said that the Vaggione approach, which sets out the difference between the microscopic and macroscopic in terms of time scales, does not aim at abolishing the threshold connecting them. What this means is that, if these two levels can be unified, their difference is nonetheless maintained: one cannot go from one level to the other solely by transposition. In Vaggione's terminology, there exists a *non-linearity* between the levels of time, an irreducibility from one to the other. It is perhaps therein that the originality of his theorisation lies: several musicians who, before or at the same time as him, also dealt with this question in the form of scales inclined more towards the principle of transposition. For Vaggione, not only do non-linearities between time scales exist but, in addition, they can be fertile for musicians (see O. Budón, 2000).

Unifying (whilst taking into account their non-linearities) electronics and instrumental also means unifying material and form. Material as well as form are composable, articulable: in the Vaggione perspective, there is no difference in nature between the terms of this duality, but a difference of scale (of time). That is why the duality could be put aside: one could then use a single word rather than a duality, a word that would be changed in keeping with the scale. It is the role that, in Vaggione's writings, the notion of *morphology* seems to play. According to him, all the time scales call for morphologies: a sample (of granular synthesis), a wave form, a figure made up of a few notes, the overall form (macroform) of a musical work can be apprehended as 'forms' evolving in a time (a time scale) specific to them.

In addition to the fact that it succeeds in unifying the field of the sonorous (by going beyond the material/form cleavage), the morphological approach offers three contributions. First of all, it postulates that the material (sound) is not neutral. In other words, it starts from the principle that there are no minimal units ('bricks') that could be assembled at will in a combinatory play to produce abstract 'forms' – i.e., totally autonomous in relation to the material (see H. Vaggione, 1999). This leads to a different approach from the parametric. If one must analyse a sound form (the morphological approach is not necessarily holistic), one will speak of its 'qualities', its 'aspects' or its 'parts', and not its 'parameters'. Moreover, the morphological approach allows for thinking of sound forms as dynamic movements, or processes, and we know that processual thought is able to 'orient' the musical discourse and 'vectorise' (H. Vaggione, 1996b; our translation) it. It also allows for providing solutions to the problem of mixing instrumental and electronic materials by establishing a 'common vectorisation' (Idem).

As an example of the morphological approach, let us take the handling of space. For Vaggione (1998c), space is composable but, unlike composers coming from serialism, he does not apprehend it as a 'parameter': space *is part* of the morphology of sound, and if it has relative autonomy, it is as morphology 'that will modulate and be modulated by other morphologies' (Ibid: 154; our translation). That is why Vaggione does not treat it with standard techniques (reverberation, panoramisation, etc.): those techniques have no relation with the morphology conducive to a sound that they 'spatialise', they are simply added to it. Consequently, they end up levelling the singularity (the morphology) specific to it (see H. Vaggione, 2003b: 26). Hence the use of microtemporal decorrelation techniques stemming from signal engineering. In the use he makes of them, they consist, for example, of generating duplications of a wave form and desynchronising their phase relations, in a microtemporal scale, which gives rise to a sensation of space closely akin to the morphology of sound (see **Example 5.51 online**).

The morphological approach is able to put the accent on a capital notion: *singularity/ies*. Vaggione's reading of René Thom was fertile. The French mathematician wrote, in a language that is almost Vaggionean, that:

> The first duty of any morphological interpretation consists of the determination of the discontinuities of a morphology and the stable parts of these discontinuities. In this interpretation appears the notion of singularity, of which, in fact, discontinuity is a particular case.
> (R. Thom, 1983: 91; our translation)

The interest of the notion of 'morphology' in music lies in relating the traditional notions of 'material' and 'form'. The idea of 'morphological singularities' specifies this connecting: it consists of challenging the neutrality of material, as well as the universality of forms.

The singularities are assembled, held, tensioned, framed by (in) something: they necessitate being placed in a context which, without for all that being neutral (or constituting a background), is not a sum of singularities but also includes less prominent elements. The problem can be put another way: with 'direct action' there is the chance that singularity *emerges*, which presupposes that it also contains less singular elements. If singularity consists of a 'catastrophe' (Thom), it cannot be measured by the standard of the continuum that it breaks.

The 'framework' in which singularities suddenly appear is called *figure*. The notion of figure, such as Vaggione uses it, is first to be taken in its traditional musical meaning: a set of a few notes (combining pitches, rhythms, nuances and playing methods) forming an entity. It is with such figures that, since *Thema* (1985, for bass saxophone and tape; see E. Justel, 2007), Vaggione thinks mixed music (electroacoustic-instrumental). The second meaning of the word 'figure': the notion can be applied to any scale of time. Vaggione (1998: 97; our translation) noted that the morphological transformations that he implements 'generalise a "figural" work that can be projected towards the most diverse temporal scales'. It would seem that this generalisation applies especially to microtime where, for example, one can think of the granulation of a sampled sound as a figural work, or else, where, thanks to the technique of microtemporal decorrelations, Vaggione (2003b: 27; our translation) implements 'composed spatial figurations'.

A figure 'can be coupled with the concept of object, the latter being a category that allows for including and making figures circulate in a network of compositional operations' (H. Vaggione, 1998: 98–99; our translation). In a sense, Vaggione's compositions consist of making the singularities bear fruit through the construction of three-storey edifices: *figures*, which we have just discussed, *objects* and *networks*. However, it must be pointed out that these 'storeys' do not designate orders of fixed (temporal) size, but can change scale.

Vaggione's notion of 'object' is borrowed from computing: it refers to the object-oriented languages which, in the 1980s, proposed an alternative to linear programming. In his music, as in his musical-theoretical thinking, Vaggione (1991) radically appropriated the computing notion of object. Objects can be 'functions (algorithms), lists of parameters (scores), scripts (chains of actions to be carried out) or sounds (products as well as sources)' (H. Vaggione, 1998b: 187; our translation).

Amongst the consequences of the use of this notion in composition, Vaggione noted that it permitted 'encapsulating' both the sound and the 'score' (in the sense given above) (see H. Vaggione, 1991: 212–213). Nothing prevents 'score' from meaning, in musical terms, the structure (or: syntax). Also, due to the notion of object, Vaggione succeeded in filling the gap of the traditional sound/structure duality – just as the notion of morphology allowed for attenuating the cut between material and form. The notions of morphology and object allow for going beyond the dualities in question for, thanks to them, the concepts they contrast can be thought of in terms of composition, articulation and writing.

As for the notion of 'network', it is closely mixed with that of object: 'Every object is [...] a network, as much as every network is made up of objects' (H. Vaggione, 1998b: 187; our translation). However, it can distinguish itself from it if one considers that the network defines an upper floor of the object. Moreover, it is also understood as the association of different types of representation, like a hypertext. One might think that, to define a network, Vaggione would also refer to computing. But he chose to quote Michel Serres: the concept of network

> stems from a situation where there was 'a plurality of points (peaks) linked by a plurality of ramifications (paths)', and in which 'no point is univocally subordinated to one or another: each has its own power [...] or zone of influence, or else its original determinant.
>
> (quoted in H. Vaggione, 2003: 99; our translation)

In a note, he adds that he gave this definition, 'relatively old and non-technical, first to show the permanence of the network concept, then because this definition was not biased by more recent connotations which tend to trivialise it' (Ibid: 114).

We will find in **Example 5.52** a 40-second excerpt from the 'score' of *24 Variations* (2001, electroacoustic music), showing the timeline elaborated with the IRIN program (see C. Caires, 2004). Each rectangle represents a 'clip' or sound sample (the vertical position of a sample within a track is not significant, not corresponding to a pitch). With IRIN, one can encapsulate figures within tracks and represent them as isolated fragments, which allows for a hierarchic construction of the mesostructure. The visual result is characteristic of the work of composition of digital networks of objects on a given timescale. As for the piece in question, one will note, with Curtis Roads (2005: 306), that it is 'the most gracefully poetic of Vaggione's electroacoustic compositions. In order to appreciate this, I also recommend listening at a moderate volume, in

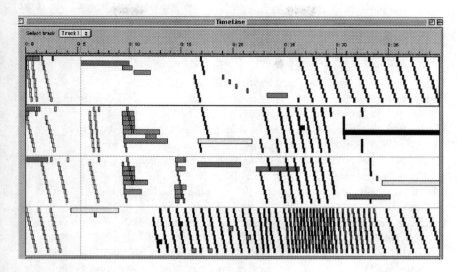

Example 5.52 Horacio Vaggione: excerpt from the 'score' (IRIN program) of *24 Variations* (version 2) (unpublished). © By kind permission of Horacio Vaggione. Screenshot; the original is in colour.

order to savour its subtleties. One is drawn in not by the expectation of spectacular climaxes, but by the originality and virtuosity of the articulations as they pass by'.[20]

Chapter 5 online examples

Example 5.7 Luigi Nono, *...sofferte onde serene...*: end of the piece (played part) (L. Nono, 1992). © By kind permission of Editions Ricordi.
Example 5.9 The EMS VCS 3 (http://www.ems-synthi.demon.co.uk/emsstory.html).
Example 5.10 Donna Summer, Giorgio Moroder, 'Love to Love You Baby': additive construction (R. Fink, 2005: 58). © By kind permission of Robert Fink.
Example 5.12 Kaija Saariaho, *Amers:* spectral analysis of the trill with greater bow pressure and *sul ponticello* position (I. Stoïanova, 1994: 54). © By kind permission of Ivanka Stoïanova.
Example 5.13 Kaija Saariaho, *Amers*, measures 1–77: approximate evolution of pitches.
Example 5.14 Fausto Romitelli, *Professor Bad Trip I:* measures 46–50 (F. Romitelli, 1998). © By kind permission of Editions Ricordi.
Example 5.17 Edgar Varèse, *Ionisation*, measures 18–20: reduction.
Example 5.19 Edgar Varèse, *Ionisation*, measures 44–45: reduction.
Example 5.21 Clara Maïda, *...who holds the strings...:* measures 64–65 (C. Maïda, 2002). © By kind permission of Clara Maïda.

198 *Composing sound*

Example 5.23 Chiyoko Szlavnics, *Gradients of Detail*: beginning of the score (C. Szlavnics, 2006b). © By kind permission of Chiyoko Szlavnics.

Example 5.24 Ivan Wyschnegradsky, *Arc-en-ciel:* p. 16 (I. Wyschnegradsky, 1956). © By kind permission of Paul Sacher Foundation, Basel, Ivan Wyschnegradsky Collection.

Example 5.25 Iannis Xenakis, *Jonchaies*, measures 10–62: sieve.

Example 5.27 Iannis Xenakis, *Syrmos*, measures 255–259: composer's graph (Archives Xenakis). © By kind permission of Mâkhi Xenakis.

Example 5.28 Iannis Xenakis, *Erikhthon*, measures 262–281: composer's graph (Archives Xenakis). © By kind permission of Mâkhi Xenakis.

Example 5.29 Iannis Xenakis, *Terretektorh*, measures 291–303: graphic transcription.

Example 5.30 Iannis Xenakis, *Pithoprakta*, measures 172–179: graphic transcription.

Example 5.31 Iannis Xenakis, *Pithoprakta*, measures 172–179: graphic transcription of three melodic curves (violin I.3, violin I.1, double bass 6).

Example 5.33 Steve Reich, *Music for 18 Musicians*, 'Pulse': the 11 chords.

Example 5.34 Gérard Grisey, *Jour, Contre-Jour:* succession of phases (J. Baillet, 2000: 56). © By kind permission of Jérôme Baillet.

Example 5.35 Gérard Grisey, *Jour, Contre-Jour:* evolution of frequencies and dynamics (J. Baillet, 2000: 73). © By kind permission of Jérôme Baillet.

Example 5.36 The WDR studio in 1966 during the composition of *Hymnen* (Stockhausen). © By kind permission of the Stockhausen Foundation for Music, Kürten, Germany, www.stockhausen.org.

Example 5.37 Milton Babbitt and the RCA synthesiser.

Example 5.39 The Moog System 55 modular synthesiser (1974) (http://www.vin tagesynth.com/moog/m55_5whole.jpg.).

Example 5.40 Iannis Xenakis, *Mycènes alpha:* 'score' (UPIC): 4'17"-5'16". © By kind permission of Editions Salabert.

Example 5.41 John Chowning, *Turenas:* bell-type synthesis sounds between 1'32" and 1'47" (after L. Pottier, 2009: 254). © By kind permission of Laurent Pottier.

Example 5.43 David Behrman: tinkered interface between a KIM 1 computer and cobbled-up synthesisers.

Example 5.44 Commented on example of programming in Csound.[21]

Example 5.45 Application of synthesis by finite elements in Modalys: first mode of vibration of a Tibetan bowl modelled by a three-dimensional mesh (IRCAM, 2010: 67). © By kind permission of Ircam-Centre Pompidou (The original is in colour).

Example 5.46 Philippe Manoury, *Jupiter*: 'large central patch' of the piece (M. Larrieu, 2018: 180).

Example 5.48 Iannis Xenakis: *Analogique A*, measures 0–2 (I. Xenakis, 1968). © By kind permission of Editions Salabert.

Example 5.49 Iannis Xenakis: *Eridanos*, meaure37–40 (brass) (I. Xenakis, 1972). © By kind permission of Editions Salabert.

Example 5.50 Horacio Vaggione, *Phases:* page 1 (unpublished). © By kind permission of Horacio Vaggione.

Example 5.51 Horacio Vaggione: simple example of microtemporal phase decorrelation (H. Vaggione, 2003b: 26). © By kind permission of Horacio Vaggione.

Notes

1 The retrograde canon characterising the second section ends at measure 44 for the first part (first stave on the reduction), whereas the third section starts at the end of measure 42 with the first part (last stave).
2 In the reduction provided, one must invert the reading of the staves: staves 4–3 and 2–1 correspond respectively to staves 1–2 and 3–4 in the first section.
3 Not to mention the description of form in traditional terms: some define it as a sonata form, with the double canon at the beginning constituting the exposition, the final double canon the recapitulation, and the central canon its development, with the themes corresponding, in this analysis, to the two initial canons.
4 'I was sensitive […] to the question of natural resonance: a chord can move away or get closer […] At the same time, if one always refers to the spectrum, if one lets oneself be completely guided by natural resonance, one constantly obtains dominant ninth chords, and it's not terribly fascinating!', wrote Pierre Boulez (in P. Albèra, 2003: 19–20; our translation). Moreover, we will emphasise that, even in a fairly arid work like *Structures I*, Boulez seemed interested, in a general way, by sound: as Pascal Decroupet wrote about this work, 'it should be noted that the finality of Boulez's research is indeed also *sound*, heard not in terms of isolated phenomenon but as polyphonic resultant and, in addition, revealing of certain specific characteristics of the initial series' (P. Decroupet, 2001: 168; our translation).
5 The *fermate* doubtless help in figuring the 'Pendulum' from the poem *Hangmen of Solitude* by René Char ('The step has receded the walker is silent / On the dial of the imitation / The Pendulum thrusts its load of reflex granite').
6 In truth, there are twelve different attack-intensities; each of the six intensities in question can also be played with an accent; moreover, let us note that there are never progressive dynamic variations.
7 Manfred Kelkel (1988: 256–261) enumerates 300 cells and analyses the rhythmic transformation procedures as equivalents of the ionisation process, basing himself on three large transformation groups: augmentation (and diminution), retrogradation, procedures of elision and filtering as well as commutation and fusion procedures.
8 Out of concern for simplification (to be able to indicate the rhythmic gestures in a general way), this reduction does not take into account the exact duration of each sound); moreover, contrary to what it indicates, the cencerro does not play in triplets in measure 44.
9 The idea of the parallel between the epistemological debate and musical research as to the question of foundation as well as the transposition of the 'intuitionism / axiomatism' opposition in the field of music is borrowed from Jean-François Lyotard (1991).
10 Xenakis drew two graphs for this passage: see B. Gibson (1994). The one I am reproducing corresponds to the published score.
11 1,142 according to Xenakis's (1956: 31) historic article, or 1,148 according to *Formalised Music* (I. Xenakis, 1963: 30); 1,146 according to my own count (see M. Solomos, 1993).
12 On this graph an 'error' will be noticed: a note in the high register (a D# which, in the score, is played by the violin II.2), in measure 177. In fact, it is not an error that Xenakis would have committed at the time of transcribing his graph in customary

musical notation: it is found in Xenakis's original graph (published in F.-B. Mâche, ed., 2001: 54–55).
13 Let us mention, however, two redundancies: violin I.6 doubles violin I.3 in measures 172-174; violin I.12 and violin II.12 play practically the same notes in measures 175–179.
14 We now know that the very first music to be produced entirely by a computer was programmed on the Australian CSIRAC computer back in 1951 (or even 1950) by the mathematician Geoff Hill (see P. Doornbusch, 2004).
15 Certain categories of the following panorama overlap the four categories (treatment of recordings, spectral models, abstract algorithms and physical models) in J. O. Smith's typology (1993), which is taken up by N. Collins (2010).
16 By 'collaborators', I mean the various people who helped the composer, in particular on the technological level, which includes, amongst others, what IRCAM called 'musical assistants', renamed 'computer music designers' (*réalisateurs d'informatique musicale*). It should be noted that the flautist Lawrence Beauregard – who died just before the piece's premiere – had already undertaken research on the dialogue between the flute and the 4X with researcher Xavier Chabot.
17 It is therefore a version realised well after the composition of the work. Generally speaking, works using technology calling for real-time electronics constantly need to be readapted to developments in technology. Numerous researchers in musical computing have worked on this question in the past few years – for example see A. Bonardi, 2011, A. Sousa Dias, 2011.
18 In the synthesis software, one works with a program running on an all-purpose computer. Material synthesis, involves the use of a special circuit, as is the case with digital synthesisers or, often, in digital signal processing units (DSP). As Curtis Roads points out, 'the distinction between software synthesis and material synthesis is sometimes blurred. Let us imagine the case of a system constructed around a DSP organ [...] with large memory. It can be possible for such a system to execute the same type of software synthesis as that of an all-purpose computer' (C. Roads, 1996: 67).
19 For an analysis of the hypothesis of a second-order sonority, see Agostino Di Scipio (1997). Di Scipio (2005) also carried on an important discussion to know whether – and possibly in what way – *Analogique A* and *B* might be failures. For an analysis of the Xenakian approach to the granular, see M. Solomos, 2016.
20 To prolong this discussion on Horacio Vaggione, see M. Solomos, 2005.
21 Thanks to Kevin Dahan for having provided me with this example and his commentary.

6 Sound–space

Representational space as operatory category

Throughout the 20th and 21st centuries, space has taken on an ever-greater importance for music. In 1967, two years before man's first steps on the moon, Gisèle Brelet (1967: 495; our translation) noted that 'in the same way as modern man, contemporary music has, in its way, conquered space', referring to musical works that broke with the frontal distribution of instruments to deploy them in the concert hall or space. One might also wonder whether, in return, space might not have conquered music. This book has already evoked the question of space, regarding the notion of sound immersion (Chapter 4). The present chapter continues the investigation in order to suggest that the importance taken by space can be explained by the fact that we are progressively oriented towards the possibility of *composed* spaces, thereby putting the finishing touches to the idea of composed sound and culminating in the general framework of *sound–space*.

While in Chapter 4 we distinguished between literal and figurative notions of space, here we shall consider two types of space: physical space, in which sound and music materialise; and representational space, a mental space in which music and sound are thought out at the time of their conception and perception. To begin with the second type of space, we have often noted that the notion slipped into music via terminology borrowed from the visual: one speaks of melodic 'lines', 'figures', 'curves'. It is, of course, the symbolic representation offered by musical notation that led to adopting such expressions; it is also due to musical notation that the field of pitches became a 'space', organised from the 'bottom' to the 'top'. What status should be granted to these borrowings from the visual sphere? Is it a matter of pure metaphors? That is the point of view of Vladimir Jankélévitch who denounced the 'spatial mirage' and its 'doubtful' metaphors, adding:

> In effect, the general characteristics attributed to music often exist only for the eye, by means of the conjuring trick of graphic analogy. The simply *particularity* of writing, which results from the symbolic projection of a musical into two dimensions as a score, will suffice for us to characterize the melodic 'arch'; and a melody that is outside all space, as a succession of sounds

and pure duration, is subjected to the contagion of graphic signs inscribed horizontally on the staff. [...] The *artifices* of staff paper end by dislodging acoustic realities.

(V. Jankélévitch, 2003: 91; our italics)

One can agree with Jankélévitch on the fact that spatial terminology in music refers to the primacy of sight over hearing, a primacy at the very foundation of western music and its system of representation, as well as, more generally, of western civilisation. However, musical notation has progressively imposed itself as a powerful tool for *thinking* music. Thus, the compositional techniques invented thanks to ruled paper – from the melodic curves mentioned above to the complex canons of Webern's *Opus 21* – constitute neither 'artifices' nor 'particularities of writing': they determine the music *itself.* More and more, the art of sounds has been composed, heard and thought in relation to the notion of space, which has ended up being naturalised.

In generalising and going back to the theoretical foundation of western music prior to the invention of solfeggio notation, one would say that a progressive *geometrisation* of music has occurred. Its birth certificate is marked by the Pythagorean analysis of musical intervals in terms of numeric proportions obtained through the study of tensions of a string as well as by the *Harmonic Elements* of Aristoxenus of Tarentum who introduced the notion of *topos*, simultaneously 'space' and place' (see A. Bélis, 1986: 135). Geometrisation subsequently increased: whereas with the Greeks, the notion of 'tone' and therefore tension, still dominated, Gregorian chant developed 'an abstract notion, the notion of sound pitch, a quantifiable, rational notion, absolutely new at the time', which imposed a 'representative spatialisation of the morphophoric low-high character (M.É. Duchez, 1989: 287 and 293; our translation). This geometrisation refers to the rationalisation of music which was discussed in Chapter 5.

Thus, representational space has been naturalised in music, allowing for thinking of it as entirely composable. So it was in the 1950–1960 period that, with serialism, the parametric definition of music appeared, allowing for decomposing in 'parameters'. At the same time, Xenakis (1992: chapter 6) used the notion of 'vector' to analyse a brief excerpt from Beethoven's *'Appassionata' Sonata* and to compose his own music. Twenty years later, spectral music would generalise this notion, Tristan Murail (2004: 56; our translation) wrote: 'The exploration of hierarchies brings out what I shall call the "vectorisation" of the musical discourse, meaning that all process is *oriented* and has a sense'. Today, we can envisage representational space as a multidimensional space where the composer defines symbolic, accountable objects of operations constituting a kind of geometry of this composable space (see G. Carvalho, 2010). In sum, we shall say with Horacio Vaggione (1998c: 154; our translation) that if 'composable' is synonymous with 'articulable' and not simply with the production of totalising mechanisms, the notion being to 'generate veritable singular events and articulate them in ever-larger ensembles without losing the sense of these singularities', the notion of space turns out to be quite useful as an *operative category*.

Composing the physical space

Towards the composability of space

At present, let us broach space in the physical sense of the term and draw up a brief history leading to its composability. Although today's music has made (physical) space a central issue, it did not, however, invent it. To tell the truth, music has always dealt with space. In traditional forms of music, physical space often constitutes a fundamental – for instance, religious rituals, which take possession of a whole temple, and where music plays an important role, presuppose that music is thought out in relation to the temple's topography. Thus space is tied to music through the *function* attached to it, which is often linked to a *place*. In the West, we have the equivalent with the music of *cori spezzati* in the sixteenth and early seventeenth centuries, which Adrian Willaert, Andrea Gabrieli, Giovanni Gabrieli and others composed for Saint Mark's basilica in Venice, taking into account the sound lags resulting from the distance between the organ lofts and the choirs. Subsequently, it was the autonomisation of music – its defunctionalisation, if one prefers – that made it lose the notion of space.

The (re)conquest of space as composable begun already in the 19th century, through the advances in terms of orchestral writing, so it is indissociable from the history of timbre. Berlioz constitutes the first outstanding point in space as a dimension that can be articulated for itself. In his treatise on orchestration, he specified the conditions of physical space with numerous details, writing, for example:

> The place occupied by the musicians, their arrangement on a horizontal plane or on an inclined plane, in a three-walled enclosure, or in the very centre of a room, with reflectors formed by hard bodies capable of transmitting sound, or soft bodies which absorb it and break the vibrations, and more or less near the performers, have a great importance.
> (H. Berlioz, 1993: 293; our translation)

In his orchestral writing, Berlioz undeniably took into account acoustic problems linked to the propagation of sound and worked on the notion of orchestral mass. Thus, his *Requiem* (1837) is 'his response to a particular technical problem, that of sonority in a vast space, and it is the response of a man who devoted a passionate interest to acoustics (something quite rare for the time)' (D. Cairns, 1994: 49). The 'Tuba Mirum' from the *Requiem* deploys four small orchestras of brass instruments [which] must be placed separately at the four angles of the large choral and instrumental mass (only the horns remain in the middle of the large orchestra) (see **Example 6.1 online**).

A few other musicians of the 19th century – Wagner, in particular – would, like Berlioz, advance the issue of space in relation to timbre and acoustics. At the turn of the 20th century, Debussy referred to space as synonymous with opening:

> One can make out a large orchestra becoming even larger with the participation of the human voice [...]. For that very reason, the possibility of music

constructed especially for the 'outdoors', all in large lines, in vocal and instrumental daring, which would play and hover over the treetops in the light of open air.

(C. Debussy, 1987: 76; our translation)

In 'Fêtes', the second of the *Three Nocturnes* for orchestra (1897–1899), Debussy created orchestral planes in order to give concrete expression to the programme: 'It is [...] the episode of a cortège (dazzling, chimerical vision) passing through the celebration, merging with it [...]' (Debussy in E. Lockspeiser et al., 1980: 670; our translation): at figure 10 [of the score], whilst the strings play a march rhythm, muted trumpets enter *pianississimo* then play 'a bit closer'. Finally, they remove their mutes and blend in with the march movement which has increased with the addition of other winds and percussion. This idea brings to mind the fleeting gesture in figure 16 [of the score] of the funeral march in Mahler's *First Symphony* (1888) (see **Example 6.2 online**), where we have the impression of a parallel world – melody in the woodwinds with the marking *äussert rhythmisch* – briefly breaking in, creating a totally different space.

At the beginning of the 20th century, Ives recalled a childhood memory:

The writer remembers hearing, when a boy, the music of a band in which the players were arranged in two or three groups around the square. The main group in the bandstand at the center usually played the main themes, while the others, from the neighboring floors and verandas, played the variations, refrains, and so forth. [...] The writer remembers as a deep impression, the echo parts from the roofs played by a chorus of violins and voices.

(C. Ives, 1933: 160)

His *Universe Symphony* (1911–1951), which was left unfinished, was to be written for a very large number of musicians, divided into orchestras; according to Henry Cowell (quoted *in* L. Austin, 1997: 183):

Several different orchestras, with huge conclaves of singing men and women, are to be placed about in valleys, on hillsides, and on mountain tops [...], each moving in its own independent time orbit, and only meeting one another when their time cycles eclipsed.

In one of the first manuscripts of the work, in the margins, the number of musicians necessary are indicated; according to Larry Austin (Ibid: 179–232), they were to have totalled 4,520!

Varèse and the pioneers of the 1950s and 1960s

Varèse was undoubtedly the first composer to consciously seek to compose space. With him, space, thought in the form of a 'sound projection', becomes a full-fledged dimension; in a lecture given in Santa Fe in 1936, he noted:

Today, music knows three dimensions: a horizontal, a vertical, and a movement of growth and decrease. I could add a fourth: sound projection (this impression that sound leaves us with the idea that it will not come back, an impression that resembles what emerges from rays of light emitted by a powerful projector): a feeling of projection, of travelling in space, for the ear and eye alike.

(E. Varèse, 1983: 91; our translation)

He situated the birth of his interest in space in his use of sirens:

My first attempt at giving music greater freedom was the use of sirens in several of my works (*Amériques*, *Ionisation*), and I think it was those trajectories of parabolic and hyperbolic sounds that led certain writers to take over my spatial conception of music, beginning in 1925.

(E. Varèse, 1983: 150)

In the late 1920s, he elaborated the *Espace* project. Even though given new impetus in 1937 with the project of a collaboration with Malraux – who travelled to the United States at the time to seek aid for saving the Spanish Republic – finally the project would come to nothing. The *Étude pour Espace* (1947) and *Déserts* (1950–1954) would advance his thinking, resulting in the *Poème électronique* (1958).

This last musical work formed a part of the multimedia performance given in the famous Philips Pavilion, built by Xenakis (then-assistant to Le Corbusier), for the Brussels World's Fair in 1958. The *Poème électronique* was diffused in space by more than 400 loudspeakers: 'The loudspeakers were piled up by groups and in what were called "sound routes" to create diverse effects: impression of music turning around the pavilion, suddenly appearing from different directions; phenomenon of reverberation, etc.' (E. Varèse, 1983: 151; our translation). The expression 'sound routes', coined by the Philips technicians, designated the sending of the sound tape over the loudspeakers according to the prepared itineraries and, during the performance, carried out mechanically using telephone selectors (see M. Treib, 1996: 205; J. de Heer, K. Tazelaar, 2017). **Example 6.3** shows Xenakis's drawings for these sound routes. Earle Brown (quoted in T. Horodyski, 1998: 321), who attended one of the performances, noted: 'It was spectacular, because you could hear a sound and it began to spin, so that you could practically follow its trace in space and follow it with your eyes'.

Following Varèse, Xenakis was one of the first to theorise the idea of a composability of space. Assessing the experience of the *Poème électronique* – for which he composed *Concret PH*, played as an 'interlude' – he writes: 'Thanks to electroacoustic techniques, we may note that the conquest of geometric space, a new step into the realm of Abstraction, is indeed realizable' (I. Xenakis, 2008: 134). Then, after another electroacoustic work, *Bohor* (1962) – one of the first compositions to think of space in the sense of immersion and not of trajectories – with the orchestral works *Terretektorh* (1965–1966) and *Nomos gamma* (1967–1968), spatial

206 Sound–space

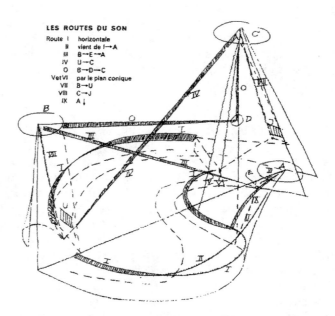

Example 6.3 The 'sound routes' of the Philips Pavilion (drawing by Xenakis) (Archives Xenakis). © By kind permission of Mâkhi Xenakis.

preoccupations became spectacular and almost political. Xenakis upset the small world of the orchestra and its audience by having the orchestra leave the concert platform: the musicians are distributed in the hall, and the audience is dispersed *in* the orchestra! **Example 6.4 (online)** shows the arrangement of the orchestra for *Terretektorh*, and the programme notes should also be quoted:

> The scattering of the musicians brings in a radically new kinetic conception of music which no modern electro-acoustical means could match. For if it is not possible to imagine 90 magnetic tapes relaying to 90 loudspeakers disseminated all over the auditorium, on the contrary it is quite possible to achieve this with a classical orchestra of 90 musicians. The musical composition will thereby be entirely enriched throughout the hall both in spatial dimension and in movement. The speeds and accelerations of the movement of the sounds will be realized, and new and powerful functions will be able to be made use of, such as logarithmic or Archimedean spirals, in-time and geometrically. Ordered or disordered sonorous masses, rolling one against the other like waves.... etc., will be possible.
>
> '*Terretektorh* is thus a "Sonotron": an accelerator of sonorous particles, a disintegrator of sonorous masses'.
>
> (I. Xenakis, 1992: 236–237)[1]

Example 6.5 proposes a transcription showing how the spatial movement of the last part (measures 352–456) of *Persephassa* (1969, six percussionists), where the musicians surround the audience, is composed. This whole passage gives rise to a huge acceleration and gigantic crescendo (certain loud dynamics that stand out in the context of the overall crescendo are indicated in **bold**), from the crotchet = 30 MM and around an *mf* to the dotted minim = 80 MM (measure 430) and around an *ffff* (measure 415). As for the tempo, the six instrumentalists (indicated by letters in the transcription), who have the whole instrumentarium at their disposal (six skins, siren, metal and wooden simantras, cymbal, gong, tam-tam, wood-block – to which are added pebbles and '*affolants*' towards the end[2]), make a minim circulate with a crotchet time-lag.[3] The tempo is double: on the one hand for the six skins, the other for the six remaining percussions (the siren does not intervene in the spatial play). The transcription (in which a line indicates the continuation of the same outline) shows that the spatial movement goes through two phases: the first (measures 352–420), quite long, is indecomposable, unlike the second, which evolves towards an increasingly minimal segmentation.

The spectacular aspect of the composition of space, combining spatial trajectories and immersion, culminates with Xenakis's *polytopes* of the 1960s and 1970s. Within these multimedia performances – combining music, light projections, actions (as well as architecture and text for *Diatope*) – the spatialisation of sound plays a major role, aiming for total immersion. Played very loud and 'travelling' round the spectator, the sound encircles the latter on all sides and is almost gut-wrenching (see Chapter 4 for the *Diatope*). In Xenakis's later instrumental output, space is far from being absent – for example, in *Retours-Windungen* (1976, for 12 cellos) or *Alax* (1985, for three instrumental groups placed in a triangle on the stage) – but it is not worked as spectacularly.

Still in the period of the 1950s and 1960s, at the same time as Xenakis, Stockhausen was also venturing decisively in the composition of space. At its first performance, in 1956, the famous electroacoustic piece *Gesang der Jünglinge* was played over five groups of loudspeakers divided up around and above the listeners. The spatial trajectories are fully composed and do not constitute a superfluous 'effect'. With *Gruppen* (1955–1957), written for three orchestras under three conductors, Stockhausen explored spatialisation in the framework of instrumental music. Having serialised the tempi, he introduced polyorchestral writing because he reckoned that a single conductor could not direct tempo superimpositions. 'I finally concluded that the only way was to split the diverse time layers and put each group in a separate place so that one didn't get distracted by the signals of the other conductors' (Stockhausen in J. Cott, 1974: 200; our translation).

In *Kontakte* (1958–1960, version for electronic sounds), certain sounds are produced using a rotating turntable (see **Example 6.6**), invented by Stockhausen himself. Around the turntable, four microphones, hooked up separately to the four channels of a four-track tape recorder, recorded the circular movement of a sound produced by a loudspeaker attached to the turntable. In *Hymnen* (1966–1967,

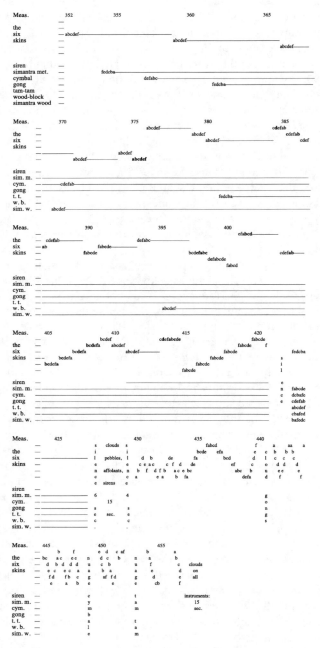

Example 6.5 Iannis Xenakis, *Persephassa*, measures 352–456: transcription of the spatial movement.

Example 6.6 Rotating turntable invented by Stockhausen. © By kind permission of Stockhausen Foundation for Music, Kürten, Germany, www.stockhausen.org.

electronic music and *musique concrète*), the German composer experimented with movements in which the rapidity exceeds six events per second. He would say:

> When one makes sounds move faster than six per second, in rotation, etc., one arrives at sounds for which one cannot make out the direction exactly. So the loudspeaker no longer exists, there is a sonic vibration that is in the body itself, inside the body.
>
> (in T. Horodyski, 1998: 351; our translation)

Moreover, in 1970, the extraordinary Osaka experiment, described in Chapter 4, took place.

The 1970s and 1980s

In the late 1960s, a trend was born that would be described *a posteriori* as 'space rock', which developed ethereal atmospheres discussed in the chapter on listening: *tenuti*, repetitive motifs and, from the point of view of sound processing, use of synthesisers, reverberation and echo, which contribute to generating the sensation of 'space' in the sense of intersidereal space. A few titles are significant: 'Astronomy Domine' and 'Interstellar Overdrive' from Pink Floyd's album *The Piper at the Gates of Dawn* (1967), the album *The Space Ritual Alive in Liverpool and London* (1973) by the British group Hawkwind, Pink Floyd's *The Dark Side of the Moon* (1973)… In the German 'Krautrock', *kosmische Musik* was developed by Tangerine Dream (see the analysis of *Stratosfear*, 1976, in the chapter on listening) and Klaus Schulze (for example, in his album *Dune*, 1979, which was initially to be the soundtrack for a film based on Frank Herbert's homonymous science-fiction novel, the realisation of which was abandoned).

In electroacoustic music, the 1970s saw the descendants of Schaeffer break with his relatively weak interest in the question of space – in his *Treatise on Musical Objects*, Schaeffer grants only meagre place to this issue. Of course, *musique concrète* had already imagined numerous setups for dealing with the dimension of space. Thus, **Example 6.7 (online)** shows Schaeffer playing the 'space desk', an invention intended to create 'sonic relief' during a performance and which was used for the first time in *Orphée 51 ou toute la Lyre* by the two Pierres (Schaeffer and Henry) in a 1951 concert. Moreover, other pioneers working at the GRM – in addition to Xenakis who has been mentioned previously – quickly became interested in space, as was the case with the engineer Jacques Poullin (1957) who, in the 1950s, published one of the first important articles on the question and invented several setups (including the 'space desk').

It is true, however, that it was not until the 1970s that a second generation of *concrète* musicians proposed a lasting solution for the question of space. This would be the task, in particular, of *Gmebaphone* of the GMEB (Groupe de musique expérimentale de Bourges), inaugurated in 1973, and the GRM's *acousmonium*. Inaugurated in 1974, the latter can be defined as an 'orchestra' of loudspeakers, these being arranged facing the audience or behind, on the sides, or even in its midst. A musician at the console, organising the projection of the sound, was often the composer himself. Beginning in the 1990s, a school of 'performers' was born, and playing the acousmonium proposed to be the (spatial) interpretation of a piece on support (which could already contain spatial information). Today, the acousmonium perpetuates the initial logic of the orchestra of loudspeakers (including loudspeakers of different makes and, consequently, having different 'timbres') whilst adding multi-channel work (5+1, 7+1, 8 channels) to it where all the loudspeakers are identical. In **Example 6.8 (online)**, we find a manuscript by François Bayle specifying the arrangement of the acousmonium for the premiere of *Morceaux de ciels* (1998). The logic espoused by the acousmonium for resolving the problem of spatial diffusion of electroacoustic music gained widespread acceptance. The 1980s and 1990s witnessed similar sound systems: the acousmatic machine of the GMVL (Groupe Musiques Vivantes de Lyon, Bernard Fort and Xavier Garcia), the acousmonium of Musiques et Recherches (Belgium, Annette Vande Gorne), the Motus acousmonium (Denis Dufour), the System of the CRM (Centro Ricerche Musicali, Rome), the orchestra of loudspeakers of the Miso studio (Lisbon, Miguel Azguime)…

Amongst the numerous pioneering works in the field of sound synthesis, we shall mention those of John Chowning. In his article 'The Simulation of Moving Sound', Chowning (1971) described how he generated a computer program controlling the apparent localisation and movement of a synthesised sound in a virtual acoustical space. This program controls a quadraphonic playback, and is used in *Turenas* (1972; see the analysis by L. Pottier, 2004) – a piece already mentioned in the previous chapter regarding FM synthesis – with such success that Jean-Claude Risset (personal communication, February 2012; our translation) would say, 'John Chowning's work on the illusions of space and movement of sound sources gave rise, with *Sabelith* and *Turenas*, to striking sensations of immersion in virtual spaces, more meaningful than the multiplication of loudspeakers'.

At the very beginning of the 1980s, the *new wave* (with, for example, the album *Faith* by Cure, 1981) systematised the use of reverberation, echo and delay, this time creating the sensation of a space with 'damp' sound (K. Blasquiz, 2010: 63). In contemporary music, the decade was marked by one of IRCAM's first major realisations, *Répons* by Boulez. Boulez had already been interested in space, for example in the version for clarinet and six instrumental groups of *Domaines* (1961–1968), which calls for the soloist to move about on stage. In *Répons* (1981–1984, for soloists, instrumental ensemble and real-time electronics), he used the 'halaphone', perfected by Hans-Peter Haller, to spatialise sounds. The piece is written for instrumental ensemble and six soloists, surrounding the audience, with the sounds of the soloists transformed and spatialised. **Example 6.9 (online)** shows the spatialisation that begins at figure 21 in the score.

The same decade also witnessed the first performance of another major work in which space constitutes a central challenge: Nono's *Prometeo* (1981–1984, revised 1985), for vocal and instrumental soloists, chorus, orchestra and live electronics. Nono took inspiration from Saint Mark's Basilica (Venice) *cori spezzati*; for this *tragedia dell'ascolto*. In Chapter 3, excerpts from the fine interview between Nono and Cacciari were quoted, showing how, for the Italian composer, the problem of space originated in the question of listening. We shall insist here on the fact that it is also linked to the question of *plurality*. As Nono wrote (1993: 490; our translation):

> The unification of spatial and musical listening is the result of the unidirectional, unidimensional use of geometry. [...] With the concentration of musical experience in theatres and concert halls, what irremediably disappears is the spatiality peculiar to places where, in a continual upheaval, innumerable geometries intermingle... [...] In the basilica San Marco, you advance, you walk and discover ever-new spaces but you sense them rather than read them, you hear them, even if there is no music.

To restore the plurality of listening, the Italian composer reconstructed the plurality of the space: multiplicity is at the heart of his musical thinking, like the libretto of *Prometeo*, which is not made up of scenes, but of 'islands', the whole forming an archipelago, as L. Feneyrou (2006) shows (see **Example 6.10 online**). As for spatialisation in *Prometeo*, it is obtained by the particular arrangement of the vocal and instrumental forces as well as by the electronics. As concerns the latter, Hans-Peter Haller (1987: 155), who assisted Nono, distinguished between transformations of sound (ring modulator, harmonizer...), sound selection (banks of filters of second, third and fifth) and, precisely, sound distribution. For the latter, he noted that 'gates' (voltage-controlled amplifiers) were used, along with a halaphone and delay devices. **Example 6.11 (online)** gives an outline of sound distribution through loudspeakers, distinguishing between movements (sounds going from one loudspeaker to the other) and static signals (sounds emitted only by loudspeaker).

The 1990s–2000s

In the years 1990–2000, reference to space tended to become widespread, doubtless because, as affirmed Hugues Dufourt (1998: 273; our translation) – who based himself on the experience of spectral music in which space is omnipresent – 'the music of our time is a music of space'. At the turn of the century, with the 1997 symposium *Space: music-philosophy* (see J.M. Chouvel, M. Solomos, ed., 1998), one notices the polysemy of the term – a polysemy such that, like Georges Perec (1974), one might speak of 'species of spaces' – which perhaps also explains its becoming widespread.

To focus on the composability of physical space, we must mention, in the field of instrumental or mixed music, the work of Emmanuel Nunes. Criticising the uses of space deemed 'anecdotal', he wished its 'musical' appropriation (see E. Nunes, 1994: 122). In his music, a youthful work, *Purlieu* (1969, for 21 strings), already worked on spatialisation with groups of musicians placed on different levels and at a distance. In *Tif'ereth* (1978–1985, for six solo instruments and six orchestral groups under two conductors), the soloists are spread out in the hall, and Nunes composed itineraries in space. *Quodlibet* (1991) systematised this idea. Recycling materials from his earlier works – hence the title – this piece, even though adaptable to other concert halls, was written especially for the Coliseu dos Recreios (Lisbon), where it was premiered in 1991, a site, Nunes specified, full of childhood memories.[4] One of the particularities of this hall is its high degree of resonance, which means that the sensation of a unique hall tends to be lost in favour of a plurality of venues. There, Nunes carried out precise location searches, chronometer in hand, for the displacement of sounds of several instruments. In the work, an orchestra and seven soloists are placed onstage, twenty-one instrumentalists are mobile, and six percussionists semi-mobile. The space is occupied both horizontally and vertically, with four levels of height being defined: the stage, the grand and upper circles, and the gallery above them. To write the piece, the composer defined a certain number of situations where the instruments have a precise place, which he calls 'tonic of situation' (see **Example 6.12 online**). Commenting on *Quodlibet*, Nunes concluded:

> It would be possible to conceive a piece of which the most of the parameters would be linked to the results and conditionings provided by the most extensive research on the site, in such an intrinsic way that its execution would be possible only in this same venue [...] It will have been understood that *Quodlibet* is not such a piece. The work is found, in the same time, *beneath* and *beyond* the potentialities of the hall.
>
> (E. Nunes, 1995)

In the *Lichtung* cycle (*I*, *II* and *III*, respectively 1991, 1996 and 2007, for ensemble and electronics), Nunes pursued his reflection on the composability of space (see P. Szendy, ed., 1998). For example, in the first 25 seconds of *Lichtung I*, which uses the first spatialisation program of the piece, the harmonic parameter is 'frozen' (a chord is held at length), which allows for enhancing the work on space. Alain Bioteau's analysis (1998: 47) shows that the spatialised sounds of three instrumental pairs create a three-dimensional sound phenomenon. The cello and percussion are associated by a triangle that would have pivoted; the clarinet and horn form, respectively, a rectangle diagonally and a diamond; the trombone and tuba complement each other to occupy the whole circle of loudspeakers (see **Example 6.13**).

A great many composers of instrumental or mixed music advanced the history of the composition of space in the 1990s and 2000s: Marco Stroppa, Xu Yi, Olga Neuwirth, Luca Francesconi, Beat Furrer, Heiner Goebbels, Jonathan Harvey,

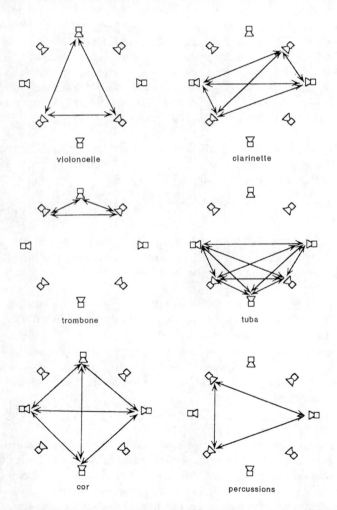

Example 6.13 Emmanuel Nunes, *Lichtung I:* first spatialisation program of the piece (after A. Bioteau, 1998: 46–47). © By kind permission of Alain Bioteau.

Isabel Mundry, Liza Lim, Philippe Leroux, Georgia Spiropoulos ... If we focus on electroacoustic music, the reflection on space is so widespread that we could go so far as to evoke 'the possibility of a new kind of music; computer-managed signal processing offers unprecedented possibilities in the control of sound fields, and the promise of three-dimensional music is on the horizon. A paradigm shift is under way' (P. Lennox, 2009: 268). Let us examine a few advances on the matter.

Techniques already known continue to be developed. The same is true of the orchestra-of-loudspeakers concept: we can think, for example, of recent developments by musicians associated with the BEAST (Birmingham ElectroAcoustic Sound Theatre) sound system founded in 1982 by Jonty Harrison, which, regarding spatialisation, closely mix research on composition and thinking about performance (see J. Harrison, 2018). In parallel, multiphony became widespread with four or eight tracks (quadraphony and octophony). One of the classics of octophony, which postulated the composability of space, is Stockhausen's *Oktophonie* (1990–1991). Realised on eight tracks, it uses electronic equipment exclusively (with a few passages where the voices of Simon Stockhausen and Kathinka Pasveer are heard). During the performance, the tracks are projected using diagrams provided in the score through eight groups of

> two or more loudspeakers, which should be directed so that the group can be heard everywhere. In this music, vertical and diagonal movements are composed for the first time, in addition to the horizontal movements of the earlier 4-channel or 8-channel electronic music.
>
> (K. Stockhausen, 1990/91: XIX)

The arrangement of these groups of loudspeakers must follow the diagram provided by the composer (**Example 6.14 online**). The contents of the eight tracks was thought out according to this spatialisation:

> In order to be able to hear such movements – especially simultaneously – the musical rhythm has to be drastically slowed down; the pitch changes must take place less often and only in smaller steps or with glissandi, so that they can be followed, the composition of dynamics serves the audibility of the individual layers – i.e. dependent on the timbres of the layers and the speed of their movements; the timbre composition primary serves the elucidation of these movements.
>
> (Ibid: XXVIII)

In contrast to multiphony, where the channels are independent, the surround technique developed, aiming at (re)constructing sound fields by combining the information contained in the tracks, a bit like stereophony was already doing. This is the case with the 5.0 or 5.1 formats, which come from cinema. With them, the number of loudspeakers is identical to the number of channels, the presence of the '1' after the decimal point indicating the existence of a channel dedicated to the sub-bass. In 5.1, the central speaker gives the illusion of localisation (it is quite useful for cinema, so that the spectator has the impression that the sound 'comes from' the image – it is, of course, very important for the human voice), the other two front speakers (left and right) reproduce the stereo and, finally, the two rear speakers add sound depth, enveloping the listener.

The setups of surround techniques, like stereophony or multiphony have a weak point: the listener must be located at an optimal listening point, called the 'sweet spot' (see **Example 6.15 online**); consequently, the ideal would be to organise concerts for a single listener. One particular surround technique seeks to avoid this drawback: ambisonics. Developed in 1974 but not becoming widespread until the 1990s thanks to, amongst others, the works of researchers at the universities of York and Derby, this process consists of encoding sound directions and amplitudes, then decoding them by creating the sensation of a 3D space. The space generated can be horizontal (panphonic system) – as with aforementioned surround systems – but can also be spherical (periphonic system). Moreover, ambisonics can be first order: in that case, one will use three coordinates, X, Y and Z, for the encoding, which are recorded on separate tracks; with ambisonics of second order or higher orders, more coordinates, and therefore more tracks, are necessary. To the degree that ambisonics consists of giving an approximation of a wavefield by a sort of 'quantisation' of directions from which the sounds come, the approximation becomes more precise as the order increases, which means it takes more tracks for the encoding and more loudspeakers for the decoding. (As an example of ambisonics, see the HOA Library developed by MUSIDANSE/CICM' lab: see. A. Sedes et al., 2014).

Amongst musicians who have ventured in this technique, we shall mention the composer Natasha Barrett, known more generally for her work on space. She wrote that, 'with ambisonics, because you can accurately compose the spatial information, you gain tighter control over the spatial musical structure and therefore allow it to play a more important role' (in F. Otondo, 2007: 12). When she works with ambisonics, she prefers third-order systems:

> The higher the order of the encoding, the more loudspeakers we need in the decoding. But a nice compromise is to use a third-order encoding, which in the horizontal axis requires a minimum of eight loudspeakers and fits quite nicely into a small concert situation.
>
> (in F. Otondo, 2007:13)

'Wavefield synthesis' (WFS) constitutes another technique for recreating space, which has developed recently. Introduced in the late 1980s with research at the University of Delft (Netherlands), it is based on a principle discovered by a 17th-century Dutch physicist, Huygens. We know that a sound source emits waves spreading in ever-larger circles: this is what is called a wavefront. When a wavefront reaches the listener, he localises the source according to the intensity and curve of this front. According to Huygens's principle, one can reconstruct a wavefront of a primary source from a multitude of linear second sources. In WFS, these secondary sources are loudspeakers forming a wall facing or encircling the listener.

By playing on the delays of the same signal through the loudspeakers, a wavefront can be simulated. To achieve a good simulation, it takes a large number of loudspeakers, treated independently, i.e., with the help of considerable calculating power. In compensation, WFS – which, like ambisonics, provides convincing listening for all listeners and not only those located in the 'sweet spot' (as is the case with stereophony, in the 5.0. type of immersion systems, or in multiphony) – is related to holophony. In the name of this technique, we find the word 'synthesis', for the sound stage is recreated artificially: the interest of WFS is being able to create complex virtual stages. Another interesting feature of this technique is emphasised by Simon Emmerson (2007: 166):

> The most revolutionary aspect of this development is [...] in its conceptualization of 'real-time' performance on such a system. At present a multichannel format requires a mix onto that specific number of channels (4, 8, 5.1, 7.1, for example); any change requires a new mix. WFS is 'object-oriented'; individual sound objects or attributes (reverberation, for example) may be defined along with their spatial positions and trajectories. It is then up to the playback software to 'allocate' these to the individual loudspeakers of the specific array (which may vary from place to place). In other words, the composer's specifications contain no loudspeaker (track or channel) information.

The technologies we have just mentioned constitute loudspeaker-based setups, but many other ways of composing the sound–space have appeared or are being developed. Thus, alongside setups with loudspeakers, binaural systems have been developed, primarily meant for headphone-listening. A history of these systems could go back to Clément Adler's *'théâtrophone'*. The French inventor, better known for his contribution to the development of aeronautics, presented at the 1881 World Fair a system allowing for broadcasting concerts or plays recorded at the Opera, Opéra-Comique or Théâtre-Français (Paris), which the audience listened to with two earphones for which Adler had perfected a recording system prefiguring stereophony (see A. Lange, undated). The history of binaural systems was then quite dense, for 'the perception that binaural is the "correct" system was, and still is, supported by the concept that if we achieve exact duplication of what the ear would hear in a natural situation, we will produce the best reproduction' (D. Malham, 2001: 35). Of course, this nearly privileged situation grew, due to the low cost of binaural systems.

We should also mention spatialisation softwares that are independent of the reproduction method and of the type of electroacoustic setup chosen for diffusion. Let us mention only the Spatialisateur (see T. Carpentier et al., 2015) developed by the Acoustique team of the IRCAM auditoria beginning in the mid-1990s up to the present day. With this program, spatialisation is realised, beginning with composition itself, using a binaural system; for playing, it can be adapted to the chosen setup. Moreover, the Spatialisateur integrates refined work in psychoacoustics: it simulates hall acoustics thanks to perceptive criteria that enable the user to specify intuitively the hall's sound characteristics without resorting to knowledge regarding acoustics or concert-hall architecture. The software can be used in real-time (the composer combines a hall effect with a sound event in the score), in postproduction and in virtual-reality setups or interactive sound installations.

The composed sound–space: a typology test

To finish this brief history of composed musical spaces, **Example 6.16** proposes a sketch of typology, distinguishing between four main categories. The first concerns the *nature of the space*, which can be real or virtual. In the second case, the musical work simulates spaces or else gives the sensation of space through work on delays, filters, panning or panoramisation, microtemporal decorrelations, etc. In the first case, it is the concrete, physical venue where the work to be given is worked on, in relation with the latter. In this way, the work exists only by and through this venue (even though one can often envisage an adaptation for other venues, as is the case with Nono's *Prometeo* or Nunes's *Quodlibet*), and, consequently, in the most successful cases, it becomes difficult to speak of 'work' prior to performance. There are numerous intermediary situations. Thus, the spatialisation of sound – to take the example of multiphony, the passage of an audio track from one loudspeaker to another – implements a real space due to the arrangement of the loudspeakers in the concrete concert venue; simultaneously, it calls for a

1. Nature of the space:	- Real			
	- Virtual			
2. Sound source:	- Acoustic:	- Setup:	- Frontal	
			- In the hall	
		- Movement:	- With	
			- Without	
	- Loudspeakers:	- Multiphony:	Spatialisation:	- Static
				- Kinetic
		- Stereo, surround:	- Stereophony	
			- Surround:	- 5.0…
				- Ambisonics
				- WFS
	- Mixed			
	- Earphones:	Binaural systems		
3. Type of writing:	- Localisation			
	- Figures			
	- Immersion			
	- Space ambiences:	- Existent		
		- Imaginary		
4. Space and sound:	- Parametric processing			
	- Morphological processing			

Example 6.16 Typology of composed musical spaces.

virtual space since the sound system has a large share of autonomy facing the concert venue.

The second main category concerns the *sources* that generate sound. The sources of an acoustic nature (musical instruments or other) can be arranged frontally, in classic configuration, or invade the concert hall; one can ask the musicians to change place or not. As concerns loudspeakers, the essential has been said previously. Overall, one will distinguish between multiphonic diffusion (orchestra of loudspeakers, octophony, etc.) and systems generating an overall space. In the first case, spatialisation can be static (one track is played by the same loudspeaker or group of loudspeakers) or kinetic (a track goes from one loudspeaker to another). In the latter, stereophony still has a bright future but is increasingly challenged by 5.0-type surround systems, ambisonics and WFS. Third possibility: the source can be mixed (combining acoustic source and loudspeakers). Last possibility: headphones and the various binaural systems.

The third category deals with the *type of writing*. Space can be used to localise sound: for example, one can assign a particular type of sound to a loudspeaker. One can develop writing that aims at bringing out spatial 'figures', i.e., movements in space that can be systematised and developed like melodic, rhythmic figures... Or else, the sought-after effect can be that of immersion, a theme that has been dealt with at length in this book. Finally, it can be a matter of creating ambiences of existing or imaginary spaces.

The fourth and final main category is interested in the connection between *space and sound*. This differs as regards the definition of sound. If it is defined in terms of parameters, space will be considered one of them; if apprehended in terms of morphology, it will become one of its aspects (or quality). Concerning this latter category, we must mention a decisive change in the way of apprehending space: parametric treatment tends to undergo a reflux in favour of morphological treatment. In fact, space has trouble constituting an autonomous dimension the way pitch was able to:

> Space is a continuous, somewhat blurry parameter in which there are no strong poles such as pitches, intervals... Thanks to space, one can merge sounds or separate them in order to heighten auditory clarity, make them move in different directions, create poles and interferences between rhythm and movements in space.
>
> (O. Warusfel, 2007: 90; our translation)

Experience shows that work on space takes on more sense when it is posed as being indissociable from sound – i.e., when it is treated morphologically – than when it is thought of as a parameter. That is why, in this chapter, we speak of *sound–space*.

The progressive awareness of this indissolubility between sound and space opens new leads: space has become, in the same way as sound, a material for composing. Thus, the interest in space, far from being exhausted since the pioneering works of the 1950s, has increased considerably. Chances are that it will continue to do so and that the amount of research still considered pioneering today, will become commonplace, whereas other research will come into being. One of the most fruitful leads consists of exploring the links between the sound–space and listening, and, at the same time, between sound–space and the body (see R. Meric, 2012).

Music, sound, place

Music and architecture

The discussion about relations between music and space can lead to reflecting on the link between music and architecture, a reflection that fascinates more and more musicians. They have always been aware of the influence of a hall's acoustics on music. Michael Forsyth (1985: 3), author of a book on music and architecture notes that

> From early times the acoustics of stone buildings have surely influenced the development of Western music, as in Romanesque churches, where the successive notes of plainchant melody reverberate and linger in the lofty enclosure, becoming superimposed to produce the idea of harmony.

Thus, preparing the ground for the effective arrival of the latter.

More generally, one could postulate 'that room acoustics has such an influence on musical composition and performance that the architectural traditions of different races, and hence the acoustic characteristics of their buildings, influenced fundamentally the type of music that they developed' (Ibid: 3). The transformation that is leading music towards sound is pushing musicians to take even greater interest in the relation with architecture, thought of as the extension of their interest in space.

On their side, architects have traditionally concentrated less on thinking about the relationship between space and sound except, of course, in the case of concert halls. However, things are progressively changing. Thus, Barry Blesser and Linda-Ruth Salter propose the creation of 'aural architecture', a new sub-discipline of architecture, which would complement acoustic architecture:

> *Aural architecture* refers to the properties of a space that can be *experienced* by listening. An *aural architect*, acting as both an artist and a social engineer, is therefore someone who selects specific aural attributes of a space based on what is desirable in a particular cultural framework. [...] In contrast, an *acoustic architect* is a builder, an engineer or physical scientist who implements the aural attributes previously selected by an aural architect.
>
> (B. Blesser, L.R. Salter, 2007: 5)

To come back to musicians, Wagner was amongst the first to have had the opportunity to reflect on the architecture–music connection. Beginning in 1850, he dreamed of building a theatre devoted to his music. He would have to wait until 1871 to achieve this dream, thanks to the support of King Ludwig II, outside the small Bavarian town of Bayreuth. The Bayreuth Festspielhaus, built by

Otto Brückwald and inaugurated in 1876, focusses on the needs of Wagnerian drama, and the seats offer excellent visibility for all spectators. Thanks to subdued lighting, a double proscenium arch and a few other effects, what is acted out on stage appears illusory, seeming to be a matter of a 'spatial beyond'. This sensation is reinforced by the artifice that Wagner came up with for transforming the sound of the orchestra: the orchestra is entirely hidden in a pit (that can contain up to 130 musicians and is 6 steps below the stage). Due to this, not only is the sound of the orchestra attenuated but does not risk covering the singers' voices too; in addition, it reaches the listener only entirely reflected and thus blending closely with the voices, it 'gives the music a mysterious, far-off tone' (M. Forsyth, 1985: 193) – an effect reinforced by the reverberation time of 1.6 seconds in the mid-range frequencies when the hall is full, a relatively long time for an opera house.

In the 20th century, one of the major contributions to the music–architecture discussion came from Xenakis. Pioneering composer of avant-garde music, Xenakis could just as well have had a career as an architect. When he moved to Paris in 1947, with his Greek degree in civil engineering, he was hired by Le Corbusier. Initially limited to calculations, his role there turned increasingly to architecture itself. After leaving Le Corbusier's studio (1959) – following the famous dispute between the two men regarding the paternity of the Philips Pavilion of the 1958 Brussels World's Fair – he would concentrate on music and carry out only a few architectural projects. Nowadays, his pioneering role in architecture is beginning to be recognised and studied, as much through his realisations or projects as through his writings (see I. Xenakis, 2008; S. Sterken, 2004; S. Bridoux-Michel, 2006; E. Kiourtsoglou, 2016).

One might rightly think that Xenakis the architect influenced Xenakis the musician. Indeed, many of the characteristics peculiar to his music are perhaps explained by this influence. He himself commented on one of the most important:

> In music, you begin with a theme or a melody [...]. You start from the mini to attain the global. In architecture however, you must simultaneously conceive the details and the ensemble, otherwise, it all falls apart. This approach, this experience at Le Corbusier's studio and side by side with him obviously influenced me (even though I sensed it all along), or at least helped me conceive my music like an architectural project: globally and in detail at the same time.
>
> (I. Xenakis, 2008: 72)

The opposite path – from music to architecture – seems to have been taken less often by Xenakis since, in the final analysis, he carried out few architectural projects. But they are perhaps even more spectacular. Two architectural realisations bear witness to this, both stemming from the founding musical work, *Metastaseis* (1953–1954, for orchestra). The first concerns the famous 'undulating glass panes' of the La Tourette monastery (**Example 6.17 online**). Xenakis (2008: 64) wrote:

> In June 1954, I was studying the glass openings, 366 centimetres high, for the level of the common rooms and the classrooms. I discovered the intoxicating

effect of combining architectural elements, after having experimented with them in music. Indeed, in *Metastaseis* for orchestra, which I was finishing at about the same time (1953–54), the central section was constructed on a combinatorial organization of melodic intervals.

The adopted solution would end up diverging from a simple transposition of the musical realisation in question, of which **Example 6.18 (online)** gives an excerpt. The fact remains that these panes of glass, because they have real 'rhythm', seem 'musical': Le Corbusier – who admired music – 'was so pleased that he wanted to call them "musical glass panes"' (Ibid: 65).

Second example: *Metastaseis* innovates by introducing the graphic method for composing. As we know, entire sections of Xenakis's earliest music were conceived using graphics on the basis of a transposition of the two coordinates: from bottom to top, the pitches (from low to high) are read, and from left to right, the time. Thus, on the sound level, straight lines can give *glissandi*, these sounds with continuous pitch variations, so characteristic of early Xenakis, which we discussed in Chapter 5. In measures 309–314 of *Metastaseis*, we encounter *glissandi* of a particular type, which, geometrically speaking, constitute ruled surfaces: **Example 6.19** shows Xenakis's graph. A few years later, the composer-architect had to design the architecture of the Philips Pavilion. Le Corbusier asked him to think of it as a 'bottle'. After several sketches, Xenakis used the drawing of

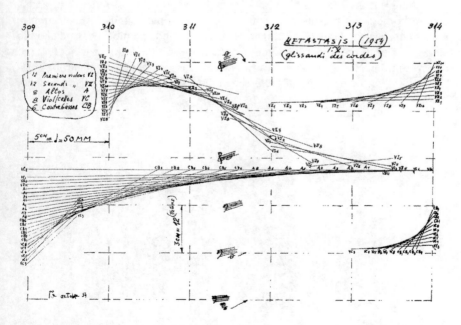

Example 6.19 Iannis Xenakis, *Metastaseis*, measures 309–314: graphic by Xenakis (Archives Xenakis). © By kind permission of Mâkhi Xenakis.

222 Sound–space

glissandi in question: the *glissandi* in ruled musical surfaces would become the famous hyperbolic paraboloids of the Pavilion (see **Example 6.20**).

A final aspect of music-architecture relations with Xenakis concerns the construction of places intended especially for music (and visual spectacles), as it is the case with his last *polytope*, the *Diatope* that was realised for the inauguration of the Centre Georges Pompidou in Paris (1978) and commented on in Chapter 4 regarding immersive sound–space and Dionysian immersion. The textile architecture of *Diatope* (see the photo in Chapter 4), which housed a spectacle where the splendid electroacoustic work entitled *La Légende d'Eer* was played along with a fully digitised visual show, takes up the form of the Philips Pavilion; however,

> the *Diatope*'s form, because of the laser trajectories, also had to conform to the following principle: a maximum of free volume for a minimum of enclosing surface. The classical answer is the sphere. But the sphere, beautiful in itself, is poor for acoustics and less rich tactilely than some other, double-curvature forms. Whence the current configuration, which is a sphere in its principles, yet open to the world by the convergence of its geometrical construction, using hyperbolic paraboloids.
>
> (I. Xenakis, 2008: 262)

This architectural structure was dismantled in order to travel. Unfortunately, it was reassembled elsewhere only once, in Bonn, before disappearing forever.

Although it is exceptional to encounter the conjunction of music and architecture in the same person, as was the case with Xenakis, music's ever-greater interest in space and that of certain architects for sound and music have led to the emergence of joint projects by a musician and an architect. This was notably the case with Luigi Nono's *Prometeo*, which we discussed previously, regarding spatialisation. For the premiere of the piece in the Venetian church of San Lorenzo,

Example 6.20 The Philips Pavilion: drawing by Xenakis (Archives Xenakis). © By kind permission of Mâkhi Xenakis.

Nono asked architect Renzo Piano (1987:167) to construct a 'musical space', not a stage set, specifying that he thought of this space as an 'archipelago', i.e., a place where one cannot embrace all the islands, but where one senses their presence. Renzo Piano (1987: 168; our translation) notes:

> From these beginnings was born the basic conception of the whole arrangement of the decor: an archipelago at the centre of which is the audience, surrounded by a musical stage that can never be seen in its entirety, all at once, but must always be perceived in its entirety thanks to the music, which, like the sea breeze, is born behind our shoulders but manifests its effects before our eyes.

Thus, 'the space [is] *read* by the sound [and] the sound *revealed* by the space' (L. Manzione, 2006: 204; our translation). The arrangement that Piano thought up (see **Example 6.21**) consisted of a large wooden arch, which resembled a lute

Example 6.21 Architectural set designed by Renzo Piano for Luigi Nono's *Prometeo*. © By kind permission of Fondazione Archivio Luigi Nono.

or mandolin, built on several levels, where the audience and instrumentalists sat, the loudspeakers playing the electronic music being outside the arch. Thus, the spectator is neither completely outside (facing) the music, nor completely inside, but located between those two spaces, overturning the traditional conception of the inside–outside relation.

We cannot conclude these few lines on music–architecture relations without mentioning the new concert halls that have been built, taking into account the need for composing space, which is apparent in new music. Such is the case with the projection space at IRCAM (1978) (see **Example 6.22 online**). This truly experimental hall, also designed by Renzo Piano, along with Richard Rogers, has a particularity: its acoustic characteristics are variable. Thus, the reverberation time can go from 0.4 to 4 seconds, thanks to the mobility of its surfaces (ceiling, floor and walls).[5] 'It is virtually a musical instrument in itself, since its acoustic adjustments appear on the scores of works' (M. Forsyth, 1985: 304). Let us also mention Karlsruhe's *Kubus* of the ZKM, finished in 2006. In this space, 39 Meyer loudspeakers totally surround the audience (360°) and are hung in such a way as to be able to orient them as desired; four others stand on the ground. The acoustic space is totally reconfigurable, and the spatialisation, achieved with the Klangdom loudspeaker system, is controlled with the Zirkonium program (see D. Wagner et al., 2014). Finally, let us mention the Sonic Laboratory of the SARC in Belfast, with its 'specialist acoustic space designed to provide a unique and exciting listening experience, in fact, the auditory equivalent of an IMAX cinema. Forty-eight strategically placed loudspeakers will project and move sounds throughout the space, including underneath the audience' (http://www.qub.ac.uk/sarc/facilities/).

Sound installations and 'audible ecosystems'

There exists a category of musical or sonic realisations intrinsically linked to space: sound installations. A sound installation consists of the exchange between a setup and the place housing it. As for the place, either it is indissociable from the installation or it can be adapted to other sites. In both cases, however, it is appropriate to speak of 'place' (or 'venue' or 'site') and not of 'space', the term 'place' designating a precise, clearly determined space. Hence the expression used in English of 'site specific' works, which is rendered in other languages like French by the Latin '*in situ*'. The art of sound installations is recent. But, since the 1970s, they were becoming an increasingly widespread practice, with artists such as Hans Otte, Earle Brown, Paul Panhuysen, Konrad Schnitzler, Peter Vogel, Maryanne Amacher, Alvin Curran, Bernhard Leitner, Rolf Julius, Annea Lockwood, Max Neuhaus, Bruce Nauman, Hugh Davies, Terry Fox, Hildegard Westerkamp, Bill Fontana, Christina Kubisch, Liz Philips, Trimpin (Gerhard Trimpin), José Antonio Orts, Christian Marclay, Nigel Ayers, Janet Cardiff, Laetitia Sonami, Don Ritter, Manuel Rocha Iturbide, Alva Noto (Carsten Nicolai), Ryoji Ikeda, Timo Kahlen, David Monacchi, Zimoun, Miguel Álvarez-Fernández....

Amongst the pioneers of the genre coming from the music field, let us mention La Monte Young and Marian Zazeela. In 1962, Young coined the term 'Dream

House', a place in which a work would be played continuously to finally exist in time like a 'living organism with a life and tradition of its own' (La Monte Young, M. Zazeela, 2004: 10) – and thereby opening listening deeply rooted in time, as was said in Chapter 3. His partner, Marian Zazeela, soon added a lighting component, and the concept expanded: 'The final configuration of each installation is determined by the architecture of the exhibition site, making each sound and light environment a unique work with its own form and proportions' (La Monte Young, M. Zazeela, 1996: 219).

Again in the United States, there is a tradition of musicians practising sound installations that doubtless could have been better described as sound setup, with, however, an anchoring in the place as strong as in the installations per se. Here we might mention Alvin Lucier and his famous *I am Sitting in a Room* (1969), which was discussed in Chapter 3: it is, in fact, a sound installation (or sound setup in powerful interaction with its environment).[6] Another realisation characteristic of the same composer is his *Music on a Long Thin Wire* (1977), where a monochord of approximately 27 metres, which is activated by an electronic oscillator, interacts with its installation space; this realisation could also be described as a sonic sculpture. Other musicians belonging to the same tradition are Pauline Oliveros, David Behrman or David Tudor.

In Europe, a tradition of sound installations was established in Germany, accompanied by theoretical thinking (see H. de la Motte-Haber, ed., 1999; U. Tadday, ed., 2008; J. Rebentisch, 2003). There we encounter figures such as Christina Kubisch, who studied both music and visual arts and whose itinerary gives us one of the origins of the idea of sound installation: 'In the works of Christina Kubisch, it is clear that the sound installation genre developed from performance art, condensing multidimensional actions' (H. de la Motte-Haber, undated; our translation). One of the most interesting artists living in Germany is the Canadian Robin Minard, with the installations *Music for Quiet Spaces* (1984), *Soundwalls* (1988), *Silent Music* (1994-2010: see **Example 6.23** and **6.24 (online)**), *Nature morte* (2008), *Outside In (Blue)* (2010)... Minard (1999: 73) writes:

> One of my primary concerns has been to establish a dialogue between the work I create, the space within which I install the work and a public who either experiences my work in passing or who lives or functions with my work over a longer period of time. My installations most often aim to intensify the public's experience of the chosen space or to provide the public with a new or enriched perception of their surroundings.

One form of sound installation which reinforces the indissolubility of sound and space is the 'audible ecosystems' of the Italian composer Agostino Di Scipio. His thinking also allows him to broach the notion of 'emergence' in the precise sense of the term, a notion that introduces the idea of composing sound from a new angle of approach. The notion of emergence was elaborated by the cognitive sciences, beginning in the late 1970s. Francisco Varela (1996) set it out as the second major paradigm of the cognitive sciences, contrasting it with the computational paradigm.

Example 6.23 Robin Minard, *Silent Music*, Stadtgalerie Saarbrücken, 1999 (www.robinminard.com). © By kind permission of Robin Minard. Photo: Tom Gundelwein, Courtesy of the Stadtgalerie Saarbrücken.

The latter – which dominated the earliest cognitive sciences from the 1950s through the 1970s, and which is far from being supplanted today – is based on the idea that the brain functions like a computer: on the one hand, it would consist of a data-processing system; on the other, calculation would bear on symbols, meaning that the (physical) support and sense are linked only by conventions. The paradigm of emergence takes inspiration from the neuronal network, which brings with it the idea of a sub-symbolic functioning: the 'upper' level (intelligence, sense, etc.) *would emerge* from the network itself. This is why Varela (1989) is one of the pioneers of the notion of autopoiesis and, more generally, the notion of autonomous systems of which self-organisation is the condition for emergence.

Di Scipio's music lies in the granular paradigm, which was discussed in Chapter 5, a paradigm that it radicalises. Whereas pioneering granular composers, such as Xenakis and Vaggione, developed this approach primarily as to microform (material), Di Scipio constructed the hypothesis that macroform itself could ensue from the granular, i.e., from microform, by a logic of emergence. In his writings, he elaborated the 'theory of sonological emergence', in which form is conceived as 'formation of timbre' – 'form' here being synonymous with macroform, and 'timbre' with microform (see A. Di Scipio 1994 and 2008). This theory postulates that one can try to 'determine a ground-level system's or process's quantitative organisation capable of bringing forth a meta-level system or process of peculiar qualitative, morphological properties' (A. Di Scipio, 1994: 205). According to this logic, the 'sounding results of composition' are apprehended as musical form, 'but in the special sense in which *timbre* – the qualitative emerging properties of the sonic structure – can be conceived as *form*. Thus [...] form can be described as a *process of timbre formation*' (A. Di Scipio, 1994: 205). In his compositions, Di Scipio would use chaos theories, for 'chaos and the dynamics of complex systems, as accessible with iterated numerical processes, represented for me a way to compose small sonic units such that a higher-level sonority would manifest itself in the process' (A. Di Scipio in C. Anderson, 2005: 13).

According to the theory of sonological emergence, the emergence of sound structures is possible because of the fact that the composer develops systems (in the sense of cybernetics) close to living systems, which are characterized by their capacity for self-organization:

> The passage of a system or process from a given structural organization to a new state of order which is recognized as a function of the qualitative properties of the former, is what we call here a phenomenon of emergence [...]. Similar phenomena can be described with rules of *morphostasis* (conservation of coherence, identity) and *morphogenesis* (dynamical behaviour, change), which together capture the main peculiarity of social and living systems: self-organization.
>
> (Di Scipio, 1994: 206)

To make sure of self-organisation in a field where this idea is not self-evident – the sound or music are not 'living' – the Italian composer uses 'circular causality', which extends the idea of feedback. For instance, in *Due di Uno* (2003, for violin, piccolo recorder and adaptive DSP), the instrumental sounds, which are electronically transformed, are also used as input for controlling these transformations (see Di Scipio, 2007).

As a result of this circular causality, Di Scipio redefines the usual notion in live electronics of 'interaction' (see Di Scipio, 2003). According to the usual notion, interaction operates as an information flow: a sound source is transformed. The system is therefore not very interactive. Or else, one can say that the underlying musical paradigm is that of instrumental playing, the agent being the musician, the setup, the instrument, with the composer being concerned solely with the (sound) *result* (see Ibid: 269). According to Di Scipio, composition could, on the contrary, consist of *composing the interactions* – the result not being what is composed directly. One would then have a truly interactive system; in this type of system:

> a principal aim would be to create a *dynamical system* exhibiting an adaptive behaviour to the surrounding external conditions, and capable of interfering with the external conditions themselves. [...] A kind of *self-organization* is thus achieved [...]. Here, 'interaction' is a structural element for something like a 'system' to emerge [...]. System interactions, then, would be only *indirectly* implemented, the by-products of carefully planned-out

interdependencies among system components [...]. This is a substantial move from interactive music composing to composing musical interactions, and perhaps more precisely it should be described as *a shift from creating wanted sounds via interactive means, towards creating wanted interactions having audible traces.*

(Ibid: 271)

Di Scipio's insistence on composed interactions is what allows for making a system 'live', considering it self-regulated and, consequently, expecting emergence. On this point, a parallel with Varela's ideas on the question of *autonomy* can be interesting. Varela criticises the conception of the brain given by the computational paradigm, for which the latter, in its contact with the world, would function like a data-processing system. This point of view, the origin of which is the computer conceived as a universal machine for resolving problems, is the point of view of the 'command' (or allonomy): the brain would be a black box with input, transformations and output. On the contrary, the autonomy point of view postulates that the brain continually interacts with the outside (see F. Varela, 1989: 7–16). Varela's autonomous (or autopoietic) systems emit the hypothesis that one cannot separate the system from its environment, which is part of the former. The emergence in question is linked to the fact that interactions and their transformations 'constitute the system as a concrete unit in the space where it exists, specifying the topological domain where it is achieved as a network' (F. Varela, 1989: 45).

Going back to Di Scipio's music, one of the strongest originalities is having developed the idea of 'ecosystem' in certain works. In the set of pieces entitled *Audible Ecosystemics* (in progress since 2002, for live solo electronics) – a set that offers the musical achievement of composed interactions in the form of pure sound installations or, more exactly, performance-installations – the ecosystem is formed by a triangular interaction between the musician, the DSP patches and the sound ambience (see **Example 6.25 online**). The performance site is closely associated with the system of composed interactions, and it should be noted that the sound ambience also includes the audience and its reactions, therefore leaving an audible trace in the work. In the first piece, subtitled '1. Impulse Response Study', the 'material' is made up only of impulses, and the entire piece consists of studying the responses of the hall to those impulses, using these responses to control, transform and develop this material. The second, '2a. Feedback Study', includes only feedback sounds, the nature of which depends considerably, of course, on the hall. The study '2b. Feedback Study, Sound Installation' also uses feedback, but several performers interfere with sounds produced with their mouth or hands 'playing' the microphone. The study '3a. Background Noise Study' is perhaps the most radical: it starts from 'nothing', i.e., no preliminary material, then the hall's background noise, amplified, goes into the system and comes out again, transformed. Finally, '3b. Background Noise Study, with Mouth Performer' (see **Example 6.26**) uses the same idea but, this time, the 'environment' is the performer's mouth.

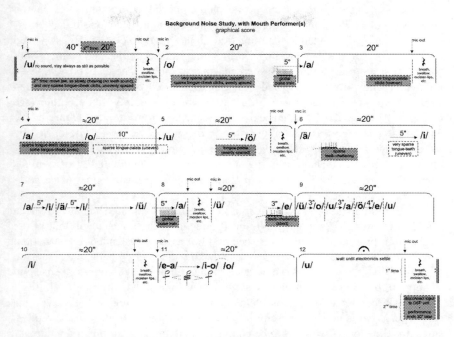

Example 6.26 Agostino Di Scipio: score for the *Audible Ecosystemics:* '3b. Background Noise Study, with Mouth Performer' (http://agostinodiscipio.xoom.it/ad iscipi/materials.htm). © By kind permission of Agostino Di Scipio.

On space, Di Scipio (1999) says:

> I'm not interested in creating any 'virtual' space. [...] I much prefer to focus on the concrete, material, historical space (hall, room, open place, etc.) hosting the performance [...], in an attempt to make the real space leave audible traces of itself within the form of the sound, within timbre. This is a way of experiencing space which, I think, is less ideologised and contrasts the notion of 'virtual reality'.

In the *Audible Ecosystemics*, space acts as both exciter and resonance chamber: the idea is pushed even further: this leads to a particular role given to noise. To simplify, we shall say that noise is no longer disturbance (traditional music) or new material to transform (contemporary music) but becomes one of the agents of interaction, since it emanates from the concrete space – the site, the environment –, which is an integral part of the system. In the *Audible Ecosystemics*, 'the role of *noise* is crucial [...]. Noise is the medium itself where a sound-generating system is situated, strictly speaking, its *ambience*. In addition, noise is the energy supply by which a self-organising system can maintain itself and develop' (Di Scipio, 2003: 271).

Another decisive aim of the work on composed interactions lies in the elaboration of a *sub-symbolic* strategy of music. The 'theory of sonological emergence' was already headed in that direction: in it, Di Scipio (1994: 207) expected the emergence of a higher level by working on grains, samples and elements not constituting symbols, for they are situated at a lower level. The work on composed interactions heightens this attitude. Di Scipio worked on interactions between *sonic signals*: all exchanges of information are of a purely sonic nature (see Di Scipio, 2003: 272). This musical strategy ensues from the very nature of the emergence paradigm. The parallel with the cognitive sciences, as described by Varela, again imposes itself. In reply to the question 'What is cognition?', computationalism states: 'The processing of information: the manipulation of symbols from rules' (F. Varela, 1996: 42; our translation), whereas the emergence paradigm responds: 'The emergence of global states in a network of simple components' (F. Varela, 1996: 77). On the musical level, the challenge had already been stated as regards the granular tradition: if one wants the upper level, that of the macroform, presented as an emergence and not as an independent construction, one must work only on the lower level, neglecting the intermediate level, made up of symbols. Even more, it is a matter of challenging the dichotomy of sense and its support, peculiar to the notion of symbol, and to postulate their indivisibility.

Composed interactions, ecosystems, sub-symbolic strategy: all these points converge. What is music? Di Scipio asks us. Is it a sound result? No, he replies, since it is the process which is to be composed and not the result. Is it a voluntary gesture (of one or several human beings, the composer and performers)? Not only that, since the environment is part of it too. Is it a language (in which the mediation of the symbol imposes a dichotomy between the support and the sense)? No. For historical musicology, Di Scipio's position is particularly interesting as it combines several post-war trends. His original aim is that all that converges on a hypothesis: music *itself* constitutes an emergence:

> For me, music is something that has no prior existence but which is finally produced, something that is always to be realised, renewed every time; it is never something that is there, already existent and delimited in an ideal or virtual form, which lends itself to being re-presented, reincarnated. In short, I do not compose music itself but rather favourable conditions that will be able to give birth to music (*my* music). The responsibility of actions to commit (for composing, playing, listening) has as much importance as the objects to be made (to compose, play, listen).
> (Di Scipio, 2007: 292; our translation)[7]

Towards the ecology of sound

When space opens even more, we encounter a last important category for this brief history of sound–space: the sound environment, that 'acoustic ecology' is one of the first trends to study. At the end of the 1960s and early 1970s, the founder of this trend, R. Murray Schafer – who coined the notion of 'soundscape' – launched the idea of the World Soundscape Project; assisted by a few students and colleagues at Simon Fraser University (Vancouver, Canada), he proposed listening attentively to the sound environment and recording in order to bear witness to the rapid changes occurring. A record was released in 1973, focussing on the city of Vancouver and including tracks entitled 'Ocean Sounds', 'Entrance to the Harbour', 'Music of Horns and Whistles' (consisting primarily of boat sirens)... Then, Schafer published his book *The Tuning of the World* (1977), which was mentioned in Chapter 2.

This book is in four parts. The first traces the history of natural soundscapes: (sea, wind, earth...), life (birdsong, insects...), rural (pasture, hunting, farm...) and urban ('Making God Listen', 'The Sound of Time'...). The second, entitled 'The Post-Industrial Soundscape', treats the industrial and electric revolutions. It is here that Schafer proposes concepts that would enjoy great success: 'lo-fi' as opposed to 'hi-fi' landscape (the urban soundscape, characterised by a magma of noises, is lo-fi, rural is hi-fi), 'schizophony' (which appears with the reproduction of sound). The third part, also quite ambitious, lays down the analytical principles of soundscapes: Schafer discusses possible notations and proposes classifications for the soundscapes, debating their perception then their morphology and symbolism ('Return to the Sea', 'The Deviousness of the Wind', 'The Mandala and the Bell'...), before focussing on noise. Finally, the fourth and last part proposes a new discipline: acoustic design Schafer prophesised that

> The true acoustic designer must thoroughly understand the environment he is tackling; he must have training in acoustics, psychology, sociology, music, and a great deal more besides, as the occasions demands. There are no schools where such training is possible but their creation cannot be delayed, for as the soundscape slumps into a lo-fi state, the wired background music promoters are already commandeering acoustic designs a *bellezza* business.
>
> (M. Schafer, 1977).

It would be impossible to mention all the ideas sketched in this part, which, to a large degree, remain to be realised.

In the lineage of Schafer, Barry Truax published a manual entitled *Handbook for Acoustic Ecology* in 1978. But Truax is also a composer well integrated into the electroacoustic music community and known in particular for his works on granular synthesis. Making a compromise between acoustic ecology and electroacoustic music, he is one of the pioneers of 'soundscape composition'. Here is how he differentiates pure electroacoustic music from the latter:

> When one captures what is sometimes called 'raw' sound on tape and subjects it to studio processing, whether for mundane sound effects or for the abstract material of the acousmatic approach, this manufacturing process with its industrial over tones suggests that one is composing 'with' the sound and using it for its desired effect and affect, essentially turning it into a consumable product. The soundscape composition typically reverses the

process because, in a sense, the sound 'uses' the composer, and ultimately the listener, in that it evokes in each a wealth of difficult to verbalize images and associations. [...] In essence, one is both composing and being composed through the sound.

(B. Truax, 1995: 95)

Hildegard Westerkamp, who was also part of the first circle of acoustic ecology, is one of the most musicianly practitioners of soundscape composition. Indeed, her works, whilst making use of soundscape recordings and through their art of mixing, display very refined musical work. Such is the case with *Beneath the Forest Floor* (1992), in which one hears, amongst other things, a raven, streams, forests in the rain or in the wind. But the piece also features a masterful transformation of the sound of the raven, which, slowed way down, is repeated several times at the beginning of the piece to sound almost like a *thorougbass*. Amongst the other 'musicalisation' elements, we shall mention the overall form, the way of composing the form locally with repetitions or else the use of a few very harmonic electronic sounds (for an analysis of the piece, see M. Solomos et al., 2015). At the same time, Westerkamp, very much an ecologist, tells us

I am no longer interested in making music in the conventional sense; I am interested in addressing cultural and social concerns in the musical idiom. That's why I use environmental sound and language as my instruments. I want to find the 'voices' of a place or situation, voices that can speak most powerfully about a place/situation and about our experience in and with it. I consider myself as an ecologist of sound.

(H. Westerkamp, 1985: 31)

In her soundscape composing, the ecological practice is shown by the fact that the intention of the works is to transmit the experience of a place to the listener. Thus, *Beneath the Forest Floor* seeks to take us 'through the visible forest, into its shadow world, its spirit; into that which affects our body, heart and mind when we experience forest' (H. Westerkamp, 1992).

The concepts of soundscape, acoustic ecology and soundscape composition are sometimes akin to other notions. They can be compared with 'urban concerts', 'environmental music' or the practice of 'soundwalks'. Concerning events that extend in the city, let us mention the bell concerts that Llorenç Barber had the opportunity of creating in several cities. With them, Barber redefined the urban space 'in a utopian perspective. His proposition could be understood as a think tank from which one might imagine new urban configurations located beyond modern spatial order' (A. Kaiero Claver, 2010: 87; our translation). For 'environmental' types of music, we shall quote Pierre Mariétan (1997: 79; our translation) who defends a 'landscaping conception of music': 'We perceive music as part of our environment. We hear it, most of the time, as a sound landscape, with more or less modelled contours, and presence more or less tolerated'. This conception stems from, amongst others the awareness that [musical] production can no longer be reserved, out of hand, to a limited group of listeners, but that there is a whole world of other listeners who are involuntary, and that their environment must be respected. Consequently, our research tends not to mask ambient sound but to enhance it.

(Ibid.: 73)

As for the 'soundwalks', they can be illustrated by, amongst others, the work of Janet Cardiff. Here, the walker-listener, equipped with headphones, listens to the instructions she has recorded: 'Go towards the brownish green garbage can. Then there's a trail off to your right. Take the trail, it's overgrown a bit. There's an eaten-out dead tree. Looks like ants. Walk up the path. I haven't been in this forest for a long time... it's good to get away from the centre, from the building noises, to idyllic nature. Ok, there's a fork in the path, take the trail to the right' (J. Cardiff, 1991), her voice tells us in her first outing, *Forest Walk* (1991), mixed with ambient sounds. 'The artist asks visitors to walk with her, to match their steps to hers and to merge their thoughts with hers. [...] The participant listens to what is said whilst she reinvents a place full of mythical and symbolic force [...] What the artist proposes is not only a geographical itinerary but also the discovery of an inner territory' (M. Fleming, 2011; our translation).

Interest in soundwalks is growing (see, amongst others, H. Westerkamp, 2006; A. McCartney, 2014; E. Biserna, 2015), joining the interest in walks that art is also experiencing (see D. Evans, ed., 2013). Moreover, we know that walking philosophies have been developing ever since Thoreau's *Walking* at least.

If we broaden our perspective, we encounter practices linked to recording such as the 'phonography', 'sound documentary' and, more generally, 'field recording'. The term 'phonography' was put forward by François-Bernard Mâche in a 1963 article, 'Le son et la musique':

Minimum abstraction will be represented by an art that remains to be created, '*phonographies*', in which any sound elements, recorded with the greatest fidelity, would be assembled, with as few splices as possible, in keeping with musical criteria and to the exclusion of any evocative, picturesque or dramatic intention.

(F.B. Mâche, 1998: 79, 2011; our translation)

For his part, in *Presque rien n°1. Lever du jour au bord de la mer* (1967–70, for tape), Luc Ferrari lets us hear a 'sound documentary' of which the

radicalness consists simply of exposing the phonography of what the subtitle describes [...with] a very literal phonography of a very simple 'real' sunrise [...] reducing to its sole sound dimension a scene that one cannot keep from associating with the *visible*.

(P.Y. Macé, 2012: 78, our translation)[8]

Generally speaking, 'field recording' consists of sound testimony. One often finds the quasi-militant gesture consisting of 'taking out' the mike (i.e., getting out of the recording studio):

> Studio recording is a way of tearing music or, more generally, sound out of the time that is passing. [...] The studio acts as an 'eraser', it decontextualises. Taking the mike out is, on the contrary, capturing a precise moment and place linked to the circumstances of the recording.
> (J.G. Muller, 2011; our translation)

Field recording was initially developed by broadcasters and recording engineers such as Ludwig Koch or naturalists such as Jean-Claude Roché. Ethnomusicologists have also contributed to its flourishing. Then artists took hold of this new medium, from Knud Viktor to Ximena Alarcón by way of Bernie Krause, Annea Lockwood, David Dunn, Peter Cusack, Gilles Malatray, Chris Watson, Francisco López, David Rothenberg, David Monacchi, Andrea Polli, Leah Barclay, Jana Winderen ... (see A. Galand, 2012; C. Lane, A. Carlyle, 2013; F. Bianchi; V.J. Manzo, 2016). Nonetheless, 'the link between field recording and creation is not necessarily obvious' (M.H. Bernard, 2016: 139): the question arises of knowing what is the limit between awareness of an environment to be preserved and the artistic gesture. Although in the past few years this limit is increasingly fluid – let us think of composer Michael Pisaro's triptych *Continuum Unbound* (2014), of which the first piece is pure field recording, the third is for five musicians, and the middle one is 'mixed' – historically, field recording does not pretend to be 'music'. We shall mention the case of the ethnomusicologist, Steven Feld, who released several CDs of soundscape recordings in regions that were long his fields of research, including the famous *Voices of the Rainforest,* subtitled *A Soundscape of a Day in the Life of the Kaluli People of the Papua Guinea Rainforest* (S. Feld, 1991), in which the tracks follow one another to compose a cycle of 24 hours. Even though his record company, profiting from the New Age trend, speaks of him as an 'artist', he himself writes:

> I think that soundscaping is first and foremost acoustic witnessing. The field part of the work is to 'be there' in the fullest way. The studio part of the work is to make that original 'being there' more repeatable, expandable, sharable, open to new kinds of participation. The idea is to turn my ear-witnessing into an invitation for your ear-witnessing, manipulating parameters and trying to feel which subtleties could be brought out a little more, which presences could be more present for uninitiated ears.
> (S. Feld, undated)

More generally, here the question arises of the relationship between Art and Nature, a debate as old as art itself. There have always been musicians to think that Nature is musical, that birds or whales sing. In their famous *A Thousand Plateaus*, Deleuze and Guattari (1987: 299) have evoked the 'becoming-animal' of music, which, in the same way as the 'becoming-woman-evolution' or the 'becoming-child', would constitute its content. By 'deterritorialising' ourselves, music makes us enter in resonance with these evolutions:

> What does music deal with, what is the content indissociable from sound expression? It is hard to say, but it is something: *a* child dies, a child plays, a woman is born, a woman dies, a bird arrives, a bird flies off. […] Why a child, a woman, a bird? It is because musical expression is inseparable from a becoming-woman, a becoming-child, a becoming-animal that constitute its content. Why does the child die, or the bird fall as though pierced by an arrow? Because of the 'danger' inherent in any line that escapes, in any line of flight or creative deterritorialization: the danger of veering toward destruction, toward abolition.

Here ecological, ethical, economic, social, political or philosophical questions open up. In fact,

> listening to the environment becomes intonation of the world and lament. Artistic, political, social and ecological planes are crossed. Consequently, thinking the sound environment and dreaming of lines of action for it must take into account the interdependence of these planes.
> (C. Pardo Salgado, 2008: 61; our translation)

Thinkers more interested in the ties between sound and the world than in the – somewhat naturalist – notion of soundscape tend to prefer the expression 'sound ecology' to 'acoustic ecology', because 'in the notion of sound(ing), it is the subject that is massively called into question and, by that, the question of listening' (R. Barbanti, 2011: 11; our translation). Unlike seeing, listening presupposes a non-separation between sound and the subject perceiving it. Owing to this, one might even evoke an 'ontological coexistence', which would refer to 'a form of immanence and *belonging* to the world, to a common vibration, which [would] put my being to resonating with the changing energies of other beings, objects or natural elements that are vibrating here and now' (Ibid: 13). In this sense, sound ecology is interested in sound as *connection*.

Chapter 6 online examples

Example 6.1 Hector Berlioz, *Requiem*: 'Tuba Mirum' (H. Berlioz, 1900–1907).
Example 6.2 Gustav Mahler, *First Symphony*, third movement: figure 16.
Example 6.4 Iannis Xenakis, *Terretektorh:* arrangement of the orchestra (I. Xenakis, 1966). © By kind permission of Editions Salabert.
Example 6.7 Pierre Schaeffer at the 'space desk' (Photograph: Maurice Lecardent, 1955). © By kind permission of INA/GRM.
Example 6.8 François Bayle: arrangement of the acousmonium in the Salle Olivier Messiaen at Radio France (Paris) during the concert of 9 January 1998 (premiere of *Morceaux de ciels*). © By kind permission of François Bayle.
Example 6.9 Pierre Boulez, *Répons:* playing arrangement and spatialisation at figure 21.

Example 6.10 Luigi Nono: diagram for *Prometeo*. © By kind permission of Fondazione Archivio Luigi Nono.

Example 6.11 Luigi Nono, *Prometeo:* spatialisation. © By kind permission of Fondazione Archivio Luigi Nono (the original is in colour).

Example 6.12 Emmanuel Nunes, *Quodlibet*: situations (after Festival d'automne à Paris, 1992: 31). The figures above the columns indicate the locations (in chronological order). The figures inside the columns indicate the musicians' position in the hall.

Example 6.14 Karlheinz Stockhausen, *Oktophonie*: distribution of the groups of loudspeakers (Ibid: XIX). © By kind permission of Stockhausen Foundation for Music, Kürten, Germany, www.stockhausen.org.

Example 6.15 Ideal configurations for stereophony, quadraphony, octophony and 5.1. surround.

Example 6.17 *La Tourette monastery*, west façade, undulating glass panes, first project: drawing by Xenakis (Archives Xenakis) © By kind permission of Mâkhi Xenakis.

Example 6.18 Iannis Xenakis, *Metastaseis:* measures 157–165 (I. Xenakis, 1953–1954). © By kind permission of Boosey & Hawkes.

Example 6.22 The IRCAM Espace de Projection (ESPRO) (photo Philippe Migeat, IRCAM). © By kind permission of IRCAM.

Example 6.24 Robin Minard, *Silent Music*, Alte Schmiede, Vienna, 1994: detail (loudspeakers) (www.robinminard.com). © By kind permission of Robin Minard. Photo P.A. Leitner.

Example 6.25 Agostino Di Scipio: composed interactions for the *Audible Ecosystemics* interface (after A. Di Scipio, 2003: 272). © By kind permission of Agostino Di Scipio.

Notes

1 For analyses of the piece, see H. Santana, 1999; B. Hofmann, 2008.
2 Simantras are 'hanging rods made of very hard *tempered steel*, approximately 20 mm in diameter by 11 cm that are struck with a triangle beater or metal head; *affolants* are 'very thin steel leaves approximately 30 x 30 cm that are held in the hand and shaken (I. Xenakis, 1969, preface).
3 The rhythmic cell passes all the crotchets from one instrumentalist to the next, whereas it is equal to a minim: also, I chose to indicate the entrance of a percussionist on the second beat of this cell, because it is the dynamic peak.
4 The information on *Quodlibet* is excerpted from: personal communications with Emmanuel Nunes; Peter Szendy, 1995; E. Nunes, 1995; the CD jacket of Emmanuel Nunes, *Quodlibet*, Auvidis Montaigne 782055; Festival d'automne à Paris (1992).
5 The mechanical movement of the surfaces is, unfortunately, not silent and can therefore perturb the performance of a work.
6 In truth, the first version of the piece – the one commented on in Chapter 3 – is for tape. Only afterwards did Lucier propose a live version, which is compared here to an installation (see A. Di Scipio, 2005b).
7 To prolong this discussion on Di Scipio, see A. Di Scipio (ed., 2014) and M. Solomos (ed., 2014). For analyses of *Audible Ecosystemics*, see R. Meric (2008), G. Rimoldi, J. Manzolli (2016), M. Mazzoli (2017), A. Eldridge, O. Bown (2018).
8 See also A. Reyna, 2016.

Conclusion

We have now come to the end of this plural adventure of the emergence of sound in music, consisting of six histories: timbre, which became a central category of composition; noise and the exploration of its musical potential; listening, with awareness having opened up to sound in itself; the increasingly intensive immersion in sound; the substitution of the composition *of* sound for composition *with* sounds; and space, which is increasingly thought of as 'composable'. It is in crossing, combining and converging that these histories have ended up provoking the change of paradigm that we are currently witnessing, where we go from a musical culture centred on notes to a culture of sound.

This major change – occurring within the very core of music – affects practically all of today's music to various degrees. The question of integrating genres on the borderline of music often arose at the moment of the book's conception. Was it necessary to open up to spheres that do not (or no longer) use the word 'music'? Was it not better to limit ourselves to music alone? The second option was preferred, and that is why only two fields that do not – yet – belong to the musical sphere were taken into account: sound installations and sound ecology, on the one hand because musicians are increasingly moving into them, and on the other because, in this book, we ended up at them via the question of space, which has become highly important for music itself.

Three other important spheres that could have been integrated were finally left out, in expectation of future works. The first encompasses sound practices – sometimes truly musical – that are encountered in the other constituted arts: visual arts, video, performance, sound poetry and others without, of course, overlooking cinema. There, the sound dimension has taken on increasing importance and often freed itself, sometimes joining certain preoccupations stemming from the emergence of sound in music. A place apart would need to be made for performance art, in particular when practised by artists coming from music and exploiting the possibilities of electronics (in several cases, the boundary between performance art and traditional musical performance but augmented with electronics is rather blurry).

The second sphere concerns musical realisations integrated into interdisciplinary artistic research: opera and other dramaturgical practices, music and image, colour and visual music, music and dance, performance art, multimedia realisations, digital and media arts. In a number of these various types of research, the idea of synthesis in the arts is poles apart from the Wagnerian total work of art: the encounter between the arts does not discount merging; they are juxtaposed and play on their complementarity and difference. 'Their demarcation lines have been eroded', as Adorno already wrote (2003: 368) in his lecture 'Art and the Arts' – music opening up in particular to the dimension of space, more characteristic of the visual arts in the past. In short, there one focusses on plurality and heterogeneity as well as on complexity. Challenging the idealistic aesthetic of *The* art in favour of the irreducibility of *the arts*, one advances their material and perceptive media, which constitute their ultimate difference, as it were: sound and the auditory, image and the visual. These researches have thus contributed profoundly to the emergence of sound.

Sound art constitutes the third sphere. We mentioned this 'new' art in the introduction, and it is difficult to predict the future of this expression: will it disappear or else become a constituted sphere that develops in parallel with other existing fields, including music? Or else, will it end up designating a new art that has *absorbed music*? At the present time, numerous artists catalogued as 'sound artists' could also be categorised as musicians' – by entering, in particular, the constantly evolving category of 'experimental music' (see J. Gottschalk, 2016, who quotes several 'experimental musicians' that can be encountered on sound art networks). Conversely, we observe that, with others, the difference exists and that it even gets bigger, whereas one might think that the emergence of sound was going to smooth it out. To explain this ambiguous situation, it could be said that, on the one hand, sound art continues to dream of ridding itself of music – remembering, in particular, from John Cage only his affirmation 'I never heard a sound I didn't like: the only problem with sounds is music' (J. Cage, 1994: 21) and remaining impervious to the most musical performances of his music (such as the one by Agostino Di Scipio and Ciro Longobardi: see J. Cage, 2012); for their part, musicians, thanks to the emergence of sound, have *already* achieved/carried out the revolution of sound art – as writes S. Emmerson (eds., 2018), 'there has [...] been an unexpected outmaneuver of this apparently irreconcilable difference between sound art and music: changing listening habits (and locations) from within experimental *music* itself'. So if the emergence of sound leads, in fact, music to a sound-based art, a sound art, the difference with what is currently called 'sound art' could subsist, were it only to mark the different relation to the temporal development that music maintains despite its sound–space evolution.

We must, however, ask the question: What could be the *final outcome* of this history of the emergence of sound in music and, more generally, the future of music? Is *Tonkunst* – the other name for music in the era of its maximal sphere of influence, Romanticism – destined to disappear? Would conservatives be right in accusing musical modernity – which has borne this history of the emergence of sound – of having destroyed music in both spirit and letter? It is interesting to observe that, on several occasions, musicians very involved in this history suggested abandoning the word 'music'. 'As the term "music" seems to me to have increasingly lost its meaning, I would prefer to use the expression "organised sound" and avoid the monotonous question "But is it music?"', said Varèse (1983: 56; our translation). The debate also arose in *musique concrète* circles. Michel Chion (1982: 12–13; our translation) wrote, not without some humour:

> Let us imagine [...] that electroacoustic music was wished and defined as an autonomous art of sounds, able to encompass traditional music just as cinema integrates theatre, painting, etc. That could be called, for example, 'telepanaphon' art'. One would go to listen to a 'tape' (as one says see 'a film') in a 'telepana' hall.

But, up until the present day, the word 'music' has always won out.

However, it is possible that this will no longer be the case in the near future. After all, the evolution has already occurred in other domains: is the expression 'visual arts' not used without having eliminated the word 'painting'? We might imagine a new sharing where, on the one hand, the word 'music' would designate music of the past as well as current practices more or less linked to the traditional definitions of music (developing melody, harmony, rhythm, instrumentation...); on the other, the expression 'sound art' in a very broad sense, or another equivalent, would group the musical practices that had drawn all the consequences from the refocussing of music on sound as well as the practices coming from other artistic fields and going in the same direction, by favouring, in particular, thanks to digital media, transdisciplinary projects. Moreover, ethnomusicologists like to remind us that numerous cultures have no equivalent for the – Greek – term 'music' (see F. Giannattasio, 2007). They thus emphasise not only the fact that there are different conceptions of music, but that the notion of 'art of the muses' is not universal: in numerous societies, there are no 'accredited' musicians, the dividing-up of domains does not allow for a practice centred uniquely on sounds to emerge, and we have no equivalent of artistic 'autonomy', amongst other fundamental differences. 'Music' could thus disappear or else be limited to a restricted perimeter (traditional notion).

Nonetheless, is this to say that, outside the restricted field of tradition, we might also be witnessing the disappearance of all symbolic activity – i.e., of all *art* – centred on or encompassing sound? Some are living out the refocussing of music on sound as a *desartisation*. Music is not *only* sound, they argue: an activity limited to sound is not art. Sometimes they are right! A number of types of contemporary music constitute only a vast catalogue of timbres and new playing methods; many electroacoustic works only juxtapose sounds; many sound installations settle for repeating one or two sounds and are impervious to temporal developments... This is the pitfall peculiar to all music centred on sound. But there it is a matter of minor works, composed without much imagination. Yet just as the successful works of traditional musical culture go beyond their own pitfalls – formalism, excess of scales, arpeggios, etc., tendency for ornamentation, combinations of meaningless notes – the successful works of sound culture open the imagination through, in, and by means of sound.

It is true, however, that there exists a major *risk* for all art of sound. This risk is inherent in audio culture and lies in the very act of its birth: the possibility of setting a sound, of cutting it off from its source and repeating it, can turn it into a meaningless object, lending itself to *fetishist* consumption. This can easily be seen in certain music of the years 1990–2000, attached to the use of samples and tortured by repetition. The sounds thus put in a loop, even if they constitute simple materials, become objects that are taken as being strange, fascinating, hypnotising and paralysing the listener. This can be clearly seen, too, in certain frenetic listening practices, where people put sound on continuously, all the time; these practices, Hildegard Westerkamp tells us (1988: 33), are based on a need that

> resembles the desire for womblike comfort. The difference is that this 'womb' is artificially created and therefore disconnected from the real world, whereas the real womb is intricately connected with it. To seek out an artificially created 'womb' is like suffering from aural addiction. It is a psychological addiction that erects a screen of illusion between us and the world as well as, and perhaps more seriously, between us and our imagination.

But can we generalise? Generally speaking, is the interest in sound synonymous with regression and fetishism, as Adorno thought (1991) in his famous 1938 article 'On the Fetish Character in Music and the Regression of Listening'? We hope to have shown in this book that the emergence of sound in music does not necessarily represent the symptom of a triumphant materialism leading to fetishist consumption practices. 'Sound', which we have discussed, is not solely an inert matter to be venerated: it can be invaded by the forces of what is called art. Two moments of our history, representing complementary poles, attest to this. The first focusses on sound to emphasise listening. Here, focus on sound is a way for us to (re)discover this powerful faculty: learning to listen, learning to analyse the miniscule details of a sound. As for the other, it resides in the moment when one speaks about sound to designate constructed entities, made according to a compositional project: the musical work, in its entirety – from micro- to macrotime – is fully articulated in it. What is more unique to the art of sounds than, on the one side, listening and, on the other, articulation?

Furthermore, being aware of the risk of fetishism, much of today's sound-based music is striving to go beyond the notion of sound as a frozen, reified object, and engaging in a critique of sound in this sense. Generally speaking, we might say with Agostino Di Scipio (2016: 37–38; our translation):

> Sound is never truly *object*. We can always receive it as the auditory trace of certain relations and interactions in the space-time unity of experience, the here-and-now. […] Never truly *object*, sound is therefore always *event*. In its temporal unfolding, in its three-dimensional propagation, sound propagates around and inside the listening body, whilst also extending through the body of the source.

Sound is marked by its properties of emergence and by its complexity, we would add. It is also inclusive – 'Sound's fluid quality saturates and surrounds us and is by its nature inclusive. We hear things and are included with those things in a common soundfield', writes Michael Stocker (2013: 21) – hence its immersive aspect, which has been treated at length here. Far from being an object, sound might be thought of as a *network of relations*. For all these reasons, today we are seeing proliferate composite expressions such as 'soundspace' – the culmination of our six histories – as well as 'soundscape', 'sound environment', 'sound ambiance' or 'sound atmosphere' and 'sound *milieu*' (see M. Solomos, 2018), which invite us to become aware of this new culture of sound that we have entered, a culture asking us to be attentive if we want to avoid the trap of reification. To be fully aware of the emergence of sound, we would have to develop an *ecology of sound*. Indeed, this paradigmatic revolution introduces considerable mutations not only inside the musical material (substitution of sound for tone), but also in the processes of subjectivisation, in compositional and listening strategies, in the ways of being music as regards the surrounding space..., in short, in the very substance of what an art is – whether it is called 'music' or 'sound art'. It is a matter of thinking sound in its relation to innumerable factors that are not sound itself and apprehending it in its relationships to its multiple environments – hence the expression 'ecology *of* sound'.

'Music is not a language. Every musical piece is like a complex rock formed with ridges and designs within and without, that can be interpreted in a thousand different ways without a single one being the best or truest. By virtue of this multiple exegesis, music inspires all sorts of fantastic imaginings, like a crystal catalyst', noted Xenakis (2008: 261). The paradigmatic change that we are going through, leading from *Tonkunst* to *Klangkunst*, from the note to the sound, is radically transforming our conception of music (or of the art called to succeed it). The birth of tonality in the early 17th century had joined music to language, providing a powerful model. In that model, music adopts the structure of language, being conceived as combinative of elementary units, the notes – the equivalent of phonemes – in ever vaster assemblages: motifs, phrases, periods, sections, parts and, finally, an entire work. As in language, these formal assemblages can be associated with a sense that the listener is supposed to understand. Thus, music is akin to a discourse: thanks to these isolated elements and significant dynamic structures, it becomes narration, suggestion, evocation. The refocussing on sound calls this model into question. Putting the combinative logic in brackets, it favours a morphological type of thinking, of which the consequential development perhaps lies in what has been described as 'space-sound'.

The emergence of sound puts forward the spatiotemporal qualities of sound, rather than its evocative power – without, for all that, renouncing it – its relation to the surrounding space, and its interaction with the body. The listener is invited to an embodied listening, the body no longer being thought of – in the manner of *Tonkunst* – as a simple intermediary between mind and matter. This type of listening is now studied by the cognitive sciences of music (see M. Leman, 2008). We know the history of this English musical critic who, having lost his hearing in one ear, and therefore the sensation of space, lost all taste for music:

> What I hear now when I listen to music is a flat, two-dimensional representation: flat as in literally flat like a sheet of paper with lines on it. Where I used to get buildings, I now only get architectural drawings. [...] I can't enter music and I can't perceive its inner spaces. I've never got much of an emotional hit from technical drawings. This is what really hurts: I no longer respond to music emotionally.
>
> (N. Coleman *in* O. Sacks, 2008: 160)

In a number of works centred on sound, music is defined as a phenomenon of energy: if it touches the listener, it is not because it was 'understood', but because, through its sound movements, it implements energy transformations that carry him along. Varèse (1983: 99; our translation) liked to say: 'The function of art is to live and communicate what is alive. What interests me first of all is music's dynamic, its emotion, which does not mean its sentiment'. And we could also quote Deleuze and Guattari (1987: 342–343): in the modern age,

> the forces to be captured are no longer those of the earth, which still constitute a great expressive Form, but the forces of an immaterial, non-formal, and energy Cosmos. [...] This is the post-romantic turning point: the essential thing is no longer forms and matter, or themes, but forces, densities, intensities.

However, it is probable that the model of language will not be totally abandoned. To tell the truth, refocussing on sound does not signal the complete disappearance of work on the note, and not only in 'music', but also in the 'art of sounds'. And the inverse: a number of works from the past, however much centred on the note, would also deserve to be listened to for their work on sound as well as for their energy work. The two models have therefore always coexisted – even though the second waited for modernity to assert itself. As Grisey wrote:

> I would tend to divide music very roughly into two categories. The first is music that presupposes declamation, rhetoric, language: a music of discourse. Berio and Boulez are in this category – just as Schoenberg and Berg have a way of saying things with sounds. The second is music that is more a state of sound than discourse. It is the difference between Monteverdi who, most of the time, says things, and the music of Ockeghem, who says 'That is the way of the world'. You can put Xenakis in this category, for example, as well as a large part of Stockhausen – even though he quite often belongs to both. And I also belong to this category.
>
> (G. Grisey, 2008: 273; our translation)

This just shows that what this book has been about is also a question of sensitivity.

References

Adorno Theodor W. (1927): 'Schönberg: *Fünf Orchesterstücke op. 16*', in Adorno Theodor W. (1984): *Gesammelte Schriften*, Francfort, Suhrkamp, vol. 18, p. 335–344.
Adorno Theodor W. (1976): *Introduction to the Sociology of Music*, translated by E.B. Ashton, New York, The Seabury Press.
Adorno Theodor W. (1991): 'On the Fetish Character in Music and the Regression of Listening', in *The Culture Industry: Selected Essays on Mass Culture*, edited by J.M. Bernstein, London, UK, Routledge, p. 29–60.
Adorno Theodor W. (1997): *Aesthetic Theory*, translated by Robert Hullot-Kentor, London, UK, Bloomsbury. [Adorno Theodor W. (1970): *Asthetische Theorie*, Frankfurt am Main, Suhrkamp.]
Adorno Theodor W. (2003): 'Art and the Arts', in *Can One Live After Auschwitz? A Philosophical Reader*, edited by Rolf Tiedemann, translated by Rodney Livingstone, Stanford, CA, Stanford University Press, p. 368–387.
Adorno Theodor W. (2006): *Philosophy of New Music*, translated, edited and with an introduction by Robert Hullot-Kentor, Minneapolis, MN, University of Minnesota Press. [Adorno Theodor W. (1949): *Philosophie der neuen Musik*, Tübingen, J.C.B. Mohr (Paul Siebeck).]
Adorno Theodor W. (2009): *In Search of Wagner*, translated by Rodney Livingston, London, UK, New Left Books. [Adorno Theodor W. (1952): *Versuch über Wagner*, Berlin, Frankfurt am Main.]
Albèra Philippe (2003): 'Entretien avec Pierre Boulez', in Albèra Philippe (ed.) (2003): Pli selon pli *de Pierre Boulez. Entretien et études*, Genève, Contrechamps.
Anderson Christine (2005): 'Dynamical Networks of Sonic Interactions. An Interview with Agostino Di Scipio', *Computer Music Journal* vol. 29 n°3, p. 11–28.
Anderson Julian (1989): 'De *Sables* à *Vues aériennes*. Le développement d'un style', *Entretemps* n°8, p. 123–138.
Ansermet Ernest (1961): *Les fondements de la musique dans la conscience humaine*, La Baconnière, Neuchâtel.
Antoine Aurélien, Miranda Eduardo R. (2017): 'Musical Acoustics, Timbre, and Computer–Aided Orchestration Challenges', *Proceedings of the 2017 International Symposium on Musical Acoustics (ISMA)*, Montréal, p. 151–154.
Antonopoulos Antonios (2008): *De la modélisation matricielle dans* Pithoprakta *de Iannis Xenakis. Approche systémique et analytique*, Ph.D. thesis, University Paris 4.
APM (Équipe Analyse des pratiques musicale) (undated), *Écoutes signées*, http://apm.ircam.fr/ecoutes_signees/.

Arbo Alessandro (2005a): 'En-transe', in Arbo Alessandro (ed.) (2005b): *Le corps électrique. Voyage dans le son de Fausto Romitelli*, Paris, France, L'Harmattan, p. 17–50.

Arbo Alessandro (ed.) (2005b): *Le corps électrique. Voyage dans le son de Fausto Romitelli*, Paris, France, L'Harmattan.

Arditti (Quartet) (1995): CD *From Italy*, MO, Paris, Auvidis Montaigne.

Arena Leonardi Vittorio (2016): *Scelsi: Oltre l'Occidente*, Crac edizioni.

Artaud Pierre-Yves (and Geay Gérard) (1980): *Flûtes au présent*, Paris, France, Jobert/Transatlantiques.

Augoyard Jean-François, Torgue Henry (eds.) (2005): *Sonic Experience. A Guide to Everyday Sounds*, translated by Andra McCartney and David Paquette, Montréal, McGill University, 2005. [Augoyard Jean-François, Torgue Henry (eds.) (1995): *À l'écoute de l'environnement. Répertoire des effets sonores*, Marseille, Parenthèses.]

Austin Larry (1997): 'The Realization and First Complete Performances of Ives's *Universe Symphony*', in Lambert Philip (ed.) (1997): *Ives Studies*, Cambridge, MA, Cambridge University Press.

Baalman Marije A.J. (2008): *On Wave Field Synthesis and Electro-Acoustic Music*, Saarabrücken, VDM Verlag.

Bailey Derek (1992): *Improvisation. Its Nature and Practice in Music*, Da Capo Press.

Bailey Kathryn (1991): *The Twelve-Note Music of Anton Webern*, Cambridge, MA, Cambridge University Press.

Baillet Jérôme (2000): *Gérard Grisey. Fondements d'une écriture*, Paris, France, l'Harmattan.

Barbanti Roberto (2011): 'Écologie sonore et technologies du son', in *Sonorités* n°6, p. 9–42.

Barrett Natasha, www.natashabarrett.org.

Barrière Jean-Baptiste (ed.) (1991): *Le timbre. Métaphore pour la composition*, Paris, France, Christian Bourgois.

Barry Wallace (1976): *Structural Functions in Music*, New Jersey, General Publishing Company.

Barthelmes Barbara (1995): *Raum und Klang. Das musikalische und theoretische Schaffen Ivan Wyschnegradskys*, Wolke Verlag.

Bartoli Jean-Pierre (1986): 'Écriture du timbre et espace sonore dans l'œuvre de Berlioz', *Analyse Musicale* n°3, p. 31–36.

Bartolozzi Bruno (1967): *New Sounds for Woodwind*, London, UK, Oxford University Press.

Battier Marc (ed.) (1994): 'Notice technique d'*Amers* (1992) de Kaija Saariaho', IRCAM.

Battier Marc, Cheret Bertrand, Lemouton Serge, Manoury Philippe (2003): CEDEROM *Les musiques électroniques de Philippe Manoury*, Paris, France, IRCAM-Centre Georges Pompidou.

Bauckholt Carola, (1995): *Treibstoff*, Freiburg, Thürmchen Verlag.

Baudouin Olivier (2007): 'A Reconstruction of *Stria*', *Computer Music Journal* vol. 31 n°3, p. 75–81.

Baudoin Philippe (1992): Linear notes for the CD Monk Thelonious (1992): *Thelonious Monk and his Quartet en concert: Olympia, mars 1965*, Trema.

Bayer Francis (1981): *De Schönberg à Cage. Essai sur la notion d'espace sonore dans la musique contemporaine*, Paris, France, Klincksieck.

Bayer Gerd (2009): 'No Class? Class and Class Politics in British Heavy Metal', in Bayer Gerd (ed.) (2009): *Heavy Metal Music in Britain*, Fanrham, UK, Ashgate, p. 161–180.

Bayle François (1993): *Musique acousmatique. Propositions… …positions*, Paris, France, INA-GRM/Buchet-Chastel.
Bayle François (1997): 'Entretiens de Makis Solomos', in Nicolas François (ed.) (1997): *Les enjeux du concert de musique contemporaine*, Paris, France, Cdmc-Entretemps.
Bayle François (2007): *L'image de son/Klangbilder. Technique de mon écoute / Technik meines Hörens*, herausgegeben von Imke Misch und Christoph von Blumröder, Redaction Anne Kersting, zweite korrigierte und erweiterte Auflage, Redaktion Marcus Erbe, Köln, Signale aus Köln, Beiträge zur Musik der Zeit, band 8.
Bayle François (2009): *Érosphère*, Paris, Magison, DVD 'Cahier d'acousmographies'.
Beaussant Philippe (2001): 'À la recherche du son perdu', in Delalande François (ed.) (2001): *Le son des musiques. Entre technologie et esthétique*, Paris, France, INA-Buchet/Chastel, p. 112–115.
Beckett Lucy (1981): *Richard Wagner: Parsifal*, Cambridge, MA, Cambridge University Press.
Bélis Annie (1986): *Aristoxène de Tarente et Aristote: Le Traité d'harmonique*, Paris, France, Klincksieck.
Berio Luciano (1955): *Nones*, Edizioni Suivini Zerboni.
Berio Luciano (1983): *Entretiens avec Rossana Dalmonte*, Paris, France, J.C. Lattès.
Berlioz Hector (1969): *Mémoires*, Paris, France, Garnier-Flammarion.
Berlioz Hector (1993): *Traité d'instrumentation et d'orchestration*, Paris, France, Lemoine. [Berlioz Hector (1843): *Grand traité d'instrumentation et d'orchestration modernes*, Paris, Schonenberger.]
Bernard Marie-Hélène (2011): *Les compositeurs chinois au regard de la mondialisation artistique: résider-résonner-résister*, Ph.D. thesis, University Paris 4.
Bernard Marie-Hélène (2016): 'Field recording et création', in Solomos Makis et al. (2016): *Musique et écologies du son. Propositions théoriques pour une écoute du monde/Music and Ecologies of sound. Theoretical Projects for a Listening of the World*, Paris, France, L'Harmattan, p. 139–145.
Bijsterveld Karin, Cleophas Eefje, Krebs Stefan, Mom Gijs (2014): *Sound and Safe. A History of Listening Behind the Wheel*, Oxford, UK, Oxford University Press.
Bioteau Alain (1998): 'Toucher l'espace', in Szendy Peter (ed.) (1998): *Emmanuel Nunes*, Paris, France, L'Harmattan/IRCAM.
Birdsall Carolyn (2012): *Nazi Soundscape. Sound, Technology and Urban Space in Germany, 1933–1945*, Amsterdam, the Netherlands, Amsterdam University Press.
Biserna Elena (2015): 'Tactiques artistiques et pratiques mobiles d'écoute médiatisée: entre "révélation", "superposition" et "interaction"', in Roy Jérôme, Sinclair Peter (eds.), *Locus Sonus. 10 ans d'expérimentation*, Le Mot et le Reste, p. 193–212.
Blasquiz Klaus (2010): 'Le sens du son à fond dans la réverb', *Home-studio. Le magazine de la création musicale* n°256, p. 33–38.
Blesser Barry, Salter Linda-Ruth (2007): *Spaces Speak, are you Listening? Experiencing Aural Architecture*, Cambridge, MA, MIT.
Block Geoffrey (1996): *Ives. Concord Sonata*, Cambridge, MA, Cambridge University Press.
Blum Bruno (2008): *Lou Reed. Electric Dandy*, Paris, France, Hors Collection.
Bodon-Clair Jérôme (2008): *Le langage de Steve Reich. L'exemple de* Music for 18 musicians *(1976)*, Paris, France, L'Harmattan.
Bogdanov Vladimir, Woodstra Chris, Erlewine Stephen Thomas, Bush John (eds.) (2001): *All Music Guide to Electronica*, Ann Arbor, MI, All Media Guide.
Böhme Gernot (2017): *The Aesthetics of Atmospheres*, edited by Jean-Paul Thibaud, London, UK, Routledge.

Bonardi Alain (2003): 'Analyse hypermédia de *Jupiter* de Philippe Manoury', in Battier Marc, Cheret Bertrand et al. (eds.) (2003): CEDEROM *Les musiques électroniques de Philippe Manoury*, Paris, France, IRCAM-Centre Georges Pompidou.

Bonardi Alain (2011): 'Approches pratiques de la préservation/virtualisation des œuvres interactives mixtes: *En écho* de Manoury', *Actes des 17èmes Journées d'Informatique Musicale* (JIM 2011), Université Jean-Monnet Saint-Etienne, http://jim2011.univ-st-etienne.fr/html/actes.html.

Bonardi Alain, Bossis Bruno, Couprie Pierre, Tiffon Vincent (eds.) (2017): *Analyser la musique mixte*, Sampzon, Delatour France.

Born Georgina (ed.) (2013): *Music, Sound and Space: Transformations of Public and Private Experience*, Cambridge, MA, Cambridge University Press.

Bossis Bruno (2004): '*Mortuos Plango, Vivos Voco* de Jonathan Harvey ou le miroir de la spiritualité', *Musurgia* vol. XI n°1–2, p. 119–144.

Boulez Pierre (1965a): *Éclat*, London, UK, Universal Edition.

Boulez Pierre (1965b): *Le Marteau sans maître*, London, UK, Universal Edition.

Boulez Pierre (1966): *Relevés d'apprenti*, Paris, France, Seuil.

Boulez Pierre (1974): 'Perspective-prospective', in Ouvry-Vial Brigitte (ed.) (1992): *Recherche et création. Vers de nouveaux chemins*, Paris, France, IRCAM/Centre Georges-Pompidou.

Boulez Pierre (1975): *Par volonté et par hasard*, entretiens avec Célestin Deliège, Paris, France, Seuil.

Boulez Pierre (1989): *Jalons (pour une décennie)*, Paris, France, Christian Bourgois.

Boulez Pierre (2005): *Le Marteau sans maître. Fac-similé de l'épure et de la première mise au net de la partition/Facsimile of the Draft Score and the First Fair Copy of the Full Score*, edited by Pascal Decroupet, Basel, Switzerland, Paul Sacher Stiftung.

Bowers Faubion (1979), Introduction to Scriabin Alexandre (1979): *Prometheus. The Poem of Fire* op. 60, Mainz, Germany, Ernst Eulenburg Ltd.

Branden Joseph W. (2016): *Experimentations: John Cage in Music, Art, and Architecture*, New York, Bloomsbury Academic.

Bredel Marc (1984): *Edgar Varèse*, Paris, France, Mazarine.

Bregman Albert S. (1990): *Auditory Scene Analysis. The Perceptual Organization of Sound*, Cambridge, MA, MIT.

Brelet Gisèle (1967): 'Musicalisation de l'espace dans la musique contemporaine', in *Festschrift Walter Wiora*, Kassel, Bärenreiter.

Brelet Gisèle (1968): 'L'esthétique du discontinu dans la musique nouvelle', in *Revue d'Esthétique: Musiques nouvelles*, Paris, France, Klincksieck.

Bridoux-Michel Séverine (2006): *Architecture et musique: croisements de pensées après 1950 (la collaboration de l'architecte et du musicien, de la conception à l'œuvre)*, Ph.D. thesis, University Lille 3.

Budón Osvaldo (2000): 'Composing with Objets, Networks and Time Scales: An Interview with Horacio Vaggione', *Computer Music Journal* vol. 24 n°3, p. 9–22.

Bull Michael (2007): *Sound Moves: iPod Culture and Urban Experience*, Oxon, Routledge.

Bull Michael (ed.) (2018): *The Routledge Companion to Sound Studies*, London, UK, Routledge.

Bull Michael, Back Les (eds.) (2016): *The Auditory Culture Reader*, Oxford-New York, Bloomsbury Academic, second edition.

Burkhart Charles (1973–74): 'Schœnberg's *Farben*: An Analysis of op. 16, n°3', *Perspectives of New Music* vol. 12 n°1, p. 141–172.

Byrne Madelyn (1999): 'Speech Based Computer Music: Selected Works by Charles Dodge and Paul Lansky', in *ICMC (International Computer Music Conference) Proceedings*, Pékin, p. 561–564.
Cage John (1961): *Silence*, Middletown, CT, Wesleyan University Press.
Cage John (1960): *4'33''*, Peters Edition.
Cage John (1981): *For the Birds: John Cage in Conversation with Daniel Charles*, Boston, MA, Marion Boyars Publishers Ltd.
Cage John (1994): *Je n'ai jamais écouté aucun son sans l'aimer: le seul problème avec les sons, c'est la musique*, traduction Daniel Charles, s.l., La main courante.
Cage John (2012): *Electronic Music for Piano* (Ciro Longobardi, piano; Agostino Di Scipio, electronics), Stradivarius, STR 33927.
Caires Carlos (2004): 'Micromontage in a Graphical Sound Editing and Mixing Tool', in *Proceedings of the ICMC 2004*, San Francisco, CA, International Computer Music Association.
Cairns David (1994), Linear notes for the CD Berlioz (Hector) (1994): *Requiem, Symphonie funèbre et triomphale*, Philips 416 283-2.
Cardiff Janet (1991): *Forest Walk*, http://www.cardiffmiller.com/artworks/walks/forest.html.
Carles Philippe (2001): 'Le son du jazz. Entretien de François Delalande avec Philippe Carles', in Delalande François (ed.) (2001): *Le son des musiques. Entre technologie et esthétique*, Paris, France, INA-Buchet/Chastel, p. 67–85.
Carles Philippe, Comolli Jean-Louis (2015): *Free Jazz/Black Power*, translated by Grégory Pierrot, Jackson, MS, University Press of Mississippi. [Carles Philippe, Comolli Jean-Louis (1971): *Free Jazz. Black Power*, Paris, Gallimard.]
Carlyle Angus, Lane Cathy (eds.) (2013): *In the Field. The Art of Field Recording*, Uniformbooks.
Carpentier Grégoire, Tardieu Damien (2011): http://recherche.ircam.fr/equipes/repmus/carpentier/orchidee.html.
Carpentier T., Noistering M., Warusfel O. (2015): 'Twenty Years of Ircam Spat: Looking Back, Looking Forward', in *Proceedings of the International Computer Music Conference*, Denton, TX, p. 270–277.
Carvalho Guilherme (2010): 'Apports grangériens à une théorie de la composition musicale', in Soulez Antonia, Moreno Arley R. (eds.) (2010): *La pensée de Gilles-Gaston Granger*, Paris, France, Hermann, p. 283–304.
Cascone Kim (2000): 'The Aesthetics of Failure. Post-digital Tendencies in Contemporary Computer Music', *Computer Music Journal* vol. 24 n°4, p. 12–20.
Castagnoli Giulio (1992): 'Suono e Processo nei *Quattro pezzi per orchestra* (*su una sola nota*)', in Castanet Pierre Albert, Cisternino Nicola (eds.) (1992): *Giacinto Scelsi. Viaggio al centro del suono*, La Spezia, Italy, Lunaeditore, p. 246–260.
Castanet Pierre Albert (1999): *Tout est bruit pour qui a peur. Pour une histoire sociale du son sale*, Paris, France, Michel de Maule.
Castanet Pierre Albert (2008a): 'L'esprit de l'ouïe. Le souffle, la prière et le rituel, bases de la "religion flottante" de Giacinto Scelsi', in Castanet Pierre Albert (ed.) (2008b): *Giacinto Scelsi aujourd'hui*, Paris, France, Cdmc, p. 83–100.
Castanet Pierre Albert (ed.) (2008b): *Giacinto Scelsi aujourd'hui*, Paris, France, Cdmc.
Castant Alexandre (2017): *Les Arts sonores – Son et Art contemporain*, Charleroi and Bourges, Transonic/École nationale supérieure d'art.
Chadabe Joel (1997): *Electric Sound. The Past and Promise of Electronic Music*, Upper Saddle River, NJ, Prentice-Hall.

Charbonnier Georges (1970): *Entretiens avec E. Varèse*, Paris, France, Pierre Belfond.
Charles Daniel (1978): *Le temps de la voix*, Paris, France, Jean-Pierre Delarge.
Charles Daniel (2001): *La fiction de la postmodernité selon l'esprit de la musique*, Paris, France, PUF.
Charles-Dominique Luc (2008): 'Anthropologie historique de la notion de bruit', *Filigrane* n°7, p. 33–54.
Chion Michel (1982): *La musique électroacoustique*, Paris, France, P.U.F.-Q.S.J. ?.
Chion Michel (1993): *Le promeneur écoutant. Essais d'acoulogie*, Paris, France, Plume.
Chion Michel (2003): *Pierre Henry*, Paris, France, Fayard.
Chion Michel (2016): *Sound: An Acoulogical Treatise*, translated by James A. Steintrager, Duke University Press. [Chion Michel (2000): *Le Son*, Paris, Nathan/HER.]
Chocron Catherine (1994): 'Les enjeux économiques du rock', in Gourdon Anne-Marie (ed.) (1994): *Le rock. Aspects esthétiques, culturels et sociaux*, Paris, France, CNRS.
Chouvel Jean-Marc, Solomos Makis (eds.) (1998): *L'espace: Musique-Philosophie*, Paris, France, L'Harmattan.
Chowning John (1971): 'The Simulation of Moving Sound', *Journal of the Audio Engineering Society*, vol. 19; reprinted in *Computer Music Journal* vol. 1 n°3, 1997, p. 48–52 [first publication: 1971].
Chowning John (2007): '*Stria*: Lines to Its Reconstruction', *Computer Music Journal* vol. 31 n°3, p. 23–25.
Christensen Erik (1996): *The Musical Timespace. A Theory of Music Listening*, Aalborg University Press.
Cipriano-Crause Marie, Montagnon Christian, Abiet Edith (1984): *Le bruit en milieu carcéral. Une double approche du phénomène*, Paris, France, Ministère de la Justice.
Clarke Michael (2006): 'Jonathan's Harvey *Mortuos Plango, Vivos Voco*', in Simoni Mary (ed.) (2006): *Analytical Methods of Electroacoustic Music*, London, UK, Routledge, p. 111–144.
Clutton-Brock A. (1924): 'The Psychology of the Gramophone', *The gramophone* vol. I n°9, p. 172–173.
Cobussen Marcel, Meelberg Vincent, Truax Barry (eds.) (2017): *The Routledge Companion to Sounding Art*, London, UK, Routledge.
Cœuroy André (1965): *Wagner et l'esprit romantique*, Paris, France, Gallimard.
Cogan Robert (1984): *New Images of Musical Sound*, Harvard, Harvard University Press.
Collins Nick (2010): *Introduction to Computer Music*, Chichester, UK, John Wiley and Sons Ltd.
Collins Nick, Schedel Margaret, Wilson Scott (2013): *Electronic Music*, Cambridge, MA, Cambridge University Press.
Coltrane John (1964): Linear notes for the LP Coltrane John (1964): *A Love Supreme*, Impulse!.
Cott Jonathan (1974): *Stockhausen. Conversations with the Composer*, London, UK, Robson Books.
Cott Jonathan (1997): 'Interview with Steve Reich', Linear notes for the CD Reich Steve (1997): *Works: 1965–1995*, Nonesuch.
Cowell Henry (1996): *New Musical Resources*, Cambridge, MA, Cambridge University Press.
Cox Christoph, Warne Daniel (eds.) (2004): *Audio Culture. Readings in Modern Music*, London, UK, Continuum.
Criton Pascale (1997): 'La perception vive', *Doce notas preliminares* n°1, Madrid.

Criton Pascale (1998a): 'Continuum sonore et schèmes de structuration', in Soulez Antonia, Vaggione Horacio (eds.) (1998): *Musique, rationalité, langage. L'harmonie: du monde au matériau*, revue *Cahiers de philosophie du langage* n°3, p. 73–88.
Criton Pascale (1998b): *Territoires imperceptibles*, Paris, France, Éditions Jobert.
Criton Pascale (2005): 'Subjectivités et formes', *Filigrane. Musique, esthétique, sciences, société* n°2, p. 119–138.
Dack John (2002): 'Histories and Ideologies of Synthesis', Sheffield, Maxis Conference Proceedings, http://www.cea.mdx.ac.uk/?location_id=61&item=86.
Dahan Kevin (2007): 'Surface Tensions: Dynamics of *Stria*', *Computer Music Journal* vol. 31 n°3, p. 65–74.
Dahlhaus Carl (1987): *Schœnberg and the New Music*, translated by Derrick Puffett and Alfred Clayton, Cambridge University Press.
Da Silva Santana Helena Maria (1999): *L'orchestration chez Iannis Xenakis: l'espace et le rythme fonctions du timbre*, Ph.D. thesis, University Paris 4, 1998 (publication: Presses Universitaires du Septentrion, Villeneuve D'Ascq).
Daughtry J. Martin (2015): *Sound, Music, Trauma, and Survival in Wartime Iraq*, Oxford, UK, Oxford University Press.
David Evans (ed.) (2013): *The Art of Walking. A Field Guide*, London, UK, Black Dog Publishing.
Dean Roger T. (ed.) (2009): *The Oxford Handbook of Computer Music*, Oxford, UK, Oxford University Press.
Debussy Claude (1987): *Monsieur Croche et autres écrits*, Paris, France, Gallimard.
Decroupet Pascal (2001): 'Varèse: la série et la métaphore acoustique', in Deliège Irène, Paddison Max (ed.) (2001): *Musique contemporaine. Perspectives théoriques et philosophiques*, Liège, Mardaga, p. 165–178.
Delalande François (1997): *'Il faut être constamment un immigré'. Entretiens avec Xenakis*, Paris, France, Buchet/Chastel-INA.
Delalande François (ed.) (2001): *Le son des musiques. Entre technologie et esthétique*, Paris, France, INA-Buchet/Chastel.
Delaplace Joseph (2007): *György Ligeti. Un essai d'analyse et d'esthétique musicales*, Rennes, France, Presses universitaires de Rennes.
Deleuze Gilles, Guattari Félix (1987): *A Thousand Plateaus. Capitalism and Schizophrenia*, translation and foreword by Brian Massumi, Minneapolis, MN, University of Minnesota Press. [Deleuze Gilles, Guattari Félix (1980): *Mille plateaux*, Paris, Minuit.]
Deliège Célestin (1989): 'De la forme comme expérience vécue', in McAdams Stephen, Deliège Irène (ed.) (1989): 159–179.
DeLio Thomas (ed.) (1996): *The Music of Morton Feldman*, Westport, CT-London, Greenwood Press.
Delume Caroline, Solomos Makis (2002): 'De la fluidité du matériau sonore dans la musique de Pascale Criton', *Revue Descartes* n°38, Paris, p. 40–53.
Denave Laurent (2007): 'L'internationalisation de la pratique du gamelan et la révolution conservatrice à la lumière du cas américain', *Filigrane. Musique, esthétique, sciences, société* n°5, p. 177–198.
Derrien Jean-Pierre (1970): 'Pierre Boulez', *Musique en Jeu* n°1.
Dessy Jean-Paul (2008): 'S(u)ono Scelsi, techniques de l'être et du son dans l'écriture pour cordes', in Castanet Pierre-Albert (ed.) (2008b): *Giacinto Scelsi aujourd'hui*, Paris, France, Cdmc, p. 121–124.
Dictionnaire de l'Académie Française, first edition, 1694; fifth edition, 1798; sixth edition, 1835.

Di Scipio Agostino (1994): 'Formal Processes of Timbre Composition. Challenging the Dualistic Paradigm of Computer Music', in *Proceedings of the 1994 International Computer Music Conference*, San Francisco, CA, International Computer Music Association, p. 202–208.

Di Scipio Agostino (1997): 'The Problem of 2nd-Order Sonorities in Xenakis' Electroacoustic Music', *Organised Sound* vol. 2 n°3, p. 165–178.

Di Scipio Agostino (1998): 'Question Concerning Music Technology', *Angelaki: Journal of the Theoretical Humanities* vol. 3 n°2, p. 3–40.

Di Scipio Agostino (1999): 'The Composition of INSTALL QRTT. An Eco-System View Of Music Composing', unpublished.

Di Scipio Agostino (2003): '"Sound is the Interface": From *Interactive* to *Ecosystemic* Signal Processing', *Organised Sound* vol. 8 n°3, p. 269–277.

Di Scipio Agostino (2005a): 'Formalization and Intuition in *Analogique A et B* (with Some Remarks on the Historical-Mathematical Sources of Xenakis)', in Georgaki Anastasia, Solomos Makis (eds.) (2005): *International Symposium Iannis Xenakis*, Athens, Greece, University of Athens, p. 95–108.

Di Scipio Agostino (2005b): 'Per una crisi dell'elettronica dal vivo. *I am sitting in a room* di Alvin Lucier', *Rivista di Analisi e Teoria Musicale* n°2, p. 111–134.

Di Scipio Agostino (2007): '*Due di Uno*. Une composition dédiée à Horacio Vaggione', in Solomos Makis (ed.) (2007): *Espaces composables. Essais sur la musique et la pensée musicale d'Horacio Vaggione*, Paris, France, L'Harmattan, p. 289–312.

Di Scipio Agostino (2008): 'Émergence du son. Son d'émergence. Essai d'épistémologie expérimentale par un compositeur', in Sedes Anne (ed.) (2008): *Musique et cognition = Intellectica* 2008/1–2 N°48–49, p. 221–249.

Di Scipio Agostino (ed.) (2014): *Polveri sonore. Une prospettiva ecosistemica della composizione*, Roma, La camera verde.

Di Scipio Agostino (2016): 'Objet sonore? Événement sonore! Idéologies du son et biopolitique de la musique', in Solomos Makis et al. (eds.) (2016): *Musique et écologies du son. Propositions théoriques pour une écoute du monde/Music and Ecologies of sound. Theoretical Projects for a Listening of the World*, Paris, France, L'Harmattan, p. 35–46.

Doflein Erich (1969): 'Schönberg op. 16, n°3. Der Mythos der Klangfarbenmelodie', *Melos* vol. 36 n°5, p. 203–205.

Doggett Peter (2007): *There's a Riot Going On. Revolutionaries, Rock Stars and the Rise and Fall of '60s Counter-Culture*, Edinburgh, UK, Canongate Books.

Donin Nicolas (2004): 'Towards Organised Listening: Some Aspects of the "Signed Listening" Project, IRCAM', *Organised Sound* vol. 9 n°1, p. 99–108.

Doornbusch Paul (2004): 'Computer Sound Synthesis in 1951: The Music of CSIRAC', *Computer Music Journal* vol. 28 n°1, p. 10–25.

Doornbusch Paul (2009): 'A Chronology of Computer Music and Related Events', in Dean Roger T. (ed.) (2009): *The Oxford Handbook of Computer Music*, Oxford, UK, Oxford University Press.

Downes Michael (2009): *Jonathan Harvey: Song Offerings and White as Jasmine*, Aldershot, UK, Ashgate.

Duchez Marie-Élisabeth (1983): 'Des neumes à la portée', *Revue de musique des universités canadiennes* n°4, p. 22–65.

Duchez Marie-Élisabeth (1989): 'La notion musicale d'élément "porteur de forme". Approche historique et épistémologique', in McAdams Stephen, Deliège Irène (eds.) (1989): *La musique et les sciences cognitives*, Liège, Belgium, Pierre Mardaga, p. 285–303.

Duchez Marie-Élisabeth (1991): 'L'évolution scientifique de la notion de matériau musical', in Barrière Jean-Baptiste (ed.) (1991): *Le timbre. Métaphore pour la composition*, Paris, France, Christian Bourgois, p. 47–81.
Dufourt Hugues (1991): *Musique, pouvoir, écriture*, Paris, France, Christian Bourgois.
Dufourt Hugues (1998): 'L'espace sonore, "paradigme" de la musique de la seconde moitié du 20e siècle', in Chouvel Jean-Marc, Solomos Makis (eds.) (1998): *L'espace: Musique-Philosophie*, Paris, France, L'Harmattan, p. 177–186.
Dufourt Hugues (1999): 'Préface', in Castanet Pierre Albert (1999): *Tout est bruit pour qui a peur. Pour une histoire sociale du son sale*, Paris, France, Michel de Maule.
Dumaurier Élisabeth (ed.) (1978): *Cahiers Recherche/Musique* n°6: *Le pouvoir des sons*, enquête réalisée par Élisabeth Dumaurier, Paris INA/GRM.
Dyson Frances (2009): *Sounding New Media: Immersion and Embodiment in the Arts and Culture*, University of California Press.
EARS (ElectroAcoustic Resources Site): http://www.ears.dmu.ac.uk.
Ehrenzweig Anton (1967): *The Hidden Order of Art*, Berkeley and Los Angeles, University of California Press.
Eldridge Alice, Bown Oliver, 'Biologically Inspired and Agent-Based Algorithms for Music', in Dean Roger T., McLean Alex (eds.) (2018): *The Oxford Handbook of Algorithmic Music*, Oxford University Press.
Emmerson Simon (ed.) (1986): *The Language of Electroacoustic Music*, London, UK, Macmillan.
Emmerson Simon (2007): *Living Electronic Music*, Aldershot, UK, Ashgate.
Emmerson Simon (ed.) (2018): *The Routledge Research Companion to Electronic Music. Reaching Out with Technology*, Routledge.
Emmerson Simon, Landy Leigh (eds.) (2016): *Expanding the Horizon of Electroacoustic Music Analysis*, Cambridge, MA, Cambridge University Press.
Eno Brian (1983): 'The Studio As Compositional Tool', *Downbeat* n°56–57, p. 50–52.
Erickson Robert (1975): *Sound Structure in Music*, Berkeley, CA, University of California Press.
Feld Steven (1991): *CD Voices of the Rainforest. A Soundscape of a Day in the Life of the Kaluli People of the Papua Guinea Rainforest*, Rykodisc.
Feld Steven (undated): http://earthear.com/feld.html.
Feldman Morton (1959): *Last Pieces*, Peters Edition.
Feldman Morton (1986): *Coptic Light*, Universal Edition.
Feldman Morton (2000): *Give My Regards to Eighth Street: Collected Writings*, edited by B.H. Friedman, Cambridge, MA, Exact Chang.
Feneyrou Laurent (2006): '*Prometeo*, dramaturgie de l'invisible', in Ferrari Giordano (ed.) (2006): *L'opéra éclaté. La dramaturgie musicale entre 1969 et 1984*, Paris, France, L'Harmattan, p. 189–208.
Ferneyhough Brian (1975): *Unity Capsule*, Peters Edition.
Ferneyhough Brian (1980): '*Unity Capsule*: An Instant Diary', *Contrechamps* n°8, in Ferneyhough Brian (1995): *Collected Writings*, edited by James Bors and Richard Toop, Harwood Academic Press, p. 98–106.
Féron François-Xavier (2010): 'Gérard Grisey: Première Section de *Partiels* (1975)', *Genesis* n°31, p. 77–100.
Ferrari Giordano (ed.) (2006): *L'opéra éclaté. La dramaturgie musicale entre 1969 et 1984*, Paris, France, L'Harmattan.
Festival d'automne à Paris (1987): *Luigi Nono*, Festival d'automne à Paris/Contrechamps.

Festival d'automne à Paris (1992): *Emmanuel Nunes*, Festival d'automne à Paris.
Fétis François-Joseph (1833): 'Du son considéré dans le timbre', *Revue musicale* tome XIII, p. 193–196 and 217–220.
Fleming Marnie (2011): 'Cardiff, Janet', *Encyclopédie de la musique au Canada*, http://www.thecanadianencyclopedia.com/articles/fr/janet-cardiff.
Fink Robert (2005): *Repeating Ourselves. American Minimal Music as Cultural Practice*, Berkeley, CA, University of California Press.
Fontaine Astrid, Fontana Caroline (1996): *Raver*, Paris, France, Economica.
Forsyth Michael (1985): *Buildings for Music. The Architect, the Musician and the Listener from the Seventeenth Century to the Present Day*, Cambridge, MA, Cambridge University Press.
Fortier Denis (1992): *Les mondes sonores*, Paris, France, Presses Pocket.
Francastel Pierre (1956): *Art et technique*, Paris, France, Denoël.
Francœur Louis-Joseph (1772): *Diapason général de tous les instruments à vent*, Genève, Minkoff reprints (1972).
Francœur Louis-Joseph, Choron Alexandre (1813): *Traité général des voix et des instruments d'orchestre, principalement des instruments à vent, à l'usage des compositeurs*, Paris, France.
François Jean-Charles (1991): 'Organization of Scattered Qualities: A Look at Edgar Varèse's *Ionisation*', *Perspectives of New Music* vol. 29 n°1, p. 48–79.
Fretwell Paul (2001): Programme notes for *Travelling Still*, London, UK, Tate Gallery, October 21.
Freud Sigmund (1962): *Civilization and its Discontents*, translated by James Strachey, New York, Norton Company.
Fubini Enrico (1991): *The History of Music Aesthetics*, translated by Michael Hatwell, London, UK, MacMillan.
Gann Kyle (2010): *No Such Thing as Silence: John Cage's 4'33''*, Yale University Press.
Gardner Thomas, Voegelin Salomé (eds.) (2016): *Colloquium: Sound Art and Music*, Winchester, WA, Zero Books.
Georgaki Anastasia (1998): *Problèmes techniques et enjeux esthétiques de la voix de synthèse dans la recherche et création musicale*, thèse de doctorat, EHESS-IRCAM-CNRS.
Georgaki Anastasia, Solomos Makis (eds.) (2005): *International Symposium Iannis Xenakis*, Athens, Greece, University of Athens.
Giannattasio Francesco (2007): 'Le concept de musique dans une perspective anthropologique et ethnomusicologique', in Nattiez Jean-Jacques (ed.) (2007): *Musiques. Une encyclopédie pour le XXIe siècle*, tome 5: *L'unité de la musique*, Paris, France, Actes Sud/Cité de la musique, p. 309–407.
Gibson Benoît (1994): 'La théorie et l'œuvre chez Xenakis: éléments pour une réflexion', *Circuits* vol. 5 n°2, p. 42–46.
Gibson Benoît (2011): *The Instrumental Music of Iannis Xenakis. Theory, Practice, Self-Borrowing*, Hillsdale, NY, Pendragon Press.
Gilles Guillaume (2018): 'Link Wray, à la poursuite du son sale et sauvage', in Proceedings of the Symposium *Quand la guitare [s'] électrise !*, Paris, France, éditions collegium musicae, forthcoming.
Gilmore Bob (undated): 'Interview with Richard Barrett', www.paristransatlantic.com.
Goddard Michael, Halligan Benjamin, Hegarty Paul (eds.) (2012): *Reverberations: The Philosophy, Aesthetics and Politics of Noise*, New York, Continuum.
Godefroy Frédéric (1994): *Lexique de l'ancien français*, publié par les soins de J. Bonnard et A. Salmon, Paris, France, Honoré Champion.

Godwin Jocelyn (1991): *L'ésotérisme musical en France*, Paris, France, Albin Michel.
Goodman Steve (2010): *Sonic Warfare. Sound, Affect, and the Ecology of Fear*, Cambridge, MA, The MIT Press.
Gottschalk Jennie (2016): *Experimental Music Since 1970*, Bloomsbury.
Gould Glenn (1966): 'The Prospects of Recording', in Cox Christoph, Warne Daniel (eds.) (2006): *Audio Culture. Readings in Modern Music*, London, UK, Continuum, p. 115–126.
Grey John (1975): *An Exploration of Musical Timbre Using Computer-Based Techniques for Analysis, Synthesis and Perceptual Scaling*, Ph.D. thesis, University of Stanford, Ann Arbor, MI, University Microfilms International, 1980.
Grey John (1977): 'Multidimensional Perceptual Scaling of Musical Timbres', *Journal of the Acoustical Society of America* n°61, p. 1270–1277.
Grey John (1978): 'Timbre Discrimination Musical Patterns', *Journal of the Acoustical Society of America* n°64, p. 467–472.
Grisey Gérard (1975): *Partiels*, Éditions Ricordi.
Grisey Gérard (2008): *Écrits ou l'invention de la musique spectrale*, édition établie par Guy Lelong avec la collaboration d'Anne-Marie Réby, Paris, France, Musica falsa.
Grisey Gérard (undated): Linear notes for the LP ERATO STU 71157.
GRM (1962): *Répertoire international des musiques expérimentales*, Paris.
Grossberg Lawrence (1993): 'The Framing of Rock: Rock and the New Conservatism', in Bennett Tony, Frith Simon, Grossberg Lawrence, Shephed John, Turner Graeme (eds.) (1993): *Rock and Popular Music. Politics, Policies, Institutions*, London, UK, Routledge.
Guillebaud Christine (ed.) (2017): *Toward an Anthropology of Ambient Sound*, London, UK, Routledge.
Guiu Claire, Faburel Guillaume, Mervant-Roux Marie-Madeleine, Torgue Henry, Woloszyn Philippe (eds.) (2014): *Soundspaces. Espaces, expériences et politiques du sonore*, Rennes, France, Presses universitaires de Rennes.
Hadja John M., Kendall Roger A., Carterette Edward C., Harschberger Michael L. (1997): 'Methodological Issues in Timbre Research', in Deliège Irène, Sloboda John (eds.) (1997): *Perception and Cognition of Music*, East Sussex, Psychology Press, p. 253–306.
Hainge Greg (2013): *Noise Matters: Towards an Ontology of Noise*, London, UK, Bloomsbury.
Halbreich Harry (1980): *Olivier Messiaen*, Paris, France, Fayard.
Haller Hans-Peter (1987): 'De la transformation des sons', in Festival d'automne à Paris (1987): *Luigi Nono*, Festival d'automne à Paris/Contrechamps, p. 35–39.
Hanslick Édouard (1854): *Vom Musikalisch-Schönen. Ein Beitrag zur Revision der Ästhetik der Tonkunst*, Leipzig, Germany, R. Weigel.
Harley James (2001): 'Formal Analysis of the Music of Iannis Xenakis by Means of *Sonic Events*: Recent Orchestral Works', in Solomos Makis (ed.) (2001): *Présences de Iannis Xenakis*, Paris, France, CDMC, p. 37–52.
Harley James (2004): *Xenakis. His Life in Music*, New York, Routledge.
Harrison Jonty (2018): 'Rendering the Invisible: BEAST and the Performance Practice of Acousmatic Music', in Emmerson Simon (ed.) (2018): *The Routledge Research Companion to Electronic Music. Reaching Out with Technology*, Routledge.
Harvey Jonathan (1980): Programme notes for *Mortuos Plango, Vivos Voco*, http://www.fabermusic.com/repertoire/mortuos-plango-vivos-voco-1154.
Harvey Jonathan (1982): *Bhakti*, Faber Music.
Harvey Jonathan (1984): 'Reflection After Composition', *Contemporary Music Review* vol. 1 n°1, p. 83–86.

References

Harvey Jonathan (1986): 'The Mirror of Ambiguity', in Emmerson Simon (ed.) (1986): *The Language of Electroacoustic Music*, London, UK, The Macmillan Press.

Harvey Jonathan, Lorrain Denis, Barrière Jean-Baptiste, Haynes Stanley (1984): 'Notes sur la réalisation de *Bhakti*', in Machover Tod (ed.) (1984): *L'IRCAM: une pensée musicale*, Paris, France, Éditions des Archives Contemporaines.

Heer Jan de, Tazelaar Kees (2017): *From Harmony to Chaos: Le Corbusier, Varèse, Xenakis and Le poème électronique*, Amsterdam, the Netherlands, 1001 Publishers.

Hegarty Paul (2007): *Noise/Music. A History*, New York, Continuum.

Helmholtz Hermann von (1895): *On the Sensations of Tone as a Physiological Basis for the Theory of Music*, translated by Alexandre J. Ellis, London and New York, Longmans, Green, and Co. [Helmholtz Hermann von (1862): *Die Lehre von den Tonempfindungen*, Brunswick].

Hendrix Jimi (2000): *Live at Woodstock*, musical transcriptions by Andy Aledort, Jesse Gress, Pete Bilmann, Hal Leonard Corporation.

Henry Pierre (1992): CD *Le* Voyage, d'après disque Vinyl Philips, 412 706-2, 1967.

Henry Pierre (1996): *Journal de mes sons*, d'après des entretiens avec Anne Rey, Paris, France, Séguier.

Hiles John (1871): *A Complete and Comprehensive Dictionary of 12 500 Italian, French, German, English and Other Music Terms, Phrases and Abbreviations*, London, UK, Brewer.

Hiller Paul (1997): *Arvo Pärt*, Oxford, UK, Oxford University Press.

Hoffmann Peter (2001): 'Analysis through Resynthesis. *Gendy3* by Iannis Xenakis', in Solomos Makis (ed.) (2001): *Présences de Iannis Xenakis*, Paris, France, CDMC, p. 185–194.

Hofmann Boris (2008): *Mitten im Klang. Die Raumkompositionen von Iannis Xenakis aus den 1960er Jahren*, PhD thesis, Diss. D 83, Berlin, Technische Universität, 2006 (Edition: Sinefonia Band 10, Wolke Verlag Hofheim).

Hofstadter Douglas (1979): *Gödel, Escher, Bach: an Eternal Golden Braid*, New York, Basic Books.

Holmes Thom (2008): *Electronic and Experimental Music. Technology, Music and Culture*, Routledge, third édition.

Holmes Tim (1995): Linear notes for the CD Branca Glenn, *Symphonie* n°9 (*l'eve future*), Point, 446-505-2.

Horodyski Timothée (1998): *Varèse: héritage et confluences (Les masses sonores – L'espace du son – La spatialisation)*, Ph.D. thesis, University of Lille, Atelier national de reproduction des thèses.

Horodyski Timothée, Lalitte Philippe (ed.) (2008): *Edgar Varèse. Du son organisé aux arts audio*, Paris, France, L'Harmattan, p. 139–170.

Institut Technique du Porc (1996): *Élevage porcin et bruit. Évaluation de l'impact sonore des porcheries*, Paris.

Hourdin Christophe, Charbonneau Gérard, Moussa Tarek (1997): 'A Multidimensional Scaling Analysis of Music Instruments' Time-Varying Spectra', *Computer Music Journal* vol. 21 n°2, p. 40–55.

IRCAM (2010): Borchure *Recherche et développement/Research and development*, Paris, France, IRCAM-Centre Georges Pompidou.

Ives Charles (1933): 'Music and its Future', in Albright Daniel (2004): *Modernism and Music. An Anthology of Sources*, Chicago, IL, The University of Chicago Press.

Jacquet Marie-Thérèse (1995): *Le bruit du roman. Le Père Goriot, Madame Bovary, Germinal, Fasano di Brindisi*, Schema.

Jameux Dominique (1984): *Pierre Boulez*, Paris, France, Fayard.
Jankélévitch Vladimir (1976): *Debussy et le mystère de l'instant*, Paris, France, Plon.
Jankélévitch Vladimir (2003): *Music and the Ineffable*, translation Caroline Abbate, Princeton, NJ, Princeton University Press. [Jankélévitch Vladimir, *La Musique et l'Ineffable*, Paris, Seuil, 1983.]
Jarocinski Stefan (1970): *Debussy. Impressionnisme et symbolisme*, Paris, France, Seuil.
Jolivet Hilda (1973): *Varèse*, Paris, France, Hachette.
Jones Carys Wyn (2005): '"We got Heads on Sticks/You got Ventriloquists': Radiohead and the Improbability of Resistance', in Tate Joseph (ed.) (2005): *The Music and Art of Radiohead*, Aldershot, UK, Ashgate Publishing Limited, p. 15–37.
Jones LeRoi (1963): *Blues People: Negro Music in White America*, New York, William Morrow & Company.
Jost Ekkehard (1994): *Free Jazz*, Da Capo Press.
Junkerman Charles (1994): '"nEw/foRms of Living Together": The Model of the Musicircus', in Perloff Marjorie, Junkerman Charles (eds.) (1994): *John Cage. Composed in America*, Chicago, IL, The University of Chicago Press, p. 39–64.
Justel Elsa (2007): 'Un "Thema", une image', in Solomos Makis (ed.) (2007): *Espaces composables. Essais sur la musique et la pensée musicale d'Horacio Vaggione*, Paris, France, L'Harmattan, p. 235–270.
Kagel Mauricio (1993): *Parcours avec l'orchestre*, Paris, France, L'Arche.
Kahn Douglas (1999): *Noise, Water, Meat. A History of Sound in the Arts*, Cambridge, MA, MIT.
Kaiero Claver Ainhoa (2010): 'Les concerts de cloches de Llorenç Barber et la conception postmoderne de l'espace urbain', *Filigrane* n°12, p. 71–88.
Kaltenecker Martin (2001): *Avec Helmut Lachenmann*, Paris, France, Van Dieren éditeur.
Kane Brian (2014): *Sound Unseen. Acousmatic Sound in Theory and Practice*, Oxford, UK, Oxford University Press.
Karajan Herbert von (1977): Beethoven, Symphony n°3, CD, Berliner Philharmoniker, Deutsche Grammophon – 419 049-2.
Kassabian Anahid (2013): *Ubiquitous Listening. Affect, Attention, and Distributed Subjectivity*, Berkeley, CA, University of California Press.
Kastner Georges (ca 1835): *Traité général d'instrumentation comprenant les propriétés et l'usage de chaque instrument, précédé d'un résumé sur les voix à l'usage des jeunes compositeurs*, Paris, France, Philipp et C°.
Kelkel Manfred (1984): *Alexandre Scriabine. Sa vie, l'ésotérisme et le langage musical dans son œuvre*, Paris, France, Honoré Champion.
Kelkel Manfred (1988): *Musiques des mondes*, Paris, France, Vrin.
Kelly Caleb (2009): *Cracked Media: The Sound of Malfunction*, MIT.
Kelly Caleb (ed.) (2011): *Sound*, London, UK, Whitechapel Gallery (with MIT Press).
Kennaway James (2012): *Bad Vibrations. The History of the Idea of Music as a Cause of Disease*, Londres, Ashgate.
Kientzy Daniel (1990): *Saxologie*, Ph.D. thesis, University Paris 8.
Kim-Cohen Seth (2009): *In the Blink of an Ear: Toward a Non-Cochlear Sonic Art*, New York, Continuum.
Kiourtsoglou Elisavet (2016): *Le travail de l'analogie dans la musique et l'architecture de Iannis Xenakis*, Ph.D. thesis, University Paris 8.
Koblyakov Lev (1990): *Pierre Boulez. A World of Harmony*, London, UK, Harwood Academic Publishers.
Koechlin Charles (1944): *Traité d'orchestration*, Paris, France, Max Eschig.

Kostelanetz Richard (1988): *Conversing with Cage*, Limelight Editions.
Kostelanetz Richard (ed.) (1991): *John Cage. An Anthology*, New York, Da Capo Press.
Kurljandski [Kourliandski] Dmitri (2004): 'Constructing with Simple Elements', interview with Makis Solomos, in *3rd International Forum for Young Composer*, Paris, France, Cdmc, p. 69–71.
Kurljandski [Kourliandski] Dmitri (2005a): *Four States of Same*, Paris, France, Éditions Jobert.
Kurljandski [Kourliandski] Dmitri (2005b): *White concerto*, Paris, France, Éditions Jobert.
Kurljandski [Kourliandski] Dmitri (2010a): 'La musique objective', in Roullier Pierre (ed.) (2010): *Dmitri Kourliandski. La musique objective*, Paris, France, collection À la ligne, 2E2M, p. 15–22.
Kurljandski [Kourliandski] Dmitri (2010b): 'Mécanicité et physiologie du son', entretien avec Jan Topolski, in Roullier Pierre (ed.) (2010): *Dmitri Kourliandski. La musique objective*, Paris, France, collection À la ligne, 2E2M, p. 43–52.
Kundera Milan (1981): 'Xenakis, "prophète de l'insensibilité"', in *Regards sur Iannis Xenakis*, Paris, France, Stock, p. 21–24.
Kurth Ernst (1923): *Romantische Harmonie und ihre Krisis in Wagner Tristan*, Berlin, Germany, M. Hesse.
LaBelle Brandon (2010): *Acoustic Territories. Sound Culture and Everyday Life*, New York, The Continuum.
LaBelle Brandon (2015): *Background Noise: Perspectives on Sound Art*, London, UK, Bloomsbury, second edition.
LaBelle Brandon (2018): *Sonic Agency: Sound and Emergent Forms of Resistance*, London, UK, Goldsmith Press.
Lachaud Max (2007): 'Une esthétique de la déconstruction. Essais sur les fondements de la musique industrielle', in *Obsküre. Chroniques des Musiques Sombres, Opus 1*, Paris Éditions Kinite.
Lachenmann Helmut (1972): *Pression*, Köln, Musikverlag Hans Gerig. 1980 assigned to Breitkopf & Härtel, Wiesbaden.
Lachenmann Helmut (1991): 'Quatre aspects fondamentaux du matériau musical et de l'écoute', traduction Jean-Louis Leleu, in *InHarmoniques* n°9.
Lachenmann Helmut (1993): 'De la composition', in Buci-Glucksmann Christine, Levinas Michaël (eds.) (1993): *L'Idée musicale*, Saint-Denis, Presses Universitaires de Vincennes, p. 225–242.
Lachenmann Helmut (2010): *Pression*, Breitkopf und Härtel, revised edition.
Laliberté Martin (2007): 'Pistes analytiques pour *Till* d'H. Vaggione', in Solomos Makis (ed.) (2007): *Espaces composables. Essais sur la musique et la pensée musicale d'Horacio Vaggione*, Paris, France, L'Harmattan, p. 161–226.
Landy Leigh (2007a): *La musique des sons/The Music of Sounds* (édition bilingue), Paris, France, MINT.
Landy Leigh (2007b): *Understanding the Art of Sound Organization*, Cambridge, MA, MIT.
Landy Leigh (2012): *Making Music With Sounds*, Routledge.
Lange André (undated): 'Le théâtrophone de Clément Adler', http://histv2.free.fr/theatrophone/theatrophone2.htm.
Larrieu Maxence (2018): *Analyse des musiques d'informatique, vers une intégration de l'artefact. Propositions théoriques et application sur* Jupiter *(1987) de Philippe Manoury*, PhD thesis, Université Paris-Est.
Leibowitz René (1949): *Schoenberg and his School*, translated by Dika Newlin, New York, Philosophical Library. [Leibowitz René (1946): *Schönberg et son école*, Paris, Janin.]

Leipp Emile (1971): *Acoustique et musique*, Paris, France, Masson.
Lemaître Maurice (1954): 'Introduction', in Russolo Luigi (1954): *L'art des bruits. Manifeste futuriste 1913*, traduction M. Lemaître, Paris, France, Richard-Masse, p. 9–17.
Leman Marc (2008): *Embodied Music Cognition and Mediation Technology*, Cambridge, MA, Massachusetts Institute of Technology.
Lennox Peter (2009): 'Spatialization and Computer Music', in Dean Roger T. (ed.): (2009): *The Oxford Handbook of Computer Music*, Oxford, UK, Oxford University Press.
Lévi-Strauss Claude (1964): *Le cru et le cuit*, Paris, France, Plon.
Levitin Daniel (2007): *This Is Your Brain on Music: The Science of a Human Obsession*, New York, Plume (Penguin).
Licata Thomas (ed.) (2002): *Electroacoustic Music: Analytical Perspectives*, Westport, CT, London, Greenwood Publishing Group.
Licht Alan (2007): *Sound Art: Beyond Music, Between Categories*, New York, Rizzoli International Publications.
Lichtenthal Pietro (1826): *Dizionario e bibliografia della musica*, two volumes, Milan, Italy, Antonio Fontana.
Ligeti György (1960): 'Wandlungen der musikalischen Form', *Die Reihe* n°7.
Ligeti György (1963): *Atmospheres*, Universal Edition, A.G. Vienna/UE 11418.
Ligeti György (1966): 'Form in der Neuen Musik', *Darmstädter Beiträge zur Neuen Musik*.
Ligeti György (1968): *Continuum*, B. Schott's Söhne.
Ligeti György (1974): 'D'*Atmosphères* à *Lontano*', *Musique en jeu* n°15, p. 110–119.
Ligeti György (1983): *Ligeti in Conversation*, London, UK, Eulenburg Books, 1983.
Ligeti György (2007): *Gesammelte Schriften*, bands 1 and 2, Mainz, Germany, Schott.
Lista Giovanni (1975): 'Russolo, peinture et bruitisme', in Russolo Luigi (1975): *L'art des bruits*, textes établis et présentés par Giovanni Lista, traduction Nina Sparta, Lausanne, L'Age d'Homme.
Liszt Franz (1995): *Artiste et société*, édition des textes en français, réunis, présentés et annotés par Rémi Stricker, Paris, Flammarion (Harmoniques).
Lockspeiser Edward, Halbreich Harry (1980): *Claude Debussy*, Paris, France, Fayard.
Lohmann Johannes (1970): *Musiké und Logos. Aufsätze zur griechischen Philosophie und Musiktheorie*, Stuttgart, Germany, Musikwissenschaftliche Verlagsgesellschaft.
López-López José-Manuel (2003): *Le parfum de la lune*, Éditions Salabert - Universal Music Publishing Classical.
Lucier Alvin (1995): *Reflexions. Interviews, Scores, Writings*, Cologne, Germany, MusikTexte.
Lyotard Jean-François (1991): 'Obedience', in Lyotard Jean-François (1991): *The Inhuman. Reflections on Time*, translated by Geoffrey Bennington, Rachel Bowlby, Stanford, CA, Stanford University Press, p. 165–181. [Lyotard Jean-François (1986): 'L'obédience', *InHarmoniques* n°1, p. 126–147.]
MacDonald Ian (1994): *Revolution in the Head: The Beatles' Records and the Sixties*, Great Britain, UK, Fourth Estate.
Macé Pierre-Yves (2012): *Musique et document sonore. Enquête sur la phonographie documentaire dans les pratiques musicales contemporaine*, Paris, France, Les Presses du réel.
Mâche François-Bernard (1998): *Entre l'observatoire et l'atelier*, Paris, France, Kimé.
Mâche François-Bernard (2000): *Un demi-siècle de musique ... et toujours contemporaine*, Paris, France, l'Harmattan.
Mâche François-Bernard (ed.) (2001): *Portrait(s) de Iannis Xenakis*, Paris, France, Bibliothèque Nationale de France.

258 References

Mâche François-Bernard (and Tremblay Gilles) (1983): 'Analyse d'Intégrales', in Mâche François-Bernard (ed.) (1983): *Varèse vingt ans après = Revue musicale* n°383–385.

Maconie Robin (1990): *The Works of Karlheinz Stockhausen*, Oxford, UK, Clarendon Press.

Maïda Clara (2003): ...*who holds the strings*..., auto-edition.

Maffesoli Michel (1988): *Le temps des tribus*, Paris, France, Klincksieck.

Maisonneuve Sophie (2009): *L'invention du disque 1877–1949. Genèse de l'usage des médias musicaux contemporains*, Paris, France, Éditions des archives contemporaines.

Malham David G. (2001): 'Toward Reality Equivalence in Spatial Sound Diffusion', *Computer Music Journal* vol. 25 n°4, p. 43–52.

Manning Peter (2009): 'Sound Synthesis Using Computers', in Dean Roger T. (ed.) (2009): *The Oxford Handbook of Computer Music*, Oxford, UK, Oxford University Press, p. 85–105.

Manoury Philippe (1987): *Jupiter*, Paris, France, Éditions Amphion.

Manzione Luigi (2006): 'Musique en tant qu'espace habitable. L'"arche" de Renzo Piano pour le Prometeo de Luigi Nono', in Ferrari Giordano (ed.) (2006): *L'opéra éclaté. La dramaturgie musicale entre 1969 et 1984*, Paris, France, L'Harmattan.

Marcus Greil (1989): *Lipstik Traces. A Secret History of Manic Street Preachers*, Harvard University Press.

Mariétan Pierre (1997): *La musique du lieu. Musique, Architecture, Paysage, Environnement, Textes, Projets/réalisations, Événements*, Berne, Commission nationale suisse pour l'UNESCO.

Masuo Hiromi (1994): *Les bruits dans À la recherche du temps perdu*, Tokyo, Japan, Surugadai.

Mathews Max (1969): *The Technology of Computer Music*, Cambridge, MA, MIT.

Matossian Nouritza (2005): *Xenakis*, Lefkossia, Moufflon Publications Ltd.

Matter Henri-Louis (1981): *Webern*, Lausanne, L'Age d'homme.

Mattin, Iles Anthony (ed.) (2009): *Noise and Capitalism*, Donostia-San Sebastián, AUDIOLAB.

May Andrew (2006): 'Philippe Manoury's *Jupiter*', in Simoni Mary (ed.) (2006): *Analytical Methods of Electroacoustic Music*, London, UK, Routledge, p. 145–186.

Mazzoli Mario (2017): 'Emerging Musical Structures in Electroacoustic Music', *Proceedings of the 9th European Music Analysis Conference*, Strasbourg.

McAdams Stephen, Deliège Irène (eds.) (1989): *La musique et les sciences cognitives*, Liège, Belgium, Pierre Mardaga.

McAdams Stephen, Goodchild Meghan (2017): 'Musical Structure: Sound and Timbre', in Ashley Richard, Timmers Renee (eds.) (2017): *The Routledge Companion to Music Cognition*, New York, Routledge, p. 129–139.

McCartney Andra (2014): 'Soundwalking: Creating Moving Environmental Sound Narratives', in Gopinath Sumanth, Stanyek Jason (eds.) (2014): *The Oxford Handbook of Mobile Music Studies*, Volume 2, Oxford, UK, Oxford University Press, p. 212–237.

Meneghini Matteo (2007): 'An Analysis of the Compositional Techniques in John Chowning's *Stria*', *Computer Music Journal* vol. 31 n°3, p. 26–37.

Méric Lison (1994): *Le bruit. Nuisance, message, musique*, Genève, Georg Editeur SA.

Meric Renaud (2008): 'Le bruit de fond est-il un son ? À propos d'*Écosystèmes audibles 3a* d'Agostino Di Scipio', *Filigrane. Musique, esthétique, sciences, société* n°7, p. 197–214.

Meric Renaud (2012): *Appréhender l'espace. L'écoute entre perception et imagination*, Paris, France, L'Harmattan.

Meric Renaud, Solomos Makis (2009): 'Audible Ecosystems and Emergent Sound Structures in Di Scipio's Music. Music Philosophy Helps Musical Analysis', *Journal for Interdisciplinary Music Studies* vol. 3 n°1–2, p. 57–76.
Merleau-Ponty Maurice (1945): *Phénoménologie de la perception*, Paris, France, Gallimard.
Merzbow (2006): 'The Beauty of Noise: An Interview With Masami Akita of Merzbow', in Cox Christoph, Warne Daniel (eds.) (2006): *Audio Culture. Readings in Modern Music*, London, UK, Continuum.
Messiaen Olivier (2002): *Traité de rythme, de couleur et d'ornithologie*, vol. VII, Paris, Leduc.
Messiaen Olivier (undated): *Quatuor pour la fin du temps*, Éditions Durand – Universal Music Publishing Classical.
Michel Pierre (2005): '*Professor Bad Trip (Lessons I, II, III)*', in Arbo Alessandro (ed.) (2005b): *Le corps électrique. Voyage dans le son de Fausto Romitelli*, Paris, France, L'Harmattan.
Middleton Richard (1990): *Studying Popular Music*, Buckingham, Open University Press.
Mila Massimo (1960): 'La ligne Nono', in Festival d'automne à Paris (1987): *Luigi Nono*, Festival d'automne à Paris/Contrechamps.
Minard Robin (1999): 'Sound Installation Art', in Bernd Schulz (ed.) (1999): *Robin Minard. Silent Music*, Stadtgalerie Saarbrücken, Kehrer Verlag Heidelberg, p. 72–81.
Minjard Jean-François (1998): Programme notes for *Paysages*, GRM-Radio France, Paris, April 10th 1998, p. 4.
Moore Allan F. (1997): *Sgt. Pepper's Lonely Hearts Club Band*, Cambridge, MA, Cambridge University Press.
Moore Ryan M. (2009): 'The Unmaking of the English Working Class: Deindustrialization, Reification and the Origins of Heavy Metal', in Bayer Gerd (ed.), *Heavy Metal Music in Britain*, Fanrham, Ashgate, p. 143–160.
Moorefield Virgil (2005): *The Producer as Composer. Shaping the Sounds of Popular Music*, Cambridge, MA, M.I.T.
Mosch Ulrich (2004): *Musikalisches Hören serieller Musik. Untersuchungen am Beispiel von Pierre Boulez 'Le marteau sans maître'*, Saarbrücken, PFAU-Verlag.
Motte-Haber Helga de la (ed.) (1999): *Klangkunst: Tönende Objekte und klingende Räume*, Handbuch der Musik im 20. Jahrhundert 12, Laaber-Verlag.
Motte-Haber Helga de la (undated): 'Christina Kubisch. Die Idee der Kunstsynthese', http://www.geelhaar.de/TR/special/text/kub/index.html.
Muller Jean-Grégoire (2011): 'Field recordings: des micros pour raconter le monde', http://www.lamediatheque.be/dec/genres_musicaux/field_recording_des_micros/index.php?reset=1&secured=.
Mumma Gordon (2005): Linear notes for the CD Mumma Gordon (2005), *Electronic Music of Theatre and Public Activity*, New World Records 80632-2.
Murail Tristan (1992): Programme notes for *Désintégrations*, Paris, IRCAM, September 11–13, p. 26.
Murail Tristan (2004): *Modèles et artifices*, textes réunis par Pierre Michel, Strasbourg, France, Presses Universitaires de Strasbourg.
Muzet Alain (1999): *Le bruit*, Paris, France, Flammarion.
Nicholls David (1990): *American Experimental Music. 1890–1940*, Cambridge, MA, Cambridge University Press.

Niklas Stefan (2014): *Die Kopfhörerin. Mobiles Musikhören als ästhetische Erfahrung*, Paderborn, Wilhelm Fink.
Nono Luigi (1992): *...sofferte onde serene...*, Milan, Italy, Ricordi.
Nono Luigi (1993): *Écrits*, textes traduits de l'italien et de l'allemand par Laurent Feneyrou, Paris, France, Christian Bourgois.
Nono Luigi (2007): *Écrits*, nouvelle édition française de Laurent Feneyrou, Genève, Contrechamps.
Norman Katharine (2004): *Sounding Art: Eight Literary Excursions Through Electronic Music*, Aldershot, UK, Ashgate Publishing Limited.
Nunes Emmanuel (1994): 'Temps et spatialité', *Cahiers de l'IRCAM* n°5.
Nunes Emmanuel (1995): Linear notes for the CD Nunes Emmanuel, *Quodlibet*, Auvidis Montaigne 782055.
Nunes Mark (ed.) (2011): *Error: Glitch noise and Jam in New Media Cultures*, New York, Continuum.
Nyman Michael (1974): *Experimental Music: Cage and beyond*, London, UK, Studin Vista.
Odiard Patrick (1995): 'De la confrontation à la conjonction. À propos de *Sonus ex machina*', *Les Cahiers de l'IRCAM* n°8, p. 39–66.
Olive Jean-Paul (2008): *Un son désenchanté*, Paris, France, Klincksieck.
Oliveros Pauline (2005): *Deep Listening. A Composer Sound Practice*, New York, iUniverse.
Osmond-Smith David (1991): *Berio*, Oxford, UK, Oxford University Press.
Otondo Felipe (2007): 'Creating Sonic Spaces: An Interview with Natasha Barrett', *Computer Music Journal* vol. 31 n°2, p. 10–19.
Ouellette Fernand (1968): *Edgar Varèse*, Orion Press.
Panassié Hugues (1965): *La bataille du jazz*, Paris, France, Albin Michel.
Paparrigopoulos Kostas, Solomos Makis (ed.) (2013–14): *Music and Ecologies of Sound. Theoretical and Practical Projects for a Listening of the World*, review *Soundscape, The Journal of Acoustic Ecology* vol. 13 n°1.
Pardo Salgado Carmen (2007): *Approche de John Cage. L'écoute oblique*, Paris, France, L'Harmattan.
Pardo Salgado Carmen (2008): 'Éthique et Esthétique de l'environnement sonore', *Sonorités* n°3, p. 41–64.
Pardo Salgado Carmen (2011): 'L'oreille globale', in Bouët Jacques, Solomos Makis (eds.) (2011): *Musique et globalisation: musicologie-ethnomusicologie*, Paris, France, L'Harmattan, p. 253–268.
Parra Hèctor (2011): *Stress Tensor*, Barcelona, Spain, Tritó Edicions.
Patil K., Pressnitzer D., Shamma S., Elhilali M. (2012): 'Music in Our Ears: The Biological Bases of Musical Timbre Perception', *PLOS Computational Biology* vol. 8 n°11, p. 93–101.
Patocka Jan (1992): *Introduction à la phénoménologie de Husserl*, traduction E. Abrams, Grenoble, Jérôme Millon.
Penderecki Krzysztof (1971): *De natura sonoris n°2*, Schott Music.
Perec Georges (1974): *Espèces d'espace*, Paris, France, Galilée.
Perone James E. (1996): *Orchestration Theory. A Bibliography*, Wesport, CT, Greenwood Press.
Piano Renzo (1987): 'Prometeo, un espace pour la musique', in Festival d'automne à Paris (1987): *Luigi Nono*, Festival d'automne à Paris/Contrechamps, p. 11–17.
Pierce John (1992): *The Science of Musical Sound*, New York, W.H. Freeman and Company, revised edition.

Pinch Trevor, Bijsterveld Karin (eds.) (2012): *The Oxford Handbook of Sound Studies*, Oxford University Press.
Pink Floyd (1984): CD *The Dark Side of the Moon*, EMI.
Polansky Larry (1983): 'The Early Works of James Tenney', in Garland Peter (ed.) (1983): *The Music of* James *Tenney, Soundings* n°13, http://eamusic.dartmouth.edu/~larry/published_articles/tenney_monograph_soundings/index.html.
Pons Jordi, Slizovskaia Olga, Gong Rong, Gómez Emilia, Serra Xavier (2017): 'Timbre Analysis of Music Audio Signals with Convolutional Neural Networks', https://arxiv.org/pdf/1703.06697.pdf.
Posadas Alberto (2005): Linear notes for *Oscuro de llanto y de ternura*, Cité de la musique, Paris, October 15, p. 43.
Potter Keith (2000): *Four Musical Minimalists. La Monte Young, Terry Riley, Steve Reich, Philip Glass*, Cambridge, MA, Cambridge University Press.
Pottier Laurent (2004): '*Turenas*. Analyses et écoutes interactives', in John Chowning (ed.) (2004), *Portraits Polychromes*, Paris, France, INA-GRM, p. 67–85.
Pottier Laurent (2009): 'Le contrôle de la synthèse sonore par ordinateur', in Pottier Laurent (ed.) (2009): *Le calcul de la musique. Composition, modèles et outils*, Saint-Étienne, Publications de l'université de Saint-Étienne.
Poullin Jacques (1957): 'Son et espace', in Schaeffer Pierre (ed.) (1957): *Vers une musique expérimentale, La Revue musicale* n°236, p. 105–114.
Pousseur Henri (1972): *Musique, sémantique, société*, Tournai, Casterman.
Pressnitzer Gil (2010): 'Arvo Pärt. La musique qui tintinnabule', http://www.espritsnomades.com/siteclassique/arvopart.html#2.
Price Peter (2011): *Resonance: Philosophy for Sonic Art*, New York, Atropos Press.
Pritchett James (1993): *The Music of John Cage*, Cambridge, MA, Cambridge University Press.
Radulescu Horatiu (1996): Linear notes for the concert, February 17, IRCAM.
Rae Caroline (2000): *The Music of Maurice Ohana*, Aldershot, UK, Ashgate.
Rebentisch Juliane (2003): *Ästhetik der Installation*, Frankfurt am Main, Suhrkamp Verlag.
Rehfeldt Phillip (1976): *New Directions for Clarinet*, Berkeley, CA, University of California Press.
Reich Steve (1979): *Violin Phase*, London, UK, Universal Edition.
Reich Steve (2002): *Writings on Music: 1965–2000*, edited with an introduction by Paul Hiller, Oxford, UK, Oxford University Press.
Reyna Alejandro (2016): *La construction de l'hétérogène dans la musique de Luc Ferrari: lieu, récit et expériences. Analyses d'Hétérozygote*, Far west news et Chantal, ou le portrait d'une villageoise, PhD thesis, University Paris 8.
Ribot Marc (2000): 'Earplugs', in Zorn John (ed.): *Arcana. Musicians on Music*, New York, Granary Books, p. 233–237.
Rice Tom (2013): *Hearing at the Hospital. Sound, Listening, Knowledge and Experience*, Sean Kingston Publishing.
Rigoni Michel (1998): *Stockhausen... un vaisseau lancé vers le ciel*, Lillebonne, Millénaire III.
Rimoldi G., Manzolli J. (2016): 'Medidas de quantificação recorrência: uma proposta de análise para Audible Ecosystems de Agostino Di Scipio', *XXVI Congresso da Associação Nacional de Pesquisa e Pós-Graduação em Música, Belo Horizonte*.
Rimsky-Korsakov Nikolaï (1964): *Principles of Orchestration*, translated from Russian by E. Agate (according to the Russian edition of 1922), New York, Dover.

262 References

Riot Claude (1995): *Chants et instruments. Trouveurs et jongleurs au Moyen Age*, Paris, France, Desclée de Brouwer.

Risset Jean-Claude (1969): *An Introductory Catalogue of Computer Synthesized Sounds*, Murray Hill, NJ, Bell Telephone Laboratories; new edition: *The historical CD of digital sound synthesis*, WERGO 2033-2.

Risset Jean-Claude (1988): 'Perception, Environnement, Musique', *InHarmoniques* n°3, p. 10–43.

Risset Jean-Claude (1990): 'Composer le son: expériences avec l'ordinateur, 1964–1989', *Contrechamps* n°11, p. 107–126.

Risset Jean-Claude (1991): 'Timbre et synthèse des sons', in Barrière Jean-Baptiste (ed.) (1991): *Le timbre. Métaphore pour la composition*, Paris, France, Christian Bourgois, p. 239–260.

Risset Jean-Claude (1992): 'Composing Sounds with Computers', in Howell Tim, Paynter John, Orton Richard, Seymour Peter (eds.) (1992): *Companion to Contemporary Musical thought*, London, UK, Routledge.

Risset Jean-Claude (1998): 'Hauteur, timbre, harmonie, synthèse', in Soulez Antonia, Vaggione Horacio (eds.) (1998): *Musique, rationalité, langage. L'harmonie: du monde au matériau*, review *Cahiers de philosophie du langage* n°3, p. 153–168.

Risset Jean-Claude, Wessel David (1991): 'Exploration du timbre par analyse et synthèse', in Barrière Jean-Baptiste (ed.) (1991): *Le timbre. Métaphore pour la composition*, Paris, France, Christian Bourgois, p. 102–133.

Roads Curtis (1978): 'Automated Granular Synthesis of Sound', *Computer Music Journal* vol. 2 n°2, p. 13–27.

Roads Curtis (1996): *Computer Music Tutorial*, Cambridge, MA, MIT Press.

Roads Curtis (2001): *Microsounds*, Cambridge, MA, MIT Press.

Roads Curtis (2005): 'The Art of Articulation: The Electroacoustic Music of Horacio Vaggione', in Solomos Makis (ed.) (2005): *Horacio Vaggione: Composition Theory*, *Contemporary Music Review*, volume 24 parts 4+5, p. 295–310.

Roads Curtis (2015): *Composing Electronic Music. A New Aesthetic*, Oxford, UK, Oxford University Press.

Robert Martial (1999): *Pierre Schaeffer: des Transmissions à Orphée*, Paris, France, L'Harmattan.

Rockwell John (1983): *All American Music. Composition in the Late Twentieth Century*, London, UK, Kahn and Averill.

Rodgers Tara (2010): *Pink Noises. Women on Electronic Music and Sound*, Duke University Press.

Romitelli Fausto (1996): Programme notes for *EnTrance*, January 26–27, IRCAM.

Romitelli Fausto (1998): *Professor Bad Trip. Lesson I*, Éditions Ricordi Paris – Universal Music Publishing Classical.

Rosen Charles (1975): *Arnold Schœnberg*, Chicago, IL, The University Press of Chicago.

Rossing Thomas D. (1990): *The Science of Sound*, Reading, MA, Addison-Wesley.

Rousseau Jean-Jacques (1995): *Œuvres complètes*, volume V, Paris, France, Gallimard-Pléiade.

Roy Stéphane (2003): *L'analyse des musiques électroacoustiques: modèles et propositions*, Paris, France, L'Harmattan.

Russolo Luigi (1986): *The Arts of Noises*, translated by. Barclay Brown, New York, Pendragon Press.

Saariaho Kaija (1992): *Amers*, Chester Music.

Sacks Oliver (2008): *Musicophilia: Tales of Music and the Brain*, New York, Vintage Books Edition.
Sakai Kenji (2009): 'Astral/Chromoprojection', http://brahms.ircam.fr/works/work/25530.
Saladin Matthieu (2014): *Esthétique de l'improvisation libre. Expérimentation musicale et politique*, Paris, France, Les Presses du réel.
Satie Érik (1997): *A Mammal's Notebook: Collected Writings of Erik Satie*, edited by Ornella Volta, translated by Anthony Melville, London, UK, Serpent's Tail: Atlas Arkhive, No 5.
Scaldaferri Nicola (2009): 'De l'événement sonore au processus de composition. Analyse de *Notturno*', traduction d'Emmanuelle Bousquet, in Mathon Geneviève, Feneyrou Laurent, Ferrari Giordano (eds.) (2009): *À Bruno Maderna*, volume 2, Paris, France, Basalte, p. 449–485.
Scelsi Giacinto (1964): *String Quartet No. 4*, Salabert - Universal Music Publishing Classical.
Scelsi Giacinto (2006): *Les anges sont ailleurs...*, textes inédits recueillis et commentés par Sharon Kanach, Arles, Actes Sud.
Schaeffer Pierre (ed.) (1957): *Vers une musique expérimentale*, review *La Revue musicale* n°236.
Schaeffer Pierre (1967): *La musique concrète*, Paris, France, PUF/Que Sais-Je?.
Schaeffer Pierre (1971): *De l'expérience musicale à l'expérience humaine*, review *Revue musicale* n°274–275.
Schaeffer Pierre (1976): 'La musique par exemple (Positions et propositions sur le *Traité des objets musicaux*)', *Cahiers Recherche/Musique* n°2.
Schaeffer Pierre (1981): 'Chroniques xenakiennes', in *Regards sur Iannis Xenakis*, Paris, France, Stock, p. 79–88.
Schaeffer Pierre (2002): *De la musique concrète à la musique même*, Paris, France, Mémoire du Livre.
Schaeffer Pierre (2012): *In Search of a Concrete Music*, translated by Christine North and John Dack, University of California Press. [Schaeffer Pierre (1952): *À la recherche d'une musique concrète*, Paris, Seuil.]
Schaeffer Pierre (2017): *Treatise on Musical Objects. An Essay Across Disciplines*, translated by Christine North and John Dack, Oakland, CA, University of California Press. [Schaeffer Pierre (1966): *Traité des objets musicaux*, Paris, Seuil.]
Schafer R. Murray (1977): *The Tuning of the World. A Pioneering Exploration into the Past History and Present State of the Most Neglected Aspect of our Environment: The Soundscape*, Random House Inc.
Schilling Gustav (ed.) (1838): *Encyclopädie der gesammten musikalischen Wissenschaften oder Universal Lexicon der Tonkunst*, Stuttgart.
Schoeller Philippe (1986): 'Mutation de l'écriture: *Éclat, Stria, Désintégrations*', *InHarmoniques* n°1, p. 197–209.
Schoenberg Arnold (1978): *Theory of Harmony*, translated by Roy E. Carter, Berkeley, Los Angeles, University of California Press. [Schoenberg Arnold (1922): *Harmonielehre*, Wien, Universal Edition, third edition.]
Schoenberg Arnold (1984): *Style and Idea*, edited by Leonard Stein, with translations by Leo Black, Berkeley, CA, University of California Press.
Schubert Giselher (1986): 'La sonate *Concord* de Charles Ives', *Contrechamps* n°7, p. 43–59.
Schulz Bernd (ed.) (1999): *Robin Minard. Silent Music*, Stadtgalerie Saarbrücken, Kehrer Verlag Heidelberg.

Schumann Robert (1891): *Gesammelte Schriften über Musik und Musiker*, Leipzig, Germany, Breitkopf und Härtel, second edition.
Schumann Robert (1965): *On Music. A Selection from the Writings*, translated, edited and annotated by Henry Pleasants, New York, Dover Publications.
Schumann Robert (1979): *Sur les musiciens*, traduction Henry de Curzon, Paris, France, Stock.
Schwartz Hillel (2011): *Making Noise: From Babel to the Big Bang and beyond*, New York, Zone.
Sciannameo Franco (2001): 'A Personal Memoir: Remembering Scelsi', *Musical Times*, July 2001, http://www.andante.com/article/article.cfm?id=10644.
Scriabin Salvatore (1988): *Infinito nero*, Éditions Ricordi.
Scriabin Alexander (1979): *Prometheus. The Poem of Fire* op. 60, Mainz, Germany, Ernst Eulenburg Ltd.
Sedes Anne, Guillot Pierre, Paris Elliott (2014): 'The Hoa Library, Review and Prospects', *Proceedings ICMC/SMS/2014*, Athens, p. 855–860.
Siedenburg K., Fujinaga I., McAdams S., (2016): 'A Comparison of Approaches to Timbre Descriptors in Music Information Retrieval and Music Psychology', *Journal of New Music Research* vol. 45 n°1, p. 27–41.
Simoni Mary (ed.) (2006): *Analytical Methods of Electroacoustic Music*, London, UK, Routledge, p. 145–186.
Smalley Denis (1986): 'Spectro-Morphology and Structuring Processes', in Emmerson Simon (ed.) (1986): *The Language of Electroacoustic Music*, London, UK, Macmillan, p. 61–93.
Smith Julius O. (1993): 'Observations sur l'histoire de la synthèse numérique du son', *Les Cahiers de l'IRCAM* n°2, p. 83–95.
Smith Pamela (1989): 'Towards the Spiritual – The Electroacoustic Music of Jonathan Harvey', *Contact* n°34, p. 31–39.
Solomos Makis (1993): *À propos des premières œuvres (1953–1969) de Iannis Xenakis. Pour une approche historique de l'émergence du phénomène du son*, Ph.D. thesis, University Paris 4.
Solomos Makis (1999): 'Schaeffer phénoménologue', in *Ouïr, entendre, écouter, comprendre après Schaeffer*, Paris, France, Buchet/Chastel-INA/GRM, p. 53–67.
Solomos Makis (2001a): 'Du projet bartókien au son. L'évolution du jeune Xenakis', in Solomos Makis (ed.) (2001): *Présences de Iannis Xenakis*, Paris, France, CDMC, p. 15–28.
Solomos Makis (2001b): 'The Unity of Xenakis' Instrumental and Electroacoustic Music. The Case of "Brownian Movements"', *Perspectives of New Music* vol. 39 n°1, p. 244–254.
Solomos Makis (2005): 'An Introduction to Horacio Vaggione's Musical and Theoretical Thought', *Contemporary Music Review*, vol. 25 n°4–5, p. 311–326.
Solomos Makis (2006): 'Le *Diatope* et *La légende d'Eer* de Iannis Xenakis', in Bossis Bruno, Veitl Anne, Battier Marc (eds.) (2006): *Musique, instruments, machines. Autour des musiques électroacoustiques*, Paris, France, Université Paris 4-MINT, p. 95–130.
Solomos Makis (2008): 'Xenakis-Varèse et la question de la filiation', in Horodyski Timothée, Lalitte Philippe (eds.) (2008): p. 139–170.
Solomos Makis (2010): 'The Post-Catastrophe World. Six Thesis to Understand Dmitri Kourliandsky's World', in Roullier Pierre (ed.) (2010): *Dmitri Kourliandski. La musique objective*, Paris, France, collection À la ligne, 2E2M, p. 87–104.
Solomos Makis (2011): 'Xenakis first composition in *musique concrète*: *Diamorphoses*', http://www.gold.ac.uk/ccmc/xenakis-international-symposium/programme.

Solomos Makis (2012): 'From Abstract to Concret: Notes on Bayle's Universe', in Erbe Marcus, Blumröder Christoph von (eds.) (2012): *Le monde sonore/The sounds world of/Die Klangwelte des François Bayle*, Vienna, Verlag Der Apfel, Signale aus Köln 18, p. 110–120.
Solomos Makis (2016): 'Xenakis e il "circolo granulare"', in Di Scipio Agostino, Zavagna Paolo (eds.) (2016): *Grani e texture sonore* = revue *Musica/Tecnologia* n° 10, p. 43–66.
Solomos Makis (2018): 'From sound to sound space, sound environment, soundscape, sound milieu or ambiance…', *Paragraph. A Journal of Modern Critical Theory* vol. 41 n°1, p. 95–109.
Solomos Makis (ed.) (2001): *Présences de Iannis Xenakis*, Paris, France, CDMC.
Solomos Makis (ed.) (2005): *Horacio Vaggione: Composition Theory*, *Contemporary Music Review*, volume 24 parts 4+5.
Solomos Makis (ed.) (2007): *Espaces composables. Essais sur la musique et la pensée musicale d'Horacio Vaggione*, Paris, France, L'Harmattan.
Solomos Makis (ed.) (2014): *Agostino Di Scipio: Audible Ecosystems*, *Contemporary Music Review* vol. 33 n°1.
Solomos Makis, Barbanti Roberto, Loizillon Guillaume, Pardo Salgado Carmen, Paparrigopoulos Kostas (eds.) (2016): *Musique et écologies du son. Propositions théoriques pour une écoute du monde/Music and Ecologies of sound. Theoretical Projects for a Listening of the World*, Paris, France, L'Harmattan.
Solomos Makis, Freychet Antoine, Duhautpas Frédérick (2015): 'Beneath the Forest Floor de Hildegard Westerkamp. Analyse d'une composition à base de paysages sonores', *Analyse musicale* n°76, p. 34–42.
Soraghan S., Renaud A., Supper B. (2016): 'A Perceptually Motivated Visualisation Paradigm for Musical Timbre', in *Proceedings of the Conference on Electronic Visualisation and the Arts*, British Computer Society, p. 53–60.
Sousa Dias António de (2011): 'Musique électronique "live" et "recasting". Trois cas d'étude', *Revue Francophone d'Informatique Musicale* n°1, online.
Sterken Sven (2004): *Iannis Xenakis, ingénieur et architecte. Une analyse thématique de l'œuvre, suivie d'un inventaire critique de la collaboration avec Le Corbusier, des projets architecturaux et des installations réalisées dans le domaine du multimédia*, Ph.D. thesis, University of Gent.
Stenzl Jürg (2006): '"Daily Life, Slavishly Imitated": Varèse and Italian Futurism', in Felix Meyer and Heidy Zimmerman (eds.) *Edgar Varèse. Composer, Sound Sculptor, Visionary*, Basel, Paul Sacher Stiftung.
Sterne Jonathan (2003): *The Audible Past: Cultural Origins of Sound Reproduction*, Durham, NC, Duke University Press.
Sterne Jonathan (ed.) (2012): *The Sound Studies Reader*, London and New York, Routledge.
Sterne Jonathan (2013): 'What the mind's ear doesn't listen', in Born Giorgina (ed.) (2013): *Music, Sound and Space: Transformations of Public and Private Experience*, Cambridge, MA, Cambridge University Press, p. 111–127.
Stocker Michael (2013): *Hear Where We Are. Sound, Ecology, and Sense of Place*, New York-Heidelberg, Springer.
Stockhausen Karlheinz (1957): *Gruppen*, Universal Edition.
Stockhausen Karlheinz (1963): *Texte zur Elektronischen und Instrumentalen Musik*, volume 1, Cologne, Germany, DuMont Schauberg.
Stockhausen Karlheinz (1968): *Aus den sieben Tagen*, Universal Edition.
Stockhausen Karlheinz (1978): *Texte zur Elektronischen und Instrumentalen Musik*, volume IV, Cologne, Germany, DuMont Schauberg.

References

Stockhausen Karlheinz (1990/91): *Oktophonie*, Stockhausen Verlag.
Stoïanova Ivanka (1994): 'Une œuvre de synthèse. Analyse d'*Amers*', *Les Cahiers de l'IRCAM* n°6, p. 43–63.
Swan Claudia (ed.) (1997): *Minimalism and the Baroque*, New York, Eos Music Inc.
Szendy Peter (1995): *Avant-textes, textes, contextes: à partir du* Quodlibet *d'Emmanuel Nunes*, PhD thesis, Paris, France, EHESS-ENS-IRCAM.
Szendy Peter (ed.) (1998): *Emmanuel Nunes*, Paris, France, L'Harmattan/IRCAM.
Szendy Peter (2008): *Listen. A History of our Ears*, translated by Charlotte Mandell, New York, Fordham University Press. [*Écoute. Une histoire de nos oreilles*, Paris, Minuit, 2001.]
Szlavnics Chiyoko (2006a): 'Opening Ears. The Intimacy of the Detail of Sound',*Filigrane. Musique, esthétique, sciences, société* n°4, p. 37–58.
Szlavnics Chiyoko (2006b): *Gradients of détail*, auto-edition.
Tache Olivier, Cadoz Claude (2009): 'Vers un instrumentarium pour les modèles musicaux Cordis-Anima', *JIM (Journées d'Informatique Musicale)*, Grenoble, France, online.
Tadday Ulrich (ed.) (2008): *Klangkunst*, MusikKonzepte, special issue.
Tenney James (undated): 'Computer Music Experiments, 1961–1964', http://www.plainsound.org/pdfs/ComputerMusic.pdf.
Thibaud Jean-Paul (2016): 'Les puissances de l'ambiance', in Rémy Nicolas, Tixier Nicolas (eds.) (2016): *Ambiances, tomorrow. Proceedings of 3rd International Congress on Ambiances* (Septembre 2016, Volos, Greece, International Network Ambiances, University of Thessaly), vol. 2, p. 689–694.
Thom René (1983): *Paraboles et catastrophes*, Paris, France, Flammarion.
Thompson Marie (2017): *Beyond Unwanted Sound: Noise, Affect, and Aesthetic Moralism*, London, UK, Bloomsbury.
Thompson Marie, Biddle Ian (eds.) (2013): *Sound, Music, Affect. Theorizing Sonic Experience*, Londres, Bloomsbury.
Thurmann-Jajes Anne, Breitsameter Sabine, Pauleit Winfried (eds.) (2006): *Sound Art: Zwischen Avantgarde und Popkultur / Sound Art: Between Avant-Garde and Pop Culture*, Cologne, Salon.
Toop David (1995): *Ocean of Sound. Aether Talk, Ambient Sound and Imaginary Worlds*, London, UK, Serpent's Tale.
Tournès Ludovic (2008): *Du phonographe au MP3. XIXe-XXIe siècles. Une histoire de la musique enregistrée*, Paris, France, Autrement.
Treib Marc (1996): *Space Calculated in Seconds. The Philips Pavilion, Le Corbusier, Edgar Varèse*, Princeton, NJ, Princeton University Press.
Trower Shelley (2010): *Senses of Vibration. A history of the Pleasure and Pain of Sound*, New York-London, The Continuum.
Truax Barry (1978): *Handbook for Acoustic Ecology*, Simon Fraser University and ARC Publications.
Truax Barry (1988): 'Real-Time Granular Synthesis with a Digital Signal Processor', *Computer Music Journal* vol. 12 n°2, p. 14–26.
Truax Barry (1995): 'The Composition of Environmental Sound at Simon Fraser University', in *Aesthetics and Electroacoustic Music/Esthétique et Musique Électroacoustique. Actes de l'Académie de Bourges*, Bourges, France, GMEB, volume I, p. 91–98.
Ungeheuer Elena (1992): *Wie die elektronische Musik "erfunden" wurde... Quellenstudie zu Werner Meyer-Epplers Entwurf zwischen 1949 und 1953*, Mainz, Germany, Schott.
Vaggione Horacio (1991): 'A Note on Object-based Composition', in *Interface* vol. 20 n°3-4, p. 209–216.

Vaggione Horacio (1995): Linear notes for the CD *Musiques pour piano et électroacoustique*, Chrysopée électronique-Bourges, LDC 278 1102.
Vaggione Horacio (1996a): 'Articulating Micro-Time', *Computer Music Journal* vol. 20 n°1, p. 33–38.
Vaggione Horacio (1996b): 'Vers une approche transformationnelle en CAO', *Actes des Journées d'Informatique Musicale (JIM) 1996, Les cahiers du GREYC*, CNRS-Université de Caen, p. 24–34.
Vaggione Horacio (1998a): 'Transformations morphologiques: quelques exemples', *Actes des Journées d'Informatique Musicale (JIM) 1998*, LMA-CNRS, Marseille.
Vaggione Horacio (1998b): 'Son, temps, objet, syntaxe. Vers une approche multi-échelle dans la composition assistée par ordinateur', in Soulez Antonia, Vaggione Horacio (eds.) (1998): *Musique, rationalité, langage. L'harmonie: du monde au matériau*, revue *Cahiers de philosophie du langage* n°3, p. 169–202.
Vaggione Horacio (1998c): 'L'espace composable: sur quelques catégories opératoires dans la musique électroacoustique', *in* Chouvel Jean-Marc, Solomos Makis (eds.) (1998): *L'espace: Musique-Philosophie*, Paris, France, l'Harmattan, p. 153–166.
Vaggione Horacio (1999): 'The Morphological Approach', in *Actes de l'Académie internationale de musique électroacoustique*, volume IV, Bourges, France, Éditions Mnémosyne, p. 140–145.
Vaggione Horacio (2003a): 'Composition musicale et moyens informatiques: questions d'approche', in Solomos Makis, Soulez Antonia, Vaggione Horacio (2003): *Formel/Informel: musique-philosophie*, Paris, France, L'Harmattan, p. 91–118.
Vaggione Horacio (2003b): 'Décorrélation microtemporelle, morphologies et figurations spatiales du son musical', in Sedes Anne (ed.) (2003): *Espaces sonores. Actes de recherches*, Paris, France, Éditions musicales transatlantiques.
Vaggione Horacio (2005): 'Notes on *Atem*', in Solomos Makis (ed.) (2005): *Horacio Vaggione: Composition Theory*, *Contemporary Music Review*, volume 24 parts 4+5, p. 339–350.
Varela Francisco J. (1989): *Autonomie et connaissance. Essai sur le vivant*, Paris, France, Seuil.
Varela Francisco J. (1996): *Invitation aux sciences cognitives*, Paris, France, Seuil.
Varèse Edgar (1967): *Ionisation*, Colfranc Music.
Varèse Edgar (1983): *Écrits*, textes réunis et présentés par Louise Hirbour, Paris, France, Christian Bourgois.
Varèse Edgar (2009): CD *Entretiens et création de* Déserts *au Théâtre des Champs-Elysées*, INA, mémoire vive, IMV075.
Varga Bálint A. (1996): *Conversations with Iannis Xenakis*, London, UK, Faber and Faber.
Veitl Anne (1993): *Politiques de la musique contemporaine*, Ph.D. thesis, University Pierre Mendès France de Grenoble, Grenoble, France.
Vinay Gianfranco (2005): 'L'invisible impossible: voyage à travers les images poétiques de Salvatore Sciarrino', in *Filigrane. Musique, esthétique, sciences, société* n°2, p. 139–165.
Vinet Hugues (2005): 'Les nouveaux musiquants', *L'inouï* n°1, Paris, France.
Vivier Odile (1973): *Varèse*, Paris, France, Seuil.
Voegelin Salomé (2010): *Listening to Noise and Silence. Towards a Philosophy of Sound Art*, New York, Continuum.
Volcler Juliette (2011): *Le son comme arme. Les usages policiers et militaires du son*, Paris, France, La Découverte.

References

Wagner D., Brümmer L., Dipper G., Otto J. A. (2014): 'Introducing the Zirkonium MK2 System for Spatial Composition', in *Proceedings of the International Computer Music Conference (ICMC)/Sound and Music Computing (SMC)*, Athens, p. 823–829.

Wang Ge (2007): 'A History of Programming and Music', in Collins Nick, d'Escriván Julio (eds.) (2007): *The Cambridge Companion to Electronic Music*, Cambridge University Press.

Warusfel Olivier (2007): 'Entretien avec Olivier Warusfel. De l'acoustique virtuelle à la réalité virtuelle', *Musique, architecture*, review *Revue Descartes* n°56.

Webern Anton (1963): *The Path to the New Music*, edited by Willi Reich, Bryn Mawr, PA, Theodor Press Co.

Weiss Allen S. (ed.) (2000): *Experimental Sound and Radio*, Cambridge, MA, MIT Press.

Wen-Chung Chou (1979): '*Ionisation*: The Function of Timbre in its Formal and Temporal Organization', in Solkema Sh. V. (ed.) (1979): *The New Worlds of Edgar Varèse*, New York, Institute for Studies in American Music.

Westerkamp Hildegard (1985): 'Acoustic Ecology and the Zone of Silence', *Musicworks* 31.

Westerkamp Hildegard (1988): *Listening and soundmaking: a study of music-as-environment*, master thesis, Simon Fraser University.

Westerkamp Hildegard (1992): *Beneath the Forest Floor*, http://www.sfu.ca/~westerka.

Westerkamp Hildegard (2006): 'Soundwalking as Ecological Practice', in *The West Meets the East in Acoustic Ecology. Proceedings for the International Conference on Acoustic Ecology*, Hirosaki, Japan, Hirosaki University, November 2–4, online.

Wilkins Nigel (1999): *La musique du diable*, Liège, Belgium, Pierre Mardaga.

Williams Andrew (2007): *Portable Music and Its Functions*, New York, Peter Lang.

Wilson Scott, Harrison Jonty (2010): 'Rethinking the BEAST: Recent Developments in Multichannel Composition at Birmingham ElectroAcoustic Sound Theatre', *Organised Sound* vol. 15 n°3, p. 239–249.

Winckel Fritz (1967): *Music, Sound and Sensation. A Modern Exposition*, translated from the German by Thomas Binkley, New York, Dover Publications. [Winckel Fritz (1960): *Phänomene des musikalischen Hörens; ästhetisch-naturwissenschaftliche Betrachtungen, Hinweise zur Auflührungspraxis in Konzert und Rundfunk*, Berlin, M. Hesse.]

Wishart Trevor (1985): *On Sonic Art*, York, Imagineering Press. New edition: *On Sonic Art*, revised edition by Simon Emmerson, OPA (Overseas Publishers Association) N.V., published by licence Under Harwood Academic Publishers imprint, 1996, reprinted in 2002 by Routledge.

Wyschnegradsky Ivan (1956): *Arc-en-ciel*, unpublished score.

Wyschnegradsky Ivan (1996): *La loi de la pansonorité*, texte établi et annoté par Franck Jedrzejewski avec la collaboration de Pascale Criton, préface de Pascale Criton, Genève, Contrechamps.

Xanthoudakis Haralambos (Haris) (1992): *Κείμενα για μια λειτουργική θεωρία της μουσικής*, Athens, Greece, I.E.M.A.

Xenakis Iannis (1953–54): *Metastaseis*, Boosey and Hawkes.

Xenakis Iannis (1955): 'Προβλήματα ελληνικής μουσικής σύνθεσης', *Επιθεώρηση τέχνης* n°9, Athènes, p. 185–189; translated in French in Solomos Makis (ed., 2001): *Présences de Iannis Xenakis*, Paris, France, CDMC, p. 11–15.

Xenakis Iannis (1956): 'Wahrscheinlichkeitstheorie und Musik', *Gravesaner Blätter* n°6, p. 28–34.

Xenakis Iannis (1960): 'Elements of Stochastic Music' (1), *Gravesaner Blätter* n°18, p. 84–105.

Xenakis Iannis (1965): 'Le déluge des sons', *Le Nouvel Observateur* n°53, November 1965, p. 38.
Xenakis Iannis (1966): *Terretektorh*, Paris, France, Salabert.
Xenakis Iannis (1967): *Pithoprakta*, Boosey and Hawkes.
Xenakis Iannis (1968): *Analogique A*, Paris, France, Salabert.
Xenakis Iannis (1969): *Persephassa*, Paris, France, Salabert.
Xenakis Iannis (1971): *Mikka*, Paris, France, Salabert.
Xenakis Iannis (1972): *Eridanos*, Paris, France, Salabert.
Xenakis Iannis (1992): *Formalized Music*, revised edition, with additional material compiled and edited by Sharon Kanach, Stuyvesant, NY, Pendragon Press. First edition: translated b Christopher Butchers, G. H. Hopkins, John Challifour, Bloomington, University Press, 1971.
Xenakis Iannis (1994): *Kéleütha*, textes réunis par Alain Galliari, préface et notes de Benoît Gibson, Paris, France, L'Arche.
Xenakis Iannis (2008): *Music of Architecture*, translated, compiled and presented by Sharon Kanach, Hillsdale, NY, Pendragon Press.
Young La Monte, Zazeela Marian (1996): 'Continuous Sound and Light Environments', in Duckworth William, Fleming Richard (eds.) (1996): *Sound and light: La Monte Young, Marian Zazeela*, Lewisburg, Bucknell University Press, p. 218–221.
Young La Monte, Zazeela Marian (2004): *Selected Writings*, ubuclassics, first edition: 1969.
Zanési Christian (2002): Linear notes for the CD Zanési Christian, *91 98 01*, INA/La Muse en Circuit, M10 275872.
Zattra Laura (2007): 'The Assembling of *Stria* by John Chowning: A Philological Investigation', *Computer Music Journal* vol. 31 n°3, p. 38–64.

Index

Bold: reference to an example in the book or online.

Ablinger, Peter, 113n6
acid house 122
acousmatic music 3, 8, 17, 62, 90, 93–5, 120, 231
acousmograph 94
acousmonium **210**
acoustic ecology 3, 10, 230–3
ACROE (Association pour la Création et la Recherche sur les Outils d'Expression) 188
Adams, John 41, 101
Adès, Thomas 41
Adler, Clément 216
Adorno Theodor W., 2, 9, 22, 26, 53, 72, 121, 137, 138, 139, 238, 240, 243; and the question of material 137–9
Alarcón, Ximena 234
Albèra, Philippe 199n4, 243
Alonso, Sydney 186
Alpet, Richard 68
Alsina Tarrés, Ariadna 13
Alva Noto (Carsten Nicolai) 79
Álvarez-Fernández, Miguel 224
Amacher Maryanne 224
ambient music 6, 8, 160, 171; and immersion 122–3
ambisonics 10, 215
Amblard, Jacques 12
Anderson, Christine 227, 243
Anderson, Julian 98, 112, 180, 181, 243
Andriessen, Louis 101
Ansermet, Ernest 136, 243
Antoine, Aurélien 243
Antonini, Giovanni 50
Antonopoulos, Antonios 12, 177, 243
Aperghis, Georges 69, 79
Aphex Twin 122

Appleton, John 186
Arbo, Alessandro 162, 244
Arcane Device 79
architecture and music **219–23**
Arditti Quartett 126, 244
Arel, Bulent 184
Arena, Leonardi Vittorio 130, 244
Aristoxenus of Tarentum 202
Artaud, Pierre-Yves 28, 70, 244
Ashley, Robert 107, 184
atonality 7, 53, 66, 69, 83, 136
Aube (Akifumi Nakajima) 79
audible ecosystem *see* Di Scipio, Agostino
audio culture 1, 2–3, 10, 240
Augoyard, Jean-François 2, 244
Augustine of Hippo 133
Austin, John 108
Austin, Larry 204, 244
avant-garde music 6, 7, 11, 41, 55, 57, 65, 66, 78, 158, 173, 174, 220
Ayers, Nigel 224
Azguime, Miguel 210

Baalman, Marije A.J. 244
Babbitt, Milton **183–4**
Bach, Johann Sebastian 22, **27**, 99, 133, 179, 185
Bachelard, Gaston 192
Bacon, Francis 162
Bailey, Derek 5, 244
Bailey, Kathryn 145, 244
Baillet, Jérôme 45n7, 181, 198, 244
Barbanti, Roberto 12, 235, 244, 265
Barbaud, Pierre 186
Barber Llorenç 232
Barclay, Leah 234
Baron, Joey 73

baroque music 4, 22, 50, 101
Barraqué, Jean 149
Barrett, Natasha 215, 244
Barrett, Richard 74
Barrière, Jean-Baptiste 188, 244
Barron Louis and Bebe 183
Barry, Wallace 172, 244
Barthel-Calvet, Anne-Sylvie 12
Barthelmes, Barbara 172, 244
Bartók, Béla 173
Bartoli, Jean-Pierre 22, 244
Bartolozzi, Bruno 70, 244
Basinski, William 79
Battier, Marc 162, 189, 244
Bauckholt, Carola **74–5**
Baudelaire, Charles 124
Baudouin, Olivier 12, 66, 187, 244
Bayer, Francis 172, 244
Bayer, Gerd 73, 244
Bayle, François 12, 60, 65, 113n4, 120, **210**, 245; and acousmatic **93–5**
Beach Boys 124
BEAST (Birmingham ElectroAcoustic Sound Theatre) 214
Beatles (The) 68, **157–8**
Beauregard, Lawrence (Larry) 189
Beaussant, Philippe 245
bebop 66–7
Beckett, Lucy 245
Beethoven, Ludwig van 55–6, **124–5**, 202
Behrman, David **187**, 225
Béjart, Maurice 155
Belar, Herbert F. 183
Bélis, Annie 202, 245
Bell Telephone Laboratories 184, 186
Berberian, Cathy 70
Berg, Alban 26–7, 242
Berio, Luciano **28**, 64, 69, 149, 182, 183, 242, 245
Berlioz, Hector 10, 16, 22, **23**, 40, **52**, 68, **203**, 245
Bernard, Marie-Hélène 12, 40, 170, 245
Bertaggia, Michele 105
Besada, Jose-Luis 13
Beyer, Robert 182
Biddle, Ian 2, 266
Bijsterveld, Karin 3, 245
binaural systems 216
Bioteau, Alain **213**, 245
Birdsall, Carolyn 3, 245
Biserna, Elena 233, 245
Blasquiz, Klaus 211, 245
Blesser, Barry 219, 245
Block, Geoffrey 245

Blum, Bruno 68, 245
Boards of Canada 79
Bodon-Clair, Jérôme 180, 245
body 126, 134, 162, 172, 209, 219, 232, 240, 241
Bogdanov, Vladimir 122, 245
Böhme, Gernot 2, 245
Bonardi, Alain 13n6, 190, 200n17, 245, 246
Born, Giorgina 10, 246
Bornemann, Fritz 121
Brown, Earle 205, 224
Bossis, Bruno 118, 134, 246
Boucourechliev, André 121
Boulez, Pierre 9, 113n7, 137, 138, 148, 149, 161, 172, 199n4, 242, 246; *Le Marteau sans maître* **150–4**; *Répons* **211**
Bourgenot, Sarah 13
Bowers, Faubion 130, 246
Boyd Rice 79
Brahms, Johannes 47
Branca, Glenn 9, 132
Branden, Joseph W. 87, 246
Bredel, Marc 164, 246
Bregman, Albert S. 14, 246
Brelet, Gisèle 5, 146, 201, 246
Bridoux-Michel, Séverine 220, 246
Brosses, Charles de 50
Brown, Frank 186
Brückwald, Otto 220
bruitism 6, 7, **55–59**, 75
Brümmer, Ludger 192, 267
Brün, Herbert 186
Bryars, Gavin 101, 149
Buchla synthesiser 186
Buchla, Donald 186
Budón, Osvaldo 194, 246
Bull, Michael 13n1, 246
Burkhart, Charles 26, 246
Butler, Samuel 131
Byrds (The) 185
Byrne, Madelyn 188, 246

Cacciari, Massimo 105–6, 211
Cadoz, Claude 188, 246, 266
Cage John IX, 5, 6, 8, 31, 60, 69, 107, 122, 137, 148, 149, 183, 238, 246–7; listening 83–9; *4'33"* **86**
Caires, Carlos 196, 247
Cairns, David 203, 247
Cale, John 68
Cardew, Cornelius 74, 182
Cardiff, Janet 224, 233, 247
Carles, Philippe 4, 66, 67, 247

Carlos, Wendy 185
Carlyle, Angus 13n3, 234, 247
Carpentier, Grégoire 43, 247
Carpentier, T. 216, 247
Carter, Elliott 28
Carvalho, Guilherme 202, 247
Cascone, Kim 79, 247
Casio VL-Tone synthesiser 187
Castagnoli, Giulio 28, 247
Castanet, Pierre Albert 70, 130, 247
Castant, Alexandre 13n3, 247
Caullier, Joëlle 12
CEMAMu (Centre d'Études de Mathématique et Automatique musicales) 78, 186
Centro Ricerche Musicali 210
Chadabe, Joel 185, 247
CHANT program 162, 188
Charbonnier, Georges 59, 247
Charles-Dominique, Luc 49, 247
Charles, Daniel 5, 84, 247
Chastagnier, Claude 12
Chen, Qigang 40
Chen, Yi 40
Chernigina, Anastasia 13
Chion, Michel 2, 21, 47, 50, 61, 82n3, 93, 118, 134, 155, 239, 248; *acoulogy* 94–5
Chladni, Ernst 17, 80
Chocron, Catherine 107, 248
Choron, Alexandre 16
Chou, Wen-Chung 164, 268
Chouvel, Jean-Marc 12, 212, 248
Chowning, John, 186, **186–7**, 210, 248
Christensen, Erik 103, 248
Christou, Jani 69
Cipriano-Crause, Marie 46, 248
Clarke, Michael 118, 248
cluster 29, 31, 58, 60, 69, 91, 127, 177; *see also* Cowell, Henry
Clutton-Brock, A. 111, 248
Cmix program 188
Cmusic program 188
Cobussen, Marcel 13n3, 248
Cocteau Twins 122
Coeuroy, André 124, 248
Cogan, Robert **97**, 248
Coleman, Anthony 73
Collins, Nick 200n15, 248
Collins, Nicolas 79, 187
Coltrane, John 9, 69, 132–3, 248
Columbia-Princeton Electronic Music Center 183, 184
Comolli, Jean-Louis 66, 67, 248
complexity 5–6, 69, 93, 129, 181, 238, 241

composed sound (history of) **136–200**
constructivism 7, 9, 75
contemporary music 4, 5, 8, 11, 50, 69, 74, 145, 160, 162, 201, 211, 229, 239
continuum 99, 109, 121, 134, 154, 155, **170–172**, 190, 195
Cordis-Anima program 188
Cott, Jonathan 116, 133, 178, 207, 248
Country Joe and the Fish 86n6
Couprie, Pierre 246
Cowell, Henry **53–4**, 60, 204, 248
Cox, Christoph 2, 123, 248
Crawford, Ruth 53
Criton, Pascale 39, **109–10**, 117, 172, 248
Crumar Synergy 187
Crumb, George 187
CSIRAC computer 200n14
Csound program **188**
Cure (The) 211
Curran, Alvin 224
Cusack, Peter 234
Czernowin, Chaya 170

D'Alembert 15
Da Silva Santana, Helena Maria 249
Dack, John 91, 187, 249
Dahan, Kevin 12, 187, 200n21, 249
Dahlhaus, Carl 35, 249
Dalbavie, Marc-André 39
Damon 133
Dao, Nguyen-Thien 28
Daughtry, J. Martin 249
David, Evans 249
Davidovsky, Mario 184
Davies, Hugh 224
Davis, Miles 21
DAW (digital audio workstation) 190
Dean, Roger T. 249
Debussy, Claude 5, 7, 17, 121, 122, 138, 147, 148, 149, 191, 203–4, 249; *Jeux* **33–4**
Decroupet, Pascal 199n4, 249
Delalande, François 32, 50, 65, 249
Delaplace, Joseph 99, 249
Delaunay, Robert 104
Deleuze, Gilles 109, 117, 131, 172, 234, 242, 249
Deliège, Célestin 117, 249
DeLio, Thomas 102, 249
Delume, Caroline 109, 249
Denave, Laurent 180, 249
Derrien, Jean-Pierre 150, 249
Dessy, Jean-Paul 130, 249
deterritorialisation 235

Deutsch, Andrew 79
Di Giugno, Giuseppe 186
Di Scipio, Agostino 12, 77, 156, 192,
 200n19, 236n5, 236n6, 238, 240,
 249–50; *audible ecosystems* **225–30**
Diderot, Denis 15
Digidesing Turbosynth 190
Dionysian aesthetic 8, 65, 125–6, 222
disco 4, 9, 160
dissonance 7, 18, 33, 35, **53–4**, 60, 66, 69,
 70, 87, 136, 139
DJ Spooky (Paul D. Miller) 79
dodecaphony 9, 83, 136, 137, 145, 173
Dodge, Charles 188
Doflein, Erich 26, 250
Doggett, Peter 82n6, 250
Donatoni, Franco 28
Donin, Nicolas 113n7, 250
Donna Summer **160**
Doornbusch, Paul 184, 186, 190,
 200n14, 250
Doors (The) 185
Downes, Michael 132, 250
drone music 171
DSP (digital sound processing) 190, 227, 228
Duchez, Marie-Élisabeth 49, 136, 202, 250
Dufour, Denis 210
Dufourt, Hugues 37, 39, 40, 70, 80, 122,
 131, 181, 212, 250–1
Duhautpas, Frédérick 13
Dumaurier, Élisabeth 251
Dunn, David 234
During, Élie 12
Durutte, Camille 130
Dusapin, Pascal 41
Dutilleux, Henri 35
DX synthesiser 186, 187
Dyson, Frances 13n3, 251

Eastman, Julius 101
echo 28, 85, 107, 121, 122, 146, 148, 161,
 182, 183, 204, 209, 211
Ehrenzweig, Anton 146, 150, 251
Eimert, Herbert 182
Einstein, Albert 190
Einstürzende Neubauten 72
El-Dabh, Halim 184
Eldridge, Alice 236n6, 251
electroacoustic music X, 4, 5, 8, 9, 10, 11,
 28, 43, 59, 61, 65, 68, 77, 93, 136, 205,
 207, 214, 216, 222, 231, 239; composed
 resonances 154–6; immersion 117–120;
 space 210–11; timbre 31; *see also* sound
 synthesis

electronic music IX, 1, 2, 4, 5, 6, 7, 9, 17,
 21, 24, 31, 34, 39, 40, 43, 59, 60, 91,
 132, 139; composing timbre 35–37;
 noise 77–80; *see also electroacoustic
 music*; *see also* sound synthesis; *see also*
 granular music; *see also* live electronics
electronica 5
Elggren, Leif 79
Elmus Lab 184
emergence 5, 226–7
Emerick, Geoff 158
Emmerson Simon IX–XI, 13, 13n6, 216,
 238, 251
emotion 2, 10, 53, 74, 87, 110, 111, 282
EMS VCS 3 synthesiser
energy 19, 21, 22, 94, 133, 134, 162, 180,
 192, 229, 242
Eno, Brian 123, 159, 251
Eric B. and Rakim 122
Erickson, Robert 172, 251
Escher Maurits 99, 101, 176
Estrada, Julio 170
Etant Donnés 72
Evans, Mal 158
Exarchos, Dimitris 12
experimental music IX, 4, 11, 60, 74, 78,
 79, 98, 149, 238
Expressionism 53

feedback 69, 79, 171, 227, 228
Feld, Steven 234, 251
Feldman, Morton **102**, 150, 251
Feneyrou, Laurent 211, 251
Fennesz, Christian 79
Fernandez, João 13
Ferneyhough, Brian 28, **29**, 70, 251
Féron, François-Xavier 45n6, 251
Ferrari, Giordano 251
Ferrari, Luc 64, 93, 233
Ferreyra, Beatriz 93
Fétis, François-Joseph 17, 80, 251
field recording 3, 10, 233–4
filter (electronic) 9, 118, 182, 183, 184
Fineberg, Joshua 39
Fink, Robert 160, 180, 251
flamenco 4, 109
Fleming, Marnie 233, 251
FM synthesis *see* Chowning, John
Fontaine, Astrid 126, 251
Fontana, Bill 224
form (musical) 8, 9, 103, 117, 118, 121,
 133, 137–8, 139, 146, 154, 155, 163,
 164, 170, 171, 180–1, 194–6
Forsyth, Michael 219, 220, 224, 252

Fortier, Denis 46, 252
Fox, Terry 224
fractals 117
Francastel, Pierre 117, 252
Francesconi, Luca 213
Franco-Rogelio, Christophe 12
Francoeur, Louis-Joseph 16, 252
François, Jean-Charles 164, 252
free jazz 6, 7, 73, 74; and noise **66–67**
Fretwell, Paul 120, 252
Freud, Sigmund 124, 126, 252
Freychet, Antoine 13
Friedl, Reinhold 12
Fripp, Robert 69
Frisius, Rudolf 12
Frith, Fred **74**
Frith, Simon 253
Fubini, Enrico 252
funk 4
Furrer, Beat 213
Futurism 122

Gabor, Dennis 190–1
Gabrieli, Andrea 203
Gabrieli, Giovanni 203
Gann, Kyle 113n1, 252
Ganru, Ge 40
Garcia, Xavier 210
Gardner, Thomas 13n3, 252
GENDYN program *see* Xenakis
Genesis 69
Genet, Jean 46
Georgaki, Anastasia 12, 118, 252
gesture 2, 110, 127, 131, 145, 167, 175, 187, 204, 230
Gesualdo, Carlo 32
Giannattasio, Francesco 239, 252
Gibson, Benoît 12, 199n9, 252
Gilles, Guillaume 82n7, 252
Gilmore, Bob 74, 252
Glass, Philip 101, 132
glissando 17, 65, 97, 114, 117, 127, 158, **170–1**, 176
glitch 79
Globokar,Vinko 28, 70
GMEB (Groupe de musique expérimentale de Bourges) 210
Gmebaphone 210
GMVL (Groupe Musiques Vivantes de Lyon) 210
Goddard, Michael 7, 252
Godefroy, Frédéric 14, 252
Gödel, Kurt 101
Godwin, Jocelyn 131, 252

Goebbels, Heiner 213
Gómez-Villagómez, Alejandro 13
González-Arroyo, Ramón 12
Goodman, Steve 47, 252
gothic rock 72
Gottschalk, Jennie 4, 238, 252
Gould, Glenn 111–12, 252
Grandmaster Flash and the Furious Five 73
granular synthesis 9, 136, 170, 174, 187–8, 188, **190–7**, 226, 230, 231
Graves, Milford 67
Greek music (ancient) 80, 105, 202
Grey, John 7, **19–20**, 253
Grisey, Gérard 9, 98, 117, 119, 131, 138, 192, 242, 253; threshold of perception **37–9**; process **180–1**
GRM (Groupe de Recherches Musicales) 93, 182, 190, 210, 253
GROOVE system 186
Grossberg, Lawrence 67, 253
Guattari, Félix 117, 172, 234, 242, 249
Guerrero, Francisco 170
Guigue, Didier 12
Guillebaud, Christine 2, 12, 253
Guillot, Pierre 264
Guiu, Claire 10, 13n1, 253
Guttman, Newman 184

Haas, Georg Friedrich 39
Hadja, John M. 18, 253
Hainge, Greg 7, 253
halaphone 211
Halbreich, Harry 34, 253, 257
Halet, Pierre 96
Hallberg, Björn Wilho 28
Haller, Hans-Peter 211, 253
Halligan, Benjamin 7, 252
Hanslick, Édouard 22, 253
hard rock 69
Harley, James 12, 175, 253
harmony X, 4, 6, 7, 8, 22, 49, 50, 52, 63, 66, 80, 83, 89, 98, 123, 127, 130, 133, 151, 156, 161, 180, 219, 239; harmony-timbre **32–40**
Harnoncourt, Nikolaus 21
Harrison, Jonty 214, 253, 268
Harvey, Jonathan 7, 9, 43, 122, 130, 132, 192, 213, 253; *Mortuos Plango, Vivos Voco* **118–119**
Haters (The) 79
Hawkwind 209
heavy metal 72, 73
Hecker, Florian 79
Heer, Jan de 205, 254

Hegarty, Paul 7, 254
Helmholtz, Hermann von 7, 17–18, 19, 35, 40, 50, 80, 192, 254
Helmuth, Mara 192
Hendrix, Jimi, 69, 254
Henry, Pierre 61, 64, 118, 210, 254; *Le Voyage* 154–5
Herrmann, Bernard 53
Hervé, Jean-Luc 39
Hiles, John 16, 254
Hiller, Lejaren 188
Hiller, Paul 149, 254
Hitchcock, Alfred 53
Hoffmann, Peter 12, 78, 254
Hofmann, Boris 206, 254
Hofstadter, Douglas 101, 254
Holmes, Thom 183, 254
Holmes, Tim 132, 254
holophony 216
Honegger, Arthur 55
Horkheimer, Max 72
Horodyski, Timothée 205, 209, 254
Hourdin, Christophe 21, 254
Hurel, Philippe 39
Husserl, Edmund 84, 90–1

Ikeda Ryoji **98–99**
Il Giardino Armonico 4, 50
Iles, Anthony 78, 258
Iliescu, Mihu 12
illusion (auditory) 18, 47, 98, 99, 127; *see also* Risset, Jean-Claude
immersion 8; history of **114–135**
Impressionism 6, 26, 40, 138
improvisation 7, 74
Incapacitants 81
industrial music 6, 7, 72
Inoue Tetsu 122
intonarumori see Russolo, Luigi
IRCAM (Institut de recherche et coordination acoustique/musique) 7, 43, 97, 112, 161, 162, 186, 188, 189, 190, 211, 216, **224**
IRIN program 196
Iron Maiden 72
Iseki, Kumiko 13
Ives, Charles 7, 55, 254

Jacquet, Marie-Thérèse 47, 254
Jameux, Dominique 151, 254
Jankélévitch, Vladimir 138, 254; and the 'spatial mirage' 201–2
Japanoise 7, 79–80
Jarocinski, Stefan 34, 254

Jeney, Zoltán 28
Johnson, Tom 101
Jolivet, Hilda 254
Jones, Cameron 186
Jones, Carys Wyn 73, 255
Jones, LeRoi 66, 67, 255
Joplin, Janis 107
Jost, Ekkehard **66–67**, 255
Judas Priest 72
Julius, Rolf 224
Junkerman, Charles 89, 255
Justel, Elsa 195, 255

Kagel, Mauricio 28, 35, 182, 255
Kahlen, Timo 224
Kahn, Douglas 255
Kaiero, Claver Ainhoa 232, 255
Kaltenecker, Martin 77, 255
Kane, Brian 113n3, 255
Kant, Emmanuel 48
Kaproulias, Thanasis (aka Novi_sad) 79
Karajan, Herbert von 255
Karplus, Kevin 188
Kassabian, Anahid 1, 255
Kassap, Roseline 12
Kastner, Georges 16, 255
Kelkel, Manfred 130, 199n7, 255
Keller, Damian 192
Kelly, Caleb 13n3, 79, 255
Kennaway, James 3, 255
Kientzy, Daniel 70, 255
KIM-1 computer 187
Kim-Cohen, Seth 13n3, 255
King Crimson 69
Kiourtsoglou, Elisavet 12, 220, 255
Klangfarbenmelodie 7, 31, 35, 146, 174; *see also* Schoenberg; *see also* melody of timbres
Knussen, Oliver 41
Koblyakov, Lev 150, 255
Koechlin, Charles 17, 117, 255
Koechlin, Olivier 94
Koenig, Gottfried Michael 24, 186
Korg synthesiser 186, 187
Kostelanetz, Richard 85, 87, 88, 255
Kraftwerk 55, 122
Krause, Bernie 234
Krautrock 209
Krenek, Ernst 137
Kubisch, Christina 224, 225
Kundera, Milan 82n1, 256
Kurljandski [Kourliandski], Dmitri **75–77**, 255–6
Kurtág, György 28

Kurth, Ernst 33, 256
Kurzweil synthesiser 187
Kyma program 190

La Barbara, Joana 70
LaBelle, Brandon 3, 13n3, 256
Lachaud, Max 72, 256
Lachenmann, Helmut 7, 41, 74, 77, 82n7, 256; *musique concrète instrumentale* **70–72**
Laliberté, Martin 12, 193, 256
Lalitte, Philippe 12, 256
Lancino, Thierry 189
Landy, Leigh 4, 13n6, 251, 256
Lane, Cathy 234, 247
Lange, André 216, 256
Lansky, Paul 188
Larrieu, Maxence 190, 256
Le Corbusier, Charles-Édouard 5, 205, 220, 221
Leary, Timothy 68
Leibowitz, René 145, 256
Leipp, Émile 97, 257
Leitner, Bernhard 224
Lemaître, Maurice 60, 257
Leman, Marc 241, 257
Lennon, John 68, 158
Lennox, Peter 214, 257
LeRoi, Jones 66, 67
Leroux, Philippe 214
Lévi-Strauss, Claude 136, 257
Levitin, Daniel 4, 257
Licata, Thomas 13n6, 257
Licht, Alan 13n3, 257
Lichtenthal, Pietro 16, 257
Ligeti, György IX, 8, 101, 117, 121, 171, 173; *Continuum* **99–100**; process 177–8, 182, 257; timbre 22–4, 28, 60, 98
Lim, Liza 214
Lindberg, Magnus 41
Lippe, Cort 189
Lista, Giovanni 55, 257
listening 1, 2, 3, 6, 8, 18, 19, 28, 30, 41, 47, 50, 77, 81, 117, 125, 129, 139–48, 164, 179, 196, 211, 216, 219, 224, 225, 230, 235; history of listening **83–113**
Liszt, Franz 16, 257
live electronics 6, 118, 154, 156, 211, 227
Lockspeiser, Edward 33, 121, 204, 257
Lockwood, Annea 234
Lohmann, Johannes 49, 257
Loizillon, Guillaume 12
loops 68, 101, 108, 159, 160, 178, 189, 240
López-López, José-Manuel **40**, 257

López, Francisco 234
Lorenzo, Mario 12
Lou Reed 69, 197
Lucier, Alvin 107–8, 225, 236n5, 257
Lyotard, Jean-François 103–5, 257

MacDonald, Ian 68, 157, 158, 257
Macé, Pierre-Yves 13n3, 233, 257
Mâche, François-Bernard 3, 28, 64, 137, 164, 173, 233, 257–8; *L'estuaire du temps* **29–30**
Maconie, Robin 36, 258
macrocomposition/microcomposition 174
Maderna, Bruno 28, 182
Maffesoli, Michel 125, 258
Mahler, Gustav 53, **204**
Maïda, Clara **170**, 258
Maintenant, Frédéric 12
Maisonneuve, Sophie 110, 111, 258
Malatray, Gilles 234
Malec, Ivo 64–5
Malham, David G. 216, 258
Malraux, André 205
Mannheim School 22
Manning, Peter 188, 258
Manoury, Philippe **189–190**, 258
Manowar 73
Manzione, Luigi 223, 258
map of timbres 7, 19, 21, 32
Marclay, Christian 224
Marcus, Greil 69, 258
Marcuse, Herbert 68
Maresz, Yann 43
Mariétan, Pierre 232, 258
Martin-Chevalier, Louisa 13
Martin, George 158
Masuo, Hiromi 47, 258
material IX, X, 4, 8, 9, 53, 54, 56, 61, 63, 70, 72, 77, 88, 93, 104, 109, 110, 117, 131, 145, 146, 154, 156, 161, 162, 164, 174, 180, 181, 190, 193, 194, 195, 196, 212, 218, 226, 228, 229, 231, 238, 240, 241; *see also* Adorno, Theodor W.
Mathews, Max **184–5**, 186, 189, 258
Matossian, Nouritza 114, 258
Matter, Henri-Louis 146, 258
Mattin 74, 258
Max/MSP program 189
May, Andrew 258
Mays, Tom 12
Mazzoli, Mario 236n6, 258
McAdams, Stephen 45n4, 258
McCartney, Andra 233, 258
McCartney, Paul 68, 158

meaning (musical) IX, 2, 87, 92–3, 173, 195–6, 202, 226
Meelberg, Vincent 248
mellotron 68
melody of timbres 6, 22, **24–8**, 31; *see also Klangfarbenmelodie*
Meneghini, Matteo 187, 258
Méric, Lison 47, 258
Meric, Renaud 4, 13, 77, 193, 219, 236n6, 258–9
Merleau-Ponty, Maurice 90, 91, 96, 259
Mersenne, Marin 15
Mervant-Roux, Marie-Madeleine 253
Merzbow **79–80**, 81, 259
Messiaen, Olivier 7, 28, **34–5**, 148, 259
metal 7, 72–3
Metallica 73
Meyer-Eppler, Werner 182
Michel, Pierre 162, 259
micro-interval 39, 57, 109
microphone X, 2, 89–90, 93, 107, 118
microtime 182, 190, 193, 195
Middleton, Richard 107, 259
MIDI norm 187, 189
Mila, Massimo 138, 259
Milhaud, Darius 53
Minard, Robin **225–6**, 259
minimalism 6, 8, 9, 39, 122, 149, 178–80; and time 101–2; *see also* Reich, Steve
Minjard, Jean-François 120, 259
Miranda, Eduardo R. 44n4, 192, 259
Miso studio 210
mixed music 6, 160, 163, 192, 195, 212, 213
Modalys program 162, **188**
modernity 55, 117, 136, 137, 238, 242
Monacchi, David 234
Monet, Claude 34
Monk, Thelonious 66
Monteverdi, Claudio 7, **22**, 242
Moog synthesiser 185, 186
Moog, Robert 185
Moore, Allan F. 158, 259
Moore, Ryan M. 73, 259
Moorefield, Virgil 157, 158, 259
Moroder, Giorgio **160**
Morrison, Jim 185
Mosaïc program 188
Mosch, Ulrich 150, 259
Mossolov, Alexander 55
Mötley Crüe 72
Motte, Helga de la 13n3, 225, 259
Motus acousmonium 210
Mozart, Wolfgang Amadeus 59, 133

Muller, Jean-Grégoire 234, 259
multiphony 214–6, 217
Mumma, Gordon 156, 184, 259
Mundry Isabel 214
Murail, Tristan **38–9**, 97, **98**, 119, 129, 180–1, 202, 259
MUSIC N program **184–5**, 188
MUSIDANSE 215
musique concrète 1, 2, 4, 5, 6, 7, 59, 77, 89, 90, 91, 93, 95, 154, 173, 182, 183, 188, 209, 210, 239; and noise 60–6
Muzak 3, 123
Muzet, Alain 47, 259
mysticism 36, 130–1, 174

nature 29, 46, 56, 57, 65, 72, 137, 139, 150, 234
Nauman, Bruce 224
network 195–6, 226, 226, 228, 230, 238, 241
Neuhaus, Max 224
Neuwith, Olga 213
New Age 122, 132, 149, 234
new wave 59, 211
New York Noise 7, 73–4
Niblock, Phill 122
Nicholls, David 53, 259
No, Stephen 13
Noise (music) 7, 79–80
noise 1, 2, 6, 7–8, 11, 16, 18, 28, 30, 31, 32, 40, 41, 43, 84, 89, 111, 122, 139, 163, 177, 228–9; history of noise **46–82**
Nono, Luigi 28, 65, 103, 108, 138, 149, 183, 211, 217, 259–60; and listening 105–7; *...sofferte onde serene...* **155–6**; *Prometeo* **211**, **223**
Norman, Katharine 260
Normandeau, Roberto 93
Nunes Emmanuel 10, 149, **212–13**, 217, 236n3, 260
Nunes, Mark 79, 260
Nyman, Michael 4, 101, 149, 260

Obermayer, Paul 74
ocanic feeling 8, 122–4, 126, 133, 170
Ockeghem, Johannes 242
Odiard, Patrick 189, 260
Ohana, Maurice 28, 35, 149
Olive, Jean-Paul 12, 260
Oliveros Pauline IX, 113n6, 122, 185–6, 225, 260
Olson, Harry F. 183
ondes Martenot 95
Ono, Yoko 122

orchestration 4, 7, 16, 17, 22, 25, 27, 31, 33, 38, 39, 40, 43, 60, 96, 149, 160, 203
Orchidée program 43
organicism 9, 25, 114, 137, 139, 180
Ornstein, Leo 53
Orts, José Antonio 224
Osmond-Smith, David 28, 260
Otondo, Felipe 215, 260
Otte, Hans 224
Ouellette, Fernand 59, 135n1, 260
Oval 79
overdubbing 72, 73

Pan Sonic 79
Panassié, Hugues 82n5, 260
Panhuysen, Paul 224
Papachristou, Ntana 13
Paparrigopoulos, Kostas 12, 260, 265
Pardo Salgado, Carmen 1, 12, 85, 235, 260, 265
Paris, Elliott, 264
Paris, François 39
Parker, Charlie 122
Parmegiani, Bernard **31**, 192
Parra, Hèctor 43, 260
Parsons, Michael 74
Pärt, Arvo 41, 132, **149**
Partch, Harry 137
Pasveer, Kathinka 214
Patil, K. 45n4, 260
Patocka, Jan 90, 260
PBK 79
Peña, Paco 5
Penderecki, Krzysztof 28, **29**, 69, 173, 260
perception 6, 7, 17, 18, 22, 62, 63, 84, 96, 109, 129, 134, 146, 148, 150, 151, 154, 171, 172, 179, 180, 181, 190, 193, 201, 216, 225, 231; thresholds of perception 37–9; and Pierre Schaeffer 90–2; composing from what one perceives 96–101
Percussions de Strasbourg 69
Perec, Georges 212, 260
Perone, James E. 16, 260
phenomenology 5, 8, 90–1
Philips Studio 184
Philips, Liz 224
phonograph 47, 88, 110–1
Piano, Renzo **223–4**, 260
Pierce, John 21, 260
Pinch, Trevor 13n1, 260
Pink Floyd 103, 122, 158–9, 209, 261
Pisaro, Michael 234
Plato 105, 133

Plomp, Reiner 19
Polansky, Larry 78, 261
Pole 79
Polli, Andrea, 234
Pollini, Maurizio 155
polytonality 7, 55
polytope 78, **124–5**, 207, 222
Pons, Jordi 44n4, 261
pop music 9, 69, 158, 162
Popp, Markus 79
Posadas, Alberto 117, 170, 261
post-modernity 6
post-punk 74
Potard, Yves 188
Potter, Keith 101, 261
Pottier, Laurent 210, 261
Poullin, Jacques 210, 261
Pousseur, Henri 150, 183, 261
power of sound (and music) 105, 133
Pratella, Francesco Balilla 55
prepared piano 60, 84
Presley, Elvis 107
Pressnitzer, Gil 132, 261
Price, Peter 13n3, 261
Prigogine, Ilya 192
Pritchett, James 86, 88, 261
process 9, 21, 65, 75, 80, 88, 98, 101, 108, 112, 131, 149, 160, 167, 168, 171; *see also* Grisey, Gérard; *see also* Ligeti, György; *see also* Reich, Steve; *see also* Xenakis, Iannis
Prokofiev, Sergueï 53, 55
protest (social) 65–72
Proust, Marcel 47
psychedelic rock 8, 122
psychoacoustic 9, 18, 91, 96–8, 101, 136, 216
Public Enemy 73
Puckette, Miller 189
punk 68, 69
Pure Data program 189
Pythagoras 49, 62, 131, 133, 202

Quartetto di Nuova Musica 129

Radigue, Eliane 71
Radiohead 73
Rădulescu, Horatiu 131, 261
Rae, Caroline 149, 261
Rameau, Jean-Philippe 7, 32, 40, **50–1**, 105
rap 4, 7, 73
rationalisation 138–9, 202
rave parties **125–6**

Ravel, Maurice 33
RCA Electronic Music Synthesizer 183
Reagan, Ronald 72
real-time electronics 6, 156, 186, 190, 192, 211, 217
Rebel, Jean-Féry **50**
Rebentisch, Juliane 225, 261
recording 1, 2, 5, 10, 47, 59, 110–1, 118, 156–60, 233
Reed, Lou 69, 107
Rehfeldt, Phillip 70, 261
Reibel, Guy 93
Reich Steve IX, 101, 122, 160, 261; *It's Gonna Rain* 178; *Music for 18 Musicians* **180**; process 178–180; *Violin Phase* **179**
representation 10, 94, 106, 107; representational space 201–2
resonance 102, 118, 136, 188, 212, 235; composed resonances **139–63**
reverberation 107, 159, 183, 189, 194, 205, 209, 211, 216, 220, 224
Reyna, Alejandro 13, 233, 261
Ribot, Marc 73, 261
Rice, Tom 3, 261
Rigoni, Michel 36, 261
Rihm, Wolfgang 41
Riley, Terry 101
Rimoldi, G. 236n6, 261
Rimsky-Korsakov, Nikolaï 16–7, 96, 261
ring modulator 182, 211
Ringo Starr 158
Riot, Claude 261
Risset, Jean-Claude 9, 12, 13n4, 17, 18, 19, 113n7, 184–5, 186, 210, 262; *Mutations* **36–37**; auditory illusions **96–7**
Ritter, Don 224
Roads, Curtis 12, 13n6, 186, 187, 191, 192, 196, 200n18, 262
Robert, Martial 262
Rocha Iturbide, Manuel 224
Rocha, Namur Matos 13
rock 4, 5, 6, 7, 67–9, 72–4, 102–3, 107, 156–9, 162, 209
Rockwell, John 101, 262
Rodet, Xavier 188
Rodgers, Tara 2, 262
Rodriguez, Federico 13
Rogers, Richard 224
Roland synthesiser 186, 187
Rolland, Romain 124
Roman de Fauvel **49**
romanticism 5, 22, 33, 87, 238
Romitelli, Fausto **162–3**, 262

Rosa, Guilhem 13
Rosen, Charles 172, 262
Rossing, Thomas D. 18, 262
Rothenberg, David 234
Rousseau, Jean-Jacques 7, 15–16, 18, 20, 32, 50, 262
Roxy Music 159
Roy, Stéphane 13n6, 262
Ruiz, Pierre 188
Russolo, Luigi 7, **55–8**, 60, 62, 64, 262

Saariaho, Kaija 39, **161–2**, 262
Sacks, Oliver 242, 262
SACR (Sonic laboraty, Belfast) 224
Saffar, Frédéric 12
Sakai, Kenji **42–3**, 262
Saladin, Matthieu 74, 263
Salter, Linda-Ruth 219, 245
San Francisco Tape Music Center 185
Satie, Érik 3, 33, 122, 263
saturation 68, 69, 79, 162
Saw Throat 122
Sawdust program 186
Scaldaferri, Nicola 182, 263
Scanner (Robin Rimbaud) 79
Scarlatti, Domenico 50
Scelsi, Giacinto 4, 8, 28, 121, 131, 133, 174, 181, 192, 263; *Fourth String Quartet* **126–30**
Schaeffer, Pierre 1–2, 4, 8, 18, 55, 94, 96, 107, 118, 182, 263; and noise 60–4; and listening **89–93**; and space **210**
Schafer, Murray R. X, 46, 230–1, 263
Schaub, Stéphan 13
Scherchen, Hermann 184
Schilling, Gustav 16, 263
Schnitzler, Konrad 224
Schoeller, Philippe 150, 263
Schoenberg, Arnold 7, 35, 53, 83, 84, 121, 136, 137, 173, 174, 242, 263; and *Klangfarbenmelodie* **24–8**
Schubert, Giselher 82n2, 263
Schulz, Bernd 263
Schulze, Klaus 209
Schumann, Robert 16, 263–4
Schwartz, Hillel 7, 264
Schwitters, Kurt 79
Sciannameo, Franco 129, 264
Sciarrino, Salvatore 28, **41**, 264
Scratch Orchestra 74
Scriabin, Alexander 9, 34, **130**, 172, 264
Sedes, Anne 215, 264
Seeger, Charles 53

280   Index

serialism 6, 28, 39, 60, 97, 132, 149, 150, 182, 194, 202; *see also* Boulez, Pierre; *see also* Webern Anton
Serres, Michel 196
Sex Pistols 69
Shepp, Archie 66
Sibelius, Jean 150
Siedenburg, K. 7, 264
Siemens-Studio für elektronische Musik 184
silence 1, 65, 73, 79, 95, 98, 106–7, 148, 158; and John Cage **84–7**
Simoni, Mary 13n6, 264
site specific 224
Skempton, Howard 74
Slits (The) 69
Slonimsky, Nicolas 164
Smalley, Denis 13n6, 43, 93, 264
Smedeby, Sune 28
Smith, Julius O. 200n15, 264
Smith, Pamela 132, 264
Solypsis (James Miller) 79
Sonami, Laetitia 224
Sonic Youth 72
sonority 4, 6, 9, 16, 17, 38, 60, 75, 77, 151–3, 191, 192, 203, 226; composed sonorities **163–81**
Soraghan, S. 7
sound ambiance 2, 241
sound art 3, 238, 241
sound aura 160–3
sound design 1, 3
sound environment 1, 231–5, 241
sound fetishim 240
sound installation 3, 10, 156, 217, 224–5, 237, 239
sound morphology 2, 62, 69, 170, 190, 194, 195, 196, 218, 231
sound object 5, 22, 37, 62, 63, 92–3, 94, 181, 193, 216
sound pain 47
sound pleasure 48, 95, 126, 162
sound presence 3, 162
sound spatialisation 8, 120–1; *see also* space
sound studies IX, 2–3, 10
sound synthesis X, 6, 9, 77–80, 96, 139, 148, 159, 174, 181–90
Sound Tools 190
sound walk 3, 10, 233
sound-space 8, 10, 11, 120–3; history of **201–36**
SoundHack (DSP) 190

soundscape 3, 230–5, 241
Sousa Dias, António de 200n17, 265
space IX, X, 6, 9–10; history of space in music **201–236**
space rock 209
Spatialisateur program 216
spatialisation of music 121, 202
Spector, Phil 157
spectral music IX, 6, 7, 9, 19, 34, 35, 192, 202, 212; and "abyss" of sound 131–2; and process 180–1; and thresholds of perception 37–40, 43, 97, 122, 138, 161–2, 170
Spiegel, Laurie 187
Spiropoulos, Georgia 214
SPK 72
SSP program 186
Stamitz, Johann 22
Steiner, Rudolf 130
Stelzer, Howard 79
Stenzl, Jürg 57, 265
stereophony 214–8
Sterken, Sven 220, 265
Sterne, Jonathan 2, 13n1, 113, 265
Stocker, Michael 241, 265
Stockhausen Simon 214
Stockhausen, Karlheinz IX, 7, 8, 10, 31, 37, 64, 84, 149, 154, 158, 170, 192, 242, 265; "abyss" of sound 131–3; auditorium of the Osaka's World Fair **121**; composing timbre **35–6**; granular paradigm 191; "inner life" of sound 116–17; *Hymnen* **182**; *Kontakte* **116**, **207–9**; *Mikrophonie I* **118**; *Oktophonie* **214**; sound synthesis 182; space **207–209**, 214; *Studie I* **36**
Stoïanova, Ivanka 161, 162, 265
Stratos, Demetrio 70
Stravinsky, Igor 7, **53–4**, 121
Strong, Alex 188
Stroppa, Marco 213
structuralism 97, 102, 150
Studio di Fonologia Musicale (Milan) 155, 182
studio IX, X, 4, 9, 10, 24, 29, 59, 61, 68, 107, 154, 182–4; the studio as compositional tool **156–60**
Subotnik, Morton 185
Suicide 122
Sun Ra 122
SuperCollider program 190
surround (spatialisation) 214–8
Suzuki, Daisetz Teitaro 87

SVP Phase Vocoder 162
Swan, Claudia 101, 265
Swedenborg, Emanuel 104
synthesiser 102, **159**, 171, 183–4, **185**, 186, 187
Syter (DSP)
Szendy, Peter 113n7, 236n3, 266
Szlavnics, Chiyoko **171–2**, 266

Tache, Olivier 188, 266
Tadday, Ulrich 225, 266
Taïra Yoshihisa 28
Takemitsu, Toru 28
Tan, Dun 40
Tangerine Dream 102–3, 122, 209
tape music 182
Tardieu, Damien 43
Tarjabayle, Benoît 12
Taverner, John 132
Taylor, Cecil **66–7**
Tazelaar, Kees 205, 254
Tchaikovsky, Piotr Ilitch 52
Tenney, James **77–8**, 184, 266
Teruggi, Daniel 93
Test Dept 72
théâtrophone 216
Theremin 157
Thibaud, Jean-Paul 2, 266
Thom, René 195, 266
Thompson, Marie 2, 7, 81, 266
Tiffon, Vincent 246
timbre IX, X, 4, 6, 7, 56, 57, 67, 69, 74, 80, 81, 91, 98, 114, 117, 127, 145, 148, 154, 161, 163, 170, 172, 181, 203, 227; history of timbre **14–45**
time 40, 52, 57, 80, 81, 98, 109, 117, 123–4, 132, 147, 150, 151, 172, 173, 175–6, 180, 191–5, 196; and listening 101–3; *see also* microtime
tonality 5, 31, 32, 50, 53, 54, 136, 137, 139, 241
Tone, Yasunao 79
Toop, David 122, 266
Torgue, Henri 2, 244, 253
Tournès, Ludovic 82n5, 110, 266
Toyama, Michiko 184
Treib, Marc 206, 266
Trimpin (Gerhard Trimpin) 224
Trower, Shelley 3, 266
Truax, Barry 192, 231–2, 266
Tudor, David 86, 107, 225
Turner, Charles 12
Tuttle, John Tyler 13

Ungeheuer, Elena 182, 266
UPIC (Unité polyagogique informatique du CEMAMu) **186**
Ussachevsky, Vladimir 183

Vaggione, Horacio 11, 13n5, 35, 47, **192–197**, 266–7
Vande Gorne, Annette 93, 210
Varela, Francisco J. 225, 226, 228, 230, 267
Varèse, Edgar X, 5, 6, 7, 8, 9, 10, 35, 64, 84, 114, 130–1, 173, 184, 191, 239, 242, 267; 'organised sound' **57–9**; *Ionisation* **163–70**; and space **204–5**
Varga, Bálint A. 175, 267
Veitl, Anne 63, 267
Velvet Underground 68, 107
Vercoe, Barry 188
Vienna School 6, 136
Viktor, Knud 234
Vinay, Gianfranco 41, 267
Vinet, Hugues 94, 112, 113n7, 267
Virgil 46
Vitiello, Stephen 79
Vivaldi, Antonio 4, 50
Vivier, Odile 164, 267
Voegelin, Salomé 13n3, 267
Vogel, Peter 224
Volcler, Juliette 47, 267
VOSIM program 188
Vuillermoz, Émile 34

Wagner, D. 224, 267
Wagner, Richard 7, 10, 16, 22, 27, **33**, 56, **123–4**, 148, 203, 219–20
Wang, Ge 184, 267
Warne, Daniel 2, 248, 252, 259
Warusfel, Oliver 218, 247, 267
Waters, Roger 159
Watson, Chris 234
WDR studio **182**
Weber, Max 138
Webern, Anton X, 5, 9, 26, 27–8, 31, 149, 150, 151, 154, 164, 202, 268; *Symphony, Op. 21* **139–148**
Weiss, Allen S. 13n3, 268
Wessel, David 19
Westerkamp, Hildegard 224, 232, 233, 240, 268
WFS (wavefield synthesis) 10, 215–6
Wilkins, Nigel 49, 268
Willaert, Adrian 203
Wilson, Brian 157
Wilson, Scott 248

282 Index

Winckel, Fritz 18–9, 268
Winderen, Jana 234
Wishart, Trevor 4, 268
world music 4
Wyschnegradsky, Ivan 9, 109, **172**, 268

Xanthoudakis, Haralambos 15
Xenakis, Iannis IX, 5, 6, 8, 9, 10, 12, 21, 28, 31, 60, 64, 82n1, 102, 113n5, 138, 186, 192, 199n10, 199n11, 199n12, 210, 226, 236n1, 268–9; *Analogique A* **191**; architecture and music **220–2**; Brownian mouvements and *Mikka* **78**; composing sound (textures and masses) **173–6**; continuum (glissandi) 170; *Diamorphoses* **65**; *Diatope and Légende d'Eer* **78**, **121**; *Eridanos* **191**; *Erikhthon* **176**; granular paradigm 191; *Jonchaies* **175**; *La Tourette*, **220**; *Metastaseis* **221**, **236**; music and language 241–2; *Mycènes alpha* **186**; noise 65; *Persephassa* **207–8**; Philips Pavilion **205–6**, **222**; *Pithoprakta* **114–115**, 175–7; *Polytope de Cluny* **124–5**; process 176–7; space 205–8; space as operative category 202; spatialisation-immersion 121, 124–5; stochastic synthesis **78–9**; *Syrmos* **176**; *Terretektorh* **176**, **206**; timbre 32; *see also* GENDY program
Xu, Shuya 40
Xu, Yi 40

Yamaha 186
Young, La Monte 9, 101–2, 122, 131, 224–5

Z'ev 72
Zanési, Christian 93, 119, 269
Zappa, Frank 72
Zattra, Laura 187, 269
Zazeela, Marian 102, 131, 224–5, 256
Zhou, Long 170
Zimoun 224
zoom 117, **119**
Zorn, John 46, 73
Zuccheri, Marino 155
Zukovsky, Paul 113n7